W9-CRD-008

GUARDIAN OF THE GRAIL

JOHN WHITEHEAD

GUARDIAN OF THE GRAIL

A New Light on the Arthurian Legend

**BARNES
&NOBLE**
BOOKS
NEW YORK

TO

MY MOTHER

Frontispiece: KING ARTHUR'S BANNER: Green, a silver cross, in
the cantel the figure of the Virgin and Child in gold; quarterly with,
azure, three golden crowns; the banner surmounted of a crown. The
staff supported by a bull sable, armed and crined or, with three golden
crowns on his shoulder, the uppermost one encircling the neck.

This edition published by Barnes & Noble, Inc.

1993 Barnes & Noble Books

ISBN 1-56619-385-0

Printed and bound in the United States of America

M 9 8 7 6 5 4 3 2 1

Contents

Illustrations

TABLES OF DESCENT

I

Perspective

F EW people cannot but have been fascinated, at some period of their lives, by the legends of King Arthur and his Round Table, his knights' quest of the Holy Grail, and his mysterious last journey to Avalon, leaving behind the lingering hope among his people that some day he will come again. Such a figure might conceivably be one of poetic imagination, built up around a man of great ideals whose deeds were enacted upon a small stage, and whose identity thus has become forgotten; but King Arthur's stage attracted the interest of all Celtic Europe, his part was admired by an international, not merely national, public. And so, it is difficult to believe he was just one of the many Britons who opposed the Anglo-Saxons ineffectually, during their long 128 years' infiltration, that is to say from their first landing in Kent to the battle which gained them Bath. A local chieftain, unmentioned in the *Anglo-Saxon Chronicle*, could hardly have assumed heroic proportions overseas; still less is he likely to have become his conquerors' own national hero. Either poetic imagination has been phenomenally vivid, or else something is at fault with the story's historical setting as it now stands. The latter, fortunately, is the truth. King Arthur lived and died very much as the legends relate; he is one of the finer characters of British history; and the aim of this book is to find him his proper place in it.

The part he was called upon to play in history may not have been decisive; that was a matter of his countrymen's choice, it was no question of his ability. Instead of joining the roll of those who have built kingdoms and empires, he is among the captains of losing sides. Fate has dealt kindly with him, therefore, by pre- serving his name as one of the great figures of romance. It seems as though his countrymen had recognized the game had been lost through their own shortcomings, despite his gallant and selfless leadership; in remorse they had tried to make amends to his memory by enshrining it in a magnificent legend of high ideals. Translating this into history in no way detracts from its beauty, but enhances it through doing his reality justice. It restores him from fantasy, enabling him to be honoured among those who 'gave their bodies to the common weal, and received, each for his own memory, a home in the minds of men, where their glory remains fresh to stir to action as the occasion comes; whose story lives on, woven into the stuff of other men's lives'.

Consequently, before embarking upon the story of his life, the perspective from which it is to be viewed must needs be given a little consideration. The historical aspect of the romance has to be brought into line with actuality, and its confused geography to be straightened out. This is a simpler task than perhaps it may sound; there is, so to speak, a single big hurdle in the course, and when once that has been cleared the remainder is straightforward going. In this chapter an endeavour is being made to sketch the revised perspective in as plain words as possible without sacrificing conviction; such technicalities as are introduced are for the satisfaction of those who read critically, they can be left unread by those indifferent to the why and wherefore; the bulk of technical detail has been kept apart in a Glossary at the end of the book. References to the Glossary are asterisked (*) against the word under which the note will be found; it is alphabetically arranged.

All of the Arthurian legend has originated from oral tradition; not for very many centuries was it ever committed to writing. But that, so far from creating doubt over its validity, may have contributed to much of the accuracy in its preservation; because, among the Celts, history was customarily passed down by word of mouth, by bards trained to meticulous accuracy in oral repetition. Conversely, however, when Britain fell into Saxon hands the more patriotic bards are likely to have lost their lives or drifted away to the Welsh and Scottish hills, while with those who remained and became absorbed standards are bound to have deteriorated. Thus by mediaeval times the 'minstrels', as the profession came to be named, pursued a rather questionable calling, which did not exclude the solace of lonely ladies. Among the sincere, traditional standards were retained to the best of their ability; but among the less scrupulous it is easy to picture licence being taken in order to enhance the atmosphere of romance.

Nor, to give bards and minstrels their due, did all the tales reach them in clear wording. Celtic Britain was not socially homogeneous; it was divided into tribal areas in which differences of dialect will have amounted almost to those of language; in southern England, for example, the difference between West Country speech and the Fenlanders' cannot have been far removed from that between Welsh and Gaelic. Stories in these dialects were passed on to English ears; and if the Saxon's receptivity to foreign tongues be judged by that of his present-day descendants, it can be realized that mispronunciation and mistakes crept in readily. As an example of what can occur, Sir John Rhys has pointed out how the Welsh *Diarwya* became the French *de Arroy* and Arroy. In turn, there were inevitably men who sought to clarify what they found obscure; and if they happened to be at fault in their attempts, the mistake would grow more complex. One such instance is of the Trent being called Humber for 'clarification', because at the time of the Danish raiding the estuary's name was more familiar to southerners than the river itself; but it so happened that the Trent being referred to was not that of Nottingham, but of Sussex, and thereby the whole geographical sense became distorted.

Another source of error was inter-tribal feud. As is well known, King Arthur lost his life through a feud; his rival's tribe have handed down a version whitewashing their disloyalty, and in the hazards of chance the rival's family has flourished, while King Arthur's faded into obscurity; consequently the falsified version has become accepted. Nor is it impossible that the bards, knowing what was being shrouded, were by no means reluctant to let history drift into romance; and there is at least one instance of corroboration for this inference, in a continental story telling the truth but followed by the remark—'one durst not tell that tale before Britons'.

This, then, is the light in which the romances are to be viewed: in substance they are likely to be true; faults, though, can be expected to have crept in through mistranslation between tongues, through glossing over unpalatable occurrences, and through embellishments of imagination. Accordingly much will always be open to dispute, and remain a matter of opinion. None the less it is hoped that the reconstruction made here is, generally speaking, accurate.

The legends as they now stand contain several chronological anomalies. One is the statement at the opening of the Neele copy of the Grail romance, that the events were recorded by Josephus;* that is to say they took place in the first century of our era. And in Malory's version (*Morte d'Arthur*, XIII, x) an event is specifically stated to have taken place thirty-two years after the Passion,* which, following the popular belief in that date to have been A.D. 33, makes the event to have happened in A.D. 65. So, are we to take these as embellishments to a tradition of the Saxon era, and if so for what purpose? Again, the Roman 'King Claudas' demands truage from Britain, but at a time when Rome was actually impotent; is this to be assumed a recollection of when Rome was at the height of her power, and attached to a later event? Or can it have been the original, under Claudius? Thirdly, Arthur's nine years' victorious sojourn abroad and his triumphant advance on Rome correspond with nothing known in history; yet they are an integral part of the story, because from his absence arose Modred's treachery; may they not be real occurrences which have become distorted?

The answers can be given summarily. The story of King Arthur belongs properly to the first century A.D. The enemy he resisted were Romans, known colloquially by the Britons as 'the pagans', and indeed called such in the romance; this term was misinterpreted 'Saxons' when the later disaster eclipsed the earlier invasion. Subsequently, to suit crusading times, the enemy was again changed to 'Saracens', giving rise to the following typical mixture (quoted from Malory, v, ii): 'The emperor made ready his Romans . . . and besieged a castle, and won it soon and stuffed it with two hundred Saracens or Infidels, and after destroyed many fair countries which Arthur had won of King Claudas.'

Arthur's period in reality began with the Claudian invasion; the words put into his mouth by Wace—'The Romans desire to make Britain their province, to grow fat with our tribute, and to bring France once more to their allegiance'—are a true memory of the time when Britain had never been a Roman province, when

Gaul had been conquered but not Britain. Seen from this angle it is possible to disentangle the confused geography of legend. The events all took place in southern England, within the province first occupied by the Romans, and called by them *Britannia Prima*; the sites of his battles are as identified by Mr Collingwood in *Antiquity* of September 1929. Arthur spent nine years at Rome; but, while national pride has pictured him going there as a conqueror, in truth he went there as a prisoner—this was the tale that 'one durst not tell before Britons'. Even so, the euphemism is not wholly incorrect; because in the end he achieved a moral victory, returning to Britain as King, chosen by the conquerors to govern the land under their suzerainty. Hence the pan-Celtic admiration for his prowess. For, at a time when Rome was all-powerful, he alone had the courage and ability to keep the field against her; it was his inspiration that brought out the best in his countrymen's character, and finally this was acknowledged by his opponents, who appointed him to maintain peace where they could not.

King Arthur in the flesh thus emerges as the historical figure of 'Caractacus', the Roman mispronunciation of Caratacos, or the modern Welsh Caradoc. Arthur was a tribal nickname, the British Arto- and Welsh Arth, 'The Bear'; it is well illustrated by his dream before embarking for Rome, when he saw a Bear being slain by a Dragon—his soothsayers interpreted it as a rival 'Bear' being killed by him as Pen-Dragon, which it proved to be; he himself though doubted whether it might not foretell his own overthrow by the Emperor of Rome. Another illustration is Gildas' designation of Cuneglas as 'thou Bear'. The custom of using such names is familiar in 'the Black Dog of Arden', 'the Boar of Tuscany', or William 'the Lion' of Scotland; and we have it today in 'the Springboks', 'the Kiwis', 'the Choughs', 'the Rams', and 'the Desert Rats'—to quote various cricket and football teams, and a well-known military division. Their leaders were styled by the name in singular, prefixed 'The', as for instance 'The Chough'; just as chiefs of Highland clans are customarily designated today. Caractacus' royal birth made him hereditary chief of several tribes: his father is sometimes referred to as 'Chough', sometimes as 'Dragon'; his own title 'the Bear' seems to have been chieftainship by adoption. This mode of speech may sound fanciful to present ears, but when it is compared with the abstruse phrases of old Welsh tales and poetry, it will be realized that much of what sounds to us involved was to them perfectly comprehensible allusion. Nor is it far removed from the current habit of 'cross-word' thinking.

Thus although Caractacus was known to the Romans commonly by that name, he was known to the Britons by another, Arwirauc, which it so happens is mentioned by Juvenal in its Roman spelling *Arviragus*. The proper spelling is of some consequence, because it is clear from a manuscript in the College of Arms (L.14.ii) that the pronunciation was with a 'w', not a 'v'; the latter is pure misapprehension and is misleading. For, Arwir represents the British attempt to sound the Gaelic *Arquhir*, just as in old Scots the English *when* is written *quhen*; the sound is not so much a different letter as merely a guttural breathing. This sound in Pictish became a dental breathing, hence Arthwir. Thus Ar'wir and Arthur are the same, 'the Bear-folk', with the one having '-auc' added as designation of the chief. When the apparent discrepancy between the names Caractacus and Ar'wiragus has been overcome, a quantity of extra traditional history becomes available; nor are traditional stories to be inconsiderately rejected, seeing that they were handed down by men especially trained to the art of oral repetition with strict accuracy, and in this case some at least of their material furnishes astonishing survivals. Accordingly the amendment of Arthur's period from the fifth to the first century enables Arviragus and Guiderius, the two sons of Cymbeline in British tradition, to be recognized easily as Caractacus and Togodumnus the two sons of Cymbeline in Roman account; the elder's death in action, and the assumption of command by the younger, render their identity sufficiently plain.

The two principal sources of British tradition are Geoffrey of Monmouth's *Histories of the Kings of Britain*, and Hector Boece's *Chronicles of Scotland*. Although it has been customary until recently to scorn Geoffrey's reliability, his latest editors Griscom and Jones have dispelled that illusion; his work is what he himself claims it to be, a record of what he has been told set down in good faith, and so is invaluable bardic history. Boece too is found to preserve some remarkably accurate chronology, testifying to the likely reliability of much else. These enable British sources to fulfil their natural function of amplifying classical accounts; nor are the Roman narratives entirely free from slips. Both sources need critical scrutiny, and some appreciable differences have to be reconciled: that of nomenclature is readily done by means of a comparative table, and one will be found in the Glossary under ARWIRAGUS; the other major disagreement is that while Geoffrey makes the scene of the fighting to have been around Winchester, Dio places it near *Camulodunum* which is usually translated as Colchester.

To deal with the latter: Winchester in the British tongue was Camelot, or more fully Camelot Dun, the Dun referring to the hill-fort overlooking the present town; Colchester also was Camelot Dun (latinized into Camulodunum). The one has been mistaken for the other; and it is Geoffrey's, not the classical, account which is correct. But the objection may be raised that Dio Cassius' description of Camulodunum having been reached after crossing the Thames refutes this view. One mistake has led to another: Dio wrote from a foreign source, and a century after the event; the river name he appears to have heard was Icen,* which for 'clarity' he thought fit to alter to the better-known name of Thames. For, in spite of Professor Eckwall's contrary opinion, the Thames is on record as having borne two names, the alternative Icen being instanced in Rhyd-Icen (Icen-ford), Oxford.* The mistaken identity is plainly exampled in Stewart's version of Boece, the Isle of Wight being put at the mouth of the Thames (*lines* 27,206-9):

> The Saxons duelland into Victa Yle,
> Fra Albione that lyis sum thing south,
> Evin richt foirnent the water of Tamis mouth.

Correctly the fighting took place where Geoffrey describes it, near Winton, Winchester, that is to say on the lower Hampshire Icen, now the Itchen. Corroboration for this is found in Dio's description of the site as 'fenny' which 'in flood-tide forms a lake'; this exactly suits the mouth of the Hampshire river, as is examined in detail in the Glossary, under ICEN. The lay-out of the Roman road* system points to the same conclusion, indicating the main base to have been where Geoffrey states the landing to have been made, round Portchester; the inadequate size of the Richborough* defences and the course taken by Watling Street evidence a subsidiary purpose.

In the other discrepancy, the difference between parental names, Caratacos being called 'ab Vran' in Welsh tradition, it is once again a matter of nickname. It has come about through Cymbeline having had a claim to Cornwall through his father (the family descent is given in the Glossary, under CYMBELINE); accordingly in the West Country he was spoken of as 'the Chough', *Vran*, while in East Anglia he was *Cuno-Belin*, 'the Hound of God'. He was also known by the traditional style of British kings, 'the Dragon'; and his people bore in battle a Dragon standard, just as the Norsemen bore a Raven whose wings flapped or sagged in omen of victory or failure, and just as the Dacians carried a Wolf's head contrived so as to howl in the wind. When, under the Saxon catastrophe, refugees from all parts of England mingled in Wales, speaking different dialects, these several names developed into separate persons.

Hector Boece's *Chronicles of Scotland* have been written from the angle of the Moray folk who migrated to Scotland after Boadicea's disastrous rising. The chieftain or 'king' under whom they fought was of Caledon, not 'Scotland' as related, and a Caledon that was adjacent to Boadicea's country in southern England; this, with the amended geography given here, is recognizable as the Weald of Surrey, the Caledonian woods mentioned by Caesar as having been entered by him. More on this subject is explained later; and with that explanation much of the otherwise confused geography of Geoffrey's earlier chapters also becomes cleared. Of the two versions of Boece, Bellenden's prose is a direct translation; but Stewart's metrical rendering adds certain extra material, which was evidently still extant in oral tradition when he wrote in 1531-5, and is not to be discounted as mere fanciful embellishment by him.

The geography of Britain south of the Thames reflects the archaeological Iron Age invasions. The area was divided into two main tribal provinces, the south-east and south-west, the dividing line between which was more or less the Test valley; it fluctuated, however, and was a constant object of strife. Super-

imposed on this border land in Arthur's time were the Belgic
Celts of the last century B.C.; but they will be treated separately.
West of the Test was Corin country, that is to say the Iron Age
invaders of 400 B.C., whose name survives in Corini-um (Cirencester) and the legendary personification Corine-us; in the romances it is called 'Cornwall', but it must be appreciated that this
Cornwall stretched over the whole of Wessex, and was in no
sense confined to the tip of the peninsula. East of the Test was the
domain of the earlier Iron Age invaders of 700 B.C., and went by
the name Albany; that name had once been given to the whole of
Britain by its first Celtic conquerors, and now was applied to the
remnants who had managed to retain some of their old identity
in the Weald, in spite of having been overflowed by wave after
wave of later Celtic adventurers. A fuller account of both these
tribes' histories and characteristics is given under their respective
names in the Glossary. The rivalry between Corin* and Albanys*
is one of the most prominent features in pre-Roman history, and
was the weakening element which ultimately caused the land to
fall into Roman hands.

Geoffrey of Monmouth's account coming from a Cornish
source mainly, the Arun instead of the Test is treated as the
boundary. At that period it bore the name Tarrant, still to be
found in Tarrant Street, Arundel. Colloquially Tarrant became
shortened into Trent; and, as has already been observed, Trent
was 'clarified' into Humber, with the result that the expression
'beyond the Humber' or 'on that side Humber' became misconstrued as 'Northumberland'. Hence the Northumberland and
Caledon and Albany of the legends have nothing to do with the
north of Britain, but are properly the Weald. In one instance the
original wording has survived, in Malory's *Morte d'Arthur* (I, xi),
where Arthur was at London and Merlin was somewhere between Dover and London, and an order was given to all people
'on this side Trent water', a much more localized meaning than it
sounds.

A map of pre-Roman Britain has been included overleaf.
Without it the vagaries of legend are impossible to follow; but
with it, not only does a great deal of traditional romance become
plain, but also the Romans' strategy in their invasion under
Claudius. Some of its principal features require comment.

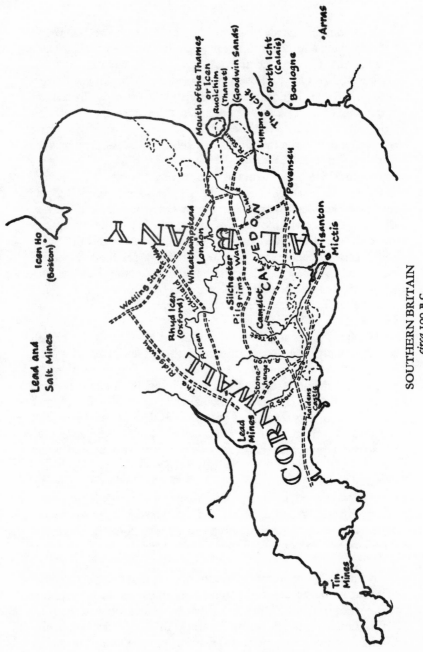

SOUTHERN BRITAIN
circa 100 B.C.

The Weald will be seen designated as Caledon, the name Albany covering a wider area. The latter has already been remarked as a national name, the former applied to the Weald more strictly as being that of its tribal population; the territorial equivalent is Caledonia, thereby aggravating the confusion with Scotland. Several relics of the name remain: Julius Caesar, in his account of operations south of the Thames, mentions having penetrated 'the Caledonian woods', a march which can be identified as along Pilgrims Way from Canterbury towards Silchester, where he had allies; again, in early charters the Hogs Back by Guildford is referred to as on the boundaries of 'Geldidon'; and Geoffrey of Monmouth pictures a figure, standing at Winchester, seeing London on her left hand and the forest of Celidon on her right. The Weald is plainly the forest of Caledon, and it is the Wealden folk who adopted the Cornish Arthur as their chief and designated him 'the Bear'; for, the syllable Cal- stands for a tribe that had for its emblem a Bear,* witness the classical story of Calisto who became a Bear, and the mediaeval French legend of St Gall (i.e. the Saint of the Cal- folk) who was led to his monastery by a Bear, and the northern epic the Kaleva-la which tells of a people prone to sacrifice to a Bear. Moreover Kaleva is identical with Caleva, Silchester.

Adjoining the southern fringe of the Weald lay a very important geographical feature in the history of the times, a river estuary that is now Spithead. In those days, or shortly before them, the Isle of Wight was part of the mainland. Even today a trace of that period is visible in the sunken turf of an old track that ran along the crest of the downs to the Needles, plainly once continuing to the region of Christchurch; and if it be followed up further in either direction, it is revealed as the old pack route from the Somerset lead mines, and perhaps the Cornish tin workings, to a harbour somewhere beyond Brading, on the east coast of Wight. Thence the metal will have been shipped to the mouth of the Seine, to connect with the overland route to Marseilles. Within comparatively recent times, therefore, the Solent and Spithead were the valley and estuary of the Christchurch Stour or Tarrant, which continued its course eastwards and was joined by the Test and Itchen to make a river mouth of considerable size. This was the *Trisanton* of classical geographers.

In imagining the old aspect of the land at this point, the amount of erosion which must have taken place, before the coast was protected by groynes, can be gauged by watching the constant gnaw of the heavy Channel tides against the foot of the chalk cliffs, and against the protective works themselves; an immense amount of land must have disappeared. And so it seems reasonable to surmise that the harbour whence metal was shipped to France lay on an island there, the one mentioned by Diodorus in 45 B.C., called Ictis, which could be reached by wagons at low tide. A century later the Isle of Wight is recorded by Pliny, so there are grounds for believing that the subsidence which separated it from the mainland took place at some time between these dates. Furthermore, a comparison of Claudius' plans for his invasion with those of Julius Caesar also suggests it happened between those two events, in other words in about the year A.D. 30. This is a matter of material concern, because on this changed geography hinges much of the history of King Arthur's times. The coastline sketched here is intermediate to that shown in Clement Reid's map of the ancient Solent* river basin.

The sunken estuary's appearance at the time this story opens was a huge expanse of mud flats, that at high tide became flooded and formed a lake, the surface of which was studded with islands, the remains of low ridges and hillocks. They were peopled by a clan whose name survives in the Kentish town of Lympne, the Leman clan, corresponding to the Lemovic of Gaul, or 'Warriors of the Elm'. On this account Lake Leman figures in the legend, but mistakenly translated as Loch Lomond; it is coupled with a remarkable recollection of its features:

set in middle-earth, with fen and with reed, and with water exceeding broad. . . . Sixty islands are in the long water. . . . There falleth in the lake, on many a side, from dales and from downs, and from deep valleys, sixty streams, all there collected; yet never out of the lake any man findeth that thereout they flow, except a small brook at one end, that from the lake falleth and wendeth very stilly into the sea.

Such was the former *Trisanton* estuary and harbour for the West Country metal traffic. Possession of its wealthy trade had been a source of strife for centuries, between Albany and Cornwall; and at the date this story begins the jealousy was even more acute, because, in the Lake's sheltered waters a still safer harbourage had been created, witnessed to by the subsequent Roman station at Portchester and by our later-day Portsmouth.

The folk of the Lake* were Gaels, in contradistinction from the Britons of south-western England and the Picts of the southeast. Not that the segregation of Britons, Picts, and Gaels was in any way absolute; far from it, the intermingling will have been almost, if not quite, as complete as it is between English, Welsh, Scots, and Irish today; only, also like the present day, each area prided itself in its separate identity, and to some extent maintained its particular characteristics. Throughout existed a Gaelic substratum, the remnants of the earliest Celtic incomers; nor have they ever been obliterated, and their traces in folk-lore are still to be found today. But being a water-faring folk, they inclined more to the marshes than the uplands. Different from them, yet amalgamated with them, were the Picts, the compound being known as the Gwyddel Ffichti—the Gaelic Picts; they were herdsmen and dwellers on the uplands, and they owned a propensity since fathered on to their compatriots—'the Gwyddel, devils, distillers'. This amalgam peopled Albany, Caledon in particular being Pictish. The third main division, the Britons, were predominant in Cornwall; that is to say they covered the whole south-west.

These three tribes had conspicuous differences in dialect, or even language. The Briton spoke the tongue from which Welsh has been derived, a 'P' Celtic dialect; the Gael, like the Gaul on the opposite side of the Channel, spoke a 'Q' dialect; while the Pict differed again from both. Consequently the tribal areas of Cornwall, Albany, and the Lake were even more distinct from one another than is Northern Ireland from Eire today, and with equally bitter antagonisms. They are to be visualized as—Cornwall, reaching as far east as the Test, speaking British; Albany, from the Test to the east coast, speaking Pictish; the south coast of both provinces, from Dorset to Kent, speaking Gaelic. The Test is being suggested as the dividing line for language, rather than the Arun, because from the story of events it seems that Alban connections remained strong in the Test and Itchen valleys, even though the rulership was Cornish. The point is scarcely of material concern, but is being made in order to provide

the probable colouring for the people who are going to occupy
the centre of the coming picture.

The two principal parties being the Cornish Britons and the
Albanys, inevitably the Gaels of the Lake figure prominently in
the role of a third party, courted by both and hostile to both. So
we will take a slightly closer look at them. Just as the Lemovic
on the Continent were Gauls, and just as Lake Geneva (then part
of Gaul) was known as Lake Leman, so were the folk on the
shores of the British Lake Leman Gaels. It is a circumstance that
has given rise to another important confusion in the geography of
the romances. For, the people of the isles were spoken of as 'the
Gwyddel', that is to say Goidel or Gael. Gwyddel, however, is
commonly translated as 'Irish'; and so it has come about that the
folk of the Lake are referred to as Irish and their territory as
Ireland.* This, after all, is no greater an error than might be made
by someone unfamiliar with the pronunciation Gallic for Gaelic,
in thinking it were synonymous with 'French'. Moreover there is
reason for believing that the Dorset kingdom of Iwerne, which
name is identical with Ivernia or 'Hibernia', Ireland, at one time
used to stretch as far east as the Arun; this was before Cornwall
became paramount, but characteristically it will have been remembered by the conquered Iwernians and recounted with a sense
of grievance.

The reason is bound up with the career of the megalomaniac
chief of the Iwerne folk, designated Iwer-awch or Ewrawc, who
built Maidens Castle in Dorset; he extended his sway, and also
built a fort named after himself Caer Ewrawc 'beyond the
Humber', which as we have seen means in the region of the Arun.
This name persisted until Arthur's day, in the romances anglicized
into 'York', so it is reasonable to suppose that the term Iwernia
for the district from the Stour to the Arun also lasted. It is a
matter of interest that the archaeologists' deduction of megalo-
mania, from the huge size of the earthworks, is borne out by
tradition:

Ebrauc, a man tall of stature and of marvellous strength . . . begat
twenty sons by twenty wives that he had, besides thirty daughters. . . .
He was the first to take a fleet along the coasts of Gaul, and carrying war
into the country to harass the provinces by the slaughter of men and the

sacking of the cities; returning thence with victory and enriched with boundless plenty of gold and silver.

Doubtless he will have said that it was the infliction of thirty daughters which drove him to pillage; yet others might believe that it was in the blood, for another Gwyddel has been especially remembered for his serene motto—'Better the grave than a life of want.'

Thus the neighbourhood of 'York',* the boundary between the rival provinces of Cornwall and Albany, each with its quota of resentful and predatory 'Irish' fain to deny allegiance to either, was one of the thornier problems of any British ruler; so we see kings and chiefs seeking to solve it through alliances by marriage, first in one direction, then in another. For this reason a short account of Arthur's forbears must be given, as they form the background of the scene on to which he stepped. His problems and decisions cannot be viewed in isolation; they are part of a steadily evolving picture of Britain, in which he during his life-time was the central figure, who is seen gathering together threads for mending a part of the material that has worn out. But always he is working on an old fabric; and it is the original weaving of that fabric which is now to be described.

2

Family Background

CARADOC AB VRAN AB LLYR is the name under which Arthur figures in Welsh records; so in order to appreciate the circumstances of his childhood, we will begin with Llyr. He is called son of Beli, to whom is given a long British pedigree; but this is plainly inaccurate, because he was of Belgic stock. Son of Beli, however, means no more than what we are all customarily christened today, 'son of God'; for Beli was the deity. Mediaeval heraldry ascribes arms to Beli, three golden crowns on a blue field, similar to those on Arthur's banner reproduced here as the frontispiece; and this heraldry, far from being meaningless caprice, as it might seem to be, is invaluable tradition of the race who venerated that deity, the British stock from whom Llyr was sprung through his mother, an East Anglian princess. Llyr and his family were remembered down to mediaeval times as the royal heirs to his mother's people.

The meaning of the Three Crowns arms is related in detail in Chapter 16; Beli's form part of a group of similar shields, and a map is provided on p. 261 showing the sites to which the group principally belongs. It is noticeable that the area they comprise corresponds remarkably closely with the finds of East Anglian Belgic coins, in particular Cymbeline's, mapped in *Archaeologia* 1944 and in *Antiquity* 1939; the coins bear out that the arms denote the Celts, while the arms themselves tell that the particular branch of Celts were the ancient semi-Gaelic stock known as the Children of Don.* The name of Llyr's sister corroborates this conclusion; she was Arianrhod,* the famous name of a daughter of Don, preserved in the constellation Northern Crown, Caer Arianrhod. At a guess, Llyr's mother may have borne that name; and an alternative shield of arms ascribed to Arthur, thirteen crowns,

26

speaks of the Welsh 'Court of Don'. We can thus think of her people in the terms of their Irish counterpart, the Danann— 'Everyone who is fair-haired, honourable, tall; every warrior, every man of music; the people of sweet string-music and of harmony; those who excel in every magic art . . . are of the posterity of the Tuatha de Danann in Ireland.' How it is that Llyr's mother came to be married to a Belgic Celt can only be surmised; probably he and his following were invited by the East Anglians to help them in an internal quarrel, and, as its romantic result, or as its less romantic price, was their princess' hand.

Classical history tells us more about this people, of whom Llyr became the king. Caesar remarks that a certain chieftain Mandubracius was the son of Inianu-Vetitius (the revised version of what used to be read as Immanuentius); while Welsh tradition remembers Mandubrauc as the son of Llyr, thus connecting Llyr with the name Inianu-Vetitius. Rather than being a personal name, though, it is evidently the king's designation; because Inianu is the name of a people, the same one as is personified by Ignoge* in British tradition, and represented by the Three Crowns arms. In the latter name the 'gn' is the obsolete letter which is the Spanish 'ñ' and the rune 'ing' X;* it varies from 'ng' or 'gn' to a plain 'n' or sometimes 'g'. Iñiañu could therefore be written Igni-agni; it is the Iana-ione of British coins, mentioned under JANUS,* and is much the same as the Greek Oenone, and the British king Oenus mentioned by Boece (Stewart, l. 2850). It is evidently the compound of two words relating to Light, instanced by the Latin *ignis*, fire, and the Sanskrit *agni*, fire; the name survives today in the surnames Innes or Ince, and Angus, which last enters into the coming story as Malory's Anguish king of Ireland or Scotland, and was also the name of 'Great Youth' of the Danann. In Chapter 16 is related how the Three Crowns stand for 'Light', and how the device of a crescent and sun is a world-wide ancient hieroglyph for 'Light', figurative though for light of mind, or Reason. Accordingly when we find that very device of a crescent and sun conspicuously used on East Anglian coins and on those of Llyr's family, we can realize that it is denoting his people by their creed, of Wisdom. Overleaf are some illustrations of the coin devices and their modern survivals, showing the consistency of the motifs.

Canaan & Phoenicia   China   Caspar   Moslem

ANCIENT HIEROGLYPH FOR 'LIGHT'

Icen   Essex   Icen   Tasciovan

BRITISH COINS

Horse brasses   John de Warenne
of Surrey, badge

MEDIAEVAL COMPARISONS

Icen   Essex

BRITISH COINS

Horse brass   Heraldic   3 'Lights'
(Surrey)   (see Glossary)

MEDIAEVAL COMPARISONS

3 Crowns   3 Conventional
of Light   Crowns

CROWNS OF 'LIGHT'

There are many other variations, too, for the Celts were imaginative and artistic, their skill probably being exercised largely in tattooing, which of course has perished; this field of artistry explains the survival of several intricate devices found in mediaeval heraldry,* clearly Celtic in origin.

Under Llyr the East Anglian kingdom grew in strength and extent. His capital seems to have been at Wheathampstead, through which ran the trade-route from the north-west to a ford across the Thames at Gravesend, and thence to the Channel port of Lympne, the earliest line of Watling Street. Wheathampstead was the frontier post on the Chilterns, between the Fenland Icen and the Trinovant of the Thames estuary; it will have been a 'thorn in the eye' for the valley folk, for the Icen were extending their dominion southwards. Eventually Llyr succeeded in conquering the Trinovant, and founded London;* in doing so he incensed the defeated people, by giving the fortress a new name instead of calling it after themselves. So they stigmatized him a foreigner, Llediaith (Lud), 'of foreign accent'. Perhaps, though, he never conquered them completely, because he lost his life in a fight on the Stour* of Kent; that was shortly before Julius Caesar's invasion, in about 56 B.C.

Llyr's family is tabulated in a Glossary note under CYMBELINE. In it he has been assumed to be the same as King Lear of an earlier chapter in Geoffrey of Monmouth's history, because, although the point is not of essential concern, it is indicated by a scrutiny of Geoffrey's sources of information, and it explains what are otherwise several inconsistencies. Geoffrey's first and second books are clearly Cornish in origin, but his fourth focuses itself on Cassivellaunus and makes Marius king of Britain, that is to say it is East Anglian or from Albany, while the third (a very confused assortment) leads up to it; thus the Lear of Book II has developed into a separate person from the Llyr of Book III, though in reality both are the same individual. Lear left no sons, but had three sons-in-law through alliances contracted in pursuit of his policy of East Anglian expansion. One daughter he married to an Albany chieftain, another to a Cornishman (almost certainly of Cirencester), and Cordelia the third to a Gaul of the Pas de Calais—Caer Icht, 'Karitia'. In the last we see the Atrebates of Silchester,* the Gauls from Arras whose chieftain Commius is known to us through Caesar's memoirs; and Llyr's action in marrying a daughter to them would seem to be the substance of the Mabinogion story of Lludd and Llevelys, when he settled the plague of a dragon of a foreign race by means of the loving cup. The traditional tale of his two elder daughters deserting him in old age is plain: in his attempt to subdue the Trinovant south of the Thames, in Kent, both his Cornish and Albany alliances failed him; only the Gauls of Silchester responded, and he met with disaster.

The tale is a sorry one, for his brother Caswallon ('Cassivel-launus') had sided with the Trinovant, and now seized his realm of East Anglia. Geoffrey's source records that he sympathetically recognized his nephews-in-law in their chieftainships of Cornwall and Kent; but little imagination is needed to detect the real scene of inter-tribal rivalry once again let loose, now that Lear's unify-ing even if acquisitive hand had been removed. Our own concern is with the Cirencester daughter and son-in-law. Their attitude during the great event of the period, Caesar's invasion, was mainly inaction. Boece says that in one of the engagements of the first campaign a Cornish contingent eventually arrived, turn-ing the scale in the Britons' favour, having deemed it better to come late rather than few in numbers. After that however they do not figure. Perhaps, like Mandubrauc, they resented Caswal-lon's domineering; perhaps they were more concerned with safe-guarding their own frontier against Silchester (which was in league with Rome), or were hoping to regain territory from it. Certainly the sons of the Cornish and Albany sisters both harried Cordelia's domain, so Geoffrey tells us. From the Cornish point of view, Cornwall was comparatively far from Kent, and like all its neighbours was unable to trust anyone; its own domestic safety had to be secured, and thus it held aloof. The inaction is not necessarily to its discredit entirely. Later events reveal the varying degrees of commonweal spirit obtaining in the different quarters of the land; the West led, and on that it is to be judged.

Lear's Cornish grandson will have been the Tasciovan whose coins demonstrate his recovering the whole of East Anglia, except the Trinovant Thames estuary. He seems to have governed East Anglia directly, but to have treated Cirencester as an independent tributary. Under him Verulam, the camp on the rising ground south of St Albans, in Prae Wood, became an important frontier station; and the trade route which used to run through Wheathampstead was now diverted past it to Dunstable. It would appear that the hill of St Albans itself remained a Trinovant outpost, and that by mutual agreement boundary ditches were dug between it and Verulam; and it can but be observed that the need for such a boundary mark must have been acute, because the ditches represent distinctly heavy excavation. At Verulam, Tasciovan established a mint, the control of the Watling Street trade evidently being of considerable importance.

Tasciovan's reconquest of East Anglia can be dated approximately as between 15 B.C. and A.D. 0. During this period two sons of his were growing up, Cuno-belin (Shakespeare's Cymbeline) and Epaticcus; their mother's name is said to have been Ywerit, an 'Irish' woman, whom we will suppose to have come from the Glastonbury district, among which marshes a people like the East Anglians continued to live a separate semi-Gaelic existence. What little we can discern about Tasciovan tells us that he was a progressive ruler, that is to say ready to incline towards Roman modernity though without surrendering native characteristics. Thus we notice an improved continental type of coinage, yet with national features; and he places the youth Cymbeline under the Emperor Augustus' tutelage at Rome, in order to school him for rulership. So, when Cymbeline succeeded his father in about A.D. 5, he was coming from the hub of fashionable society, the Imperial Court; and he had in addition experienced a campaign with the legions, in Germany. He was up to date and unsophisticated.

If the reason for the last remark be queried, it can be told from the intriguing designs on his coins; the spirit is British, though the form has a nicely classical touch from Rome. In place of the two crescents, set back to back, is the two-faced Janus;* and instead of the sun and moon, the true heavenly twins, are a pair of horses reproducing it would seem the Roman twin horsemen. But, making allowance for youthful impressionability, we can suppose that Cymbeline had seen through the gaudiness and sensuality of the great city; and he will have observed that, magnificent though it were to the material view, it lacked some of the

soul of his more simple native ways. At his age he may not have
been able to detect all the flaws, nor diagnose their import;
nevertheless he may well have recognized the brutality of public
displays and the licence in private life. Even if the appalling sen-
sualism of the Caesars after Augustus, described so disillusively by
Suetonius, had not yet set in, he must have encountered the
Roman mentality that was to accept it among their very emperors;
and he cannot have been but disgusted at the idea voiced by no
less a man than the famous philosopher Cicero—'It is the greatest
pleasure in life to see a brave enemy led off to torture and death.'

In contrast he will have heard the respect paid to the Britons'
fighting qualities, in recollections told of Julius Caesar's campaigns; and he will have seen the young bloods of the City driving
about in chariots, imitating the British battlefield dash, and have
noticed the girls dyeing their hair red—'It's so British, you know.'
He will have felt a tinge of pride at the thought that his countrymen were admired for their masculinity, and a touch of contempt
at the inhumanity of the superficially polished bully; and he may
perhaps dimly have appreciated that what was surrounding him
was a worldly civilization, deficient of the moral spirit which
made the roughest Briton a nature's gentleman, even if not up to
date with the fashions of the era.

Thus when he took his father's place in about A.D. 5, Cymbeline will have embarked on his duty imbued with his father's
policy of bringing the country up to date with Roman life,
though without relinquishing its native morality, and determined
to complete his aim of regaining all Lear's possessions, and more
—of achieving a united Britain, that is to say Britain south of a
line from the Wash to the Severn. With little delay he seized the
Trinovant territory in the Thames estuary, whose chieftain
Dubno-wellaun then appealed to Augustus for help; but otherwise
he seems to have followed his father's practice of forming a
commonwealth of provinces, ruling personally the Catuuellaun
and Trinovant area (Chilterns and Thames valley), while leaving
the Fens and Cirencester both independent but leagued with him,
and acknowledging him as High King. South of the Thames it is
difficult to be sure of what took place at Silchester and in the
Weald, and in Kent. From the coinage we see the Silchester
chieftain Epillus being replaced by Verica at about this time, yet

Epillus reappearing as ruler in Kent; Verica's position at Silchester is maintained for over a quarter of a century, suggesting recognition by Cymbeline, yet during the latter part of his time Cymbeline's brother Epaticcus appears to be exercising some sort of authority in conjunction with him.

Perhaps a clue to what was taking place there is to be found in Boece's Caledonian chronicle. Under the term 'king of Scots', implying Caledon, the Weald, it tells the story of what seems unmistakably the Atrebatan chieftainship of Silchester; it ends with a Caratak of Caledon, who can thus be identified with the CARA of a coin struck in the Weald. Under CALEDON in a Glossary note has been traced the outline of events in the district's rule. Boece's chronicle relates that now, round about A.D. 5 (regarded as the date of Christ's 'breith'), Augustus sent a legate to Verica and Cymbeline, calling for their alliance with Rome. As Cymbeline was already on close terms of friendship with the City, and as Verica responded by sending the Emperor a golden crown in sign of compliance, we may perhaps interpret the tale as a euphemism for Rome having bid Silchester, which was already her tributary, to recognize Cymbeline as Rome's representative and acknowledge him as High King. It would be typical of tribal dignity for the Weald to maintain that its vassalage was to Rome, and that acknowledgement of Cymbeline was out of courtesy to Augustus' request that it should be made.

One of Cymbeline's first acts after his accession must have been to marry; and although there is no direct evidence as to whom he chose, there is a certain amount of reason for believing that it was a princess of the house of Caledon. It will be seen in the forthcoming narrative that various Caledonians laid claim to the crown during the next generation, as though holding some inherited right to it; and such claims would appear to have been derived through this marriage. In romance, too, his trusted adviser is Ulfin, an anglicism for Alpin, the name of Caledon's hereditary kings, still perpetuated in the Highland *Siol Ailpein* today. His wife bore him a son and two daughters, the son being named Gwydr Togo-dumnus, in which the -dumnus or -dubnus is reminiscent of Dubno-wellaun of Kent and of a later Cogidubnus; it raises the thought that it may have been titular, the equivalent of 'Prince of Wales'. For, such was the child in the

Caledonians' eyes, a boy of their own blood as heir to the realm.

The Queen died, however; and for his second marriage Cymbeline turned to Cornwall, possibly with the feeling that having satisfied his duty by providing the kingdom with an heir of Alban stock, he might now justifiably take a maid of his own kith. According to story the lady of his choice, Ygerne, was already the wife of a Cornish chieftain. But it is highly improbable that Cymbeline's marriage could have been irregular, negotiated as it was by two druid ministers of state; something peculiar was certainly involved, as will be discussed later, but nothing outrageous or that was not custom. It was a political affair which needed to be conducted with absolute propriety. Hence Cymbeline's first step was to send an Albany druid to discuss the matter with the renowned Cornish druid Merlin. And here it must be remarked that 'druid' does not imply anything awesome or addicted to magic; it merely denotes men who had been trained to a high intellectual standard, with the characteristic faculty of judging problems impartially. Some druids had religious, scientific, or medical functions, and some conceivably used to abuse their calling by trading on men's superstitions; but in general they were philosophers of high, even international, repute, and statesmen, while kings customarily were druids. They were the counterpart of modern university doctors of letters, science, medicine, and divinity.

Without labouring the suggestion, it seems possible that the particular druid sent on this occasion, from Albany, was the writer of the old Welsh poem 'The Avallenau'; its scene is Celidon, and the events attached to it are not appropriate to Cadwaladr's day, as they stand in its present form. If it is correct that the poem really belongs to Cymbeline's day, then a wise-woman foretold Arthur's coming; and a delightful old-time romance is disclosed, between her and a philosopher, when in earlier years she had been a dryad.

Let us assume, then, that this poem was written originally about pre-Roman times, and that subsequently, like the Arthurian romance itself, it was given a Saxon background. Reading it, we see an aged druid making his way through the forest of Celidon, to a wise-woman who dwelt under a venerable apple-tree; they are old friends, and he discusses with her the shadow of Rome that is falling over the land. She answers him prophetically, though in veiled terms:

> I prophesy truth without disguise—
> The elevation of a child in a secluded part of the South.
> A golden rod of great value will for bravery
> Be given to glorious chiefs, before the Dragons;
> The diffuser of grace will vanquish the profane man.
> Before the child, bold as the sun in his courses,
> Pagans shall be eradicated, and bards shall flourish.
> All shall have their rights, and the Brython will rejoice,
> Sounding the horns of gladness, and chanting the song of peace
> and happiness.

It is clear that the birth of a great leader is being foretold. The druid bids her farewell, and sets off on his way back to Alpin's household. As he steps along the woodland path his memory recalls how, fifty years ago, he was doing the same; how he used to make long journeys to visit the maiden of the famed Apple-tree, spending the night under some forest oak before joining her, to eat a meal prepared by her own hands. And he reflects, 'She is still the same to me as she was, my "fair sportive maid, a paragon of slender form".' At length he reaches his journey's end, and in due course recounts her words to his chief; it is on this account that he is chosen to bear the King's proposal to Merlin.

We have now come to the scene of Arthur's birth; and the curtain rises on a woodland vista somewhere in the West Country, with two scholarly looking Britons discussing ways and means for helping the King accomplish his purpose.

3

Boyhood

'HE[1] SHALL posess the fair Ygerne, and he shall beget on her what shall widely rule; he shall beget on her a man exceeding marvellous. So long as is eternity, he shall never die; the while that this world standeth his glory shall last. All shall bow to him that dwelleth in Britain; of him shall gleemen goodly sing; of his breast noble poets shall eat; of his blood shall men be drunk; from his eyes shall fly fiery embers; each finger on his hand shall be a sharp steel brand; stone walls shall before him tumble; chieftains shall give way, and their standards fall. Thus he shall well long fare over all the lands, people to conquer, and set his laws. These are the tokens of the son that shall come of the King and of Ygerne.'

It was Merlin replying to his Alban colleague; and thus was Arthur heralded into the world. The Cornishman had agreed wholeheartedly with the proposal. What followed has to be sifted from the fictitious overlay in the romances. Imaginary, of course, some of the romancers' scenes and wording are, but they are attractive through the way they carry us back into the past; and there is always the chance that mixed up in them may happen to be some fragment of real tradition. The following immediate sequel to the two druids' conference (which was taken from Layoman) is quoted from Malory; it shows how fifteenth-century England visualized kings on an ultra-masculine scale. Anticipating if not moulding Henry VIII, Cymbeline has arrived at Ygerne's residence; his Minister, Alpin, says to the assembled Court:

---

[1] Uther's proper identity as Cymbeline is explained in the Glossary, under WEALDEN BATTLES.

'Our King is a lusty knight and wifeless, and my lady Ygerne is a passing fair lady; it were great joy unto us all, an it might please the King to make her his Queen.' Unto that they all well accorded, and moved it to the King; and anon, like a lusty knight, he assented thereto with good will. And so, in all haste they were married in a morning, with great mirth and joy.

Then back to Layoman's narrative:

Ygerne was with child by the King; (and) the time came that was chosen, then was Arthur born. So soon as he came on earth elves took him; they enchanted the child with magic most strong—they gave him might to be the best of all knights; they gave him another thing, that he should be a rich king; they gave him the third, that he should live long; they gave to him the prince virtues most good, so that he was most generous of all men alive. This the elves gave him, and thus the child thrived.

Yet much of his nature must actually have been derived from his mother, Ygerne; and it is a pity that there is practically no record whatsoever of her character. Attention becomes focussed inevitably on Cymbeline's share, on account of his known deeds. But some of Arthur's fine qualities are bound to have been an endowment from her; for she came from a distinguished West Country stock, being a daughter of Amlodd,* which name is accompanied by the designation *Wledig* or 'Count', and three of her sisters are renowned in tradition as mothers of saintly families. Of Ygerne herself the only description is Layoman's— 'Ygerne is chaste, a woman most true; so was her mother, and more of the kin.' These words seem more than fictional, and to be the dim survival of an oral memory, seeing that the comment about 'more of the kin' being chaste is scarcely usual. They call for an examination of the expression 'daughter of Amlodd'.

At this same age in the world, there were in Greece and the Near East sacred institutions known as the 'daughters of' various names; one of such was the 'daughters of Dan' in Phoenicia, instanced in the mother of the craftsman sent to Solomon for decorating the Temple (mentioned in *II Chronicles* ii, 14). Similar to them, so it would seem, were the 'daughters of Diocletian' in

Syria, legendary forbears of the Cromarty Gaels, and the 'daughters of Danaos' in Greece, also reputed to be ancestors of the Gaels in Britain. About these, the fabulous story of murdering their husbands on their wedding night can be discounted as the garbled memory of an ancient and gruesome rite, belonging to an ideal known as 'perpetual youth'; the rite, though, had long since been discontinued. They were religious and scientific institutions, and it can be assumed philosophic also. It is possible, therefore, that the daughters of Amlodd in Britain were a similar body; in which case Ygerne came of a stock devoted to public service, no matter how peculiar some of its customs may appear to modern ways. Part of this may be conjecture, but not without foundation; it is put forward as worth consideration, so that we may appreciate as much as possible the kind of woman who was Arthur's mother, and the nature she transmitted to him.

Boece's Caledonian chronicle is so insistent that Arthur's birth was illegitimate, in contrast to his sister's, which was in wedlock, and it indicates so clearly that this was slandered against him during his lifetime, that the legend as told in romance cannot be passed over cursorily. For the reasons already given, the tale that Ygerne was already the wife of the Earl of Cornwall, and that Cymbeline deceived her with the aid of Merlin's magic, encompassing the Earl's death as David did Uriah's, can be dismissed as fable; yet it must have been built up around some unusual circumstance. And as other daughters or grand-daughters of Amlodd conceived children under curious conditions, it seems possible that the mystery represents some custom associated with the name. One old custom which comes to mind is the feudal abuse known as the 'droit de seigneur', which may well have been derived from something far older, such as the Serpent of Aesculapius practice described by Sir James Frazer; it amounted to early eugenics, the seigneur's prototype having been the noblest in the land, its king or high-priest. So, as a guess, let us suppose that it was customary for girls born as 'daughters of Amlodd' to undergo such a rite before being wedded; but it must be regarded as undergone for a privilege, not out of crudity, the seigneur in Britain being a revered druid. As Cymbeline was himself one, he could have complied with the time-honoured custom before being technically married to Ygerne; and around this could have been woven the legendary sensational story. The supposition is being made with the purpose of finding a basis for the fiction.

. . . . .

Where and when Arthur made his debut into the world can be surmised with reasonable probability as having been at Verulam, Cymbeline's capital, in about A.D. 20. The site will have been the old British township, now crumbled back into natural soil, beneath the timber of Prae Wood on the hillside across the valley from St Albans. It is to be pictured mainly as a closely packed group of wattle and daub huts, surrounded by a palisaded ditch for protection; beyond which, after a short stretch of cultivated land, lay dense forest that only thinned where the ground rose to chalky uplands. The surroundings on which his eyes opened could hardly be called pretentious; we can imagine him in a small bare room, with walls of whitewashed plaster, opening on to a verandah with a courtyard beyond, where men would loiter about waiting for a summons to the King's adjoining apartment. It will have been the first adaptation of Roman building to British native conditions; for, after his imperial upbringing, and having made himself master of all south-east England, Cymbeline is almost bound to have built a 'modern' palace, to add to his prestige as well as serve his comfort.

And so, although the building would in our eyes have resembled a spacious staging bungalow more than a palace, and though we would have remarked on the bareness of its furnishing and the cattle-yard degree of cleanliness of the outer court, yet its reputation throughout the kingdom will have been one of unparallel magnificence, with huge rooms and lofty ceilings, all shining white. There Arthur will have grown up, with his sister Anna and elder half-brother Gwydr and two half-sisters, taught and his character shaped by his mother, his nurse, his appointed druid teacher, and by the various retainers with whom he was in daily contact. Chief of them will have been his foster-father Cynyr, parent of Kai, destined to become Arthur's seneschal. From them too he will have heard, as he grew older, news and gossip about current events in Britain and across the Channel, as well as from the travelling merchants and visiting chiefs' retinues when he mingled with the crowd or played with other children.

Let us pause for a moment to picture the traffic that used to journey up and down the pack-route past Verulam. Pedlars, travelling quacks, wandering bards, an occasional merchant seeking new fields for enterprise, or a wise-man looking for discourse, will have made up the groups of wayfarers keeping together for mutual interest and protection; they will have stopped at Verulam to spend the night behind the safety of its palisades. And there, in a travellers' courtyard, they will have been buttonholed (if the anachronism be forgiven) by the local gossips to glean their news. Trains of pack-ponies will likewise have jingled in and out, usually arriving in the evening and leaving at daybreak, and spending the night in the vicinity of the toll-booth. On the up journey their panniers would be laden with goods from the Continent—jewelry, attractive cloth or pottery of foreign design, Baltic amber, even a high-valued Roman glass; or there might be British ironwork from the Weald, sword-blades, spear-heads, arrow-heads, for local craftsmen to turn into finished weapons. On the return journey they would bring mainly raw materials from the north and west—salt and lead from the Stafford and Derby mines, copper ingots from North Wales, or bronze articles forged from it, and occasionally a carefully guarded package of goldsmiths' work from Ireland. From the accompanying traders, or rather from overhearing persons who had talked with them (for Arthur was only an urchin hanging about the crowd), he will have learned the latest talk from the Continent. Amongst it he may well have heard the Emperor's recent words to the Senate quoted approvingly—'A well-disposed and helpful prince ought to be the servant of the senate, and often of the citizens as a whole'; and the local yard-corner politicians will have been careful to let him hear their echo—'Ay, servant to the state', and (in British)—*Trech gwlad n' arglwydd*, 'The country is above the King', emphasized with a noisy expectoration.

Arthur will have watched interestedly, with his brother, the toll being collected from the traders, and being shared out with a Trinovant official, as the Thames folk's due from time immemorial. We can imagine the brothers becoming friendly with that official, and making their way to visit him at his home on the top of St Albans hill, which will have been a clay-plastered hurdlework hut, one of several at the foot of a turf tower, predecessor to the present clock-tower. Thence they may have wandered to the nearby holy well, mindful of their mother's bidding never to touch the elder-trees round it, lest that be taken by the people for an intentional insult. And they may have become familiar with the Goat* beneath the elders, no four-footed creature but a learned druid, inclined to be asperse with youngsters not of his persuasion; and they may have watched him at the annual Lewy's Fair, escorted by the crowd from his elder-grove to the tower, garlanded with greenery, to preside over it like his namesake at Kilorglin. But they will have heard from their father that these Ruis (elder) folk are never really to be trusted; it was they who gave Julius Caesar his safe landing at Ru-oichim (Thanet), by the Cave of the Verdant Green Edge. Arthur will have grown up to know, too, that he had a Trinovant cousin Cartimandua, grand-daughter of the traitor Mandubrauc who had allowed the landing; she was married to a chieftain with whom his father was on reasonably friendly terms, the lord of Brigance* in South Sussex.

We can also picture him visiting aged relatives at Wheathampstead, listening to them as they sat gathered round the hearth of a simple hut, regretting how the place had lost its importance. When the Gravesend ford had been in use, all the traffic that now flowed through Verulam used to come to them; but something had happened to the river bed, it had deepened and there was no longer a ford, the traffic had to cross the Thames* higher up at London, near the Yew-tree (St Paul's). So, when Arthur's grandfather Tasciovan was having trouble with the Trinovant, he had changed the line of the road to its present one through Verulam; it was shorter, and Wheathampstead's old prosperity had gone for good.

At times he will have accompanied his father to Colchester and London, Colchester being one of the ports for continental trade, and the site of an important mint. London he will have learnt to look on as a growing place, the gateway to Gaul and Rome from his father's domain north of the Thames. Periodically too he will have visited Cirencester, and his mother's home beyond it in the West Country. There he will have noticed a changed attitude amongst the country folk towards himself; no longer will he have been treated as the younger brother, but as the people's favourite. His father was affectionately known to them as Vran, 'Chough', or Pen-Dragon; while he himself was given to know that one day he would be their prince, for they wanted no Albany ne'er-do-weel interfering with their affairs.

.   .   .   .   .

At much the same time as this has been portrayed, when Arthur was about ten years old, say in A.D. 30, a catastrophe took place that will have caused his father to ride off post-haste from Verulam to the Hampshire coast, the first of several scenes to have fixed themselves in Arthur's memory. The news which reached the Court was that the sea had broken into the valley of the lower Christchurch Avon, the Camel or Dyfi* as it was then called. The whole of what is now the Solent, Southampton Water, and Spithead, which previously had been a low-lying wooded valley, had been turned into a huge island-studded lake, or, when the tides receded, a vast expanse of mud. Pwyll Avallawch's domain of Annwvyn,* the lower Ann or Test, had been swamped; what remained of it, the higher ground south of the Dyfi, was now an island, the Isle of Wight. The loss of life was enormous; and the trade rou which used to run from Christchurch over the Wight downs to an island harbour of Icht (*Ictis**) had been severed. Cymbeline will have had two problems to solve: the immediate one of finding sustenance for such survivors as had managed to reach dry land; and the one of later development, the rearrangement of the trade system which now used a new harbour near Portsmouth, in Albany not Cornish territory. The latter problem was hedged with difficulties, in that where previously there had been no question of sharing the trade dues, now there was a bitter wrangle because all the West Country trade was being shipped through Albany hands. For months there will have been tense bargaining over the terms, with feelings running high. Old claims will have been resurrected; for at one time Cornwall had ruled as far east as the Arun, yet at another the Test valley had belonged to Albany. The Picts of Netley preserved the memory that Winchester, Camelot, had been founded by them:

> The king of Picts, who was called Camelon,
> Founded a city called Cameli-dun;
> Which after was a city of honour,
> Of wisdom, strength, of riches and valour.

So writes Boece (Stewart, ll. 1425–30), though he sites the town in Scotland; but this can be taken as to conform with the transferred tradition. The point is not of material consequence, because other lines in Boece speak of the Ordul Picts of the neighbourhood; but the description seems worth quoting for the interest of an apparently transferred tradition. Considered critically, the Scottish site had no such conspicuous past; while the preceding lines refer to a prosperity apparently gained in Arthur's time:

> . . . of Caledon the first king
> (Who) in his time did many a noble deed.
> Peace and policy, riches and renown,
> Wealth and welfare in castle, tower and town,
> Pleasure and plenty, all were in his days,
> With law and justice . . .
> Over all Europe his fame did spread and spring,
> In Albion for the most famous king.

Here Caledon has been substituted for 'Scotland', and with that alteration it is difficult to believe that the memory does not relate to Arthur; because there is no one else of whom it could be said that his fame spread over all Europe. Let the idea be taken not as proven, but as conceivable.

Cymbeline's settlement of the rival claims was to admit neither, but to constitute Camelot a separate royal 'earldom', under his brother Epaticcus or Manawyddan;* and he included in it Pwyll Avallawch's land in the lower Test, called 'Rhiannon',* Pwyll remaining as chieftain of Wight and presumably receiving some other compensation. But as long afterwards his niece was complaining that her mother had been unjustly reft of his lands in the Valleys of Camelot, the compensation may have been in the nebulous terms of expediency. Thus Camelot became called sardonically 'Belgian Market', *Venta Belgarum*. The name was a taunt, by the Albany folk; to the Cornish it continued Camelot. The royal family was in no sense Belgic; fifteen-sixteenths of its blood was British. Never since Cymbeline's great-great-grandfather had there been a Belgic parent; nor was it he but his queen who was regarded as ancestor of the family, and she was an East Anglian Gael. Arthur will have learnt from one of his earliest recollections how bitterly his family was resented in the Weald.

Considerable interest lies in what can be gained from Welsh stories about Manawyddan. An anomaly in them which needs explanation is the entry of Caswallon's name; the person intended is Arthur's brother Gwydr, as will be apparent later; it is possible that he was referred to as 'The Catuwellaun', the customary mode of styling the chief of the Catuwellauni, and thereby he has become mistaken for Cassiwellaunus. In a triad Manawyddan is called One of the Three Golden Shoe Makers of the Island of Britain, implying that he travelled much 'when he was as far as Dyfed laying restrictions', from which we gather that his duties after the flooding of the Dyfi valley were incessant. More about the circumstances which brought him the name of Golden Shoe Maker is told in the Mabinogion story of him, though its allusions are so abstruse as to be doubtful. One comprehensible incident is that 'the illusion cast over the seven cantreds of Dyfed' was the result of Pwyll Avallawch's son having grasped a golden bowl on a slab by a fountain; this corresponds exactly with the custom of the Black Man of the Fountain described in a later chapter, and, as the flooding of the Lowland* Hundred is said to have been caused by the Maiden of the Fountain, it deserves notice for it is connected indirectly with Arthur and the Holy Grail.

During the next few years Arthur himself must have accompanied Cymbeline on some of his frequent visits to the growing Camelot, which before long was developing into an entrepot of foreign trade, a miniature Southampton. There he will have talked with Pwyll Avallawch, and heard from him the story of his disaster. This is what he will have been told, though in more picturesque language and with place-names long since forgotten, here replaced by their modern equivalents:

From Christchurch to the Isle of Wight, which then reached much further out into the Channel, there used to lie a forested valley that ran into the sea far eastwards opposite Portsmouth, where it opened out into an estuary called Trisanton.* Between Hengistbury Head and the Needles the valley was divided from the sea by a low neck of land. Along it ran the trade route that carried the West Country tin and lead traffic to a small island harbour off Culver; this could be reached by wagons at low water, and was called by foreigners Icht, after the name of the English Channel. The Hengistbury-Needles neck of land bordered a bay formed by the Frome estuary, and was always a source of anxiety, due to its being constantly gnawed away by the Channel tides.

Seithenyn, son of the chief of Dyfed, was responsible for the upkeep of the sea wall against this erosion. He was given to good living, and may have been neglectful of his charge; but that was not the real cause of the sea bursting through. The land sank. It may be that it subsided a few feet only, but with a spring tide and a gale blowing up the Channel the effect was calamitous; the neck of land was breached, and the gap quickly became worn wider. At low tide the water would recede, but at high tide it would return; it was impossible to repair the breach. In the matter of a few years the gap was a mile wide; and in the former valley most of the trees had been uprooted and washed away, or they had been broken off leaving only their stumps, the whole area being turned into a desolate waste of mud flats. Here and there hillocks remained as islands; but the old scourge of the tides ate them away one after another.

Most of the people were overwhelmed in the first rush of water; only a few, near the eventual shoreline or on the knolls, managed to escape with their lives. But they reached land without food, homes, or livelihood. None of the fishermen's coracles could stand up to the surge of water and flotsam; those folk perished wholesale. The peasant survivors' plight was terrible; at the best of times there was little food to spare among the widely scattered hamlets, in the forest clearings, so that the mainland people were hard put to it to feed the refugees, and in many cases literally unable to do so. The problem then arose as to whose responsibility it was to provide them with land, and to accept them until they could produce their own livelihood. The site of the catastrophe was borderland between Cornwall and Albany; both claimed part of the shoreline, neither wanted the refugees. Both tended to send the wretched surplus to the border, telling them it was theirs, and that the refugees might take what land they could and keep it.

The King's intervention was necessary for peace; and he found it best to create a royal estate, where the now divided trade tolls could be regulated, and the refugees absorbed. It was the wisest solution, though all the surrounding chiefs had to have their territories shorn, which left grievances in every direction.

.   .   .   .   .

Boys and girls who were to figure prominently in after years will have played with Arthur as children at Camelot. We can imagine Aaron Rheged* bringing his family over from Chichester; and we can see him carrying Arthur's sister Anna on his back, or chasing her round the playground, little thinking she will one day be his wife. With him are his first wife, Modron,* and her twins Owein and Morvyth, both to become famous—Morvyth as the passionate desire of one of Arthur's counsellors, Owein who was to be known as one of the three knights of battle in the Court of King Arthur. Owein and Arthur play chess together, as they were to in later years, and inevitably quarrel about their parents' rival Ravens. The two boys are separated by Cynon, then a grown man but already captivated by Morvyth's charm; already is he showing the good sense by which he is to become one of the three renowned counsellors, who—'whatever dangers threatened Arthur in any of his wars counselled him, so that none was able to overcome him; and thus Arthur conquered all nations through three things which followed him, and these were: good hope, and the consecrated arms which had been sent him, and the virtue of his warriors'. Even at this age, from his boyhood games and quarrels, we can picture Cynon perceiving in Arthur the determination that in after years was to distinguish him, the unquenchable good hope or strength of will which never let him give in.

Another visitor to the Court, at a slightly later date, is Caratak of Caledon and Brigance, who has just succeeded his father-in-law Verica in the chieftainship of Caledon; with him is his widowed step-mother Voeddig, also called Cartimandua, and her daughter, his half-sister Voada. Arthur was perhaps scarcely old enough to appreciate that Cartimandua was a lady with a roving eye, or that at the moment it was lighting single-mindedly on one

Venutius, also a chieftain of Brigance (Boece amends Tacitus), a
man of sturdy character; but his father might have passed the
cryptic remark that cousin Voeddig seemed to like soldiers. She
for her part cannot help casting her eyes on Cymbeline's two sons,
and wondering whether some day a daughter of hers may not
marry one of them; but Arthur and Voada will have played together as boy and girl, of maybe fifteen and ten years' age, un-
concernedly and without suspecting the stern part that she is
destined to take in history, under the Roman mistaken name
'Boadicea'.

Then there are closer relatives who come to the Court; and
if their names sound strange to English ears, let it be understood
that by nephews and nieces they will have been called by pet
abbreviations. There is Aunt Tywanwedd, an aged but aristo-
cratic-looking woman, formerly one of the 'daughters of
Amlodd'; with her is her own daughter, Cousin Yglais, wife of
Paul Avallawch and 'Lady of the Valleys of Camelot'. And there
is another 'daughter of Amlodd', Aunt Gwyar from Cornwall,
with her husband Erbin and son Geraint, the lad who is to have
so curious a romance with his long-suffering Enid. Occasionally
Arthur sees Aunt Branwen, married to Matholwch the 'Irishman'
of the Dorset sea-marshes, a sad-faced woman whose marriage
was intended to secure the allegiance of that chieftain but has
brought her no happiness. Also comes Cousin Kilhwch from
Caledon, a dashing youth whose appearance has been so delight-
fully described a few years later, when he

pricked forth upon a steed with head of dappled grey, four winters old,
firm of limb, with shell-formed hoofs, having a bridle of linked gold on
his head, and upon him a saddle of costly gold; and in the youth's hand
were two spears of silver, sharp, well-tempered, headed with steel,
three ells in length, of an edge to wound the wind and cause blood to
flow, and swifter than the fall of the dewdrop from the blade of reed-
grass upon the earth when the dew of June is at the heaviest. A gold-
hilted sword was upon his thigh, the blade of which was of gold,
bearing a cross of inlaid gold of the hue of the lightning of heaven;
his war-horn was of ivory. Before him were two brindled white-
breasted greyhounds, having strong collars of rubies about their necks,
reaching from the shoulder to the ear; and the one that was on the
left side bounded across to the right side, and the one on the right

to the left, and like two sea-swallows sported around him. And his
courser cast up four sods with his four hoofs, like four swallows in
the air, about his head, now above, now below. About him was a four-
cornered cloth of purple, and an apple of gold was at each corner, and
every one of the apples was of the value of an hundred kine. And there
was precious gold of the value of three hundred kine upon his shoes,
and upon his stirrups, from his knee to the tip of his toe. And the blade
of grass bent not beneath him, so light was his courser's tread as he
journeyed towards the gate of Arthur's palace.

Other visitors constantly coming for consultation with the
King, or passing through on their way to the great College of
Stonehenge, are druid ministers of state and professors. All of
them are styled Birds, with names such as 'Raven', 'Nightin-
gale', 'Finch', reminiscent of mediaeval heralds; but if we treat
these as modern surnames, prefixing them with 'Mr' or better
still 'Dr', we get a true picture of perfectly ordinary men going
about their everyday business. It would be right to disillusion the
mind of any fanciful notions when coming across the term 'druid';
it implies nothing more unusual than at the most does the word
'professor' today. So, when we read in old Welsh legend of Arthur
having a conversation with an Eagle, or when Geoffrey of
Monmouth relates that an Eagle* foretold events at Shaftesbury,
we can visualize the words as coming from two Britons blessed
with a liberal (or was it a conservative?) education.

Most conspicuous among these Doctors of Letters to be seen
making his way about the streets of Camelot is Merlin, the Black
Bird (i.e. Chough) from Cornwall, that is to say from the West
Country, for almost certainly he will have come from Stonehenge;
it is difficult to believe he would have resided elsewhere than at
that famous circle. But more frequently met with are the local
'Ravens', a kindred and more ancient establishment belonging to
the Gaels of the sea-marshes; both Aaron Rheged and the King
have their Ravens, who, like Irish priests today, are able to exercise considerable influence over their people. Another institution
among the Lake Leman islanders are the 'Eagles'; they are accustomed to frequent Camelot, particularly just before May-day,
when the Eagles from all the islands of the Lake gather together
and foretell events—in other words, lay down the law for the
year. Also among the heterogeneous Court crowd are to be found

'Nightingales' from St Leonard's Forest, 'Swallows' from Celidon, Ickle 'Woodpeckers' from the Fens, and occasionally a 'Heron' from the Lake; which last brings to mind the curious mediaeval dialogue between a Heron and a Chough, recounting the New Testament story of the Flight from Egypt.

As the years go by, and Arthur grows old enough to stand the fatigue of a long day in the saddle, he is to be seen accompanying his father and Gwydr on protracted journeys to Cornwall; there the collection of dues on the tin trade with the Mediterranean needs careful checking, while on the journey's course discussions are held with local chieftains, and justice delivered in disputes. Sometimes they follow the coast route through Maidens Castle (Dorset), Exeter and Totnes; alternatively they may travel by the north-west frontier station of Cirencester, then past the Somerset lead mines to Geraint's land of Cerainwg in North Devon, and, if we are to accept legend, to Ygerne's old home at Tintagel. Near Lands End, in the neighbourhood of Looe, they pay a visit to Aunt Rhieinwylydd, a very old lady and formerly a 'daughter of Amlodd', with her half-Phoenician husband Bicanys; in his time he had been a prominent tin trader, but now his travelling days are past, and the business is in the hands of his son Joseph. From them the royal party would hear news about their cousins Joseph and Anna, both of them settled in Palestine, the one at Arimathea, the other married to a Temple priest Joacim, with a daughter Mary who had a growing family. Indeed it is within the bounds of possibility that on one of such visits Arthur may have met his cousins.

.   .   .   .   .

We now come to A.D. 37, a year in which an event took place that was to exercise considerable influence on the subsequent history of the time. In view of the relationship mentioned, Joseph of Arimathea,* when the early Christians were expelled from Palestine, came to Britain and asked his cousin Cymbeline for leave to make a home here for his persecuted Church. Cymbeline granted the request, thereby earning for himself the affectionate appellation 'the Blessed Chough', Bendigeid Vran. Malory tells the story:

Ye have heard much of Joseph of Arimathie, how he was sent by
Jesu Christ into this land for to teach and preach the holy Christian
faith; and therefore he suffered many persecutions the which the
enemies of Christ did unto him, and in the city of Sarras he converted a
king whose name was Evelake (Avallawch). And so this king came
with Joseph into this land—Carbonek.

(*Morte d'Arthur*, XIV, iii & ii)

Thus we see that Joseph landed in Avallawch's territory, the lower
Anton valley, the name applying to the shores of Southampton
Water, which before the flooding of the Lowland Hundred had
been the valley running to the estuary Tris-Anton; it is not impossible that Saris-bury may retain the name, but be that so or no
it serves as a guide to the approximate locality. There Avallawch
was at war with a cousin, whose lands were on the marches of
Loegria* (Albany/Cornwall); but with Joseph's aid he was victorious, and so became converted. Thence the two of them
crossed the water; but opposition was encountered, and Joseph
was temporarily held a prisoner (*Morte d'Arthur*, XIII, x); ultimately
he was released, and established with Avallawch at 'Carbonek'.*
The location of this place is a matter of consequence. Correctly
the name is Caer Bannawc, anglicized alternatively into 'Benewick'; it lay by the Wasted Land, and was not far from the
Valleys of Camelot. Its ownership was contended, but throughout
the coming narrative it remains in the hands of Avallawch, and
has thus become known by his name—Avalon.* It is the Inys
Witryn, the Isle of Wight. The apples* that Avalon and Avallawch
signify can be likened to the apple badge of the present Highland
clan Lamont; they bring to mind the apple-tree in Caledon beneath which the bard (p. 34) used to court his maid, and the hoar
apple-tree that overlooked the battlefield of Senlac—they were
typical of the region. But Avallawch's right to Carbonek was challenged by one Ban of Benewick; the enmity of his family is constantly referred to in romance, and operated adversely against the
Church's start; it is probably one of the Wasted Land legacies
from the disastrous flooding of the Lowland Hundred. Why
Joseph should have been given so unpropitious a site may invite
surprise. The reason would seem to be that the main sponsors for
his venture were his two women cousins, Yglais wife of Aval-

lawch, and Ygerne wife of Cymbeline; perhaps it was all they could persuade Cymbeline to provide him with in their neighbourhood.

Not that the new Church ran counter to the people's current beliefs; on the contrary its teachings were extremely similar, but in purer form. The bard Taliesin writes—'Christianity may have been a new thing in Asia, but there was never a time when the druids of Britain held not its doctrines'. And Malory, in his *Morte d'Arthur* (XVII, v-vii), tells of the tradition that when Solomon instituted his Temple at Jerusalem, a branch of it found its way to Britain. This there is every reason to believe, because, in a Glossary note under ECCLESIASTES, that book will be found so closely paralleled by the relics which remain to us of druidic philosophy, that it is impossible to doubt the connection; Phoenician trade might be suggested as the medium, yet the source could be older still. Little heed customarily is paid to the degree of moral intellect obtaining in Britain, shrouded as it is by the backwardness of the material culture, and by the veiled mode of speech used; but there is food for thought in the druidic triad: 'Three things came into being at the same moment: light, man, and moral choice' ('light' being light of understanding, knowledge).

As a test, which shall we say is the more accomplished view of human nature: the one preached by this triad, that goodness is inherent in man; or the one of modern psychology, that goodness is only acquired by default? Moreover it needs to be remembered that Yesu in the druidic trinity was the spirit or will for goodness which inspired men to renovate or re-create the future. Cymbeline's grant of sanctuary to Joseph's Church was the natural outcome of this country's predilection for moral speculation, apart from cousinly sympathy.

In order to see the occurrence in better perspective, we will go back to what had taken place a few years earlier. The Crucifixion was not only known in Britain, but was learnt of with great sadness; the references to this in British folk-lore are of so consistent a pattern as not to be ignored justifiably, while Irish tradition relates it direct. Conchobar MacNessa, so it is told, was revealed the death of Christ on the cross at the time it happened, by the druid Oetno; he was so impressed that he became a Christian, and died from over-exertion in attacking a forest of trees

with his sword, which he mistook for Jews. In more prosaic language, he had a druidic grove of trees felled in retribution. The
trees we can surmise to have been elders, since Iscariot is the same
as the Cornish Yscau, elder-tree, which explains the legend that
Judas hanged himself upon one in remorse. MacNessa was punishing Judas' deed. Then, we are told by a Vatican manuscript,
in A.D. 35 when the Christians were expelled from Palestine,
Lazarus and his sisters, with a handmaid and a disciple, and Joseph
the Decurion of Arimathea were set adrift in a boat without oars,
which finally reached Marseilles; thence they passed into Britain,
where, after preaching the Gospel, Joseph died. And so persistent
is this legend in France, that all gypsies still make an annual
pilgrimage to where they came ashore at the mouth of the Rhône.
Joseph will have followed the tin route across France and the
Channel; this will have brought him to the Lake, as the flooded
valley of Southampton Water was called, and to his women
cousins who were to become the famed ladies of the Lake in
romance.

With him Joseph brought the relics that are so beautifully
perpetuated in the story of the Grail; and he became, again to
quote Malory, 'the first bishop of Christendom, the same which
Our Lord succoured in the city of Sarras in the spiritual place'
(*Morte d'Arthur*, XVII, xx). Thus began the moral endeavour which
runs so closely in conjunction with the military endeavours of the
period. But we have to picture the Church at the outset being
faced with all the prejudice that would be aroused today by any
departure from engrained custom, the aversion being aggravated
by its being planted on land claimed by an influential local an-
tagonist. Arthur is bound to have absorbed some of his mother's
interest in it; but beyond that, as a youth of some seventeen years'
age, his mind will have been more intent upon the everyday
excitements in the news of the time.

    •   •   •   •   •

By now Arthur will have begun to listen to and take stock of
rumours about the emperors at Rome, told to him by his father
and talked of at Court. There the complaint will frequently have
been voiced that it was degrading for Britons to pay tribute to

the degenerate power at Rome; and he is bound to have heard criticism passed on his father for doing so. The present emperor, Tiberius, was being referred to by the wags as Biberius, 'the drinker'; yet that was the least of his vices. One of the tales going round was of his having been entertained by a lustful old prodigal with nude girls waiting on them; and another of a woman, who had refused his advances, stabbing herself to death after openly telling people of the ugly old man's obscenity, so that the expression now ran in Rome that 'the old goat was licking the does'. It was known too that he wanted money, and that men and women were being driven into taking their lives or murdered judicially for it; while political advisers and unwanted relatives were being done to death cruelly wholesale. Men were committing suicide when summoned to defend themselves, rather than face the torture that would follow; even the ancient custom which secured maidens from death was being evaded, by having them first violated by the executioner; while the emperor himself was in the habit of watching the tortures and of devising new ones. So foul was his behaviour that the King of the Parthians was known to have written to him, charging him with the murder of his kindred, and with shameless and dissolute living, and counselling him to gratify the citizens' intense hatred by voluntary death as soon as possible.

Arthur will have shared the general resentment, and must have asked his father why decent-living Britons should subsidize this sort of bestiality. The answer was that, loathsome though it were to do so, it was politic; it would be unwise to try Britain's strength against Rome, because British resources were precarious, disunity could at any time destroy them. There were men and women still alive who could remember the lack of common concert which let Julius Caesar impose this tribute, even though his legions had been fought to a standstill and feared the Britons. Before Rome could be ignored, this country must forgo its addiction to party strife.

Soon enough the need for his father's acquiescent policy was verified. One of his daughters, Clarine, Arthur's half-sister, was married to a Briton called in Roman history Adminius of the Coritani; these are possibly the Coranians of the Arun (the 'Humber') that were treasonable in Caesar's day. In British romance Adminius is Ban of Benewick,* of the Lake, the same region. This son-in-law of Cymbeline now rebelled, deserting to the Romans on the Continent, with a small following; this will have been the result of, or the cause of, Benewick having been granted to Avallawch and Joseph. A new emperor had just succeeded Tiberius, by name Caligula; he was courting popularity, and common report was thankfulness for the change. Adminius' defection to him may have looked ominous. Before long, though, appearances altered. The nature of Adminius' reception must have been heard in Britain with astonishment, followed by half-credulous scorn. Caligula was on a campaign in the Netherlands at the time, but achieving nothing; the Britons' arrival was hailed as a great victory. A grandiloquent letter was sent to the Senate, conveying the impression that the whole island had submitted; the couriers carrying it were granted special privileges for speed, and were charged to deliver it before the consuls in full Senate and in the temple of Mars the Avenger, where great victories were wont to be celebrated. Other stories of the campaign will also have trickled through: how that, finding no enemy, the Emperor had concealed a few Germans from his bodyguard on the far side of a river, and had had the news delivered to him, with every semblance of alarm (after lunch), that the enemy were at hand. Upon that he had dashed out with friends and some cavalry to the woods nearby; whence, after cutting some branches and adorning them as trophies, he had returned by torchlight to taunt those in camp as cowardly, and to decorate his party with crowns. Another tale was that some hostages were taken from a school and secretly sent on ahead of him; he suddenly left a banquet, with some cavalry, and pursued them as though they were runaways, bringing them back in fetters. And to cap the farce, he had sent a stern edict to Rome rebuking the Senate and people because—'While Caesar was fighting and exposed to such dangers, they were indulging in revels and frequenting the theatres and their pleasant villas!'

What kind of a man was this for Britons to pay tribute to? The scathing question is bound to have been asked all over the country, with the corollary—Why was Cymbeline doing it? Perhaps, they will have concluded, he was ageing; he was over fifty. So his troubles began to multiply. The next to rebel was a brother-in-law, the Gael of the Frome estuary in Dorset married to his sister Branwen. The date of his outbreak can be taken roughly as A.D. 39. The quarrel was one of long standing, and concerned a 'cauldron' which Cymbeline had once taken from Matholwch's territory, and had subsequently returned to him as part atonement for an insult given him by a Briton at his wedding. The 'cauldron' was a much venerated object, one of the Thirteen Treasures of Britain, but which for the purposes of this narrative can be regarded as having been a fixed object with land pertaining to it. The ill-feeling lingered in spite of the gift, and amounted to the fact that the Dorset 'Irish' wanted to be independent.

Cymbeline went thither with an armed force, which prompted the Gaels to agree to a compromise, in the shape of the land being transferred nominally to Cymbeline's nephew, son of Branwen and Matholwch; but there was evidently an under-current in the proceedings, which, at a guess, was that the Briton, perpetrator of the original insult, coveted it. At any rate the nephew gave his allegiance to Cymbeline, and to his brother and cousin (the insulter); but it is noticeable that neither of the King's two sons, Gwydr nor Arthur, was present. The cousin then murdered the boy treacherously, bringing on a battle in which the Britons were worsted and Cymbeline mortally wounded. His dying behest is a curious story that in some veiled way relates to Arthur, in that Arthur is said to have infringed his wish; its interpretation though is to be questioned, so the story will be told more fully. But apart from whatever it may mean, the fact is self-evident that from now onwards ill-will continued over that tract of Dorset territory, apparently an island near the mouth of the Frome (in the legend near Aber Ffraw*), between its 'Irish' inhabitants and their Briton neighbours.

As Cymbeline lay dying, so the story runs, he bid his men cut off his head and take it back to the 'White Mount', Bryn Gwyn, where they were to bury it with his face towards France; so long as it remained thus buried no invasion would come from overseas. They would take four-score years and seven over the journey—'and all that time the head will be to you as pleasant company as it ever was when on my body'. This they did, and remembered nothing of their journey; they were 'unconscious of having ever spent a time more joyous and mirthful; and they were not more weary than when first they came to (one of their halting places), neither did any of them know the time they had been there; and it was not more irksome to them having the head with them, than if Bendigeid Vran had been with them himself'.

Some comments are called for. Firstly, although Bryn Gwyn is generally assumed to be the White Mount at the Tower of London, it must properly have been the Hill of Winchester, which went by the name of Caer Gwyn, taking its name from the stream at its foot, the Gwyn, still known occasionally as the Win or Winnal. Secondly, the four-score years and seven of the journey appear to represent the time lapse between the two Roman invasions, 54 B.C.—A.D. 43; that is ninety-seven years, a ten seemingly having been lost. Thirdly, therefore, the head borne with them on their journey will mean the tribute that was paid during the period, and was found no burden. Thus Cymbeline's dying behest that they should bury his head with its face towards France (beyond which lay Rome) must have meant for them that besides carrying his head to the Camelot he yearned to keep free, they should continue paying the tribute. Legend goes on that Arthur, disregarding the enjoinder, disclosed the head—that is to say, refused the tribute; he is said to have trusted to his own prowess to defend the realm, which was one of the 'fatal uncoverings' for Britain. The decision, though, was not Arthur's but his elder brother's; and that is the subject of the next chapter.

4

The Gathering Storm

WITH pipes wailing and women keening, we can picture the
Venerable Head of Cymbeline being borne up the Bryn
Gwyn. In front marched a choir of bards, amongst them the
counterparts of the Ferdan and Seanachaidh, singing praises of
his goodness and valour, and the accounts of his deeds and those
of his ancestors. Behind was led his favourite war-horse. The urn
was laid in a grave on the summit, salt was placed within; around
it were laid weapons and dead boars; then his steed was slaughtered and placed beside it, sods of turf and stones were cast over
the grave, and the company wended its way down the hill again.
Men's faces began to brighten, that is to say some of them, others
wore even graver expressions; but, as they sat down to a huge
feast signs of keen anticipation were to be seen, for now the great
business of the occasion was about to get into full swing—that of
jockeying for position in the new reign.

Succession to the kingship passed to Gwydr without dispute;
neither had Arthur the temperament to be disloyal to his brother,
nor, even had he wished to indulge in rivalry, was he old enough
to organize a substantial faction. Nevertheless a big change at
Court took place; the balance of power had now shifted to
Albany from Cornwall, all the appointments in the royal household as chief officers of state were open to revision. For those who
hankered after them, no time was to be lost in engineering support for their claims. Trinovant, Caledon, and numbers of lesser
chieftains, Chichester, Pevensey, and the Lemana Weald of Kent,
all could expect consideration; and without doubt they applied
themselves assiduously to securing support.

Manawyddan* had magnanimously withheld from making
any attempt to supplant his nephew; in the words of a triad, he

was one of the humble princes of the Island, who, after the death
of his brother Vran (mistermed 'captivity'), became a bard. In
reward he was confirmed in his Test valley estate. The Mabinogion tale of his being offered Rhiannon* in marriage is figurative for the district Rig Anton, Royal Anton; yet the grant of
it is likely to have been earlier in reality, and to correspond with
the appearance of his coins in the area (p. 33), while on the
present occasion he was being confirmed in its possession when
he made no claim for greater power. Thus we see him tendering
his homage to Gwydr at Rhyd Icen, the ford over the Itchen (misconstrued as Rhyd-Ychain, Oxen-ford); and, according to the
story—'honourable was his reception there, and highly was he
praised for offering his homage'.

Likewise did Arthur, who now became what may be called
Duke of Cornwall, with feudal independence over its internal
administration and justice, only acknowledging his brother as
High King for matters of external moment. Accordingly he made
his seat in the West Country, Armorica as it was called, the land
by the Great Sea. To what extent he was invited to join in counsels
over external affairs can only be guessed; judging from human
behaviour as we know it today, it is probable that the King's new
advisers made it abundantly clear to him that they did not want
their advice referred to Cornwall. Albany south of the Thames
was similarly treated as independent under Caratak of Caledon,
so it would seem, Gwydr's personal domain being the land north
of the Thames, as had been Cymbeline's.

In Caledon, however, the chieftainship was not uncontested;
for it seems likely that it was at this juncture that the Beric of the
Brigant, who is mentioned in classical history, began to press his
claims. Later he had actually deserted to the Romans; now he will
have been preparing to do so if he could not get what he wanted.
From what is indicated by Boece's chronicle it is fairly plain that
his defection was rivalry with Caratak of Caledon and Brigance;
for, Beric being synonymous with the name Verica of known
coins, and Caratak's inheritance of Caledon having come through
his mother (tabulated in the Glossary under CALEDON), there can
be little doubt but that some relative of the late Verica of Caledon
was laying claim to both Caledon and Brigance, in fact to Albany.
Conceivably behind the claim there may have lain some racial

factor; Beric's family was Atrebatan, while Caratak's family paternally was British; Beric could offer the Romans the prospect of his recruiting them aid in the Pas de Calais.

Whether for this or for some other cause, the Roman Emperor, Caligula, assembled an army at Boulogne and a fleet in the Seine, threatening invasion; this was in A.D. 40. The Britons correspondingly gathered together some craft, the command of which was given to Arthur. But the threat can only have been bombast, without intention of coming to grips seriously; as its abandonment is one of the more astonishing scenes on record. R. W. Morgan's description will be quoted:

Caligula, who felt a morbid gratification in burlesquing the most momentous measures of state, and scandalizing his subjects by the maddest freaks of imperial caprice, held a grand review of his splendid expeditionary force on the sands at Boulogne. At its termination, ascending the tribunal, he expatiated on the glory which already encircled his brow as one who had led his troops like Bacchus, Hercules, and Sesostris, to the confines of the earth-surrounding ocean. He asked if such renown ought to be jeopardized by an armed exploration of an island which nature itself had removed beyond the power and jurisdiction of the gods of Rome, and which the campaigns of the deified Caesar himself had only succeeded in pointing out to the wonder of the continental world. 'Let us, my comrades,' he continued, adopting the well-known phrase of the great Julius, 'leave these Britons unmolested. To war beyond the confines of nature is not courage, but impiety. Let us rather load ourselves with the bloodless spoils of the Atlantic ocean, which the same benificent goddess of nature pours on these sands so lavishly at our feet. Follow the example of your emperor—Behold,' he added, suiting the action to the word, 'I wreathe for laurel this garland of green sea-weed around my immortal brow, and for *spolia optima* I fill my helm with these smooth and brilliant shells. Decorated with these we will return to Rome, and, instead of a British king, Neptune and Nereus, the gods of ocean themselves, shall follow captives to the Capitol behind our triumphal car. To each of you, my fellow soldiers in this arduous enterprise, I promise a gratuity of a year's extra stipend in merited acknowledgement of your services and fidelity to your emperor.'

This singular harangue, which we are tempted to regard as the practical sarcasm of a despot not altogether insane on the ambition of the whole race of conquerors, was welcomed with thunders of acclamation. The projected expedition had been from the first viewed

with extreme distaste by the soldiery; and despite the indignation
openly expressed by the officers, they did not hesitate to give vent to
their satisfaction, and, with military jests and peals of laughter, imitate
the example of their imperial master.

Rarely can there have been such a puerile display by armed
men; and even if it be a contemporary exaggeration in order to
ridicule Caligula, it is the kind of report that will have reached
Britain. It is scarcely surprising that the Emperor was murdered
the next year, A.D. 41. He was succeeded by an uncle, Claudius,
who had only been left alive because his nephew knew him to be
too feeble-minded to be a rival. The Britons must have heard of
his character, and perhaps of the unedifying circumstances under
which the Empire's figurehead had come to the throne. . . . On
hearing that his nephew was murdered, Claudius stole away to a
balcony in terror, where he hid himself behind the curtains
covering the door. But a soldier, who was wandering around
aimlessly, saw the feet and wondering whose they were pulled
him out; he recognized him, whereupon Claudius fell at his feet
in abject fright. The soldier however saluted him, and took him
to his comrades, who for some time were undecided whether to
get rid of him too or not. Eventually, in response to some sort of
popular demand and after he had bribed the soldiers heavily, he
was elected.

To men of this country it must have been incomprehensible
that such masters of the world were really to be respected. 'Like
master, like man'; if the Romans chose degenerates to rule them,
there could not be much stamina in themselves. The Emperor's
defects were well known, moral and physical. His legs used to give
way beneath him when he walked; and when he was in anger he
would foam at the mouth and trickle at the nose, while his head
was at all times shaky. He hardly ever left his dining-room until
he was stuffed and soaked, when he would go to sleep, lying on
his back with his mouth open; his throat used then to be tickled
with a feather, so as to make him sick and ease him. He was cruel
and bloodthirsty by nature, given to watching tortures and execu-
tions of the most brutal kind; and he invariably gave the sign of
'no quarter' for a disabled gladiator, even for one who slipped
accidentally, so that he might watch their faces as they died.

This was the third of such emperors that the generation now growing up in Britain had known. It was Gwydr's generation, and it was Arthur's. There can have been little other sentiment than intense disgust and contempt, accompanied by an insistent demand that out of self-respect for themselves they should throw off the yoke of tribute. Accordingly Gwydr called for the return of Adminius and his deserters; and, when this was rejected, he refused to pay further tribute. Having with them two potential leaders for dissension in Britain, the Romans decided upon invasion. The trial of strength was on.

     ·   ·   ·   ·   ·

Thus the spring of A.D. 43 saw a Roman army again assembling at Boulogne, with Gwydr and Arthur making ready to meet its assault on Britain. The feeling among the people of this country will have been that they owned a moral culture (scarcely yet touched upon in this book), which they did not intend to surrender to the coarse materialism of Rome. The enemy was formidable, but he was approaching them in the spirit of *oderint dum metuant*, 'Let them hate so long as they fear'; it made men the more determined, as in 1940. They had outfought Julius Caesar's legions; they would outfight Claudius'.

At this stage, preparation against the coming attack was a task involving kingcraft as much as military strategy, because where the blow would probably fall was a very moot point, and a tribe which thought its safety neglected would be half-ready to compromise with the enemy. Nor is such an attitude to be judged too harshly: land was food, and food was life; a refugee people had only the charity of their neighbours to depend upon, and with limited resources charity were likely to begin at home. The situation bears little comparison with today, when we are accustomed to organized food supplies, rations, and Government stocks; in carrying the mind back to the past, we have to visualize everyone fending for himself, every man taking the field risking his livelihood if disabled, and with his wife facing dependence on her family for charity—all in all, public spirit demanding far greater sacrifices than we ourselves have to make.

Arthur and his brother will have had constant discussions on the subject; and will have argued the situation repeatedly with every chieftain, seeking to arrive at a common point of view. The problem will have appeared to them as in the map below, which has been turned so that the reader can picture himself in their place, standing at the centre of the kingdom and looking towards the French coast. The curious romance expression that Oxford was the centre of the kingdom indicates this very aspect; and although it is difficult to say exactly how the Britons would have visualized their country's physical outline, in an age without

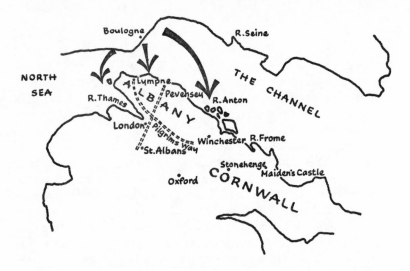

maps, it is probable that having a good knowledge of relative distances, from the times taken to reach various points, they will have pictured the problem much as it has been mapped here. Nor need it scarcely be remarked that they had not been brought up to thinking of land always as facing north. Thus from Oxford they will have conceived the Wash, the Thames estuary, and the islands of the Lake to be lying approximately on the edge of a semicircle, with East Kent as an outlying promontory. Accordingly, East Kent was a potential danger spot, being the least readily accessible to themselves, yet closest to the enemy. So let us imagine Arthur and his brother and the greater chiefs conferring on the problem, if not at Oxford then at some fairly central point like St Albans or Silchester. No attempt will be made to reproduce their contemporary mode of thought, because some of the factors governing their views will have been so familiar at the time as to have been understood as second nature, and unvoiced; it will be set down in the form in which it appears to modern eyes.

The first question is, what is the enemy likely to do? From his assembly position at Boulogne he can sail in any of three directions—eastwards (like Julius Caesar) to Thanet, or straight across to Lympne, or westwards to the new harbour of Portchester, or even further down-Channel to the mouth of the Frome in Dorset. Of these the Lympne crossing is the shortest, it lands the enemy in a conveniently remote area, where the populace is not particularly hostile to foreigners, on account of its trading connections, and where the valuable Wealden iron-fields lie open for capture; against it, though, is the lack of a harbour big enough to shelter a large fleet of transports. The storm damage wrought to Julius Caesar's shipping is a lesson of experience not to be forgotten; the route is possible but perhaps not probable, and the same applies to Pevensey.

Next to be considered is Portchester: here there is ample harbourage, and the disaffected 'Irish' of the Lake will undoubtedly help the invaders; but this route puts them ashore at a point where the Britons can most readily assemble, at the junction of Cornwall and Albany, and consequently where the greatest resistance is to be anticipated. It is certainly a practicable point; but a prudent enemy might well prefer somewhere more remote, where the characteristically non-co-operative Britons would be less incited to co-operate. The Frome estuary is one such place, where Cornwall is isolated from Albany; but it seems unlikely because of the long sea passage from Boulogne.

Thirdly is the possibility of Thanet: it provides adequate shelter for the transports; the local Trinovant may well turn 'quisling' (just as Mandubrauc did for Caesar, and his family are known to hate the sons of Cymbeline); and Thanet is the most difficult point for Britons other than the Albanys to reach, being distant from Cornwall and cut off from East Anglia by the Thames, which in flood becomes unfordable. Conversely for the Romans it is a comparatively short crossing. It seems the most likely place for their landing. And when discussing this, the Britons may even have been astute enough to forecast that from there the enemy would be able to shorten their sea communications with Gaul, by opening up fresh routes through Lympne and Pevensey as they worked their way westwards. It would be wrong to underestimate the ancient Britons' fighting intellect; men who have been brought up from the cradle to the pros and cons of how to outwit their rivals gain an intuitive sense, which might be deemed unspoken reasoning.

Having assessed what the enemy is likely to do, the Briton conference then argues about how to meet him. The first inescapable fact is that the Britons cannot collect in sufficient strength on the beaches to prevent his landing; word will certainly reach them from Boulogne when the Roman camp begins to stir in readiness, but their first definite news can only be the sight of the galleys themselves, nor can they then be sure of where the fleet is making for until the actual event. Only men from the immediate neighbourhood therefore will be able to assemble; men from further afield have got to remain at their homes until they know where to go. Hard economic limitations oblige them to wait on the enemy's choice: neither can fields nor flocks be left untended, nor can enough food be carried by each man to enable him to spend time in waiting; for, each has to furnish his own supply, and sparingly though everyone is accustomed to feed (like the Highlanders of 1745), the amount that can be carried or what wild produce can be foraged will last for a matter of days only. In consequence, immediate opposition to the enemy can hardly be more than guerilla harrying of his scouting and foraging parties, or, when he starts to penetrate, against his advance and flank guards; no stiff resistance can of necessity be contemplated until the distant contingents, from the further parts of the West Country and East Anglia, have reached the area.

Arrangements have to be agreed upon, accordingly, as to what the local chieftains shall do, wherever the attack falls; and undertakings have to be given by those likely to be remote from the site, as to what strength they will bring and how promptly. As regards the first, it seems that the initial brunt is bound to fall upon Albany, in one quarter or another; and much bargaining has to be done over sharing the burden. Cornwall and East Anglia would like Albany to adopt a 'scorched earth' policy, leaving the Romans nothing to benefit from, and, harassing their movement with guerilla tactics, preserving their own strength until a combined force has been gathered powerful enough to inflict defeat on the enemy. (Here a comment must be inserted on the word 'defeat'. It has to be appreciated, if not already apparent, that defensive fighting cannot be contemplated; the country's economic circumstances will not allow it. The blow when struck must be decisive, and the enemy be driven back, so that the fighting men can see the prospect of positive success from staying in the field, and can be induced to stay for the spoil to be gained.) Thus on Albany falls the likely part of having to carry the load on her shoulders alone, for at least a week; and who can tell how much she may not be called upon to sacrifice to an impetuous enemy in a week's offensive? Cornish and East Anglian chiefs have to assure her that they will arrive at the Kentish iron-fields within that period, and that the only folk on whom suffering cannot be prevented from falling are the Trinovant of the Canterbury Plain, supposing Thanet to be the place of landing. What then is to be offered to the Trinovant to persuade them not to make terms with the Romans, but to harry them despite retribution? Let us suppose the offer is that the spoil shall be wholly theirs. 'Wholly' though is a flexible term; all understand that nothing can prevent any individual, Cornishman or Fenlander, from carrying away what he can; all however are aware that there is a limit to what a man can carry for a long journey, and that the bulk of the Roman weapons, armour and stores will remain and be the fair share of the Trinovant, or of whichever coastal folk has to sustain the first onslaught.

But—and this will have been not the least part of the bargaining—promises are like piecrusts: Gywdr Togodubn must give some personal pledge that he will keep Albany's interests first in precedence, if he is to expect Albany to forgo them for the common good. He is now High King; and though he bears the proud Albany title -Dubn, he may forget it when in another province with persistent Cornishmen and Fenlanders tugging at his purse strings. Albany must be given a firm bond. The High King must marry an Albany princess. And he should do so now, so that there may be no retraction under prolonged warfare. His father was enticed away, after his mother's unfortunate death; the Albanys know well what devices the other provinces will use to gain his favour for themselves. So let the bond be welded now. (This negotiation is conjecture; but something of the kind is bound to have happened, as will be seen when the story further unfolds itself. Probably it had already taken place, and Gwydr was betrothed if not married; but as that has not been mentioned by any of the chroniclers, it is introduced here in order to complete the picture.)

Yet another point to be settled is the feeding of refugees. Albany cannot by herself provide for a really effective 'scorched earth' policy; Cornwall and East Anglia will have to contribute food, or else it will be impossible to dissuade folk facing the Roman landing from coming to terms with them. It is a thorny matter: unless the corn is given to Albany in advance, it will not be ready at the critical moment, nor can people be kept starving while it is tardily collected; on the other hand the Britons know the Albanys well enough not to accede to a payment in advance. We have to suppose that over this point some vagueness shrouds the outcome; in consequence the agreement on harrying the enemy is left plausibly to local enterprise, with promises that when the time comes food in aid of resistance will be furnished.

Albany stipulations having been satisfied more or less adequately, the Cornish and Fenland chiefs are called upon to give undertakings as to what forces they will contribute, and how promptly; consent has also to be obtained from Albany over what routes they shall follow when traversing her territory, because the passage of a host means the local denudation of provender, as well as high-handed incidents—it is a permission to be given with reserve. Geography provides the answer: the East Anglians will assemble at London, and the Cornishmen at Winchester; thence they will keep to the beaten traffic routes, which run from London to the coast and from Winchester along the South Downs, as dictated by Albany according to circumstances. At London and Winchester household troops will be kept in immediate readiness from now on; and the general levies will assemble as soon as the alarm is given, coming in gradually as a stream from far and wide, most of them reaching the rendezvous within four days. So, no matter when or where the enemy may come ashore, thither two steady streams of armed Britons will converge, from the north and from the west, swelling to full numbers within a week. As regards numbers, the Romans are said to be assembling about 60,000 men; the Britons (this is conjectural) will endeavour to muster the same, dividing the responsibility according to tribal strengths. Cornwall therefore will provide half, and Albany and East Anglia a quarter each, though Albany being the province directly assailed, it is hoped she will produce more.

Thus, in summary, the Britons' plan is this—Wherever the Romans may land they will be harried in guerilla fashion by men of the neighbourhood; all other persons will be urged by their chieftains to remove themselves, their corn and their cattle to the interior, where food will be supplied by their Cornish and Fenland fellow-countrymen. The chief of Albany will assemble his people and direct the guerilla fighting, but will avoid becoming involved in a pitched engagement. Gwydr and Arthur, from London and Winchester, will send their household troops to Albany's aid immediately, and will follow with their levies as soon as sufficient have gathered. On his reaching the fighting front Gwydr will take command, and when enough strength has been accumulated will give battle. In the meantime, until the invasion is launched, Gwydr will remain in East Anglia and Arthur in Cornwall.

And so, during the early summer we can imagine Arthur on the *qui vive* at a suitable place in his own province, moving to and fro between Maidens Castle and Cirencester, but mostly keeping near to the Anton valley. Periodically rumours from Gaul reach him, telling of Roman intentions, and more constantly rumours from the south-coast 'Irish'; at times speculation flags, at times it rises to a crescendo, and he wakes with pleasurable excitement— Will today be The Day? Young and full of patriotism, the prospect of measuring British strength against an avaricious invader cannot but have fired his indignation and spirit, causing a single idea to dominate his mind—the land they all loved was about to be attacked and wrenched from them; it behoved everyone to deal the enemy such a blow as would terrify him from ever again attempting to disturb its peace. Where he made his headquarters can only be guessed; possibly they were at Old Sarum, whence he could visit coastal and inland townships in every direction, checking local defence arrangements. Let us suppose he is testing the defence scheme for the hill-fort overlooking the sea by Christchurch, then fronted with a wide stretch of sea-marsh through which the Avon made a navigable approach: Was a regular look-out being kept on the Isle of Wight beacon? Was the fort's own beacon ready for immediate kindling? What was the alternative system for news in case of fog? If the enemy tried to land, where would he be fought, and where would the women and children be sent (for the fort was an out-of-date site, built before the sea had broken through between the mainland and the Isle of Wight)? Was there a definite agreement with the folk of the proposed refugee district that they would accept them? Were the men prepared for guerilla fighting if outnumbered, and what places had they selected for hampering the enemy's progress? Where would be the best point to which reinforcements should be directed? If the enemy landed elsewhere, were the men ready to go at once to the appointed rendezvous? The whole atmosphere will have been one of keen anticipation. (Should the likelihood of such meticulous preparation be queried, let the sceptic study General Skene's account of Pathan tactics in his *Passing it On*. Experience against them has taught the lesson: 'Never relax any precautions . . . the enemy is always there, and looking for you to make a mistake.' And that is exactly what the Britons will have been preparing to do to the Romans.)

.   .   .   .   .

On the other side of the Channel, however, a very different spirit was pervading the Roman camp. Perhaps this was not entirely unknown to the two brothers, from their spies amongst the Gallic camp-followers, sutlers and boatmen, and in subservient chieftains' retinues. There was rooted aversion for the expedition. The feeble spirit lay with the rank and file; the general, Aulus Plautius, was a fine soldier renowned for his capacity for swift manœuvre and strict discipline. Yet something was wanting in the system; he was unable to infuse the legions with his own morale.

So, when the critical moment arrived, the Roman soldiery

refused to embark. They would march anywhere within the world, they said, but not outside it, making clever use of the late Emperor's description of Britain as 'beyond the confines of Ocean' as an excuse for evading the hazardous task. Word was sent to Claudius at Rome, who despatched his favourite freed slave, Narcissus, to bring them to obedience. It is impossible to conceive a parallel in our own army today; the nearest is to suppose that some British regiments ordered on active service overseas refused to leave their barracks, in spite of their general's efforts at persuasion and appeals to their sense of honour, so the Prime Minister sent them a personal message through the hands of a foreign film-star. In this case the imperial agent was a eunuch; so when he ascended the platform, Narcissus was greeted with sarcastic shouts of 'Pansy' (the actual word used was a reference to the Saturnalia custom of slaves dressing up in their masters' clothes); these subsided to silent indignation, until he announced that he would himself lead them to Britain. This was too much for their self-respect; with shouts of anger the legionaries rushed to Plautius' tent and demanded to embark. He took advantage of the opportunity; the men were quickly marched on board, anchors weighed, and into the haze of a summer horizon the oars of the galleys swung, the troops knowing no more than that they were sailing westwards and their commanders had secret orders as to their destination.

Unaware of this last-moment incident, Gwydr at St Albans and Arthur at Old Sarum will have gone to rest that night with their usual feelings of happy-go-lucky confidence, their followers' apprehensions blissfully forgotten, after the customary nightly carouse. Let us assume the date is June 14th, the same night as that on which another Arthur, Duke of Wellington, more than seventeen centuries later was to attend the Brussels ball, firm-heartedly awaiting news of where his opponent was about to strike. Waterloo and Old Sarum may be far apart in time and space, but each saw a resolute man facing the same uncertainty; and each met it the same way, coolly holding his hand until the essential news came in.

5

The Storm Breaks

IT WILL have been during an early forenoon when the smoke of
a watchfire warned Arthur that the enemy were in sight, somewhere along the coast. With one exception nothing was to be
done other than order the household troops to stand in readiness
for an immediate march, and wait for news by runner of where
and in what strength they had been seen. All other action was
automatic: the signal taken up by chains of beacons sped to the
Cotswolds, to the Mendips, the Devon Moors, and to Lands
End; everywhere men left their fields or flocks, and, collecting
arms and a skin of meal from their homes, set out for their
appointed rendezvous. The one special measure needed by Arthur
was the despatch of a trusted youth, the equivalent of a staff
officer, to the Frome estuary to ascertain the reaction among the
'Irish'—Were they quiet, or were they hastening to arms?

Late at night a runner will have reached Old Sarum with
accurate news: the enemy were ashore near Portchester at three
points, in huge numbers; and the local 'Irish' were befriending
them. Arthur had only a few brief orders to give runners to go to
every appointed centre in Cornwall, ordering men to assemble at
Winchester; the Dorchester chieftain to garrison Maidens Castle
strongly until the attitude of the Frome 'Irish' was known. And
he himself with chariots and household troops dashed off into
the night, for Camelot.

The term 'runner' is far too prosaic, though, for the times
when these events were being enacted. Let us instead imagine
such men as the three described in a contemporary tale:

With Henbedestyr there was not anyone who could keep pace,
either on horseback or on foot; with Henwas no four-footed beast

could run the distance of an acre, much less go beyond it; and as to Sgilti, when he intended to go upon a message for his lord, he never sought to find a path, but knowing whither he was to go, if his way led through a wood he went along the tops of the trees—during his whole life a blade of reed grass bent not beneath his feet, much less did one ever break, so lightly did he tread.

It recalls the Anglo-Indian injunction—'Bringing master *chota peg*, running, hopping, skipping, jumping, never minding corners!' Which may serve to bring to the mind's eye the kind of master who was sending out these runners: lighthearted like any modern soldier off duty; but uncompromisingly efficient when under arms.

Turning to the invaders, from their point of view the first day's operation was a complete success: no opposition had been encountered, and on the other hand they had received some help from Adminius' islanders. They had made their landing in three divisions, one near Portchester, one at Bosham, and the third probably between them; the Portchester division was now attacking a British fort in the neighbourhood, but that was a small matter. During the next two or three days the disembarkation will have been completed, and the landing of stores begun. Plautius then may well have breathed a sigh of relief: he was ashore, concentrated, and in overwhelming force; he had four of the best legions in the Empire, the IInd, IXth, XIVth, and XXth, as well as some German auxiliaries; while in command of the IInd was Vespasian, already a distinguished leader.

To Arthur, looking down on this assembly and its outposts on Ports Down from Walderton Down above Bosham, the prospect must have been forbidding: forty thousand well-armed and trained men; there were not quite so many as their spies had reported from Boulogne, but that was not to say a second convoy might not follow. The orderliness of their ways made the spectacle the more imposing. Parties moved about in close-formed bodies, unlike the straggling bunches of independent and heedless Britons; to waylay them would be harder, which meant bigger ambushes and more difficult to conceal. Their camps were in neat rectangles, with wide clear streets leading to the centre of each face, so that reinforcements could move quickly to any point— Arthur could remember his father telling him about this, in his experiences of his German campaign, and how seasoned generals had kept on repeating to him that disciplined methods served to enhance strength. He could see signal stations already sending messages from camp to camp, telling that their commandants were ready to co-operate with one another. He was in for stiff fighting.

Against them it was true that his brother and he were assembling a great host; but would all the agreements be kept? As yet there was no word from Albany, nor were the folk round Portchester showing much enthusiasm; rather than take up arms they seemed more concerned with removing their goods and families into hiding in the woods. A messenger sent to Chichester had come back with a non-committal reply. They were an uncertain people. Perhaps they were afraid that some of the Roman army from Boulogne would make for Thanet, and that this landing was a stratagem to mislead the Britons over their real intention. Anyway his own duty was clear, as had been agreed upon, to harry the enemy. And he must have begun to plan in his own mind possible places between Portchester and Winchester where he could hamper their advance; because Camelot was surely the point they were aiming for?

It will have been somewhat of a surprise, therefore, when a few days later the heavily armed and well-drilled columns headed eastwards instead of west, and when he saw them form into a huge compact army on the downs, marching towards the Arun and skirting the forest of Caledon. This beginning stage of the campaign is told in the legend of Arthur's hunting the Boar of Caledon. In it, a prince of Caledon enlists his help against a 'Boar', a king who had been turned into a swine for his sins. British invective has not changed much through the ages! However, a more serious alternative clue to the term can be seen in the boar* embossed on a Roman shield recovered from the bed of the Thames. The legend goes on to describe the column of spearmen's appearance as it wound its way across the open downs or through the woods in the valleys intersecting them—'(the Boar's) bristles were like silver wire; and whether he went through the wood or through the plain, he was to be traced by the glittering of his bristles'.

A small but happier tradition to relate is that there were at least some staunch men among the Gaels of the Lake. The story is taken from *Kilhwch and Olwen*, where the scene is laid in Ireland. But as has already been explained (p. 24), 'Irish' means the generic term Gaels, while 'Ireland'* can apply to any of the territory south of the downs. So, in the following quotation, 'Irish' is being rendered Gaels, and 'Ireland' the Lake, although with the understanding that the coastal flats by Chichester are also included. The story runs that Arthur went to the Lake with a following, where he evidently succeeded in rallying some resistance, though not in sufficient strength to stop the Boar's progress:

When Arthur had landed in the country, there came unto him the saints of The Lake and besought his protection; and he granted his protection unto them, and they gave him their blessing. Then the men of The Lake came unto Arthur, and brought him provisions. And Arthur went as far as the place where the 'Boar' was with his seven young pigs; and the dogs were let loose upon him from all sides. That day until evening the Gaels fought with him, nevertheless he laid waste the fifth part of The Lake.'

Read in this light the story seems to preserve remarkable accuracies: Arthur persuaded the people through their druids, they then brought him provisions, and then they endeavoured to check the Romans, bringing upon themselves due retaliation. The site of their resistance must have been between Chichester and the Arun.

At the crossing of the Arun, though, it is to be feared that the Coritani lent the Romans their assistance; for there is no record of opposition at a place where it might have been expected, and where they were settled. If they are the same people as the Coranians, they had been treacherous before, in Lear's reign; they were regarded as one of the three plagues of the Isle of Britain. Contrastedly at the next river, the Adur, traces of a battle have been found near Beeding, which legend seems to indicate was fought by Arthur's household troops before he himself had arrived; this could be explained by his having returned to Winchester to hasten the march of the Cornish contingents as soon as they reached it. The Roman plan of operations was now beginning to take shape: they were evidently marching along the downs, parallel with the coast, being supplied by sea and aiming for a harbour that would give them a shorter communication with Boulogne.

From now on the British resistance is headed by Arthur, who endeavoured to hold the line of the Sussex Ouse, near Lewes— 'The first battle in which he was engaged was the mouth of the river Glein', writes Nennius the Briton historian. This has been identified by W. G. Collingwood as the Glynde, familiar today through the Glyndebourne musical festival. Excavation has revealed that the Britons hastily refortified the derelict Caburn hill defences above it, but it was stormed by the Romans. Slightly anomalously, the classical historian Dion Cassius relates that the Britons would not come to close quarters, taking refuge instead in swamps and forests, hoping to wear out the enemy by fruitless efforts, and that Plautius had a great deal of trouble in searching them out. Dio's version does not accord with this or with after events, however; it reads rather like the post-war reminiscences of a veteran, whose unit was with the main body and did not happen to be engaged. We can hear that warrior telling his friends: 'We used to have a spot of bother at the marshy river-crossings, but otherwise never caught sight of a scallywag; all I remember was day after day of trekking across the open downs in scorching sunshine, not a breath of air stirring, and by Jove wasn't the sun on our armour hot!' In point of fact, so far from finding difficulty in coming into contact with the Britons, Plautius encountered Arthur's opposition at almost every stream. It may be that Arthur's tactics were to hold up the advance guard until the heavily armed main body had deployed and come up in support, and then, when a set attack had been 'all buttoned up' (to use modern jargon), he would slip away into the woods; but those were the very tactics for the circumstances. Under his crippling disparity in numbers and armour, they resulted in his resistance never being broken; it was bent, but remained resilient.

The Romans having forced the line of the Ouse, Anderida* (Pevensey) now fell into their hands, giving them good and closer communication with Boulogne. It was turned by them into an advanced base, Portchester continuing as the main one. How did it come about, the question may be asked, that a stiffer resistance was not made on the Glynde? Within twenty miles of the heart of the Weald, and with the valuable port of Anderida at stake, the

Britons might have been expected to flock there in thousands; instead of which a legionary gained the impression that his general was having difficulty in getting to close quarters with them. The answer seems to be that the people of the district were half in league with Rome; trade figured higher in their minds than liberty. The name Anderida is reminiscent of the personal name Andrauc, who was the chieftain (alternatively called Mandubrauc) that allowed Julius Caesar an unopposed landing in Thanet. In the Glossary it is shown how the town can be recognized as having belonged to the Leman 'Irish'; disloyalty was manifesting itself.

Having established themselves at Pevensey, the Romans turned northward into the Weald, following the British track which led to London ford, and clearing it as they went into a straight unmetalled road. Gwydr now joined the battle-front and took command. What had kept him away is not told, but everything points to its having been political necessity: maybe the Trinovant of Essex were proving undependable, for the Romans are bound to have tried to resurrect Mandubrauc's disloyalty; maybe Silchester was showing signs of wavering, under the banished Beric's influence, supported with Roman gold. Between the brothers, on the other hand, perfect concord is clear: Arthur was the trusted second-in-command, whose leadership was relied upon until the elder were in a position to take it over himself; and when that happened, Arthur dropped back loyally into his due role, fighting with such verve that the subsequent battles have been customarily associated with his name.

Slowly the methodically made Roman road* thrust itself forward through the Weald, maintaining at its head a fighting force of irresistible strength. The Britons strove obstinately to check it, wherever the thick undergrowth of a stream or river gave their guerilla tactics a chance; but despite the two brothers' efforts it forged steadily ahead like a steam-roller. Nennius states that Arthur's next four battles were fought on the river 'Duglas', which is to say the Black Stream, a name that clung to the Kent Water even down to mediaeval times, and was applicable to all the rivulets of the Black Country feeding the upper Medway. Today, as seen when motoring along the highway towards Eden-bridge, the heather-covered folds of the Ashdown Forest are bare of cover for an ambush; but then, before heedless felling and the

voracity of the charcoal burners' goats had stripped them of
timber and thicket, they were a tangle of ash-tree, hazel and
briar. In imagination the scene can be re-created: a jungle, and out
of it a javelin might flash, or a sling stone find its mark with a
sudden thud, bringing down a careless flank-guard in spite of his
armour. Or, names such as Hammerwood and Furnace Pond
help to conjure up another picture: the shallow dip in the ground
terraced into a chain of ponds by mill-dam after mill-dam, feeding
the water-wheels that drive the smithy hammers; behind these,
facing the enemy through the trees, is a throng of Britons lined
up for battle, aware that the heavily armoured legionaries will only
be able to plough their way across the muddy bottom with difficulty. We can appreciate the Roman commander's problem:
Could he rely on his troops' fighting discipline to carry them
through? or, had he better send pioneers forward to break the
dams and drain the ponds, before ordering the assault? or, when
the pioneers had done their work, would it be safer to pause for
a day or two until sunshine had dried the pond-beds a little?
Morale will have been a governing factor; and it may well be that
the invader found himself obliged to bolster it up with careful
organization. Thus, with a powerful combination of sheer
strength and skilful method, Aulus Plautius penetrated deeper
and deeper into Gwydr's Britain.

For, sad to say, it was Gwydr's domain he was fighting, not a
United Britain. Lack of gallantry never caused the brothers' inability to stem the tide. Lack of will to take up arms was the
unhappy reason; political discord was acute. This can be read
between the lines of Dio's narrative, when he states that after
Arthur and Gwydr in turn had been defeated—'a part of the
Bodunni who were under the overlordship of the Catuellaun'
capitulated. The overlordship was festering. Once again the
classical wording seems to have caught an echo of local resentment; the Briton who had used the word Catuellaun was speaking
scathingly, it was tantamount to saying 'foreigner' and it was
partisanship, for Gwydr's generation was four removed from
that of the Belgic Catuellaun, and his family primarily regarded
themselves as Gaels—Icen fenlanders—not even as Cornishmen.
(This is evidenced by the traditional pedigrees and by the fabulous
arms assigned to them in the Middle Ages.) 'Catuellaun' was an

insinuation, uttered to conceal a selfish refusal to join the national cause.

Bodunni* is perhaps a mistaken rendering of Dobunni; and although that folk are mentioned elsewhere as having been in the Cirencester neighbourhood, spelt as Dobounoi, they can have been in the Weald too, for the word is a nickname—Dobona, the people of the Black* Country. So, when Dio relates that after their surrender, 'Leaving a garrison there, he advanced further and came to a river,' we can interpret and amplify the words as that Plautius, after clearing the Black Country as far as the Eden valley, posted a detachment to guard his left flank and then, wheeling right-handed towards East Kent down Pilgrims Way, came to the lower Medway (*see* map p. 80). The site of the garrison is indicated by the romances, which call it Caer Lindecoit, the Camp in the Linden Wood; this corresponds with Nennius' name for the region, Linnuis. It implies a clan whose badge was the Linden, like the Scottish Lindsay, and whose groves were of Lime* trees; Geoffrey of Monmouth calls the district 'Lincoln', which is indicated by the Linkelne, south of Edenbridge, though the actual post will have been west of the line of advance, more towards the Laencan of Lingfield. Probably it was held for the Romans by the Dobunni who had now become 'friendlies'.

The Roman plan of campaign is now clear: they intended to capture and consolidate the isolated south-east corner of Britain, the counties lying between the Thames and the Channel—Sussex, Surrey and Kent—before making their next move. It was political strategy, that would deprive the rest of the country of Albany's assistance in men and trade; it would be a lever for making the rule of Lear's house unpopular, and pave the way for replacing it with a nominee subservient to them.

Plautius, having secured his communications against interruption, from Pevensey to Pilgrims Way, by means of the Lindecoit detachment, aimed at crossing the lower Medway and subduing East Kent. Resistance, though, did not flag. Near Ightham he found himself obliged to storm Oldbury Camp; and on the Medway Gwydr and Arthur strongly resisted him, a two-day battle taking place at the ford below Aylesford. In Nennius' account this is Arthur's sixth battle, Lussas, a name which

has been preserved in the stream and district of Loose near
Maidstone; local tradition around 'Kits Coty House', a cromlech
overlooking the ford, also retains the story that two Roman
generals fought in an action here, a singularly accurate recollection of the fact that both Plautius and Vespasian were present.

The landscape then will have differed greatly from its present
appearance. Instead of open hillsides sloping down to the river in
cornfields and pasture, there was a thick carpet of forest, oak and
beech, changing in the low ground to willow and alder, with an
undergrowth of thorn-bushes and brambles; the very name 'Kits
Coty', apparently a corruption of Cat Coit, the Battle of the Wood,
presents a picture of such a covering over all the land downhill
of Pilgrims Way to the banks of the river, a long slant of forest
brakes within which the fight was to ebb and flow. Skirting its
upper edge, where chalk replaced the clay and where timber
would not grow, ran the track known later as Pilgrims Way.
Other place-names enable features to be reconstructed: at Boxley
will have been a small clearing, with a sacred grove of box-trees
and a hamlet belonging to a Chatti settlement, one of a group
stretching over the hill to Chatham and Chattenden. Not pure-
blooded Gaels these, but Cymry* from the valley of the Rhine
although calling themselves 'Irish', and either not disposed to
combine with, or not welcomed by, their neighbours of the
Weald. Even today the difference is maintained between the
people east and west of the Medway, between the 'Men of Kent'
and the 'Kentish Men'; trivial though it may sound, it has lasted
for over three thousand years, bringing home to us the acuteness
of the disunity which Arthur and his brother had to face. Supposing the men who so sturdily resisted the Romans on the
Medway had added their endeavours earlier to the opposition on
the Weald: surely the enemy would never have reached Pilgrims
Way?

Dio describes the battle:

The barbarians thought that the Romans would not be able to
cross (the river) without a bridge, and consequently bivouacked in
rather careless fashion on the opposite bank; but (Plautius) sent across a
detachment of Germans, who were accustomed to swim easily in full
armour across the most turbulent streams. These fell unexpectedly upon
the enemy, but instead of shooting at any of the men they confined

themselves to wounding the horses that drew their chariots; and in the confusion that followed, not even the enemy's mounted warriors could save themselves. Plautius therefore sent across Flavius Vespasian also ... and his brother Sabinus, who was acting as his lieutenant. So they too got across the river in some way and killed many of the foe, taking them by surprise. The survivors, however, did not take to flight, but on the next day joined issue with them again. The struggle was indecisive until Gnaeus Hostidius Geta, after narrowly missing being captured, finally managed to defeat the barbarians so soundly that he received the *ornamenta triumphalia*, though he had not been consul.

A word must be said about the term 'barbarians', lest a wrong impression be gained as to the nature of British manners. Among other characteristics it was applied by the Romans to people who wore breeches instead of their own long tunics; so much so, that a customary phrase for becoming civilized was 'to discard the breeches'—one can only comment, *altera tempora altera mores!*

The battle was decisive, British opposition collapsed; for the time being Gwydr and Arthur could do no more. Plautius for his part, also, was fain to rest; so, as winter was approaching, he withdrew his army to Portchester for a double purpose—to await the Emperor's arrival in the spring, when Claudius might finish the campaign and reap its glory, and to refit. But he left behind two garrisons in hill-forts to secure such territory as had submitted to him, the one in the Weald at Caer Lindecoit, the other on the South Downs by Chichester; also, though it is nowhere mentioned, there must have been one at Pevensey. These, together with the battles of the summer, are shown on the map overleaf.

In the romances the South Downs hill-fort goes by the name 'York';* this represents the British name Eurawc, and has no connection with the North Country site, but was derived from the Dorset chieftain Evrawc who had built both it and Maidens Castle. It is described in Geoffrey of Monmouth's history as 'beyond the Humber'; the narrator though was looking westwards, because Maidens Castle comes third in his enumeration, so 'beyond' is to be interpreted as 'west of' the Arun. It seems most probably to have been on the downs above Chichester, in continuation of the Ports Down line of outposts, at a point where the intricate and thickly wooded valleys afforded the Britons great opportunities for collecting and harrying the coast camps;

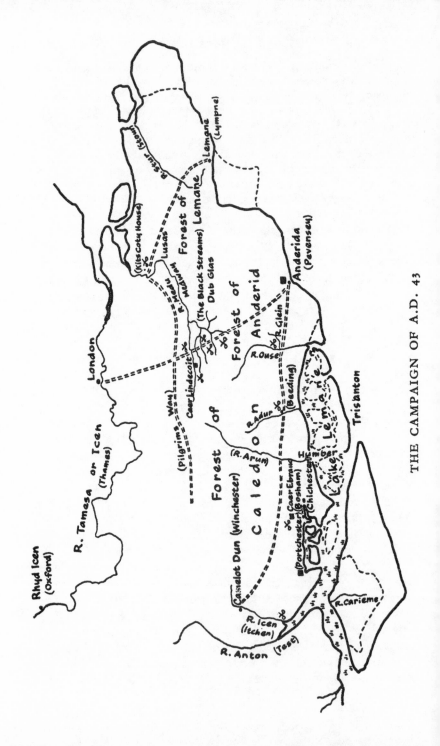

THE CAMPAIGN OF A.D. 43

it would also strengthen the allegiance of the Regni of the district, who were disposed to be friendly, as well as of the Coritani whose disloyalty to the Britons might well bring down retaliation. A comparison between the Roman and British accounts of this strategic move is amusing: according to the classical historian, the Britons 'retired' to this point and the Romans followed them (but, as has already been remarked, the source of this account does not appear too reliable); according to the British tale of Arthur, the enemy had been discomfited and fled to York, while another party (i.e. the Portchester garrison) waited by the coast for reinforcements from overseas. The plain truth scarcely needs mention: Plautius was doing what the Romans were so good at, and which modern British practice is not—he was going into winter quarters.

.   .   .   .   .

The principal scene of activity is now transferred from the Weald to the region of Portchester, where the Romans' action in garrisoning 'York' brought down on themselves a hornets' nest. Up to date the men of Caledon had held aloof, perhaps deceived into thinking that the enemy only wanted the East Weald and would leave them independent; the presence of a permanent detachment in their territory, though, disillusioned them, and from now onwards they enter loquaciously into the opposition. Boece's Caledonian account correspondingly becomes an additional source of information, containing much detail, some of which reads as though the verbatim repetition of an eye-witness' story. A point about his chronicle needs some explanation, however. Arthur's deeds are recounted under the name Arwirauc; and at the same time a Caradoc who is not he enters prominently into the narrative, Caradoc of the Caledonian Weald, whom he calls 'king of Scots'. He is the King Carados of Scotland in English romance. Later, though, Boece turns this Caradoc of Caledon into the Caractacus of Tacitus' history, making him the hero while Arwirauc fades out; yet we know from Geoffrey of Monmouth's record, and from other British tradition, that Arwirauc continued to rule after the point at which this happens. It is a mistake which has to be corrected. Whether the error was an early one, and had anything to do with Arwirauc receiving the designation 'the Bear' and becoming 'Arthur', is a matter for consideration; either it was this mistake, or else it was that the Caledonians were now identifying their lot with him so closely, that they spoke of him as their king and dignified him with their own especial title.

The course of the following operations has been taken from various sources in the romances; a table reconciling them is provided in the Glossary under WEALDEN BATTLES.

According to Boece, Gwydr appeals to the Caledonian chief for aid:

I think it reasonable, most illustrious prince, that they who seek support from strange and uncouth realms, as we now do, even though no friendship nor kindness be deserved by them for good deeds, should show them what we desire, so as to be honest and profitable. For this reason, we Britons . . . oppressed with heavy wars and destitute of all supplies and help, save only of you Scots and Picts, are coming humbly to you. . . . Now is the time to assail our enemies in battle; while we have strength, and while we may, by help of each other, be sufficient to withstand them. Soothly, if the Albion men will join together, all of one mind, they shall recover as much from the Romans as they have won from any other people. Wherefore, let the power of Scots, Britons, and Picts, join together to defend the common liberty. Let us take our weapons at once, to resist the injury appearing. And though we may be vanquished (which God forbid), it would be no reproach to us; for we would not have been vanquished by one people, but by the power of the world. And if we be victorious, as our just action firmly believes, the victory shall be no less glorious and of profit to you than to us, and ye shall be perpetually esteemed by all people.

To this the Caledonian replies:

Had ye Britons not refused our support, freely offered to you, when Julius the Roman consul invaded you in unjust battle, it should not have been necessary to you this day to seek support from us. [And so on, there being plainly a lingering sense of grievance. However he agrees to let bygones be bygones.] By joining of all our strength together, we might easily have vanquished them, and been delivered of all dread, rejoicing our homes in Albion with perpetual rest; yet better is, as they say, late than never thrive. It is not to be devised now how we might have daunted the Romans in times bygone, but how we may eschew the great danger now appearing. [Then he continues, exasperatingly,

himself the chief offender!] Ye are divided among yourselves by internal sedition; and so long as ye stand so, your common weal shall
never be free. . . . Best is to settle all sedition among yourselves, super-
seding your wars for a season; and set your labour, with most crafty
ingenuity, to transport this dangerous battle to France.

To work this prudently, ye must solicit the Normandy, Picardy,
Breton, and German folk, with all other peoples lying on the border
of France, to rebel against the Romans, in hope of recovering their
liberty; and if ye do this well, ye shall eschew this battle that the
Romans intend to force on you, and transfer it to France. Thus shall
both ye and we be delivered of all fear of our enemies, and live the
remainder of this year in quiet; and (we shall be) the more able next
year for battle. And if there be no way to eschew this most dangerous
battle, then think I best to assemble all the people of Albion together,
to fight with honest battle to the death, without regard for our lives, but
alone for glory and honour; for no people can die more honestly than in
fighting for their liberty and faith against the lords of the world.

If this reply was repeated to the two brothers word for word,
they must have felt that indeed adversity was bringing them an
unpleasant bedfellow; such bland superciliousness could wreck
future concert, just as it had evaded it in the past. Whatever it
stood for, it was not sense. However, for better or for worse
they had got an ally of some sort, and it were best to make full
use of the opportunity while it lasted. So Gwydr sent appeals for
help to the various Gauls, and at the same time gathered a force
on the lower Itchen to harry the Roman camps.

Plautius, like a good soldier, recognizing the menace on the
Itchen, went out to meet it. The prompt decision is to his credit,
as men of a lesser calibre might have hesitated in order to 'let the
situation develop'; it is a point for remark, because it must have
been noted by Arthur, and helped give his brother and him the
measure of their opponent's character, a factor that would influence the future. In the face of the Roman advance the Britons
withdrew across the sea-marshes, but made a stand on the far
side of the river, probably near Calshot. The classical account of
the battle is as follows (with the word 'sea-marsh' substituted for
Thames, for the reasons already given on page 17):

The Britons easily crossed the sea-marsh, because they knew where
the firm ground and the easy passages in this region were to be found;

but the Romans in attempting to follow them were not so successful. However the Germans swam across again, and some others got over by a bridge a little way upstream; after which they assailed the barbarians from several sides at once, and cut down many of them. In pursuing the remainder incautiously they got into swamps, from which it was difficult to make their way out, and so lost a number of men. Shortly afterwards (Gwydr) perished; but the Britons, so far from yielding, united all the more firmly to avenge his death.

Boece gives a vivid picture of the firm stand made by the Britons:

Gwydr, seeing no way to avoid his enemies, gathered all his people together in arrayed battle, and closed them with wagons and carts on every side, except the part facing their enemies, to that end that none of them shall have hope to flee; and put the wives in the said wagons and carts, to exhort their husbands to fight valiantly for their lives and lands. On the other side, Plautius divided his army in three divisions; and, by blast of trumpet, came so fiercely on the Britons that they had no space to shoot their arrows. Then the Britons flung their bows from them, and fought with their swords. The wives exhorted them with loud cries to deliver them from Roman servitude. This battle was cruelly fought; but at last the Britons were discomfited, and Gwydr their king slain. Many of all the women were smothered in the carts, by the press of them that fled. The chase ceased not till the Britons were driven to the river of Garieme, six miles from the place where the field was discomfited. This victory was not right pleasant to the Romans, for Gneus Senicus, with many other Roman nobles, was slain.

The river Garieme is possibly the Carey-brook, from which Carisbrooke takes its name; the mouth in those days would have been somewhere in the Solent, and so about six miles from where the action was fought. From this river's mention, and from the following account by Geoffrey of Monmouth, the Britons evidently left the field for their homes in two directions, the Caledonians by way of Southampton, the Isle of Wight folk by way of Carisbrooke; the Romans accordingly pursued them in two columns. Gwydr's death, so it seems, took place on the Carey, the Cwm Kerwyn where Arthur's 'son' Gwydr was slain in the hunting of the Twrch Trwyth.

Geoffrey gives a fuller narrative of his death, euphemistically inverting the British flight into 'pursuit' of the Romans, for which due allowance must be made; and there is a slip in tradition in calling Plautius 'Claudius', which here has been corrected:

Already Plautius was betaking himself to his ships, already were the Romans well-nigh scattered, when the crafty Lewis Hamo [a native traitor] casting aside the armour he was wearing, did on the arms of a Briton, and in the guise of a Briton fought against his own men. Then he cheered on the Britons to the pursuit, promising them a speedy victory. For he had learned their tongue and their customs, seeing that he himself had learnt nurture along with the British hostages at Rome. By this device he made shift by degrees to come close up to Gwydr, and when he found an opening to get at him, just when he least suspected any peril of the kind, slew him by the edge of the sword, and slipping away betwixt the companies of his enemies, rejoined his own men with his ill-omened victory.

But Arthur, as soon as he espied that his brother was slain, straightaway cast aside his own armour and did on that of Gwydr, hurrying hither and thither and cheering on his men to stand their ground, as though it had been Gwydr himself. They, not knowing that the King was dead, took fresh courage from his cheering, at once held their ground and battled on, doing no small slaughter among the enemy. At last the Romans gave way, and abandoning the field flee shamefully in two divisions, Plautius in the one, betaking himself unto the shelter of his ships, and Hamo, not having time to reach the ships, slipping away into the forest. Arthur therefore weening that Plautius was fleeing along with him, hurried in pursuit, and never once stinted of chasing him from point to point, until he came to a stand on the sea-coast, at the place that is now called Hampton . . . and unexpectedly coming down upon him slew (Hamo) on the sudden.

.   .   .   .   .

That evening, as night fell and Arthur's thoughts could turn from the immediate business of stark fighting to a wider range, the day's misfortunes must have beset him almost with despondency. He had lost a brother and a battle. The brother meant more to him than just kith; he was the only leader under whom the country would unite. Already Arthur had the cause of Britain at heart; young though he was, he had been brought up to put its needs before all else by a high-principled father, and now first and foremost in his mind will have been the bitterness of its defeat. The hardly gained concert of Caledon had suffered disaster at its first trial—was there any chance that it might continue? He himself would step into his brother's shoes, and the West would follow him; but would the East? There, jealous self-interest absorbed the people; it had cost his country the Glynde battle, it had cost it the Weald, and it had cost it the Medway; would the rot ever stop? Before today's fight luck had seemed to be turning in his favour; and he had hoped that, spurred on by Caledon's example, the rest of Albany would pull itself together and rise against the invader; but instead—Caledon's support had been lukewarm (else the site of the battle would have been near the enemy camp, on the slopes of the downs, not at a distance in a Cornish valley); treachery had been able to find itself a place on the field, and the one man who could have held the loose allegiance together had fallen. He was facing complete catastrophe.

However, to bemoan fate would gain him nothing. If he were to retrieve anything from the wreck, he must act at once. But he wanted to hear calm wisdom at this juncture, not the typical rash bombast; so he sought out Merlin, and confided in him his grief for his brother and his fear for the country's future. The druid responded; pointing to the sky he drew his notice to a comet,[1] a ball of fire like a dragon's head, from the mouth of which came two great beams of light, one directed towards the Meon valley where lay a traitorous 'Irish' gathering, the other across the Channel towards Gaul, and said: 'Arthur, be not altogether cast down, since from Death there is no return. Bring to an end this business of the war. Give battle to thine enemies, for tomorrow shall see both Romans and Irish vanquished. Fight boldly on the morrow; so shalt thou conquer, and be crowned king of Britain. Hearken to the interpretation of the sign. The dragon at the end of the beam betokens thee thyself, who art a stout and hardy knight. One of the two rays signifies a mighty conquest, made beyond the borders of France; the other ray which parted from its fellow betokens a daughter, whose sons and grandsons shall hold the kingdom of Britain in succession.'

These words must have heartened a worn out and distressed youth. Whether he accepted them in blind faith or not, some hope had been given him to cling to. Arthur could lie down to rest, ready to face the future.

[1] The source of this story is given in the Glossary under UTHER.*

6

Arthur Takes the Helm

WITH the morning Arthur rose the rightful leader of Britain, rightful in so far as he could prove it by force of character and good fortune, for his critics were not men to make allowances for bad luck. If, therefore, he did not follow Merlin's advice strictly to the letter, it was because that representative of the Church militant was advocating something in the nature of divine thunderbolt precipitancy, while he himself felt the need to proceed with more earthly caution. A youth of some twenty-two summers only, he was not going to be welcomed universally; tribes with older chiefs and a shadow of some past claim to kingship would resurrect their rights, and disparage his ability. Their goodwill must be enlisted; and not until he had made his personal position secure could he be ready to strike.

The internal situation was for a while uncertain: Cornwall recognized his succession to the crown immediately, at a gathering at Cirencester; Albany however temporized, with designs of her own. In Caledon rumours circulated that Arthur had been born out of wedlock, he was illegitimate; the legal succession passed through his sister, married to the chief of Chichester, and it now devolved on her young son Modred whose father ought to be governor on his behalf until he came of age. And Aaron Rheged, seeing the advantage of Roman support for his claim, was taking care not to compromise his policy of non-hostility with them. Boece relates their representation in all its bluntness—'Arthur, the which was ane bastard.' And he goes on to tell, much in these words and calling Aaron 'Lot', that 'Loth,* as king of the Picts, sent a deputation to the Britons (Cornish) asking them to acknowledge himself as their prince in right of his wife, until such time as his bairn should come of age. The *Cornishmen* replied that they would have no Pict over them, but only a Briton . . . upon which Loth turned to the enemy for help.' Nevertheless in the end a compromise was agreed upon: Arthur should marry the late chief of Caledon's* daughter, and, should he lose his life without an heir, the succession to Cymbeline's kingdom would pass to Rheged's son Modred.

The authority for these terms is Boece, who relates a great deal about the promised marriage to the girl who was subsequently to become famous as Boadicea* (the Roman mispronunciation of Voadicia). The Caledonians claimed that Arthur actually married her; but there seems no likelihood of truth in this, although on the other hand there is every reason to accept that he pledged himself to do so. Similarly they claimed the bond to be that Arthur should only rule for life, and that on his death the crown should pass to Modred. But that proposition does not seem tenable; neither the Cornish nor Arthur could be expected to entertain so slighting an agreement; the terms put forward here, that if Arthur fell without an heir then the succession should pass to Modred, as Cymbeline's grandson, are perfectly rational and can be presumed the true ones.

Arthur's feelings for his bride to be, the young girl Boadicea, can only be surmised from after events; they are likely to have been ones of frank good nature, without any colour of affection. Perhaps she may already have been showing signs of a masterful nature; and quite possibly her mother's propensity for intrigue jarred him. All the same he was perfectly ready to marry, as was she, in order to promote an alliance for their peoples' good; so he promised that high-spirited girl his hand.

This 'purpose of marriage' effected, and Albany's co-operation obtained, Arthur could turn his attention to the enemy without the gates; and the question was, where to attack them? His immediate need was to gain a success without risking a reverse; confidence in general had to be restored, and his own prestige established; this was no occasion for a hazardous venture. Two exposed enemy detachments offered targets: the one at Caer Lindecoit in the Weald, and the other at 'York' by Chichester. Of the two, the first entailed the least risk; it was far from enemy support, the nearest Roman force being the garrison at Pevensey. Doubtless there were additional factors to be taken into account, such as the attitude of local clans who may have been in enemy pay; but all in all they indicated Caer Lindecoit as the weakest spot. So, in conjunction with his Caledonian allies, Arthur challenged the enemy by placing himself across the line of communications through Ashdown Forest, on the stream Duglas, thereby obliging the Romans either to attack him on ground of his own choosing or to leave the detachment cut off.

His action had the desired result: the Romans moved out of Pevensey to attack him. Thus began a series of engagements known as his seventh battle, the Wood of Celidon. The descriptions quoted here are a miscellany from Wace, Layamon, and Geoffrey of Monmouth; their choice is explained under WEALDEN BATTLES in the Glossary.

To the Roman commander the prospect can have been little more than routine procedure in colonial warfare: the Britons had been beaten time and again; now they were only hesitantly interfering with his communications, they had not the spirit to attack his camp; provided he could get them to stand, he ought to be able to punish them severely. But to Arthur, as he watched the column advance in close formation up the road, in well-disciplined order with advanced and flank parties skilfully disposed, there must have been a trace of anxiety—in close order their armoured ranks were too formidable; would he ever get a chance to manœuvre them into a disadvantage? Against them, a battle had to be fought with wits as well as with courage; the latter alone could not win the day, as he had experienced too often.

The column drew close; his own skirmishers fell back, sometimes with a muttered tale of casualties, sometimes with a man brandishing excitedly a Roman sword he had captured. Faster and faster the minutes flew by, and then of a sudden the two main bodies were at grips:

On a broad ford the hosts them met; vigorously their brave champions attacked; the fated fell to the ground. There was much blood shed, and woe there was rife; shivered shafts; men there fell. Arthur saw that; in mood he was uneasy; Arthur bethought him what he might do, and drew him backward on a broad field. When his foes weened that he would fly, then was (the Roman) glad, and all his host with him; they weened that Arthur had with fear retreated there, and passed over the water as if they were mad.

Arthur called upon the Britons to counter-attack:

Now is the day come that he shall lose the life and lose his friends, or else we shall be dead; we may not see him alive. The *foreigners* shall abide sorrow, and we avenge worthily our friends. Up caught Arthur his shield before his breast, and he gan to rush as the howling wolf, when he cometh from the wood behung with snow, and thinketh to bite such beasts as he liketh. Arthur then called to his dear knights: Advance we quickly, brave thanes! All together towards them; we all shall do well, and they forth fly, as the high wood when the furious wind heaveth it with strength! Flew over the wealds (three) thousand shields, and smote on the Roman knights, so that the earth shook again. Brake the broad spears, shivered shields; the foreigners fell to the ground. The Roman gan to flee, exceeding quickly; and his horse bare him with great strength over the deep water, and saved him from death. The foreigners gan to sink—sorrow was given to them. Arthur hastened speedily to the water, and turned his spear's point, and hindered to them the ford; there the foreigners were drowned, full seven (hundred). Some they gan wander, as the wild crane doth in the moorfen, when his flight is impaired, and swift hawks pursue after him, and hounds with mischief meet him in the reeds; then is neither good to him, nor the land nor the flood; the hawks him smite, the hounds him bite, then is the royal fowl at his death-time.

The Romans suffered an overwhelming defeat. It seems that they retreated to Pevensey and were evacuated from there by sea to Portchester; Caer Lindecoit was left to hold out as best it could. Arthur's relief at so successful an outcome to the operation will have been intense; 'York'* was his next objective, and thither he led his Britons in the flush of victory, to strike while the iron was hot. In the romances his march has caused the mistaken idea that the enemy had retreated in that direction, which is impossible; a force based on Pevensey could not retire to a flank across country after being severely beaten; yet 'Colgrim' after being defeated on the Duglas reappears at 'York', so, if that is true, the move must have been made by sea. And from the Roman angle, Plautius may well have felt it desirable to recall a now useless detachment.

Reading between the lines of the romances, the degree of Arthur's success reacted upon his men unfortunately; a quantity of loot fell into their hands, with the result that many of them dispersed to their homes to store it, thus depleting his ranks at a

juncture when good strategy called for a second blow with enhanced momentum. Even so he delivered the blow, assailing
'York', the outpost on the downs near Chichester.

The melley was right sharp and grievous. Many a soul was parted
from the body. The heathen played their parts as men, and contended
boldly with the sword. The Britons could do them no mischief. They
might not force their way into the *camp*, neither could those within
prevail to issue forth. The Britons might endure the battle no longer.
They gave back in the press, and as they fled, the pursuing enemy did
them marvellous damage.

Such was the reward for ill-discipline; though characteristically the punishment did not fall on the guilty, but on those who
had resisted the temptation of loot. They were pursued to some
hills crowned with a hazel thicket, evidently a Caledon sacred
grove (judging from the Gaelic *cal*, meaning hazel); a glance at the
map suggests that this almost certainly must have been the hills
around Haslemere, on the natural line of retreat. Determined to
retrieve the situation, Arthur consulted the Cornish chief, who

was a man of much counsel and ripe of age. No need, saith he, of
beating about the bush and making long speeches, for we must make
the best use of what remains of the night. What is most wanted just
now is valour and hardihood, if ye would fain enjoy your lives and
liberties. The multitude of paynims is huge and hungry for fight, while
we are but a handful. If we wait until daylight overtaketh us, better I
ween not fight them at all. Up, then, while the darkness lasteth, and
coming down upon them in close order, let us rush their camp by a
sudden surprise. For, whilst they have no suspicion and never dream of
our falling upon them in such wise, if we make the rush with one
accord and put forth our hardihood, I doubt not but we shall win the
day.

Often has the same counsel been proffered amongst the hills of
North-West India, though with the tables turned, when it has
been Pathan tribesmen who have been fain to enjoy their liberty,
and Cornish infidels have been seeking to wrest it from them. And
just as in our time it has been firearms that have made the men
with inferior weapons resort to night attack with the knife, so in
Arthur's day it was Roman armour which caused these tactics.

Let us ponder therefore over the sequel to the Cornishman's advice, and consider whether his words may not yet be re-echoed on some future battlefield, when enemy armour has outnumbered Briton soldiers but not crushed their determination.

The assault was a complete success:

The Britons came amongst the pagans lying naked (of their armour) upon the ground, and fast in sleep. The swordplay was right merry, for the slaughter was very great. The Britons thrust their glaives deep in the breasts of the foe. They lopped heads and feet and wrists from their bodies. The Britons ranged like lions amongst their enemies; they were as lions anhungered for their prey, killing ewes and lambs, and all the sheep of the flock, whether small or great. Thus the Britons did, for they spared neither spearman nor captain. The heathen were altogether dismayed; they were yet heavy with sleep, and could neither get to their harness, nor flee from the field. No mercy was shown them for all their nakedness. . . . If any escaped from the battle, it was only by reason of the blackness of the night. He who was able to flee ran from the field; he tarried not to succour his own familiar friend. But many more were slain in that surprise than got safely away.

Arthur then beleaguered 'York' again; and Plautius had to send support to it from Portchester, where he (termed Colgrim's 'brother')

tarried by the shore, awaiting the coming of the *Emperor*. . . . Plautius made no further tarrying; he broke up his camp, and marching towards 'York', set his comrades in ambush, within a deep wood, some five miles from the host. Together with the folk of his household, and the strangers of his fellowship, Plautius had in his company six thousand men in mail. He trusted to fall upon Arthur by night, when he was unready, and force him to give over the siege. But certain of the country who had spied him spread this snare, ran to the King and showed him of the matter. Arthur; knowing of the malice of Plautius, took counsel with Cador, Earl of Cornwall, a brave captain who had no fear of death. He delivered to the earl's care seven hundred horsemen, and of spearmen three thousand, and sent him secretly to fall upon Plautius in his lurking place. Cador did the King's bidding. The Romans heard no rumour of his coming; for the host drew to the wood privily without trumpet or battle cry. Then when Cador was near the foe, he cried his name, and burst fiercely upon the heathen with the sword. In his combat there perished of the Romans more than three thousand men. Had it not been for the darkness of the night, and the hindrance of the wood, not one might have fled on his feet. . . .

The way in which Arthur received news of the Roman plan is told with slightly more detail by Layamon. It is not an entirely savoury acknowledgement of British duplicity, but deserves quotation in order that both sides of the picture may be presented. 'Breaking up his camp' is an over-statement; Plautius evidently decided on sending a relief column to 'York' by night, hoping thereby to break through the British investing line by surprise, a testimony to the fighting obstinacy now being shown.

But all it otherwise happened, other than he weened; for Plautius had in his host a British knight; he was Arthur's relative, named Maurin*. Maurin went aside to the wood, through woods and through fields, until he came to Arthur's tents; and thus said soon to Arthur the king: Hail be thou, Arthur, noblest of kings. I am hither come; I am of thy kindred. Here is Plautius arrived with warriors most hardy, and thinketh in this night to slay thee and thy knights, to avenge his brother, who is greatly discouraged; but God shall prevent him, through his mickle might.

The tale continues with a picturesque but impossible description of how the relief was effected; impossible because it visualizes a walled mediaeval castle instead of a palisaded outpost. The simple truth is that even though the Britons had gained news of Plautius' intentions, and had managed to lay an ambush for his night march, nevertheless the Roman column succeeded in getting through; its commander knew his business. But from both Arthur's and Plautius' methods it can be discerned that the two leaders had begun mutually to appreciate each other's worth.

It is possible, though, that Plautius' second operation was a much more prolonged and deliberate move than the romance tells. For, there is a Roman road running from near Chichester across a shoulder of the Haslemere hills, which eventually ends at Silchester. It has not been aligned with the point-to-point directness which characterizes Roman roads, so one is led to doubt whether its original purpose was to join those two places; instead, it is conceivable that the first portion, by Chichester, was a temporary operational road, and that it was subsequently extended to form a secondary route to Silchester. It is for consideration, therefore, whether Plautius after his first set-back may not have decided on a methodical punitive expedition to quell the Haslemere nuisance thoroughly; accordingly he made a slow and deliberate advance towards the hills, supported by an engineered line of communication, his first objective being the British camp in Hammer Wood, north-west of Iping. If this be so, then time has slightly distorted the romance, and the site of Cador's attack is likely to have been somewhere on that road as the road-head neared Hammer Wood.

The Roman column's method will have much resembled a modern punitive operation, likewise the Britons' resistance; and we can imagine that after Cador's attack and repulse the Britons had shot their bolt, and they withdrew to recover fresh strength. So too Plautius went back to Portchester, to await Claudius' arrival. Legend tells the same story: After a while news came that the Emperor Claudius

had come to a haven in Caledon, with a fleet of five hundred galleys, and was speeding to 'York'. Plautius knew and was persuaded that Arthur dared not abide his onset. This was a right judgement, for Arthur made haste to be gone. The King called a council of his captains, and by their rede decided not to await the Emperor at 'York', neither to give him battle, because of the proud and marvellous host that was with him. . . . Arthur took his captains at their word. He let well the siege . . . that he might . . . choose his own battle ground, and trouble his adversary the more surely.

.   .   .   .   .

Making allowances for embellishments to satisfy national pride, and the rosier tints given by Time, the narratives quoted here seem to be substantially a true picture of what took place. The possibility of fiction cannot of course be ignored; but when it is observed that Arthur's conduct of the campaign against a supposedly unorganized Saxon invader, in meaningless geography, proves remarkably appropriate for a highly organized Roman operation, it must be concluded that there is a strong substratum of genuine tradition. For example, what could have conceived the idea of a Saxon 'Kaiser' coming 'with all the power of Rome', other than an original tradition of a Roman Caesar so coming? Likewise if we examine the account of the night attack devised so as to catch the enemy 'naked' of their armour, we are led to the same conclusion. For, it could scarcely have originated in Saxon times, when there was no heavy armour; nor could it be Layamon's imagination drawn from current Welsh practice, because Gerald the Welshman had just recorded the reverse: 'They will expose their defenceless bodies to the attacks of mail-clad knights, will engage without weapons fully-armed men, and will rush on foot against masses of heavy cavalry. And often in such encounters their mere nimbleness of movement and their indomitable courage will win for them the victory.' The source is surely accurate tradition from the Roman event? A consistent pattern for Arthur's character is also beginning to evidence itself, which conforms with what can be inferred from Roman history of the invasion; it reveals a tenacity that commands admiration.

Not all the decisions over the fighting are to be attributed solely to Arthur. His position in command had not yet the assured feature it bore through after events. This was his first venture with supreme status, his lieutenants did not know his calibre, some indeed were bound to be sceptical; risks which he himself might be ready to accept could only be entertained on older men's advice or with their consent. The chosen objective of cutting the enemy's communications in the Weald can be taken as a council of war measure; and it is possible that the backward movement from the Duglas ford was forced on him by the enemy, rather than feigned. On the other hand the quick seizure of the opportunity to counter-attack when the enemy were across the ford, grasped in the heat of battle, must have been Arthur's own initiative; advice may have been at his elbow, but the vigour of the order and its inspiriting tones tell that his heart is speaking. And as all soldiers know, the moral determination required for turning from defence to the counter-stroke is great; yet after events show that this is more typical of Arthur's character than anything else. Similarly, after the over-hasty assault on 'York' and the forced retreat to the Haslemere hills, when it would seem that

Roman armour was proving an insuperable handicap, the advice to overcome the disadvantage by a night attack came from the Cornish chief, but the leadership was Arthur's; he had consulted the Cornishman not in despair but in resolution to win, and he evoked the response he deserved.

The enemy is not to be underrated: the pursuit to the Haslemere hills evidences firm-hearted command in a by no means happy situation; timorousness would have contented itself with remaining in camp, under the security of entrenchments, after the attack had been beaten off. Plautius' determination to retain the initiative can be discerned; Arthur was facing an opponent of like mettle to himself.

    •   •   •   •   •

We have now reached the point marked by Geoffrey of Monmouth's Book IX, ch. ii, in his *History*. Arthur sent an appeal to the Gauls for help, and a contingent of them landed at Southampton; with their aid he set about harrying the Dobunni 'friendlies' post near Edenbridge; he had transferred the centre of his opposition further inland. What happened at Caer Lindecoit has to be disentangled from the various other romances, because Geoffrey's story skips several months of packed events, when it carries the enemy from there direct to Totnes in Devon. The corresponding point in Malory's story is evidently I.x, where Arthur is at London having sent for aid to Gaul whose people are at war with a 'King Claudas', plainly the Emperor Claudius. Accordingly Malory's 'Bedegraine' is Caer Lindecoit; and the tale of its harrying is amplified by his account of how a second Gaulish contingent was brought to Dover, where Merlin ordained that—'there should no man of war ride nor go in no country on this side Trent water (the Arun) but if he had a token from King Arthur, where through the king's enemies durst not ride as they did tofore to espy.' Apparently before this the enemy had been helped treasonably, which is reminiscent of the aid Julius Caesar had received.

At the same time as he did this, Arthur left Aaron Rheged in command of the opposition round Portchester, where Plautius was awaiting Claudius' arrival. Aaron in the romances figures as

'Lot of Lothian', a designation taken from part of his domains; but the circumstances of the two figures, each married to Arthur's sister and each chieftain of The Lake, leave no doubt as to their common identity. Boece's wording, consequently, is here altered to the more comprehensive name Aaron Rheged:

> The rumour ran that *the enemy* had roused the whole of *their empire*, and had fitted out a passing mighty fleet, intending to return unto the island and destroy it. . . . Whereupon the army of Britain is given in charge unto Aaron Rheged to keep the enemy at a distance. For he was . . . a right valiant knight and ripe as well in years as in counsel, and, his prowess approving him worthy thereof, *Cymbeline* had given unto him his daughter Anna. . . . He in his campaign against the enemy was oftentimes repulsed by them, and had to betake him unto his cities, but yet more often did he put them to flight and scatter them, forcing them to flee at one time unto the forests and at another unto their ships. For the issue of the battles betwixt them was so doubtful that none could tell unto which of the twain the victory should be accorded. That which did most hurt unto the Britons was their own pride, for that they did disdain to obey Aaron's summons unto arms, whereby coming fewer into the field, they were unable to overpower the greater numbers of the enemy.

The word 'disdain' is, though, a thinly veiled excuse; Wace is more explicit: 'It befell that the Britons despised Aaron; they would pay no heed to his summons, this man for reason of jealousy, this other because of the sharing of the spoil . . . whilst the folk of the country said openly that the captains were but carpet knights who made pretence of war.'

The truth is out in the last sentence: without the incentive of Arthur in person, insincere endeavour and selfish consideration were hampering the Britons, even in the face of the enemy. But the root of the disunity is a far blacker story than the romances disclose; some of them conversely, Layamon's for example, clearly come from a source that whitewashes the principal knave's character. In truth, Aaron or Lot was preparing to play a double game. Married to Cymbeline's daughter he was in a position to lay claim to the kingship; in Arthur's defeat he saw a way open for him, and to his shame he was scheming to take that advantage. He was running with the hare and hunting with the hounds. In his fellow-Britons' eyes he was unlucky in his conflicts with the enemy; as seen by the Angel of Judgement his efforts were half-hearted, he was looking ahead to the time when he might come to terms with the enemy, and be appointed native king under Roman suzerainty. It is sad to contemplate what the position of his wife, Arthur's sister, must have been under these circumstances.

Aaron's character enters into the history of these events so considerably as to deserve comment. He was ambitious, but without the strength which could go whole-heartedly right or unscrupulously wrong, and he lacked the generosity which precludes ill intent. He craved petty independence, yet was readier to seek it in vassalage to Rome rather than accept the overlordship of a fellow-countryman, appreciating that even though he might be subject to a local Roman praetor, such an official's power would not be absolute but under remote control from Rome, whereas a British king's power was absolute. The temptation of being able to appeal against his immediate superior, even to a foreign overlord, counted for more with him than taking his place in a free nation. We constantly encounter men of his kind today, heading national assemblies which insist on maintaining a petty independence, glad to appeal to a distant international authority, but unwilling to join with their immediate neighbours in sensible union. The mentality inspiring this may be cloaked in ostensible patriotism, but is truly evasion of the self-denial needed for the common good. On a small scale the same type figures in party politics; and though men of this kind may appear impressive under normal conditions, they fail under stress, when a crisis reveals them in their true nature as—carpet knights. Such was the man whom Arthur left to face the enemy at Portchester; and the natural question is, why did he do so?

Over choice of individual, though, he had no option: Aaron was chieftain of the neighbourhood and in a position to gain the allegiance of the 'Irish' of the Lake, for their blood ran in his veins. Nor, maybe, had Arthur any cause to think him insincere; he may have been distinctly inactive up to date, but a man of Aaron's calibre could easily produce plausible reasons in explanation—his desire not to provoke retaliation, the wisdom of awaiting a favourable opportunity, even the safer strategy of enticing the enemy further inland and striking him when entangled in the forests. Wace's narrative gives the impression that this was actually mooted: 'Let the king fall back upon London, said the lords, and summon his meinie about him; the king's power will increase daily, and if *the enemy* have the hardihood to follow, with the more confidence we shall fight. Arthur took his captains at their word; he let well the siege of '*York*' and came to London, that he might strengthen his *position*, choose his own battle ground, and trouble his adversary the more surely.' And he sent to the Gauls for assistance; which, as has been related, they gave, and with which he harried Caer Lindecoit.

Whether the Roman 'friendlies' post fell or not is not clear. According to Geoffrey and his group of romancers it did; but according to Malory, 'Bedegraine' was a drawn fight, and this seems the more probable. Malory's story adds an interesting sidelight, telling that Aaron Rheged, the 'Irish', and a chieftain from beyond the Arun ('Northumberland'), amongst others, were hostile; active hostility is an exaggeration, nor at this stage will their treasonable intentions have been properly known, yet even so Arthur may have been beginning to have qualms. However, Merlin reassured him: 'These kings have more on hand than they are ware of, for the pagans ("Saracens") are landed in their countries . . . that burn and slay, and have laid siege at . . . and made great destruction.' Merlin's words were slightly ahead of time, but only a little; Claudius' arrival was imminent.

To prepare for Claudius and a spring campaign, Plautius managed to stir up dissension among the Britons, inducing a petty chieftain near Winchester to take up arms against a neighbour; this it was which caused Arthur to raise the siege of Caer Lindecoit in Kent ('Bedegraine'), and go to the loyal chief's assistance. In Malory the assailant's name is Rience of 'North Wales', and the assailed is Leodegrance of Cameliard. Both those places can be identified. North Wales is Gwynedd, that was the district of the Winchester Gwyn* and mistaken in tradition for the Snowdon-Flint area; this is dealt with more fully in the Glossary. As Rience is also called king of 'Ireland', the locality tallies; for it shows his domain to have been at the mouth of the Gwyn, Itchen, and to have included some of the islands of the Lake. Cameliard is the district of the upper Christchurch Avon, indicated by a lost mediaeval name Camelham, and by Camelos having been once the river's name, as is apparent when the name

Dyfi* for its lower reaches is examined. Plautius' strategy is clear: in order to draw Arthur away from Caer Lindecoit, or to distract Cornish support from going to Kent, he was inducing some of the estuary Gaels to create a diversion in the direction of Stonehenge.

News of this came to Arthur when he was in the London area, in the shape of a message from Rience to say that he had overcome eleven chieftains, from each of whom he had taken the beard to use for a trimming to his mantle; there was space for one more beard, would Arthur be good enough to send him his? Arthur's reply was that either Rience would do him homage on both his knees, or that he would lose his head.

By the time that Arthur had reached the scene of the fighting the insurgents were besieging a fort called 'Terrabil'; Rience had already been captured, but his brother had succeeded him in command and had brought with him men of the Orcin* isle ('Orkney') that belonged to Aaron Rheged. Aaron is said to have been kept away by the wiles of Merlin; but that plausible tale can be interpreted as that he kept himself away, though without preventing his people from joining the insurrection. Arthur gained a complete victory; no details of the fight are given, except that Rience's brother was killed with other leading men, all of whom were buried at Camelot, from which it is to be gathered that the engagement took place very near there.

In Malory's story, Aaron ('Lot of Orkney' and husband of Arthur's sister) then arrived and fought a second battle, losing his life in it to a man named 'Pellinore'* who, for reasons given in the Glossary, can be recognized as Pwyll Avallawch. This so-called battle, like much of the jousting in the romances, seems to have been metaphorical for political warfare. Something evidently took place at this time, between Aaron and Pwyll, in which Aaron came off the worst and for which his family ever after bore the other's a grudge; what that something was will now be related; it was both the beginning of the Round Table and of the feud on which that noble institution foundered.

7

A Beacon Light

IT IS clear that Arthur had all along been experiencing negative
support if not open disaffection from most of Albany, in
particular from the folk of its southern coast, the shore of the
Lake, and from the eastern Weald. Their disloyalty was wholly
illogical: men whose souls were wedded to the idea of independence were yielding their allegiance to a foreigner, rather than
grant it to one of their own countrymen; jealousy was operating,
they were cutting off their noses to spite their faces. Arthur had
now to counter this in one way or another; and two alternatives
offered themselves, apart from force of arms which was ruled out
by the enemy in their midst: either the dissentients might be persuaded by their druids to be loyal as a matter of faith, or, if the
religious appeal failed, then by a call to their sense of reason.

As regards the first alternative, Arthur had already helped his
brother, Gwydr, in an attempt of the kind. This is to be de-
ciphered from a story in the romances about an enterprise of
Uther and a brother, because the two brothers' joint action has
clearly been transposed from one scene to another, and the deeds
should be ascribed to Gwydr and Arthur. It would seem that
as soon as the Romans went into winter quarters at Portchester,
the two sought to resuscitate local morale by an appeal to the
faith, the centre of which was at Stonehenge. This stone circle
was only one of many circles, some of stone, some of timber
posts, and others of trees, studded about the countryside, all of
them local centres of a faith that approximated to a social creed.
One of these, which had a considerable reputation, lay on an
'Irish' island in the Lake; so, in order to link that people's sentiment with the Britons, Gwydr proposed the transfer of its stones
to Stonehenge, for amalgamation with the existing structure

there. A similar transfer had been made in the past, many centuries earlier, when the blue sarsens were brought from Pembrokeshire, apparently for the same purpose of cementing a union; and the importance with which it was viewed can be gauged from the magnitude of the transportation feat involved. It is conceivable, also, that a further reason was urged for the transfer now mooted, in that the island site was being threatened by encroachment of the sea. However, the idea was not welcomed by the 'Irish', and Arthur was entrusted with bringing them away forcibly. According to the romances he did so; but the two rows of unfinished holes at Stonehenge evidence the contrary, and doubtless the attempt came to an end with the Britons' defeat on the Itchen, when Gwydr's life was lost.

There followed the series of engagements in Celidon and at 'York', during which Arthur's prestige as a leader became established; and after these, when he had gained men's confidence, Arthur embarked on a different method of unifying the uncontrolled spirit. He inaugurated a moral revival of remarkable boldness, personally adopting the new faith brought to the land by Joseph of Arimathea, and encouraging his followers to do likewise. The first occasion when this is mentioned is at the harrying of Caer Lindecoit. In Layamon's words: 'That was the first man, that there gan to shout, Arthur the noble man . . . keenly and loud, as becometh a king: Now aid us, Mary, God's mild mother; and I pray her Son, that he be to us in succour!'

Today such a step is almost bound to appear in a very much more subdued light than when it was taken, seeing that we ourselves have grown up with a creed that has been established for almost twenty centuries; it is part of our natural background, and we look on it as a world-wide moral force. But in Arthur's day it was nothing—a superstition that had been banished from the Roman Empire, whose adherents could be numbered in dozens, and which was face to face with a traditional and benevolent philosophy, druidism,* that had been the country's creed for thousands of years. How many of Arthur's closer advisers must not have said to him: 'keep clear of controversy', or 'do not swap horses when crossing a stream'? It is difficult to understand on the face of the matter how it is that he did not forfeit more allegiance than he gained, seeing that men's emotion is often more fiercely aroused by a threat to their faith than by an appeal to it. Supposing, for example, that during the Battle of Britain an attempt had been made to introduce a revised State creed: would not a host of persons who never go near a church have denounced it as scandalous?

The explanation seems to be that Joseph's Church must have been very much akin to the best features in druidism, which in fact reverenced a God that was pure abstract spirit and the essence of reason; it must have appeared, therefore, more as the revival of a purified druidism than a substitution for it. This is made clear in the Glossary, under ECCLESIASTES, and is borne out by the contemporary observation of Taliesin: 'There was never a time when the druids of Britain held not its [Christianity's] doctrines.'

The persons who advocated the measure are, some of them, unexpected; they were his mother Ygerne, his sister Anna, and the druid Merlin, besides the chieftain on whose island the Church was established, Pwyll Avallawch of the lower Test valley and the Isle of Wight. That Ygerne's influence was the foundation of Arthur's decision can be discerned from the contrast in her step-son Gwydr's appeal to the old faith, while both of her own children turned to the new. Moreover, at this period in Malory's romance, Ygerne is accused of treason because of Arthur's illicit concert with his sister; in the story the concert is portrayed as incest, but this is no more than a disparaging reference to spiritual relationship in physical terms.

The offspring of this pretended misconduct is said to have been Modred; the implication is not clear, unless it is that Modred was baptized and that Arthur was his godfather, which has been misrepresented as being his human parent, for purposes of disparagement. This would accord with the instance noted at the end of the last chapter, in which political action was described metaphorically in physical terms.

Everything points towards Ygerne's support of Christianity having been derived from her being a 'daughter of Amlodd'. Through that strain, Joseph and Pwyll Avallawch both were cousins, their mothers Rhieinwylid and Tywanwedd also having been 'daughters of Amlodd'. Whatever the expression may mean (and the suggestion has already been put forward that it stood for an instutition—on p. 37), it permeated the West Country, and even Celidon, where Kilydd the chieftain who requested Arthur to hunt the Boar there was son of another such 'daughter'. Thus the foundation of the Church in Britain was very much of a family affair; and contributing to it in a most material degree are to be numbered the many other forgotten 'daughters of Amlodd' and their families, whose ways must have prepared the soil for the seed Joseph brought.

Merlin's part in advising Arthur to sponsor the new faith is remarkable, seeing that he remained chief druid while doing so; yet his sincerity is plain. Possibly, therefore, he was exercising an extremely farsighted and broadminded outlook. It may be that, as arch-druid, he recognized only too acutely the shortcomings of his own creed, and the weak hold it retained over the people in consequence. Aware of this, he saw the need for its anomalies to be discarded; but he appreciated that more good would come from a fresh sapling being planted alongside the old tree, and from both being allowed to grow side by side in harmony, letting the old die a natural death, rather than from rooting up the outworn one at once—because, were only the fruit of the new to be relied upon, it would be small in quantity for years, nor could anyone be sure that the sapling might not fail. If this surmise be correct, then he saw his own part to lie in maintaining the old in harmony with the new, and using the influence of his venerable position to help the new take root and flourish. The change would be gradual and spread over several lifetimes; in this way, old persons could die undisquieted in the faith to which born, while young ones would grow up free to make their own choice, none being vexed with bitter sectarian strife. A moderate and tolerant attitude of this kind was what the situation wanted; we cannot but comment that Providence was kind in setting so statesmanlike a character in the chair he occupied, under circumstances when wisdom and single-hearted will were so sorely needed.

Closely associated with Arthur's adoption of the new faith was his sister Anna. As the wife of Aaron Rheged, who among his many designations was known as 'of Lychlyn' or 'of the Lake', she became the Lady of the Lake. His territory did not include the Isle of Avalon, wherein the Church was established, as it was part of Avallawch's domain; nevertheless her interests were closely bound up with it, and both she and Pwyll Avallawch must have been two of its first adherents. The charming story of Arthur receiving his famous sword from the Lady of the Lake will be known to many readers; but before it is recounted, a word needs to be said about the nature of the metaphor 'a sword'.

Its meaning is identical with that used by St Paul within a few years of this date—'the sword of the spirit, which is the Word of God'; yet its usage is far more ancient still, going back practically to the dawn of what is known as civilization, when picture writing as well as human thought had reached a very advanced stage, despite primitive material conditions. The metaphor of 'light' for wisdom has been remarked; and among its numerous emblems was the sword, one example to illustrate this being the word 'brand' for both weapon and flame. The pre-Christian use of 'light' to denote divine wisdom has been recorded by the Greek Megasthenes, writing of India, whose words deserve repetition because they represent so clearly the parallel usage in Britain: 'They hold that God is "light", but not such light as we see with the eye, nor such as the sun or fire; but God is with them the Word, by which term they do not mean articulate speech, but the discourse of Reason.' Even in the distant past, strict theologians eschewed portraying the Deity in human form, because that tended to introduce misconception; druidism in particular regarded the Deity as wholly abstract, pure mental light, the spirit of unworldly wisdom. Accordingly the 'hand of God' in its direction of human affairs was depicted as an arm stretching out from a cloud, holding in its grasp a sword (or other emblem). This device is familiar in heraldry as a crest; but it should be appreciated as having an origin far older than mediaeval times, having been adopted by heralds from existing usage, presumably from a tattoo design popular among the descendants of the Gaelic Picts in England (the Gwyddel Ffichti). It is one of many and more intricate Celtic devices that have passed into heraldry, hence the inference of tattooing.

It is apparent, therefore, that part of Joseph's Church was a revival of the pure belief in a Deity of unworldly wisdom, symbolized by the device of an arm reaching from a cloud, and wielding the sword of the Spirit. But the arm was also pictured as stretching upwards from water, probably on account of the very

ancient concept of Heaven as being in the 'cloud sea'—the
Biblical 'waters above the firmament', from which rain fell;
though possibly indifferent tattooing caused the cloud to be mistaken for water. This device of an arm holding a sword and lifted
upwards from water was the symbol of the faith undertaken by
Arthur, from his sister, when he enrolled himself in Joseph's
Church; and around it has been built the delightful legend of his
having received Caliburn* ('Excalibur') from the Lady of the
Lake.

In Malory's book the incident is slightly out of place, though
that is immaterial; he has placed it after the harrying of 'Bedegraine', but actually it must have been before. The prelude is of
considerable interest, describing, in the allegorical language commented upon, Arthur's conversion to the new faith by Pwyll
Avallawch, the 'Pellinore' of his story; so, when we read of a
'fight' between the two, we have to understand it as having been
an encounter of words, of persuasion, in which the weapons were
'keen reasons penetrating the souls of men' (to quote Lucian's
words in describing the Gallic deity's arrows). With that in mind,
the mediaeval legend is best read in its old wording:

As (King Arthur and Merlin) went thus talking, they came to the
fountain and the rich pavilion there by it. Then King Arthur was ware
where sat a knight armed in a chair—Sir knight, said Arthur, for what

cause abidest thou here, that there may no knight ride this way but if he joust with thee? I rede thee leave that custom.

This custom, said the knight, have I used and will use, maugre who saith nay; and who is grieved with my custom, let him amend it that will.

I will amend it, said Arthur.

I shall defend thee, said the knight.

(Then follows a description of the fight in which Arthur is eventually worsted, but has his life preserved by Merlin; after which Merlin says to him: 'There liveth not a better knight than he; and he shall hereafter do you right good service, and his name is Pellinore.')

And as (Merlin and Arthur) rode, Arthur said—I have no sword.

No force, said Merlin, hereby is a sword that shall be yours, an I may.

So they rode till they came to a lake, the which was a fair water and broad, and in the midst of the lake Arthur was ware of an arm clothed in white samite, that held a fair sword in that hand.

Lo, said Merlin, yonder is that sword that I spake of.

With that they saw a damosel going upon the lake.

What damosel is that? said Arthur.

That is the Lady of the Lake, said Merlin; and within that lake is a rock, and therein is as fair a place as any on earth, and richly beseen; and this damosel will come to you anon, and then speak ye fair to her that she will give you that sword.

Anon withal came the damosel unto Arthur, and saluted him, and he her again.

Damosel, said Arthur, what sword is that, that yonder the arm holdeth above the water? I would it were mine, for I have no sword.

Sir Arthur, king, said the damosel, that sword is mine, and if ye will give me a gift when I ask it you, ye shall have it.

By my faith, said Arthur, I will give you what gift ye will ask.

Well, said the damosel, go ye into yonder barge, and row yourself to the sword, and take it and the scabbard with you, and I will ask my gift when I see my time.

So Sir Arthur and Merlin alit and tied their horses to two trees; and so they went into the ship, and when they came to the sword that the hand held, Sir Arthur took it up by the handles, and took it with him; and the arm and hand went under the water. And so they came unto the land and rode forth. . . .

Then Sir Arthur looked on the sword, and liked it passing well. Whether liketh you better, said Merlin, the sword or the scabbard? Me liketh better the sword, said Arthur.

Ye are more unwise, said Merlin, for the scabbard is worth ten of the swords; for whiles ye have the scabbard upon you, ye shall never lose no blood be ye never so sore wounded; therefore keep well the scabbard always with you.

．　　．　．　　．　　．

Just as with other seemingly fantastic happenings, Merlin's remark about the scabbard deserves a passing thought; because, however incomprehensible it may appear, we may be sure that it would not have been spoken unless it held some meaning, couched in the peculiarly abstruse imagery the bards were wont to adopt. A suggestion will be attempted.

From the opening words of Malory's Book II, it is clear that Book I comes from a different source; and when Book I is read critically, it will be noticed that its events are in a confused order; Book I therefore is probably an assortment of tales collected from several sources, and the story in it of how Arthur came to be chosen as king has a different origin from the one just related as to how he gained Excalibur. Or, it may be a distorted version of the same occurrence.

In that story, Arthur was chosen as king through a test arranged by Merlin and Pwyll Avallawch, the Head of the Church ('Archbishop of Canterbury' being an anachronism): a stone was said to have been found in the churchyard of the capital with a sword sticking out from it; whoever could draw the sword from the stone would be rightful king. Many tried, but only Arthur succeeded in freeing it, wherefore he was crowned king. The story entirely differs from events as told elsewhere; its meaning is presumably allegorical. Nor is it the only tale of its kind. When the adventures of the Grail began, a stone was seen floating on the river at Camelot, with a sword sticking from it that was only to be drawn by the best knight in the world; Lancelot declared himself unfit to try, and finally it was pulled out by Galahad, who had just been appointed to the Round Table seat of honour. And there is another instance in the romance of 'The Seven Champions of Christendom'. In short, there existed a recognized metaphor of 'drawing a sword from stone'; it is reminiscent of the current expression of competence to 'draw blood from a stone'.

As a guide to its interpretation, there existed also the converse metaphor of a person 'being turned into stone'. Lot's wife, the Witch of Wookey, and the power of the Earth-born Gorgon's eye, are instances. The punishment is noticeably connected with worldliness.

Indeed a contrast between the spiritual character of the sword and the worldly nature of stone seems to be the underlying meaning: in the one instance people with worldly longings are pictured as eventually succumbing to them; in the other, men of conspicuous goodness are portrayed as able to draw the true spirit out of 'stony-hearted' institutions. Corroboration comes from the East, from the 'Sathapatha Brahmana', where this metaphor is used about a stone circle with an altar at the centre, corresponding to those of druidic Britain. The passage says that the altar and its encircling stones are to be likened to the terrestrial world with the heavens around it, and to the human body which the Deity who built the altar permeates, who is pure unworldliness.

Thus 'stone' implies a worldly outlook, and the 'sword' is the unworldly spirit within, which needs to be drawn out in man's character. Certainly Galahad was chosen because of his high-mindedness to fill the seat of honour in the Round Table; and these stories about Arthur seem to indicate that he was chosen for a similar purpose. It would appear that Merlin and Pwyll Avallawch had both recognized that the spirit of Britain was dead, the country was like a figure of stone shifted about at other people's will, answering to a conscienceless expediency; it needed revivifying and in Arthur's nature they saw the character capable of doing this. So they advised him to take hold of 'the sword' (of the Spirit—the new faith) and draw it out of the 'stone' of the old creed, out of the druidic circles which had ceased to preach the unworldly call of duty.

Merlin's druidism must not be mistaken for a pagan creed; classical descriptions of it relate mainly to continental practice, not British, and on the Continent it was corrupt. In Britain, though, much of the purity of its original conception had been retained. The Deity was regarded exactly as by us today—as pure abstract spirit, the wisdom that governs nature and is characterized by goodwill; it was referred to by the same metaphor, as 'the light' of the world, meaning spiritual light, the light of understanding. The sun was no more than a token of this; it was never worshipped in itself, the druids' reverence was for the invisible Power that moved it. This will be found amplified in the Glossary, under DRUIDISM. Thus, when Merlin and Avallawch counselled Arthur to take hold of the 'sword' of the new faith, he would be drawing the true spirit from out of the stones of the old.

Should there still be doubt over what Excalibur signified, let Wace's description of Arthur's armour be compared with St Paul's figurative passage, both of which are here reproduced side by side:

Wherefore take unto you the whole armour of God, that ye may be able to withstand in the evil day, and having done all to stand. Stand therefore, having your loins girt about with truth,

Arthur got him into his harness. He donned thigh pieces of steel, wrought strong and fairly by some cunning smith.

and having on the breastplate of righteousness; and your feet shod with the preparation of the gospel of peace;

His hauberk was stout and richly chased, even such a vesture as became so puissant a king.

above all, taking the shield of faith, wherewith ye shall be able to quench all the fiery darts of the wicked.

He had set his shield about his neck, and certes showed a stout champion, and a right crafty captain. On the buckler was painted in sweet colours the image of Our Lady St Mary. In her honour and for remembrance, Arthur bore her semblance on his shield.

And take the helmet of salvation,

His helmet gleamed upon his head. The nasal was of gold; circlets of gold adorned the headpiece, with many a clear stone; and a dragon was fashioned for its crest.

and the sword of the Spirit, which is the Word of God.

He girt him with his sword, Excalibur. Mighty was the glaive, and long in the blade. It was forged in the Isle of Avalon, and he who brandished it naked in his hand deemed himself a happy man.

In his hand the king carried his lance, named Ron; sharp it was at the head, tough and great, and very welcome at need in the press of battle.

Thus to mediaeval minds the sword Caliburn had an entirely moral significance; while its meaning, the 'Hard Cleaver', conveyed to them: 'the Word of God quick and powerful, and sharper than any two-edged sword, piercing even to the dividing asunder of soul and spirit, and of the joints and marrow, and a discerner of the thoughts and intents of the heart'.

There remains to be explained Merlin's curious advice to Arthur about the scabbard, that it was worth ten of the swords, that it would preserve him from losing blood, and that he should keep it always with him. Many people will be aware from Megasthenes' record, written several centuries before the Christian era, that the doctrine of the Word was already then in being; and, from a comparison between its various survivals, it can be seen that it was far older still, and common to both East and West. Attached to it was a code of certain recognized precepts, one of which was Determination; in token of this the sword not only represented the whole doctrine of the Word (hence the custom of picturing it as coming from a man's mouth—as in the figure of Prester John of Chichester See), but also the principle of its being upheld with determination. The symbol is still with us, in the Sword of Justice borne before the Sovereign; for Justice was also one of the Word's precepts. The sword signifies its defence even more than its execution—'With this sword do justice, stop the growth of iniquity, protect the holy Church of God, help and defend widows and orphans,' runs the Coronation injunction; from which it is easy to recognize that the scabbard stood for forbearance—mercy in justice and temperance over unsheathing the blade for war, yet without any slackening of resolution. Merlin's counsel could have come from the lips of a modern elder statesman.

.   .   .   .   .

The stage was now set for the second act in the piece. Plautius had done all he could to prepare the way for the Emperor's arrival; Arthur likewise had done his best to impede it. But the Roman had organized strength behind him, while the Briton commanded woefully uncertain allegiance. To remedy his weakness Arthur, besides endeavouring to stimulate morale, was pledging his hand to a wavering chieftain's daughter, to assure his neighbours of fair dealing by offering them a share in the throne. But here Fate intervened! During the operations against the Irishmen's inroad—'there had Arthur the first sight of Guenevere, the king's daughter of Cameliard, and ever after he loved her'. The calls of political expediency became fainter. Which path was a very human monarch to follow?

The enemy came to his rescue, unwittingly:

Right so came into the Court twelve knights, and were aged men, and they came from the Emperor of Rome, and they asked of Arthur truage for this realm, other-else the Emperor would destroy him and his land.

Well, said King Arthur, ye are messengers, therefore ye may say what ye will, other-else ye should die therefore. But this is mine answer: I owe the Emperor no truage, nor none will I hold him, but on a fair field I shall give him my truage that shall be with a sharp spear, or else with a sharp sword, and that shall not be long, by my father's soul!

Once again the beacons blazed from hill to hill. Boadicea and Guenevere faded into oblivion; and Arthur assembled the Britons.

8

Heavy Seas

THE news was alarming. First came the report: 'The *Caesar* . . . is in *Caledon* arrived in a haven . . . he hath a host brave, all the strength of Rome. He saith with his boast, when men pour to him the wine, that thou darest not in any spot his attacks abide, neither in field nor in wood, nor in ever any place; and if thou him abidest he will thee bind, destroy thy people and possess thy land.' Following on that were dire tidings: the Emperor had brought elephants, 'fifty giants which had been engendered of fiends, and they were ordained to guard his person and to break the front of the battle of King Arthur'. This was a new hazard, an unknown quantity; and the Britons' apprehension will have been like that of the Germans when tanks first burst upon them, a mixture of alarm and stubborn resolve—the resolution of that nameless and very gallant German who, when the first tank rumbled over his trench, stood fast, and crouching beneath it noticed an opening in the gun-sponson floor above him, and thrust his bayonet through it into the gunner (rendering his victim unable to sit down for weeks!). In such a spirit did the Britons face the elephants.

Here a note in commentary must be made, for those who study the romances critically. The mention of elephants has been taken from a later episode (Malory v, ii); but it is there out of place, and as classical history tells us that Claudius brought them, the episode needs to be transposed. Evidently they were used in a fight on the Adur, in the South Downs, as the remains of an elephant have been unearthed there, together with traces of a battle.

Another point of detail for remark is that Malory's mention of Rome at the end of the preceding chapter, and Layamon's in the above quotation, both support the contention of this book that Arthur's real enemy was Roman, not the anomalous 'Saxon' which has crept into the romances.

Claudius' first action on landing will have been to relieve the beleaguered detachment at Caer Lindecoit (near Edenbridge in Kent), and to reopen its communication with Pevensey or perhaps with Richborough. This would explain the engagement on the Adur. He then turned his attention westwards, advancing on Camelot. Undaunted, Arthur made a stand against him in the river-marshes. This has been handed down in tradition as his eighth battle: 'near Caer Guinnion, where Arthur bore the image of the Holy Virgin, mother of God, upon his shoulders'. In Guinnion we can see the Gwyn of Winton, Winchester, already mentioned.

For both sides the issue was critical: for Plautius, fighting under the eye of his emperor, and responsible for the safety of his person, failure spelt ruin; for Arthur, a victorious enemy established between Albany and Cornwall spelt partition and defeat in detail. So, amidst the alder thickets and reed-beds of the Itchen, the fighting was fierce and resolute; and at sundown each claimed the victory. The Romans were fought to a standstill, and had lost an eagle—judging from the one dug up at Otterbourne, which can hardly have been left there, unrecovered, on any other occasion. The Britons were able to remove their wounded; no prisoners fell into Roman hands. But with that, parity ended; the Britons had again shot their bolt, the Romans had the recuperative power of organized force. Tactically it was a drawn battle, but strategically a Roman victory.

Amended in this light, Geoffrey of Monmouth's traditional account of the fight and its aftermath becomes not only comprehensible but intriguing—from Portchester, he tells us, Claudius

pursued *Arthur* to Winton, within which city he had taken refuge. He then besieged that city, and endeavoured to take it by divers devices. But *Arthur* when he beheld himself besieged, mustered his forces and opening the gates sallied forth to fight. Howbeit, just as he was preparing to charge, Claudius sent messengers unto him, bearing word that he was minded to make peace. For he feared the hardiness of the King and the valour of the Britons, and chose rather to subdue him by prudence and policy than to run the hazard of a doubtful encounter.

He therefore proposed a reconciliation, and promised to give him his daughter, so only he would acknowledge the kingdom of Britain to be a fief of the Roman Empire. The aldermen of his court accordingly counselled him to lay aside his warlike preparations and accept the promise of Claudius. For no disgrace was it, they said, unto him to become a vassal of the Romans, seeing that they had possessed them of the empire of the whole world.

This advice, wise though it might be, must have been a bitter draught for Arthur; it meant that whatever were his own feelings he could not count upon much more resistance from his following. Yet he too must have realized that the situation was hopeless. Let us try to view it with his eyes. . . . For the last fortnight, ever since Claudius' transports arrived, it has been only too clear that the odds are heavily against him; unless the enemy is to make a mistake in handling his affairs, little hope really remains. Until now there has been a chance of this happening, for, Cornwall and Albany have been in a position to act in concert, the one opposing the enemy in front, the other harrying his rear. But now, with Camelot in Roman hands or practically so, the enemy can ward off Cornish blows while turning their main strength against Albany and crush it; the end is inevitable unless a miracle should happen. Is he therefore justified in expending further life and hardship on a hopeless prospect? His aldermen say 'No'. But are their hearts as firm as they should be? To give up the struggle after a bare two weeks in the field, and after a single battle, is not the promised fight to the death. For his own part he would rather draw the enemy further inland, into difficult ground of his own choice, and at least give the miracle the chance of happening. But he knows the tone in which his followers' advice has been given him: he cannot count on them, and it has sounded the knell for his hopes. He must swallow his own will, and keeping up a bold appearance take what comes to him; yet while doing so, he will always remain ready to seize an opportunity if something unexpected should occur.

With thoughts of this nature in his mind, Arthur came to Claudius' camp to hear the terms; and fortunately for us, what reads like an eye-witness account of the proceedings has been preserved in the pages of Boece. The scene of the gathering, at the foot of the little hill of Camelot, on which a Roman piquet was posted scanning the countryside, will have resembled many a *jirga* held beneath the rugged mountains of the Indian frontier. In the centre of one side of a hollow square of onlookers, under an open sunlit sky, sits the Emperor; he is flanked by officers of rank, while behind him and on either side of the square, filling its two wings, is a great assembly of officers and men. Facing him on the fourth side are the submitting Britons, sullen faced, surrendering only to Fate and to their foe's more powerful armament. As a precaution against tempers being lost, with a last desperate resort to knives, all weapons have been handed over for the occasion, and are piled in a heap at the camp entrance under the watchful eyes of sentries. Everywhere guards stand on the alert against treachery. The Emperor opens the proceedings, his words trans-lated by an interpreter; and the following is the Caledonian memory of what was said (making allowance for a not wholly sympathetic feeling for the 'English' plight!):

When Claudius had demanded of them why they broke their faith, they fell on their knees, confessed their offence and prayed him, since they were sufficiently punished by the Gods, to receive them again to his mercy and to spare their lives, under what conditions or servitude he pleased; and made solemn oaths never to rebel in times coming, and, if they failed, all vengeance on earth to fall on them and their posterity. Some of the Romans gave counsel to Claudius to punish their rebellion, and to slay the principal movers thereof, otherwise the Britons' good-will might not be holden. Naught the less, Vespasian persuaded him by many reasons to mercy; for a prince without mercy may well be dreaded, but never loved. Also, nothing pertained so much to the majesty of the Roman people as to show mercy to their subjects, and defend them from all injury by enemies; for, by that way the empire of Rome had grown, and should endure by the same way, to the end of the world. These words of Vespasian impressed the Emperor in such manner that he chose rather to be named a merciful prince than a vengeful tyrant.

Vespasian's magnanimity stands out in pleasant relief; and un-doubtedly to him Arthur owed his life.

Accordingly, conditions of submission were agreed upon; Arthur was to remain native ruler of South Britain, but under Plautius' governorship:

Plautius was to stuff all the strongholds and towns of Britain with strong garrisons of warmen; to administer justice by the laws; to keep Britain in peace, and defend them from all injury by peoples lying round about them, especially from the Scots and Picts who were a warlike people and impatient of servitude: and to seek no occasion of war against them; and, if it were necessary to have battle, then to keep a stout watch both at home and in the field; having no less the object of keeping the Britons' goodwill than to extend their empire. And finally he exhorted the nobles of Britain to remember the affliction fallen upon them by their rebellion, and to keep their faith in time coming, for the weal of themselves, their bairns and goods.

The terms give a vague impression that the 'Scots and Picts', Caledon and Brigance, were excluded from Arthur's rule. And, another typical irritation, an old enemy was appointed Supplies* contractor for the Roman army!

.   .   .   .   .

Arthur was now, in A.D. 44, for better or for worse a Roman vassal. At the best he would be in a position to exercise an honourable and assured rule over his countrymen, standing between them and their conquerors, and safeguarding their interests. At the worst—well, if the Romans meted out gross injustice, he could always take to the field again. Then there was Claudius' proposal about his marriage to a natural daughter of his, the Emperor's. He was getting terribly entangled over these matters of political expediency, with Boadicea already on hand, but with his heart set upon Guenevere; however it would be several months before his latest feminine reckoning, Venus Julia, could be presented to him, and in the meantime it had yet to be ascertained how the kingdom would settle down under the new regime. All depended upon the victors' behaviour; some of them were given to arrogance, and he had his doubts. Fears, though, were never his master; 'Sufficient unto the day' was as far as he would foresee.

It was in a mood of this kind that he received a summons to the presence of his prospective and domineeringly aloof father-in-law. By him he was informed that he, the Emperor, proposed to return to Rome shortly; he would be sailing in a few days' time, and wanted some prisoners to take with him for his triumph; Arthur was to produce two or three hundred straightway. We can well imagine a look of black fury coming over Arthur's face—he, a Briton, being ordered to betray his country-men shamefully, and send a drove of them for brutal slaughter; which is what a triumph meant. And this after a fair fight, in which the Britons had succeeded in holding their own despite Roman numbers and armament! The man was an unvarnished and con-temptible bully. Then in a flash an idea came across his mind. It was the same lightning-like mental process as has been so vividly described by the Duke of Wellington: all in a moment a whole train of thought, with every implication and involved action, passes through the mind; yet what flies through in a second might take a couple of hours to set down on paper. So with Arthur. He saw the solution; and with a grave impassive face he replied that it would be done as ordered.

True to his word, when Claudius' galleys and escorts an-chored off the Orcin* island a few mornings later, Arthur was ready on the beach with a few hundred dejected Britons to be handed over for shipment. As they were taken on board they pro-tested vehemently that they were friendly, and had helped the Romans in their invasion, and begged that Aulus Plautius be con-sulted. But the galley-masters only laughed; they had been warned to expect this subterfuge. Arthur himself was present to vouch for their being untrustworthy scoundrels, accustomed to feign friendliness and then murder surreptitiously. Claudius was not disposed to linger; they were despised by their own king, whose concern it was; he had got his prisoners, and that was all to him that mattered. And so the fleet set sail, carrying away with it the men who, on Roman behalf, had treacherously beset Cameliard a month earlier; they would ornament a pinchbeck triumph and then be publicly slaughtered—a fitting end for traitors. Arthur must have laughed sardonically.

How Arthur cleared himself with Plautius, when the Governor learned what he had done, is not on record. But the two men were beginning to know each other's character and to develop a mutual regard; it may be that Plautius said to himself that this was an occasion when a wise man stands back and lets well alone, it was Arthur's province. For, he himself had a greater pre-occupation on his mind.

·   ·   ·   ·   ·

Arthur's troubles as native king started at once. The Orcin islanders' kinsmen of the Itchen valley raised a conspiracy against him, with the support of the Caledonians, who were incensed at his apparent repudiation of their princess in favour of a more gaudy Roman attraction. The Itchen valley folk were evidently connected with the Orcin, for the latter's chieftain who had been shipped to Rome with the prisoners bears their name, Gwyn-was; in the romances he is Gunvasius* of Orkney. Boece's Caledonian chronicle contains a detailed account of the resentment and its repercussions. Written fifteen hundred years after the event, it none the less reads convincingly; and the plentifulness of its detail bears witness to the degree to which the subject rankled. It is here being quoted at length, so that those who care to judge its contents may do so for themselves. The mediaeval Scottish wording has occasionally been altered to current idiom, in order to make the reading easier; and the word 'Wales' has been changed to Gwynedd, indicating the Gwyn district of the Itchen, which in tradition has become confused with the old North Wales province. Yet the error is clear from the revolt having been made in conjunction with the folk of the Isle of Wight. The discontent was voiced on a moral note:

Sundry princes of Britain were right concerned that *Arthur* had repudiated his queen in this manner; and tried to persuade him, for many reasons, to abandon the Roman lady and to adhere to his lawful wife.... After that they shewed what profit might be had from them, if his enemies happened some time to invade his realm; and prayed him to eschew that he, by rage of lust and deceitful words of the Romans, drew not himself and the Britons from the friendship of their old confederate friends.

The inevitable suspicion of self-interest had arisen. However, they urged in vain; so by force they carried away Boadicea, from where he was said to be detaining her.

Arthur then thought fit to make a public explanation of his behaviour.

(He) wrote to the great princes of his realm, showing that his friends the lords of Gwynedd, in whom he most confided, took indignation that he had preferred a Roman lady to his first wife; as it had been unlawful to him to have sundry wives at his pleasure; howbeit, neither the laws nor the custom of Britain impaired his action: affirming also, the said marriage was not for any rage of lust, but only that Britons and Romans might prosper together, under one blood and friendship. Further, he desired them, if the lords of Gwynedd happened to conspire against him, that they keep their faith promised to the Romans.

This did not satisfy the complainants, who replied 'that it was unlawful for him in any way to prefer a new wife to his first one; and, for that reason, they were not content over the injury done to her'. This is the Caledonian version; in actual fact it does not seem likely that the arrangement had gone further than a promise of marriage. Nevertheless feeling ran strong; it was a national slight that a foreign bride should have been preferred, and a number of men withdrew their allegiance from him.

Arthur was no waverer, however; having once made up his mind for sound reasons, he was not going to alter it. So, in consultation with Plautius, he took a combined force of Romans and his own men into Gwynedd, to bring the objectors to book. They resisted him, and were punished; but other places also rebelled, so that, in Boece's words—'from thence, Plautius had little confidence in the Britons, and sent to France for *reinforcements* to support his army; and then garnished all his strongholds with fresh warriors and victuals.' The Gwynedd chieftains next plotted secretly for a general rising.

At last it was concluded that all people under their rule should gather, on a certain day and place, to expel the Romans out of Britain, or else all together to die. By the same counsel it was decided that messengers should pass to the lords of *the Weald** to solicit them to the same effect. In the harvest following their princes aforesaid assembled at *Coremyn,** *at the head of the sea-marsh*, where they, by long regret of Roman injuries, lamented heavily the fickleness of Arthur, who had more desire to be a servant of Rome than king of Britain. Notwithstanding with whole mind and strength they agreed to recover their ancient honour and liberty.

But then began no little contention who should be captain of the army; for few of them would give place to an other. Then *the chief of Gwynedd* said in this manner: We may soon gather, most valiant men, a greater army of our people and friends than may easily be resisted, so let everything be governed by military wisdom; for therein stands all victory and glory of battle. Naught the less, sedition, discord, and ambition of honour, are so contrary to it, that where they sprout neither ardour nor warlike skill can have place, nor victory be had over our enemies. Therefore, all ambition is to be forfeit, and all dissensions are to be made expire; and finally, one man is to be chosen, to whom the remaining people shall be obedient; by whose authority this force shall be led, and, if we intend to gain the victory, to whom we shall be obedient. And because we are all of us nearly equal to one another in power, therefore it is best to send spokesmen to Caratak of Caledon, who is a most bitter enemy of the Romans, and ask him to join us in avenging the hurt done to his sister Boadicea, and to defend his kinsman whom the Romans intend to defraud of the crown of Britain; and to exhort him to take over the government thereof, while the boy is of imperfect age; and they are to obey him in all circumstances as they arise; for the more affection that he have for his sister and kinsman, the more easily may this matter be solicited.

Soon after, spokesmen were sent to Caratak, and showed him all this matter at length, as has been described. He answered that he was more grieved that Arthur had married a Roman lady, in contempt of himself and his realm, than at any injury done to his sister or kinsman; knowing well how the Romans, by false fellowship and guile, subdue imprudent kings to their dominion. Nevertheless, he promised to come, in the spring of the year, to support them with his army, as he thought was most expedient.

Caratak of Caledon now enters the story. In Boece he is King of Scots, as has been explained on p. 81 (Caratak and Caradoc being the same name); but properly he was Chief of Caledon, the Weald, half-brother to Boadicea, and Arthur's rejected brother-in-law to be. The heir designate to the kingdom, called here his 'kinsman' in substitution for Boece's word 'nephew', was Modred; but over this a great deal of confusion has arisen. The two Carataks have become mistaken for one another, in the following way: Modred was Arthur's sister's son and was Arthur's nephew, that is to say he was correctly spoken of as Caratac's sister's son and as Caratac's nephew; but the Caratac who was Arthur has been mistaken for Caratak of Caledon, whose sister Boadicea has accordingly been assigned an imaginary child.

A great deal of capital is made in Boece's Scottish chronicle over this reputed son of Arthur and Boadicea; but when the circumstances are examined, it seems almost a physical impossibility, let alone improbable. Their marriage was first mooted in the autumn or winter of A.D. 43; the Roman counter-proposal came in the following spring, and this grievance was being ventilated (traditionally) in the autumn or winter of the same year, A.D. 44. Several doubts therefore arise: Would the Roman proposition ever have been made if Arthur were already married, and if it were, would he have entertained it? It is entirely contrary to his character. Again, is it likely that Boadicea could have borne him a son within a year of the proposal first being mooted? She is not known even to have been of marriageable age at the time.

Two flaws in the supposition that he wedded her can be detected. The first is that there is no evidence of his having married Claudius' daughter; in which case he remained wedded to Boadicea—if ever wedded. The Genuissa whom he married was not Claudius' daughter, whose name was Venus Julia; Genuissa is a variation of Guenevere, it is the Latin version of Gwen Iu-wys, 'Gwen of the Yew-folk', just as Guenevere is Gwen-hwyvar, 'Gwen of the Yew'. Nor would Claudius' daughter have had much time to reach Britain before (as must be remarked prematurely) Arthur had broken into revolt and terminated any agreement made with the Emperor. It is unlikely that all these actions happened so promptly. The second flaw is that, if Arthur were being regarded as illegitimate, it would be inconsistent to look upon any son of his, even by Boadicea, as the rightful heir to Cymbeline's kingdom. The notion of Boadicea's son seems to be a later addition to the story, and to have arisen from a misconception as to the sister under reference; and the emphasis laid on it, like that on Arthur's slandered birth, witnesses the degree of partisanship with which he was having to contend.

Modred must not be pictured as having any personal connection with affairs at this period; he was in the nursery. His mother can hardly have been married before A.D. 39, judging from her birth having been after Arthur's, and from Arthur having been an unmarried youth at the time the Romans came; so Modred will only have been born at the earliest in A.D. 40, and more probably a year or two later. The policy pursued on his behalf emanated from Caratak of Caledon; Caratak was leading an extreme anti-Roman party; Arthur's illegitimacy and Modred's rightful position as heir were the excuses for Caratak's nomination as 'governor' of Britain. This policy must have been embarrassing for the boy's father, Aaron Rheged, who was pursuing an identically opposite policy, that of close subservience to the Romans.

Thus the Caledonian attitude at this stage was: Arthur, they argued, was casting in his lot with Rome; under any circumstances they did not want him as ruler, though they had acknowledged his brother Gwydr, born of an Alban mother; they chose to regard his sister's son Modred, whose father was Alban, as the rightful heir to the crown; Arthur had been born under peculiar conditions, he could be said to be illegitimate, and he had insulted their race by spurning a Caledonian princess in favour of a Roman girl. Accordingly a spokesman on their behalf suggested that Caratak should come forward as the national leader in place of Arthur, and on behalf of Modred; discontented Britons could be expected to rally to a nationalist anti-Roman call, and Caratak should be appointed governor of Britain until Modred came of age. To this Caratak consented. The awkwardness of Arthur's position will be apparent: officially he was committed to keeping the peace, but in popular British opinion he would be expected to turn a blind eye to anti-Roman activities; privately, though, he was painfully aware that this was a partisan measure to weaken his position in the realm.

The effect on Boece's chronicle, of Caratak's appointment as governor, is that he has been interpreted in it as the Caractacus of classical history, Arthur figuring as the Arwiragus of British tradition; yet, as has been pointed out in the first chapter of this book, there is no cause to doubt that the two brothers Togodumnus and Caractacus, sons of Cymbeline in classical history, are the same as the two brothers Gwydr and Arwiragus, sons of Bran in Geoffrey's history. Moreover Boece's translator, Stewart, was evidently aware that Arwiragus and Caractacus are the same person, because when referring to Arwiragus he remarks, 'As I shall tell when I have come to the time,' and when the time comes he follows Tacitus' narrative and tells of the incident in the name of Caractacus. Caratak of Caledon is therefore not that individual; he is the King Carados of Scotland in Arthurian romance, fighting alongside Arthur certainly for most of the time, yet not always so.

To return to the story: All took place as arranged between the would-be rebels and Caratak; and in the spring of A.D. 45 the men of Gwynedd and Caledon, with the Picts, gathered in revolt at 'York', by Chichester.

As soon as Plautius and Arthur were notified of this, they assembled their folk. Nevertheless they thought it unprofitable to give hasty battle, knowing well their enemies were full of ire and hatred; and therefore decided to irk them with long waiting, walking, work and shortage of victuals, rather than to jeopardize themselves against so huge a multitude of people, all enraged against them at once, who could not be vanquished without terrible slaughter.

This pays tribute to Arthur's handling of a situation in which he had every reason to want to avoid bloodshed.

The men of Albany, by this delay in fighting, came to such a pass that they could not be kept together, for the multitude of them; for such dearth and hunger arose in the army that sundry of them left their camp to look for food; of whom some were captured and brought to Plautius, and showed that the Britons by hunger, walking, and trouble, were near beaten.

Plautius, on the morrow, made his army ready for battle. Caratak, warned of this, assembled his folk and joined battle. There followed a sharp engagement, and continual fighting with uncertain result, until nightfall drew them apart. Plautius, on the morrow, seeing that he must replenish his army, returned to headquarters, after most of his horsemen had been beaten. Caratak, having suffered in the same manner, came with the remnant of his army to 'York', and commanded all his folk to return home, until further orders.

Plautius, after this unhappy battle, sent messengers to Caratak, to say he was greatly surprised that Caratak should have invaded Roman territory and aided their enemies, without any occasion of having been injured; and taking no account of the Emperor Claudius' humanity, who with little difficulty could have subdued his realm and people, but who had abstained and had visited his wrath on the Orcin instead. Therefore, he required him to make reparation for all damage done, and to refrain therefrom in times coming, else he should be regarded as an enemy to the Romans.

It was answered by Caratak, that it was not a matter for surprise that he should have defended his kinsman, defrauded of his just heritage and kingdom. And to the remaining points he answered—It was for no favour that Claudius had not invaded the realm of Caledon, but only because he knew that it was not possible to conquer it except by extreme jeopardy and chance in battle: and, for that cause, he passed on to the rough and unarmed people of Orkney, who might be soon vanquished: to that end, that he, the glorious and valiant Emperor, among feeble creatures, might have a feigned glory of triumph. For this reason, the Romans should redress both the new and old injuries done to Gaels and Picts, and depart hastily out of Albany with their folk; otherwise naught was to be trusted, both Gaels, Picts, and Britons, whom they held in great contempt, should be their perpetual enemies, for defence of their liberty and native gods.

Plautius by this answer was greatly incensed, and thought it right unworthy that a people neither powerful in riches nor warlike strength should so pertly despise the power of Rome: and swore, therefore, to revenge this proud contempt shown by Caratak. Many other Romans took oaths in that same manner.

.   .   .   .   .

We will now transfer ourselves to Roman headquarters, and see developments from Aulus Plautius' angle, in order to get a broader point of view. That general will not have been deceived by the hollowness of the Emperor's superficial settlement and hasty departure; and when Claudius, before sailing, gave him parting secret instructions to subdue the remaining districts of South Britain, he cannot but have felt that the more difficult part of the task was yet to come, and that (to use a modern colloquialism) he was being left to carry the baby. He was too experienced a soldier not to have read the sullen resentment on the Britons' faces when making their submission, nor to have known that any fresh encroachment on their freedom might rouse the whole country in arms again. He will have held many a conference with Vespasian and other seniors, and have heard the policy advocated—'Let sleeping dogs lie', for a while at any rate.

Accordingly his first policy must have been to allow the province to settle down quietly under its native ruler, with himself standing at his elbow, so to speak, ready to support his authority with the legions. And very soon Arthur's authority was being challenged, as has been related, by the Itchen valley folk. The reason so far quoted is not wholly clear; it was connected with the Caledonian princess Boadicea, but the tale that Arthur had imprisoned her, and that the Itchen folk took it upon themselves to liberate her, does not ring true. At a later date in history she is found as wife of the Itchen chieftain Prasutawg; so, the bald truth seems to be that she was kidnapped. Plautius gave Arthur some cohorts to help quell this disturbance; after which, to judge from Boece's chronicle, he received warning of a more extensive rising being planned, and brought over more troops in readiness.

Early in the following year, A.D. 45, the insurrection he had been warned of broke out, near Chichester. He and Arthur put it down between them, reducing the hill-fortress of 'York' by hunger, and obliging the rebels to disperse without much bloodshed. Arthur was giving him loyal assistance; but Caratak of Caledon was recalcitrant, posing as the national champion for a free Britain.

During this period a framework of roads was laid out for the captured territory, recognizable in the four main roads which meet at a single point in London; they are those from Chichester, Pevensey, Colchester, and Royston. At this stage they can only have been planned, and their rough preparation as grass tracks just begun—with wide clearance on either side, to prevent ambushes; metalling will not have been carried out until later. For the present, the clearance and drainage of the ground's natural surface, and bridging, are all that is to be visualized. A fifth short road connected Richborough, where there was a small garrison, with Pilgrims Way at Canterbury, the British track being used apparently as a subsidiary communication route. Thus the army was being supplied from three sea-ports: the Portchester–Chichester base area, Richborough, and Colchester; Pevensey was perhaps used for civil commerce only, as was Newhaven. London was already figuring as the administrative centre. The frontier south of the Thames ran just west of Winchester and Silchester; while north of the river it ran along the foot of the Chilterns, more or less coinciding with Icknield Way.

Having discouraged further unrest by the prompt suppression of the two revolts, and feeling reasonably assured that he could rely upon Arthur's adherence, Plautius was faced with the task of his secret orders to subjugate the remaining districts. It would have been folly to expect Arthur to remain quiescent while preparations for doing so were being made; consequently Plautius resorted to a subterfuge. He gave out that some of the legions would be returning to Gaul, and embarked them under Vespasian's command on a fleet of transports. They disappeared down Southampton Water; and the Britons saw thankfully some of their hated burden being removed. To appreciate the intensity of their feeling a whiff of Celtic sentiment is needed; and Layamon provides this, who drew his touch from the Welsh Border, where memories of Saxon encroachment still rankled. Time has gilded his picture into the enemy having been forced to go, and to do so entirely, which is very likely to have been the rumour that reached outlying districts; so his wording has to be altered from being spoken by Arthur himself, and the same words put into the mouth of another Briton, as is being done here, abbreviated. For, Arthur was well aware that only part of the legions were sailing, and that the Governor would be remaining. Thus the scene to be imagined is some distant Devon coombe, when the news 'they say' reaches the village:

Then laughed the headman with loud voice—Thanked be the Lord, that all dooms wieldeth, that Caesar the strong is tired of our land. Our land he hath divided to all his knights; us he thought to drive out of our country, hold us for base, and have our realm. But of him it is happened, as it is of the fox when he is boldest over the weald and hath his full play; he weeneth to be of power the boldest of all animals. But when come to him the men under the hills, with horns, with hounds, with loud cries; they drive the fox over dales and over downs; he fleeth and seeketh his hole. So is it with Caesar, the strong and the rich; he thought all our kingdom to set in his own hand, but now we have driven him to the bare death. Now will we give him peace, his prayer will we receive; hostages we will have of the highest of his men, their horses and weapons, ere they hence depart. So they shall as wretches go to their ships, sail over sea to their good land, and there tell tidings of Arthur our king, how he for his father's soul and for our freedom solaced the wretches.

The story continues from Wace:

The *enemy* set out across the water, until their sails were lost to sight. I know not what was their hope, nor the name of him who put it in their mind, but they turned their boats, and passed through the channel between England and Normandy. With sail and oar they came to the land of Devon, casting anchor in the haven of Totnes. The heathen breathed out threatenings and slaughter against the folk of the country. They poured forth from their ships, and scattered themselves abroad amongst the people, searching out arms and raiment, firing homesteads and slaying Christian men. They passed to and fro about the country, carrying off all they found beneath their hands.

Arthur's reaction was prompt. Any misgivings as to his sincerity, which may be felt over his facile submission to Rome, accepting the crown at their hands and undertaking to become the Emperor's son-in-law, can be set at rest. On learning of the Roman landing at Totnes he immediately relinquished all semblance of compromise, called the country to arms again, and within seven days was himself attacking their camp at Exeter. Their trickery stung him acutely; his words are quoted from Geoffrey:

> For that these *Romans*, of most impious and hateful name, have disdained to keep faith with me, I, keeping my faith unto my God, will endeavour me this day to revenge upon them the blood of my countrymen. To arms, therefore, ye warriors, to arms! And fall upon yonder traitors like men; for, of a certainty, by Christ's succour, we cannot fail of victory!

His chagrin can be imagined. He had been duped. The native royalty, which the country needed so badly for stability and welfare, had been but a painted bait offered to him and swallowed. The Caledonians now were angered, and he could no longer count upon their support with certainty; the Gauls were holding aloof cannily, mistrustful at his sudden change of front; the 'Irish' of the Lake were up in arms, enraged at his raid on Orkney. He had put his cards on the table; but he was up against a card-sharper and had been had for a mug. With a crash he upset the table and left the room, saying to himself philosophically: 'Anyway that settles the Venus Julia racket!'

Boece's version naïvely centres the initiative on the Caledonian chief, and construes Arthur's defection from the Romans as sheer opportunism. It exemplifies perfectly the semi-hostile mentality of the tribe, and the extremely clever distortion of truth with which Arthur was having to cope, when trying to weld the country into a single-hearted kingdom. Even if it be conceded

that he may have been glad to be relieved of Boadicea's partnership, he had had little option from the turn of Fate that did it; nor
did he know that Claudius was playing a double game behind his
back; and if he had relinquished a loveless affair of State, he was at
the same time forfeiting the girl of his heart, Guenevere. Thoughts
of that kind, however, had been left behind by Arthur; he was now
in the field.

Exeter is his ninth battle, and is termed in tradition 'Caer Leon
in Lloegria', to distinguish it from Caer Leon in Wales. This designation 'Camp of the Legion' is derived from its having become
later the headquarters of the IInd Legion. But in Boece's Scottish
chronicle it is called York; and the circumstances under which
this misunderstanding arose afford an excellent example of corruption in oral tradition. The true name for Exeter in tradition
was Caer Wysc, the Camp by the Exe; but to mediaeval Scotland
the river Wysc meant the Yorkshire stream of that name, now the
Wiske, because nearby had been fought the disastrous battle of
the Standard. Consequently, with the intention of clarifying the
story's geography for Scottish listeners, the Camp by the Wysc
was translated into 'York'. Its local name is given by Geoffrey,
'Caer Huelcoit (*Howel's Wood*) that is called Exeter.'

By a classical account we are told that on the eighth day of
Vespasian's operations against the place, Arthur surprised the
Romans in their camp. So swift and furious was his onslaught that
Vespasian was almost killed in his tent; he owed his life to his
son Titus, who charged the Britons at the head of a cohort of the
XIVth Legion, and rescued him. The assault will have resembled
encounters which our infantry used to experience with Pathan
tribesmen during the last century, and it can be visualized—The
camp at rest after nightfall, sentries alert round the perimeter,
outlying piquets on knolls or overlooking places where the
Britons might gather unseen. Perhaps a badly posted piquet or a
careless sentry, but the Britons succeed in assembling stealthily
within a short distance of the camp wall. All of a sudden there is
a roar of shouting, and a torrent of men pour against a single
point in the defences; the few men on guard are swept away in a
trice, and the flood bursts into the camp, spreading outwards in all
directions, hacking down every man in its way. But with the discipline born of experience, the troops fall in in squares at their

alarm posts, snatching up swords always kept ready at hand for an emergency. The Britons hurl themselves at the squares; some they break and cut to bits, others stand fast. Then, those squares which have withstood the rush move forward themselves; shoulder to shoulder the soldiers steadily advance to the help of their comrades, their compact formation giving the enemy no opening to penetrate. Yard by yard they gain ground against the Britons, gathering momentum as they go, until at last at a slow double they are clearing the havoc and coming to the aid of pressed knots of survivors. For a while the issue hangs in the balance; then, realizing that their now scattered numbers have lost their power, the Britons break and fly. As imperceptibly as they came, they disappear into woods and dells. Behind them, the soldiers re-establish their defence line around the camp perimeter, tend the wounded and collect the dead; while their commanders, thankful at having averted the catastrophe, double their precautions against another surprise.

The Romans succeeded in repulsing Arthur; after which he is likely to have retreated northwards, to the neighbourhood of the Quantocks, beyond where lies the site of his tenth battle, at the mouth of the Somerset Brue. Boece relates of a battle having been fought twelve miles from Exeter, by a marsh. There is no ground of that nature, however, near Exeter, so it is probable that the miles* were Welsh ones, four times the distance of the English measure, and that the fight was at Ham Hill near Ilchester, an important British fortress. But although not stated in words it appears that lack of concert was marring the Britons' effort; the Albany men did not take part in the fight at Exeter, they seem to have come as far as Ilchester where they fought largely on their own, accusing the Cornishmen of treachery, after which they abandoned the struggle and returned to Sussex. It is a sorry tale, and only to be recounted for the purpose of deriving some benefit from history; in that recognition of what harm was wrought by disunity in the past might perhaps help avoid recurrence of some similar failure at the present.

The Albany account runs as follows:

Vespasian raised his tents, and was led by certain treasonable Britons to where the Albany men were. There soon followed a dangerous and terrible battle; for the Albany men stood in strength beside a marsh, not twelve '*leagues*' from Exeter. The Romans that fought on the right wing were nearly beaten, nevertheless Vespasian supported them with a new legion; and because of its coming their courage was so raised that, notwithstanding their heavy wounds, they renewed the fight; and when they were pierced through the body, they died not till they had slain the enemy before them. Others fought so cruelly that, when their hand and sword were cut off, they fell on their enemies and gnawed them with their teeth. Nevertheless the fated victory, given by divine behest to the Romans, could not be prevented that day, either by numbers, manhood, nor long perseverance in battle; by the antipathy of the gods, who had determined to subdue all realms to Rome: and the Albany men, although they left nothing undone that might pertain to valiant campaigners, were finally beaten. Arthur, oppressed with heavy grief at the slaughter of so many noble companions, would have slain himself; but he was stopped by his friends, in hope of better fortune. *The Chief of Caledon*, saved with a few of his people, went to Brigance. Illithara, king of the Picts, desiring not to live after the slaughter of his dear friends, reft off his coat armour and was slain soon after, none knowing who he was.

Two points in this narrative call for comment: firstly the story of Cornish betrayal, and secondly the battle-site. As regards the first, Stewart amplifies the circumstances, saying that the Romans were led across the hills and caught the Albany men unawares. To suppose deliberate treachery at this stage is irrational; a normal picture would be that the Romans got hold of local guides, and, under a skilled commander as was Vespasian, made a dash across the hills to the north-east and caught the Albany men by surprise. It is possible that the Albany contingent had not yet made contact with the defeated Cornish, who were further west near Bishops Lydeard (where some traces of a battle have been found), and that they fought alone; for this reason, having lost the fight, the Albany men went home. Arthur, it must be supposed, when he heard that they were being attacked came to their assistance, but, unable to save the situation, was obliged to withdraw again northwards in the direction of the Brue estuary. The Caledonian account that he (Arwiragus) made peace after this differs from the romances, which tell of yet another heavy battle; the indirect truth is that the Caledonians, having left the field, had no tradition of continued resistance.

Brigance,* whither the Albany men went, was in the neighbourhood of Caledon according to Boece's geography, between it and the islands of the Lake; and as its people are mentioned in the transactions with Julius Caesar, the district would appear to correspond with present-day East Sussex.

Arthur again retreated northwards; and Vespasian, having disposed of the Albany insurgents (as they will have appeared in Roman eyes), seems to have opened up an overland line of communication with Winchester, establishing a temporary post on Hod Hill above Blandford. Possibly at this time also he built the camp near Wiveliscombe, west of Taunton, to control the Exmoor Britons; but this post may alternatively have been made at a slightly later date.

Arthur then made a stand at the mouth of the Brue, where he fought his tenth traditional battle, 'Tribruit', the Traeth Brue. Near there at Brent Knoll was a religious institution, which we hear of later on; so perhaps it was with the aid of its influence that he succeeded in rallying the Britons. However he must have been defeated, because the romances next tell of his fighting at Bath, still unyielding to despondency. This will not have been his twelfth battle, Badon, but an earlier fight on the same battleground. His fortitude in these constant endeavours, in which we see him grasping every slightest hope that offers itself, truly commands admiration; it throws into clear relief the handicap under which he was labouring—disunity. Never could he muster more than local resources. At each endeavour he would get together all the opposition that he could collect; yet always it would prove too little. Seen in retrospect, had all those who rallied to him for local defence carried their loyalty to a higher pitch, and had they joined him for a single great national effort, Britain would never have fallen under Roman sway.

The depressing disappointment to him as commander, always seeing thin ranks and hearing half-hearted forecasts or excuses, must have lain as a perpetual load on his shoulders. Men were ready to give their lives for their immediate interests, when faced with some visible threat, yet not for the indirect common good; they were throwing themselves away piecemeal rather than help one another. They were playing into the enemy's hands; and the enemy must have known it.

So, having retreated from the Traeth Brue, Arthur gathered together the slender resources of Gloucestershire and what remained of Somerset resistance, at Bath; and taking post on the hill south of the Avon, he stood to meet the Romans. His followers knew the hazard; they were well aware of Vespasian's irresistible progress up to this point. Even so, they were going to pit themselves against him:

The *Cæsar* won all that he looked on with eyes; he took Somerset, and he took Dorset, and in Devonshire the folk all destroyed, and Wiltshire with hostility he greeted; he took all the lands unto the sea strand. Then at the last, then caused he horns and trumpets to be blown, and his host to be assembled, and forth he would march, and Bath all besiege, and eke Bristol about *assail*. This was their threat, ere they to Bath came. To Bath came the *Cæsar*, and belay the castle there; and the men within bravely began; they mounted upon the stone walls, well weaponed over all, and defended the place.

Thus writes Layamon; and from his account it can be discerned that the Britons made three desperate stands, this the first, at the hill camp south of the river. Driven thence they fought on the river bank; then, when a crossing had been forced, they fought again on the hill north of it. A gallant endeavour.

Layamon's vivid picturesqueness is delightful, and will be quoted, shortened. If there are anachronisms, and if Arthur chases the enemy from point to point, whereas in reality it was he who had to give ground, they are half-pardonable poetic licence, for which allowance can be made. The pretence unspokenly covers remorse felt at the disgrace of a lost cause: 'If only the waverers had held fast' is the heart's reproach. But it is the spirit of those who did hold together and fight that it is desired to illustrate, their steadfast resolve that Britain should be for the British.

Then called Arthur with loud voice: Lo, where here before us the heathen hounds, who slew our ancestors. Now march we to them, and avenge worthily our kindred and our realm. March we now forward, fast together; and when we come to them, myself foremost of all the fight I will begin.

The Britons laid on them, they gave bitter strokes with axes and with swords. Arthur with his sword wrought destruction; the king was all enraged as is the wild boar, when he in the beech-wood meeteth many swine. *The enemy* saw this and gan him to turn, and bent him over the Avon to save himself. And Arthur drove them to the flood; there were many slain, so that all Avon's stream was bridged with steel. The enemy over the water fled, to the hill that standeth over Bath; they thought on the hill to withstand. When Arthur saw where they eke battle wrought, then called the king, keenly loud: My bold thanes, advance to the hills! Now it is to him all as the goat when the wild wolf approacheth. I am the wolf; so will I now today the enemy all destroy. Yesterday was the Roman of all knights boldest, but now he standeth on the hill and beholdeth the Avon, how the steel fishes lie in the stream!

Nigh all so swift as the fowl flieth, the brave men followed the king; they smote upon the enemy with exceeding smart strokes. Then called Arthur with loud voice: Here I come, Roman! To the realm we two shall reach; now we shall divide this land as shall be to thee loathest of all! Even with the words, his broad sword he up heaved and hardily down struck, and clove his helm in the midst. Then laughed Arthur, the noble king: Lie thou there, Roman; thou wert climbed too high. Now set I all this kingdom in your own hands, dales and downs, and all my good folk! Here shall your bones lie, beside Bath; and we shall here in this land live in bliss.

It is happier that the battle's memory should live in this fashion, rather than the sadder truth of failure; because, driven from the field though he may have been, Arthur won the day in his foe's admiration. Once again he had earned Vespasian's and Plautius' esteem; and for the second time Plautius generously invited him to bow to the inevitable, and become ruler of Britain under the suzerainty of Rome. He accepted the offer; nor could he have done better for the country.

All Britain south of the Thames now became a Roman province; and throughout the Roman occupation of this island that approximate boundary was retained, *Britannia Prima*. North of the Thames, Gloucester was garrisoned as an outpost, so also were the Chilterns and Colchester on the other flank. These represent the limits of Arthur's kingdom; and in it, the first task for Briton and Roman was to restore law and order.

9

Into Calm Water

JUST as after a gale the surface of the sea does not change all at
once from storm-lashed waves to tranquil placidity, but for a
while heaves with a swell, so had some little time to elapse before
Britain's state of turmoil could sink into rest. Arthur's first attention had to be given to quelling the Picts and Scots of the Lake
who had beset his allies the Gauls at Alclud,* one of the hill
fortresses on the South Downs above Portsmouth. From the
topography of the Downs this would seem most likely to have
been Butser Hill. Thither he summoned a band of Cornishmen;
but on the way an unfortunate incident occurred. Under their
chieftain Cador, praiseworthily termed 'a crafty captain', they
found the Roman ships in the Teign unguarded. The temptation
was too strong for a party of needy adventurers. They put the
crews to the sword and looted the ships.

The occurrence must have been awkward for Arthur to explain; but readers who have served abroad under like conditions
will perhaps themselves have encountered the technique. We can
picture Arthur reporting the news to Plautius with a very grave
face, saying that an 'accident' has taken place; he deeply regrets
the losses, but he has not yet had time to bring the outlying districts under control; and he manages subtly to infer that the
sentries had been caught off their guard, which is fair game.

The Britons' behaviour was blatant; they revelled in the feat.
The Cornishmen had found the galleys empty, the watch ashore;
they got aboard before disturbing the Romans, and then when
the alarm was given and the guards hastened to their ships
in twos and threes, cut them down. Other Britons who had surrounded the haven chased the Romans down to the river:

Cador the huntsman came winding upon their slot. . . . Those who escaped from Cador they made their way from every part to the ships; there they were slain by the archers, or perished miserably in the sea. The Britons took no captives; he who cried for mercy perished alike with him who strove with his sword. The rest of the enemy fled to the coverts of the woods and the mountains; in such desolate and waste places they lurked and hid from their enemies until hunger and thirst put a term to their miseries.

Wiping his sword, Cador collected his men and continued on his way to join Arthur. Time enough to explain when he got to the far end! Delicacy may prevent the Duke of Cornwall's Light Infantry from claiming Totnes as battle honour, but nevertheless it is one of their 'off the record' engagements. Such things happen in war.

‘   .   .   .   .

By the time the Cornish party reached him, Arthur had relieved the Gauls in the hills by Portsmouth. The Scots (by whom seem to be implied 'Irish' from the Lake) and the Picts withdrew, first to Moray and then to the islands of the Lake. Here they received full measure of Arthur's wrath; he hunted them out in boats or starved them out, and if they stood to fight him he thrashed them in battle. Their rescue came from the Church newly established in the area; its ministers pleaded on their behalf, and he acceded to their petition:

Thou hast overcome us, every one; destroy us not from the land, but suffer us to live of thy bounty. Grant that we and all our race—so be it thy pleasure—may find peace in the king's service. Have mercy on thy poor Christians. We hold the faith that you, too, count dear. How foully then should Christianity be wronged, if you destroy the whole realm. Alas, has not mischief enough been wrought already!
Arthur was tender of heart and marvellously pitiful. He took compassion on this doleful company of ladies, and by reason of those holy *relics* and those fair prelates, he granted life and member to his captives, and forgave them their debts.

Thence he returned to 'York', which for all intents and purposes will have been Chichester, where he spent Christmas. He disbanded his own men who were under arms, and sent the Gauls back to Brittany; evidently there had been trouble between the Caledonians and the Gauls at Alclud, and this ended when the latter went home. His reputation now stood high in the land: he had bravely defied the Romans, with the reward that Britain, even though vanquished, still had its own king; and he was vigorously asserting his authority among the lawless. Nennius proudly records that in the days of Claudius no tribute was received from the Britons, but that it was paid to a British king; and Wace's description of the disbandment of his forces runs: 'The host went therefore each to his own place, loudly praising the king; even in Brittany men told that there was no more valiant captain than he.'

According to the Scottish chronicle the Picts were subdued in the summer following Arthur's wintering with Vespasian at 'York', together with other recalcitrants, Caledonians, Mona* ('Isle of Man'), and the Isle of Wight; but here it has been assumed that the operations against these were the ones related in English tradition as against Moray.* The purpose of that fighting, so the romances tell, was to aid the Gauls in Alclud, which is to say in a hill-fort above the river Clwyd. That river, owing to the usual transcription of Caledon as Scotland, has become regarded as the Clyde; it is a misapprehension which may have come from another source as well, in that the Clyde lay near a district called Saluria, while there used also to be a Saluria* in West Sussex. The latter is possibly evidenced today in the group of place-names Selsey, Selborne, Selham, Selhurst, Selwood; thus the Gauls can be pictured as hemmed in at the earthwork on Butser Hill, above the Rother. To confirm this identification is its traditional construction by the same man as built the 'York' fortress, near Chichester; he was the expansionist Dorset chieftain of Maidens Castle. Another remark to be made about the district name Saluria is that, besides the two regions just mentioned there was a third, in South Wales; it is usually spelt Siluria, but the difference is immaterial, the pronunciation was the same.

Whether as an act of his own grace, or on Roman instigation, Arthur at this juncture conferred on his brother-in-law, Lot of Llychlyn, what was probably some debatable land. The romance's wording is of interest in the way it couples the Humber with Lyonnesse, corroborating that both were close to each other:

'And thou, Loth, my dear friend—God be to thee mild—thou hast my sister to wife; the better it shall be for thee. I give thee Lyonnesse, that is a land fair; and I will add thereto lands most good, beside the Humber.' Although in story Lot is portrayed as one of three brothers—Lot of Lyonnesse and Llychlyn and Lothian, Urien of Rheged and Moray, and Angwysel of 'Scotland' —it appears right, because of the disintegrating habit of tradition, to regard the three as a single individual though variously styled according to his several capacities. His many designations are tabulated in the Glossary, under RHEGED. So, from now on he will be treated under either name, Lot or Urien Rheged, as chieftain of the Chichester Regni; and under his rule are to be comprehended the Lake, Moray, and Lothian, and the familiar Lyonnesse of romance. His son is the knight Gawaine—'as yet a damoiseau, young and debonair'.

In this manner drew to a close the turbulent year of A.D. 45.

·   ·   ·   ·   ·

Having flitted like a butterfly around two political flowers, and found no honey in either of them, Arthur next winged his cheerful way towards a bloom of great beauty. Not that there had been anything really amiss with Boadicea of Caledon; it was merely that an interfering gardener had disturbed the Red Admiral while he had been dallying round, and before he could return she had been monopolized by a Cabbage White.

His romance needs to be told in the actual wording of legend. In it, the mysterious form of Merlin comes and goes, watchful over Arthur's welfare like a guardian angel. This is the story, as Malory gives it:

Arthur, after he was chosen king by adventure and by grace . . . for the most part the days of his life was ruled much by the counsel of Merlin. So it fell on a time King Arthur said unto Merlin: 'My barons will let me have no rest, but needs I must take a wife, and I will none take but by thy counsel and by thine advice. . . .'

'It is well done,' said Merlin, 'that ye take a wife, for a man of your bounty and noblesse should not be without a wife. Now is there any that ye love more than another?'

'Yea,' said King Arthur, 'I love Guenever the king's daughter,

Leodegrance of the land of Cameliard, the which holdeth in his house the Table Round that ye told he had of my father. And this damosel is the most valiant and fairest lady that I know living, or yet that ever I could find.'

'Sir,' said Merlin, 'as of her beauty and fairness she is one of the fairest on live, but, if ye loved her not so well as ye do, I should find you a damosel of beauty and of goodness that should like you and please you, if your heart were not set; but there as a man's heart is set, he will be loth to return.'

'That is truth,' said King Arthur. . . .

Then Merlin desired of the king for to have men with him that should enquire of Guenever, and so the king granted him, and Merlin went forth unto King Leodegrance of Cameliard, and told him of the desire of the king that he would have unto his wife Guenever his daughter.

'That is to me,' said King Leodegrance, 'the best tidings that ever I heard, that so worthy a king of prowess and noblesse will wed my daughter. And as for my lands, I will give him, wist I it might please him, but he hath lands enow, him needeth none, but I shall send him a gift shall please him much more, for I shall give him the Table Round, the which *his father* gave me, and when it is full complete, there is an hundred knights and fifty. And as for an hundred good knights I have myself, but I lack fifty, for so many have been slain in my days.'

And so Leodegrance delivered his daughter Guenever unto Merlin, and the Table Round with the hundred knights, and so they rode freshly, with great royalty, what by water and what by land, till that they came nigh unto *the Court*.

The story then tells of Arthur's pleasure, and of his ordering Merlin to find him fifty knights who would complete the Round Table's complement. Merlin, though, could only find twenty-eight; and this left two seats vacant. The discrepancy between the thirty and fifty is not explained; it is possible that fifty is a mistake which has crept in, and that thirty was the correct number. The point is of some moment, because the Round Table evidently contained thirty distinguished seats, which were one of its features.

Arthur's nephew, Gawaine, then asked to be knighted so as to fill one of the empty seats; which Arthur promised he would do. Another youth also made the same request, who turned out to be son of Pellinore, the chieftain who had aided Arthur in his raid on Orkney, and who had injured Gawaine's father. By chance Arthur knighted this youth before Gawaine.

'What is the cause,' said King Arthur, 'that there be two places void in the seats?'

'Sir,' said Merlin, 'there shall no man sit in those places but they that shall be of most worship. But in the Seat Perilous there shall no man sit therein but one, and if there be any so hardy to do it he shall be destroyed, and he that shall sit there shall have no fellow.' And therewith Merlin took King Pellinore by the hand, and in the one hand next the two seats and the Seat Perilous he said, in open audience, 'This is your place and best ye are worthy to sit therein of any that is here.'

Thereat sat Sir Gawaine in great envy and told his brother, 'Yonder knight is put to great worship, the which grieveth me sore, for he slew our father King Lot, therefore I will slay him, with a sword that was sent me that is passing trenchant.'

'Ye shall not so,' said *his brother*, 'at this time, for at this time I am but a squire, and when I am made knight I would be avenged on him, and therefore, brother, it is best ye suffer till another time, that we may have him out of the Court, for if we did so we should trouble this high feast.'

'I will well,' said Gawaine, 'as ye will.'

Thus, unhappily, from the very outset the seeds of jealousy were sown in the Fellowship of the Round Table, through Pellinore having been chosen by Merlin for the coveted honour, and through Pellinore's son having been knighted before Gawaine; the house of Pellinore was in fact receiving preference. This was justifiable, as events were to prove, but it aggravated an existing family feud; so, all the while in the coming story, the rivalry has to be appreciated as rankling beneath the surface. For the moment, though, the imagination can return to a happier scene:

Then was the high feast made ready, and the king was wedded at Camelot unto Dame Guenever in the church of Saint Stephen's, with great solemnity. And (after a number of strange quests) the king established all his knights, and gave them that were of lands not rich, he gave them lands, and charged them never to do outrageousity nor murder, and always to flee treason; also, by no means to be cruel, but to give mercy unto him that asketh mercy, upon pain of forfeiture of their worship and lordship of King Arthur for evermore; and always to do ladies, damosels, and gentlewomen succour, upon pain of death. Also, that no man take no battles in a wrongful quarrel for no law, nor for no world's goods. Unto this were all the knights sworn of the Table Round, both old and young. And every year were they sworn at the high feast of Pentecost.

In modern phrases, the oath of the Round Table, to which its fellowship was sworn every year, was

Always to be chivalrous to women.
Never to commit murder or outrage; and to be merciful.
Never to engage in strife for an unjust cause, or for worldly gain.
Always to be loyal to the realm.

Time has passed on, and, in today's revival of the Round Table as the Order of the Garter, there may be no need to bind its knights with an annual oath not to commit murder; but if the old rules are read in the light of the allusion pointed out on p. 100, that physical terms such as jousting were a romantic description for political strife, it is possible that they are not so archaic as appears at first sight. 'Battles' for worldly gain are perhaps to be interpreted similarly. Arthur was seeking to unify a disunited community; he had to be on guard as much against dissentient manœuvres as against open rebellion, so the allusion is by no means impossible.

And so, in the curious quests that the three selected knights —Pellinore and his son, and Gawaine—had to perform, before the fellowship was fully instituted, let us consider whether instead of a headless lady slain for a White Hart, the deed may not have been the suppression of some old and perhaps disreputable feminine custom in connection with a now forgotten practice, like the one called Herne the Hunter. It is a detail that is of interest, for it throws further light on the family feud already mentioned. Gawaine carried out his quest too drastically and earned a reproof, while Pellinore's son was rewarded with an earldom; but Pellinore too earned a reproof from Queen Guenevere, for the zeal which led him to bring one of the ladies of the Lake to Court at the expense of another lady's 'life'. The old and the new schools were clashing; and Guenevere, fresh from

Cameliard with its prized dowry of the Table Round, was still of the old.

.   .   .   .   .

Curiosity naturally makes us wonder what the Round Table may have been. It was something of great sentimental value, rather than intrinsic; it carried with it the service of 130 knights; it was situate in the land of Cameliard; and it had an awesome seat —the 'Siege Perilous'.

The Table can scarcely have been what the English word implies, a piece of furniture around which men sat; a short calculation will show that no room could have been built in those days to hold an object over a hundred feet wide, let alone the fact that such articles had not come into household use. And so, one's scrutiny is drawn to the original of the word for table, which in the language of one of the principal romances, Latin, was *mensa*. That seems to have been the translation of the Old Welsh *mwys*, both of which words come from the same source; but *mwys* in English means 'measure', as survives in Cornish dialect in a '*mease*' of herrings. However, 'measure' is also related to *mensa*, for example in the word 'mensuration'; the Table was something to do with calculation.

Lancelot Hogben, in his book *Mathematics for the Million*, has explained how the calendar used to be measured from the sun, by means of shadows cast from poles erected round a circular space; the circles were gigantic plane-tables, on which lines were drawn and measurements made in the sand. The eastern 'tables' were the origin of the stone circles in Britain, their early use possibly forgotten, but their conventional form and honoured associations retained. King Arthur's Round Table was one of these venerated circles.

Their use needs to be touched upon, in order that several colloquial references to them may be understood, and the daily life around them visualized. Apart from their functions for religious ceremony, they were also college centres, law courts, and the meeting places for old rites. Sometimes they figure in legend as 'cauldrons' or 'baskets', said to be endowed with magic properties such as turning food for one man into enough for a hundred, which is best explained as being the prototype of

Father Christmas' sack—the Source of Plenty. They were also sometimes connected with a very ancient, and practically obsolete, rite of 'perpetual youth'; this entailed mortal combat within them, and must have been very rare as by this date human life was usually compounded for some other offering. However, a scene of the old kind is realistically depicted in the story of Enid and Geraint: Around the site was a hedge surmounted with a row of stakes, on the top of each a human head; in the centre stood an apple-tree, a horn hanging from one of its branches, and a tent beside it; within the tent was a maiden. The challenger for possession of the 'cauldron' would enter the circle, passing through the hedge and a concealing maze, and then sound the horn; whereupon he would be fought by the present keeper. If he won, he gained the girl; if he lost, his head went to crown another stake. The maid was assured of a virile spouse. Fortunately today the test for manliness is carried out with a tennis racquet.

And so, the bare rings of stones which we see standing on open turf are to be pictured formerly as enclosed with hedges, guarding their sanctity; at the centre will have been either a stone or a tree, not the altar of sacrifice of popular belief, but as described in the Sathapatha Brahmana, the residing place for the Divine Spirit. The circles were open-air temples; and where the soil was fertile they will often have been surrounded by trees, or may have had trees in place of stones, whose branches arched to form a canopy overhead. Does not the tracery of vaulted roofs, springing from Gothic columns, in our churches reproduce in stone this natural covering? In Gaelic the expression for going to church is 'going to the stones'; we in the twentieth century are not so entirely removed from the days of King Arthur.

Which, then, of the old stone circles of Britain will have been Guenevere's dowry? The Round Table belonged to the land of Cameliard, part of Cymbeline's domain; that name takes us to the upper Wiltshire Avon, once called the Camelaria. The famous Round Table was Stonehenge.

The hundred knights who accompanied the Table, and the thirty furnished by Arthur, call for remark. The latter number of 'seats' corresponds with the stones of the great lintelled circle; they were apparently allotted to the more distinguished Fellows, while the 'Siege Perilous' for the Head of the Fellowship will have been at the centre. One hundred seems to have been the standard establishment of druids for a circle, although the number may have varied among sects; as an indication, the Cornish 'mease' stands for five score, 100 (or alternatively 500), and the property of a certain circle of providing food for 100 probably has the same allusion. Thus, when Leodegrance made his gift, he undertook to transfer the circle's establishment with it, but left it to Arthur to fill the places of honour.

.   .   .   .   .

For a moment let us hearken to Merlin, and learn the story of how this great ring came into being. It begins when Salisbury Plain was known as Caer Eryri, the Eagles' Abode; that is to say when it belonged to the Eagle druids of the Gaels, one of whom has already been mentioned, the Eagle of Shaftesbury. Among their people there was civil strife; whenever they attempted to build up national defence, in metaphor a 'tower', it came tumbling down. So, exactly like the Sikhs at Philaur, they resorted to magic ritual; they looked for a fatherless boy, one sacredly conceived, whom they might sacrifice and with his blood make the foundation firm. However, the true cause of their structure's weakness was explained to them—underground strife; and they were advised to make a 'cauldron', a sacred ring, and within it the warring factions were to drink together the loving cup of peace. This was done, and 'the fierce outcry ceased'. From then onwards the site was known as Dinas Emrys, Mount Ambrose,* which name stands for the 'Heavenly Brewers'. Their cauldron, the first built, is represented today by the bank and ditch inside which stood a ring of timber posts. It was said to have had an establishment of 300 priests, a trebled dignity.

Ambrose is a Pictish name. Reading between the lines, the circle had been built at Pict instigation, but subsequently there was a rift between Gaels and Picts. Then came reconciliation; and the strength of popular feeling must have been immense, because a complete Gaelic stone circle was brought from Pembrokeshire and re-erected at Stonehenge. The undertaking was enormous: the stones had to be carried from the Prescelly Hills to the shore, loaded on to wicker and skin barges, towed by sea to the Bristol Avon, taken up the river and then overland to the Wiltshire Avon, down it by water, and finally overland to the Plain. In the process, only one stone was lost, and that nearly at the end of its journey, at Bulford. These are the blue-stone circle, horse-shoe, and central stone, the memorial of a determined alliance for peace.

When the Cymry came, in order to enhance the sanctity of the site, they rearranged these stones and built around them the loftier lintelled structure which now dominates the eye. This in turn passed into Cornish hands, though still retaining its original identity; and thus its arch-druid bore the style of Merlin Ambrose —'Chough, the Heavenly Brewer'. Throughout the changes and chances of secular conquest it had stood supreme, the cauldron of goodwill, within which conquerors and conquered drank together the loving cup of mutual devotion to the common weal.

Lastly, Arthur's brother Gwydr endeavoured to gain the alliance of the 'Irish' of the Lake, by repeating the tradition and transporting stones from one of the circles in the sunken Anton estuary to Stonehenge, a project that was never finished. And in his turn, Arthur set about reviving its fellowship as a Christian order. The adventures of its knights, the quest of the Holy Grail, and the honourable striving for the Seat Perilous, are the story of the 'Old Law' of Britain being converted to the new; they are the efforts of men to prove themselves worthy to become the Church's head. As is well known, that feat was eventually accomplished by Galahad, the knight *sans peur et sans reproche*.

The Round Table bequeathed us by our forefathers is an unequalled inheritance; it is the visible sign of the idealism which has been our national aim for verging on four thousand years. The idealism is indicated in the name of its founder—Myrddin, later to become Merlin. 'John the Divine called me Myrddin' writes Taliesin cryptically, referring to Reason, the *logos* of the first verse in the Gospel; it was the watchword of Gaelic Britain, called affectionately Clas Myrddin, the Green Isle of Reason. Maligned though we may be as selfish imperialists, we can point to the sequence of Stonehenge, the Round Table, and its revival in the Order of the Garter, as four thousand years' worship of the converse—the rulership of Chivalry and Sense. For 4,000 years that ideal has been our intention; an appalling number of paving stones along the road to Hell must bear the quarry mark 'Made in Britain'!

.   .   .   .

Earlier in this chapter it was remarked that after being made a knight of the Round Table, Pellinore brought to Court one of the ladies of the Lake; her name was Nimue. Through her, Merlin came to an end. What exactly the tale as told in romance may mean can only be hazarded. According to its veiled expressions, Merlin fell into a dotage on her; finally he told King Arthur that he felt his end to be near, and repeating his advice always to keep carefully the sword and scabbard, warned him that they were going to be stolen from him by the woman he most trusted. 'Also he told King Arthur that he should miss him—Yet had ye lever than all your lands to have me again.' Arthur chided him that if he could foresee the future, then let him by the same craft put away the misadventure. 'Nay,' said Merlin, 'it will not be.' And with these words he left the Court, never to return to it again.

After a while the Lady of the Lake also left the Court, and wherever she went Merlin accompanied her. Together they visited a district where the Britons were fighting with the Romans; and Merlin comforted the Britons. Pointing to their chieftain's baby boy, he foretold: 'Take none heaviness, for this same child within this twenty year shall revenge you on King Claudas, that all Christendom shall speak of it; and this same child shall be the most man of worship of the world, and his first name is Galahad.' From there Merlin and the damosel of the Lake went to Cornwall, where he showed her a great wonder in a rock beneath a stone; and she induced him to go beneath the stone himself, then 'by her subtle working . . . she wrought so there for him that he came never out for all the craft he could do'. Thus does Merlin fade from the romance.

How are we to interpret this? Two things seem clear: that the old creed of Merlin was being supplanted by the new, as represented by the damosel Nimue, and that Merlin had warned Arthur it was premature for his creed to be discarded—trouble was ahead, and its aid would be missed. But Arthur treated the caution lightly, 'dropping the pilot' as another youthful emperor was to do in modern times. His troubles were yet to come; it was now the year A.D. 45, but not until A.D. 64 (almost twenty years later) were the Britons' wrongs to be righted. What seems indicated is that proselytizing zeal was acting prematurely; it was breaking with the old faith, yet Merlin was striving to keep the two in unison, 'doting on the damosel, and following her every-where'. Is it that Arthur took a false step at this point? It is to be feared that he did; nor is it the only occasion in history when a reformer's zeal has swept away existing practices that were better kept. Whoever Merlin in person may have been, he was a truly statesmanlike character, and one whom the country sorely needed. We bid him a sorrowful farewell.

.　　　.　　　.　　　.　　　.

Let us now return to Guenevere, the winsome object of Arthur's third adventure in royal matrimony. 'Marvellously dainty was the maiden in person and vesture, right queenly of bearing, passing sweet and ready of tongue; Arthur cherished her dearly, for his love was wonderfully set upon the damsel.' But like any other man, Arthur will also have taken some care to learn something of her family before committing himself; in the days when witches and warlocks went about disguised as ladies of the household and secretaries of state, a person could not be taken at her or his face value. Guenevere however passes muster with the best. On her mother's side she is said to have come from a noble Roman house, referring apparently to the house of Amlodd as an institution which later wielded Roman authority; also she was cousin to Cador of Cornwall, in whose family she had been brought up, and on this account one likes to think that after his improper raid at Totnes Cador sent his attractive young cousin a souvenir.

Her father was Ogyrvans,* a learned man and fond of poetry, but otherwise with a rather vague biography as a giant, possessed of a cauldron from which came three muses. In more sober idiom he was the equivalent of Dean of Guild to the Round Table, his title Ogyr being taken from the deity, who in a later age figures as Ogier the Dane, the forefather of Prester John* the emblem of Chichester diocese. All of which goes to show that not only was she charming in outward appearance, but had the bluest of blue blood, almost divine.

Her name Gwen of the Yew may sound severely dull, but alternatively its Celtic significance, the Happy Maid of York, has a different ring. Yew links her with the clan, though not necessarily the family, of 'York' the royal Mormon who built Maidens Castle. And, as one of his daughters was 'the fairest of all that time living in Britain or Gaul', the clan were evidently endowed with a discriminating taste in daughters—which Arthur had not been slow to observe.

A Welsh poem recites an amusing argument between her and Arthur, in the Gilbertian style of 'Sing, Proper Pride is the horse to·ride, and Happy-go-lucky, my lady, O'. It starts off with Arthur and she flaunting to one another their respective family colours—his black, for the Cornish Chough, hers green, for the Yew-tree—and it goes on with Guenevere teasing him by saying that he has failed to keep a promise, and that Kei Sevinson is the more impressive man, for he, Arthur, is unfortunately too small to be noticed in a crowd. So we can picture the two clad in their family tartans, Arthur in a black and yellow, like MacLeod, Guenevere in a green, such as Campbell, chaffing each other good-humouredly and drawing from him at least one untranslatable rejoinder. The Welsh character of the lines tends to read prosaically, but looking between them, Guenevere's bright face and provoking tongue peep out:

Arthur: Black is my steed and brave beneath me, no water will make him fear, and no man will make him swerve.

Guenevere: Green is my steed of the tint of the leaves. There is no disgrace like his who boasts and fails; he is no man who fulfils not his word.

Arthur: . . . .

Guenevere: . . . in the forefront of the fray no man holds out but Kei the Tall, son of Sevin.

Arthur: It is I that will ride and will stand, and walk heavily on the brink of the ebb; I am the man to hold out against Kei.

Guenevere: Pshaw, young man, it is strange to hear thee! Unless thou be other than thou lookest, thou wouldst not, one of a hundred, hold against Kei.

Arthur: Gwenhwyvar of the bright face, do not insult me small though I be; I would hold against a hundred myself.

Guenevere: Pshaw, young man of black and yellow! After scanning long thy looks methought I had seen thee before.

Arthur: Gwenhwyvar of the — face, tell me, if you know it, where you saw me before.

Guenevere: I have seen a man of moderate size at Arthur's long table in Devon, dealing out wine to his friends.

Arthur: Gwenhwyvar of facetious speech, it is a woman's nature to banter; there it is thou didst see me.

From now on her life becomes shared with his; and there is only one matter in it to be commented upon before continuing with their combined story. The illusion of her unfaithfulness with Lancelot needs to be dispelled; when the time comes, there will be found no place for it in history. Lancelot's character suffers; but that is no reason for Guenevere's being smirched in order to whiten his. The sordid truth of his so-called romance is that the queen he craved was not Guenevere, but Arthur's other wedded love—his country. Lancelot sought the crown. So, too, Modred is said to have married Guenevere, when he seized the crown during Arthur's absence, although in actual fact Guenevere was absent also. But in after years, Lancelot's branch of the family flourished, while Arthur's and Guenevere's faded from power; in consequence her memory has had to bear a stain that never soiled it in life. In the coming pages, therefore, more fittingly let us think of her as the perfect queen who shared Arthur's stormy life, buoying up his hopes through anxiety, gladdening his happiness in success, and the cynosure of a Court remembered as the pattern of noble-mindedness.

.   .   .   .   .

A curious incident is now recorded by Boece, which cannot be reconciled with anything in other narratives. He tells of Vespasian laying siege to Camelot, and capturing there a royal crown and magnificent sword, which weapon he used for the rest of his life. The picture of a revolt at Camelot is entirely contrary to what appears to have been the real situation, one of settled order under strong Roman domination; it seems that a misrepresentation has arisen from the use of a metaphor, and that Vespasian's so-called spoil was a sword of the same category as Arthur's Excalibur, and the crown likewise. In other words Vespasian either embraced or appeared to embrace privately the new creed; around this has been built the misconception of a revolt. This suggested interpretation is the more probable seeing that his senior, Plautius, was also inclining in that direction. It indicates a beneficently sympathetic attitude towards a conquered people.

At the same time, less happily, the Romans began to introduce law officers, and erected a stone temple at Camelot with two statues in it, the one of Victory and the other of the Emperor

Claudius. This tactless emphasis on victory carried with it the unpleasant indication that the country's lot was to be 'Britain for the Romans', instead of 'the Romans for Britain'; and it hints at conflicting views over policy being held at Roman headquarters. Plautius' and his lieutenant's comprehending firmness has been demonstrated; but contrastedly there are signs of an *oderint dum metuant* group, the same one that would have executed Arthur after his first surrender. Thus there are grounds for speculating whether it may not have been the influence of that group which caused Arthur to grant Aaron Rheged the lands beside 'Humber', the Arundel Trent or Arun, after the Bath calamity. As this grant coincides with a revolt in East Sussex, Brigance, we may conclude that East Sussex was being put under the rule of Chichester, and that the Brigance folk resented it. At any rate a rising did occur at this time, and was quelled by Plautius himself, the offenders fleeing to various places including the Isle of Mon, in the Lake.

Accordingly, in the spring of A.D. 46, Arthur and Vespasian made a joint expedition to punish the islanders of Mon. Just as operations were about to commence, though, Vespasian was diverted to either Kent or the Isle of Wight, to settle another disturbance, and thence he was recalled to Rome for a higher appointment; Arthur consequently conducted the expedition on his own, with complete success. Layamon's account of the peace terms is vivid, if unauthentic, but a passing comment must be made on his having quoted Exeter as the assembly point for the force; it is a confusion between the Caer Leon in Devon and another Caer Leon in Hampshire which is shortly to come on to the scene. The terms of settlement were given at a banquet, in the course of which the defeated 'Irish' chief, when he saw that Arthur was in the right mood, addressed him:

'Lord Arthur, thy peace! Give me limb and give me life, and I will become thy man, and deliver thee my three sons, my dear sons, to do all thy will. And yet I will do more, if thou wilt give me grace: I will deliver thee hostages exceeding rich, children some sixty, noble and most mighty. And yet I will more, if thou givest me grace: each year of my land seven thousand pounds, and send them to thy land, and sixty marks of gold. And yet I will more, if thou wilt give me grace: and all the steeds, with all their trappings, the hawks, and the hounds, and my rich treasures I give thee in hand, of all my land. And when thou hast this done, I will take the reliques . . . and swear to thee in sooth, that I will thee not deceive; but I will love thee, and hold thee for lord, hold thee for high king, and myself be thy underling.'

Arthur heard this, noblest of kings, and he gan laugh with loud voice, and he gan answer with gracious words: 'Be now glad, be not thy heart sore; for thou art a wise man—the better therefore shall it be to thee, for ever one ought worthily a wise man to greet—for thy wisdom shall it not be the worse for thee; much thou me offerest, the better it shall be to thee. Here forth-right, before all my knights, I forgive thee the more, all the half-part, of gold and of treasure; but thou shalt become my man, and half the tribute send each year into my land. Half the steeds, and half the garments, half the hawks, and half the hounds, that thou me offerest, I will relinquish to thee; but I will have the children of thy noble men, who are to them dearest of all; I may the better believe thee. And so thou shalt dwell in thy honour in thy kingdom, in thy right territory; and I will give to thee, that the king shall not do wrong to thee, unless he pay for it with his bare back.'

It is a very human picture of the bargaining. The defeated chieftain, who has found every mouthful of the feast a mockery, begins by offering what he knows he will have to forfeit; then he increases his offer, item by item, in descending order of importance, his eyes closely following the victor's features at each rise of his bid. At last he sees signs of satisfaction, and closes the offer. The victor, in good humour after a hearty meal with plenty of good wine, has none the less his wits well about him. Having induced his captive to a figure beyond his means, he can afford to be magnanimous; he replies, in so many words, that the vanquished may keep half the junk but he is going to take the hostages, just in case the other's memory should slip; and in that way they will be able to live on good terms with one another.

The romances relate that after this Arthur subdued Iceland, Orkney, Gothland and Finland, then Norway and Denmark. Orkney has already been identified as an island of the Lake; the others are the same, as is explained in the Glossary under LAKE; there is no need to suppose impossible voyages. To close this chapter is Layamon's description of his return to England, and of the peace the land now enjoyed.

Arthur, having brought all the islands of the Lake into submission:

held communing with his good thanes, and said that he would return again into this land, and see Guenevere the comely queen of the country. Trumpets he caused to be blown, and his army to assemble; and to ship marched the thanes wondrous blithe. . . . That heard soon the highest of this land, and to the queen came tiding of Arthur the king, that he was come in safety, and his folk in prosperity. Then were in Britain joys enow! Here was fiddling and song, here was harping among; pipes and trumps sang there merrily. Poets there sung of Arthur the king, and of the great honour that he had won. Folk came in concourse of many kind of land; wide and far the folk was in prosperity. All that Arthur saw, all it submitted to him, rich men and poor, as the hail that falleth; there was no Briton so wretched that he was not enriched.

Here man may tell of Arthur the king, how he afterwards dwelt here twelve years, in peace and in amity, in all fairness. No man fought with him, nor made he any strife; might never any man bethink of bliss that were greater in any country than in this; might never man know any so mickle joy, as was with Arthur and with his folk here.

He now reconstituted the Round Table. And at its gatherings we must imagine a concourse on the sunlit turf around the great stones of Stonehenge, rather than about a wooden table of fiction; the 'board' is a wide lawn, on which by rule goodwill reigns, and all envy is forgotten:

Knights then spake each with other as if it were his brother; all they sate about, there was none without. Every sort of knight was there exceeding well disposed; all they were one by one seated, the high and the low; might none there boast of other kind of drink other than his comrades, that were at the board. This was the same board that Britons boast of, and say many sorts of leasing, respecting Arthur the king. It is not all sooth nor all falsehood that minstrels sing; but this is sooth respecting Arthur the king. Was never ere such king, so doughty through all things! Then was Arthur most high, his folk most fair; so that there was no knight well esteemed, nor of his deeds accounted brave or aught, unless he could discourse of Arthur and of his noble court, his weapons and his garments and his horsemen; say and sing of Arthur the young, and of his strong knights, and of their great might, and of their wealth, and how well it them became. Then were he welcome in this worlds-realm, come whereso he came, and though he were at Rome; all that heard of Arthur tell, it seemed to them great marvel of the good king.

10

A Falling Barometer

I N S U C H a manner the years A.D. 46–9 rolled slowly by. Arthur's name spread in high repute over the whole western world, and in particular the Celtic world; a Celt of the Celts, he had stood up to the might of Rome, against the Emperor himself, and not once but twice had defied the legions. In response the Romans had honourably accepted him as worthy to rule; and now he reigned in terms of practical equality with the Governor. Moreover, although forced to yield to the material superiority of Rome, he was maintaining the country's moral independence: he was reviving the much valued ancient philosophy in conjunction with a new creed; and whereas that creed was being rigidly forbidden at Rome, it was being openly adopted in Britain. To salve their conscience, people persuaded themselves there was no shame in falling under the material sway of the legions, so long as they retained some degree of moral freedom; and they observed with pride that the Roman governor of Britain and his chivalrous lieutenant found themselves attracted to the creed practised in the land. Nor did other Celtic peoples question how it was that Arthur had not succeeded better in his physical resistance; for the Gauls had experienced the obstruction of local jealousy at Alclud, the Belgians were aware that their name was used as a taunt against his family, all were familiar with the Celtic addiction to feud, and kept silent. And with magnanimous understanding the Governor was unashamed to show an affectionate admiration for his former opponent, by marrying Arthur's sister Gladys; she, according to custom, took a Roman name Pomponia Graecina, with reference to her marked ability in Greek literature.

So too a Roman praetor at Chichester, Pudens, was learning to like the race; and in after years he was to marry one of Arthur's daughters, also called Gladys. And a British chieftain at Chichester, known to the Romans as Cogidubnus, was obtaining from Pudens a site on which to build a college for engineers and religious teachers, dedicated, though, to Roman gods. The land was reconciling itself philosophically to circumstances, making the best of them. In the term 'engineers' we can detect the overseers needed for supervising the large gangs of labour employed on road-making; because the beginnings of the great Roman system were now being driven with undeviating directness through forest and marsh, up hill and down dale, from Portchester to the outlying garrisons.

Beneath the surface of affairs, though, a nasty undercurrent was setting. Albany hankered after independence from Arthur's rule, but was divided within itself: a national anti-Roman party was headed by Modred's kinsman Caratak, under Modred's name, while a pro-Roman party was headed by Cogidubnus who was receiving 'certain states' for his 'unswerving loyalty' to Rome— at the expense of Britain. Bombastically the 'Modred' extremists might claim that Arthur was not doing enough (they themselves not having kept in the field for the critical fight at Bath); but behind their words was the thought of the boy's claim to kingship, and the self-interested prospect of Britain being ruled by the house of Albany. Cogidubnus and his kind, on the other hand, preferred to seek independence from one of their fellow-countrymen by allegiance to the foreigner; yet to what extent Arthur's jurisdiction reached into their concerns is doubtful, it was probably more nominal than effective. Thus the otherwise serene outlook was marred with shadows from two hostile political parties, jealous of Arthur's national following that was honouring the agreement made with Plautius. There was a so-to-speak 'fascist' element, ultra-national; and there was a so-to-speak 'communist' element, toadying to the strength of alien and irreligious materialism. The latter of these was reflected at Roman headquarters, where it seems plain there was a body of opinion in its favour, who advocated a 'divide and rule' policy and disparaged Arthur; but the flaw in their opinion lay in their misappreciation of the human factor—they were siding with men who would not subordinate their personal ambitions to anything, but would use all comers, including deluded foreigners, as tools for their selfish ends.

Nevertheless, under Plautius' firm and generous control, sense kept the upper hand. Arthur and the Britons of his circle could see the prospect of Roman and British administration going hand in hand, with the latter gradually increasing and the former gradually dying out, until Britain were restored to the position she had enjoyed under Cymbeline—independent although paying tribute to Rome. Tribute could rightly be regarded as honourable: Rome represented the concert of Europe; there was nothing amiss in forming part of it for the benefit of external security, even under her name, so long as she did not attempt to interfere over internal affairs. Arthur could look forward to securing his country her proper place in the world; and the key to success rested in his Round Table fellowship living up to its obligations.

To make a happy prospect happier, Guenevere presented him with a son, whom they named Gwydr after his brother. Although the Caledonian account states the boy to have been Boadicea's child, the misapprehension is plain, apart from the contrary appearances of circumstances, because it states that her two daughters were his as well; that is to say she had 'borne to him', as the chronicle specifically says, three children in the space of six months. The reason seems to have lain in a desire to disparage Arthur in favour of Modred.

It will be recollected that while Arthur was making his expedition to Mon, in the spring of A.D. 46, Vespasian was summoned to Rome. Taking advantage of this change, Caratak once again raised the Brigance folk in revolt and called upon Mon and the neighbouring peoples to join in; this appears to be the same opposition to Aaron Rheged as Geoffrey and other romancers designate as made by the men of Llychlyn, 'Norway'.* So far as can be discerned, Aaron's title to Brigance was in the right of his first wife, now dead; he was in consequence not wanted by the Brigant people, who in Wace's words declared emphatically that: 'They would have no alien for their lord, nor suffer a stranger to meddle in their business, lest he should give to *outsiders* what was due to the dwellers in the realm.' So Caratak, in his pose of ever-readiness to support 'nationalism', had no compunction in heading a revolt. Aaron appealed to Arthur for help; and he must have done so with a smirk: 'If he wants to be king, let him do the dirty work.' Plautius, however, took charge himself, and in conjunction with Arthur routed the rebels; Caratak fled, first to a marsh and later to Saluria, which in this instance seems to have been South Wales. The older men of his followers advised him to try no more pitched battles, until a new generation had grown up which had forgotten the pains of defeat; so, crossing the border, he spent the next two years in harrying the north-west frontier of the Roman province.

After this abortive effort, Boece tells us, many Britons who had not previously submitted to Roman rule came in and yielded themselves. From the road system's development this would appear to refer to the area Oxfordshire–Peterborough; the system at about this date, A.D. 49, is reproduced on a map on p. 163. Two roads in particular seem to have been laid out at this period: one is the route from Cirencester through Alchester to Colchester, which has the distinct appearance of a lateral line of communication to serve a temporary frontier; the other runs from Poole Harbour through Bath to Cirencester, for the control of the West Country. The utilization of sea communications is noticeable; the interior of Britain was far from secure. If Exeter were garrisoned at this date, it will have been supplied by sea; the road system can only have been developed gradually, and it does not seem likely that it will have stretched out so far west. Nor does it seem likely that Lincoln will as yet have been occupied; the station near Water Newton (Peterborough), called Durobrivae, is noticeably south of the Nene, giving the impression of that river having been a temporary frontier. The comparatively short geographical neck of land between the Wash and the Severn appears to be as far as Plautius will have cared to reach at this date.

These roads will have been built with mixed feelings by British labour, under British overseers trained at the Chichester college. Many will have voiced disgust at the land being opened up for legions to tramp through, followed by their trains of supplies; others will have tried to evade their knowledge that freedom was being forfeited, by pointing to the benefits of modernization; while the overseers will have felt satisfaction at their position in government service with assured pay. Who, it may be asked, was the Cogidubnus, founder of the engineer

college? He must surely have been Aaron Rheged, to whom
territories were given in reward for loyalty to Rome? The name is
explicable by regarding it as a title, his new one, in which
-Dubnus stands for 'The Dobunni', their chief, and referring to
the people of East Sussex, who had submitted early in the initial
invasion; there had once been a Dubno-wallaun in Essex, whose
territory might quite well have extended to the Black Country of
the Weald, which is what Dubh implies.

Thus during the three years A.D. 46–9 we can picture the
country slowly settling down to its new mode of existence, with
Arthur holding court at Camelot, and with Plautius governing
from Silchester. At Stonehenge the grand old institution of the
Round Table had sprung into fresh life, and annually in the early
summer there was being held a gathering of all British nobles, in
its precincts, for renewing their oath of loyalty to the realm and
chivalry to the weak. Only one gap was to be seen in it—Merlin's
empty place; and sad regrets will have been felt for that absent
figure, with its venerated tradition and sage wisdom. Likewise in
Avalon the Round Table's ancient philosophy, that contentment
is to be found through pursuing ideals rather than material gain,
was being preached by the new Church to an ever widening
circle; together Church and State were teaching concord. Trade
had started to flow more freely everywhere, especially through
the rapidly growing city of London; while a steady stream of
trade and military traffic passed up and down the roads from the
sea-coast ports. The Cornish and Somerset mines, the Forest of
Dean, the Weald, North Wales and the Derbyshire hills were
delivering more and more metal to the merchants' assured
security; and in return Roman and continental wares were
appearing in shops throughout the country, and in many a town
Roman buildings were rising, Roman fashion was slowly in-
truding itself. And if the arrogance of the foreign soldiery jarred
on the garrison towns' populace, there was the consolation that
they brought money—it was an ill wind that blew nobody any
good.

.   .   .   .   .

In this atmosphere of peaceful orderliness, one which Britain
had never before known, Arthur's Court gathered around it a

reputation that was enhanced as it passed from lip to lip. Told by an imaginative people, we see in its legends a picture of the prowess they liked to conjure up in their minds—men of giant stature, ability of magic strength, and beauty transcendent. Feckless they were, and it was undeniable wishful thinking; nevertheless through it we can look into their minds, where we see idealism and poetry and would-be heroism, goodness abundant, only lacking the will to turn fancy into reality. And we see the flaw happily concealed in good humour. So let us take a glance at some of the Court's legendary figures, even if their names' pronunciation entails painful gymnastics for a Saxon tongue. Time has bestowed on them amazing properties.

There was Kay the Seneschal, who could hold his breath for nine days and nine nights under water, who could increase his height at will, until as tall as the highest tree; also, so great was the heat of his nature that, even when rain was pouring its hardest, whatever he held remained dry from a handbreadth above to a handbreadth below his grasp. There was Bedivere the cupbearer, one of the three swiftest-footed men in the land; although one-handed he could shed blood on the field of battle as fast as three other warriors. There were Menw, who could safe-guard people by making them invisible; the archer Medyr, who in a twinkling could send an arrow from the Court to an island in the Lake, shooting a wren through both her legs; the swordsman Gwiawn, who could cut a haw from the eye of a gnat without hurting the creature; and the tracker Ol, who was able to trace his father's swine, that had been carried off seven years before he was born, and bring them back.

And there were Arthur's engineers: Gwadyn, who used to clear the way for him when any obstructions were met, the soles of whose feet used to emit sparks of fire when they struck on anything hard; Osla, who used to make bridges for Arthur and his host, by placing his short broad dagger across a narrow part of any torrent met; Glwyddyn, the architect who built Arthur's hall called Ehangwen, and the red-bearded Uchtryd who could spread his beard over the forty-eight rafters in it. Skilled in demolition was Arthur's attendant Rhacymwri, who with his flail could shatter the beams in any barn to fragments the size of oats.

Then there was Bedwini the bishop, who used to bless Arthur's meat and drink; and several trencher-men of repute— Hierwm and Hiratrwm, who when they made a visit would leave neither the fat nor the lean, neither the hot nor the cold, the sour nor the sweet, the fresh nor the salt, the boiled nor the raw; Sugyn the broad-chested, who would suck up a sea on which rode three hundred ships, leaving nothing but dry strand; and Huarwar from whom none could get a smile until he were satisfied, and who obtained from Arthur a boon which proved to be the third great plague of Cornwall. Gilla was at the Court, the chief leaper of Ireland, who could clear three hundred acres at a bound; Drem, who when a gnat arose in the morning with the sun in North Britain could see it from Gelliwic in Cornwall; and Clust, who, though buried ten feet below ground, could hear an ant rise from her nest fifty miles away!

Truly those were the days when men were men; and truly with a retinue of that kind Arthur could face anyone, even the Emperor of Rome, on equal terms. And Arthur himself, when he heard echoes of those feats bantered round the fire in his hall, could catch the self-confidence in their note. Yet from time to time memories must have cautioned him, memories of his two campaigns in Albany and Cornwall, and he must have pondered— would this heartiness prove to be strength of character under adverse conditions? No need to worry, though: the Roman governor had an affection for this people; he compelled their obedience kindly if forcefully, at the same time quelling any attempt from his own officials to show domineering snobbery, as some of them would have liked to affect. Not that they were of stouter character than the Britons; far from it, their courage was less, their power came from the disciplined organization to which his own people were loath to submit. Yet in self-discipline lay the country's salvation, as Arthur could see; and in enforcing it he felt that he and the Roman governor were kindred spirits, between whom the land was on the way to prosperity. Both loved the good-humoured self-satisfaction for what it was worth, valuing it at not a penny higher; and Arthur could tell that under Plautius and himself, strength was at the helm, nor mattered it much from which quarter the wind blew.

.   .   .   .   .

So it was with grave concern that Arthur received the news, in the spring of A.D. 49, that Plautius was to return to Rome. No reason has been handed down in classical history for his recall; Boece says that he was suffering from dysentery. Whatever it was, he returned covered with credit, and was given the exceptional honour of an ovation at Rome, the last ever awarded to a private citizen under the Empire. But one cannot help wondering whether mischievous tongues may not have been at work—'the Governor was going native', a sterner rule was needed; the principle of overawing the Britons must be maintained, Rome had not enough real strength to take risks in the island, and unless there were a rigid dividing line between conqueror and conquered the latter would one day take advantage of laxity and rebel. Moreover, failure in Britain would start a general conflagration in the Celtic world.

What took place between Plautius' departure and Ostorius Scapula's arrival, in his replacement as the Governor, can be conjectured from the state in which the latter found the country when he landed in the autumn. According to Boece, Caratak in Saluria (which evidently is West Sussex) had appealed to Arthur to raise another rebellion; and this seems true from what Tacitus describes —the south of Britain in commotion, a devastating incursion into states in alliance with Rome (which seems to indicate Cogidubnus' realm of Chichester), and it was being openly surmised that a new commander would not embark on a winter campaign. It is alternatively possible that Caratak was doing this from the South Wales Siluria, and that Britons from there were raiding Romano-British territory round Cirencester; it depends upon whether Boece's Coremyn* is the Cori-hill of the West Sussex Coranians or of the Cirencester Corini. A passing comment needs to be made on Tacitus' value as a historian, because from now onwards he will be quoted frequently: he can be regarded almost as contemporary, for his father-in-law Julius Agricola was serving in Britain as a young officer only fifteen years after this date, and must have heard a lot of first-hand accounts of what took place; the *Annals* are not only of proved reliability, but bear the stamp of local colour received from his father-in-law.

Evidently on Plautius' departure relations between the Britons and Romans deteriorated rapidly; but they must have been worsening beforehand, because Ostorius came as a 'new broom'. Perhaps Caratak's skirmishing on the frontier had been effective in encouraging surliness and restlessness elsewhere, embarrassing to Arthur and beyond his power to prevent; time alone could have worn it down, suppression would have come ill from him, and time he was not given. It seems as though some of Plautius' commanders may have been sending complaints to Rome that they were being required to be unreasonably tolerant, where conciliation only bred contempt. After his recall, therefore, we can surmise a change in attitude of Roman officials towards Arthur; in place of the old good-natured trust it is possible that some of the subordinate commanders became dictatorial, men who had been overruled in some small dispute now took the opportunity for spite. Correspondingly Arthur, on his part, may not have been above adopting a similar measure to what we in our own time have watched happen; he may conceivably have allowed friendly tribesmen from across the border to raid 'quislings' within his territory, and under one pretext or another have refrained from interference. For he was in a false position: his authority was being undermined by Caratak's 'fascist' patriotism, just as much as it was by 'quisling' derogation of him to the foreigner; while he himself was torn between honouring his agreement and natural sympathy with his countrymen's mistimed zeal.

If that be so, then we can picture what took place when he was summoned to Ostorius' headquarters and called upon to explain why he was not exercising control. His reply will have been the same respectful bluff as with which he had answered for Cador's inexcusable behaviour; to him it was a game, he knew he was not umpiring with strict fairness, but if the foreign governor were ready to treat it as a game then he would settle the affair. So it may be that his answer was seemingly offhanded—the raiders were not under his control, they came from beyond the border; he could not understand why the local garrison gave alarming reports about their numbers. The prevarication will have exasperated Ostorius, who had been warned what to expect, and was only ready to accept precise conformity with his wishes; the result was an incisive—'Are you, or are you not, going to govern your land? Very well then, I shall do it for you.' This is reading between the lines; and now we return to Tacitus' history.

Without hesitation Ostorius promptly organized a column of light troops, and himself led it against the raiders. Catching them by surprise he inflicted heavy losses on them, and gave their dispersed bands no chance of uniting with one another. Nor was he satisfied that this was enough; in order to guard against repetition of the inroad, he started to build a chain of forts from the Nene,* that is to say from about Peterborough, to the Severn.

On Arthur the arrogant abruptness will have been heartbreaking. For all that he may have assumed a careless pose, at the root his intention was to co-operate, on terms of equality. Instead, though, orders were being flung at him as to an inferior; he was being disdained, which did not imply so much him as an individual as it did his people, the foreigners were holding them in contempt. What future could be built on that? Herein lay the weak spot in his mental equipment—he loved his country. Had he been a hard-skinned, self-seeking character he would have acted differently; he would have cast in his lot with the new governor just as with the old, dipping deeper into his conscience's purse to pay the price. As it was, we know that the two men's ways conflicted, and we know that the country had been happy under the old regime, but was at discord under the new; his first feelings in the conflict must have been of anguish more than anger.

For a while he waited to see which way events would turn. One after another they went against him: the new commander took the field under conditions which he had hoped were impossible; the trans-border Britons were caught off their guard and shattered; his countrymen were enslaved to dig the new defences. He himself will have become an object of scorn. Senior and junior Roman officers who used to pay him deference will now have adopted a supercilious tone; the bubble had been burst, they and their military strength were what really mattered in the land, he was a nonentity. That is the tragedy, or foreign blunder: his heart was ready for Rome, but it was spurned.

Although Fate was against him, he was not prepared to bow to her spinelessly. Roman security in Britain was precarious; the legions' food, fuel, and forage for animals, and the safety of small parties travelling between stations, all depended upon the populace's goodwill. An iron-clad legion might be a fatal object to assail when formed up for battle; but when scattered foraging it was vulnerable, and the further afield it had to range the easier a target it became. Accordingly, rather than let native British authority sink into servitude, he challenged the invaders with revolt. Calling upon the people to take up arms, he raised the standard of rebellion at Maidens Castle.

.   .   .   .   .

At this stage, a glance must be taken at the dispositions of the Roman Army of Occupation in Britain. Below is a map

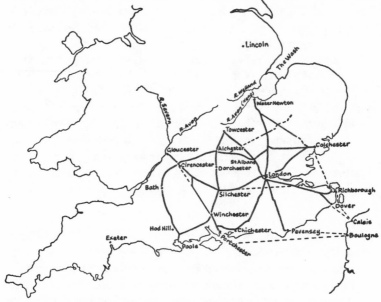

ROMAN OCCUPATION AND ROAD SYSTEM
circa. A.D. 49

showing the framework of military roads at this date, A.D. 49. There will have been the old British tracks as well—Pilgrims Way, Icknield Way, Cloven Way—but these have been omitted so as not to cloud the military lay-out. All the roads shown will not necessarily have been completed, some may only have been in the making; but their framework as a whole illustrates the military situation for which they were designed.

The main features of the system are: the base was at Portchester, serving headquarters at Silchester; subsidiary base ports were Colchester, Dover, and Richborough. Pevensey will no longer have been a military port, though available for use in case of need. Sea traffic went from all of these to Calais (Portius Itius, the Icht), or to Boulogne and to the mouth of the Seine. London was a commercial rather than a military centre, but had a garrison. The province was divided into military Districts (to use a modern term), the responsibility of which was not only to guard against the enemy from beyond the borders, but to keep internal security within. The Districts can be surmised from the Legions' headquarters at a slightly later date; at this period they will have been developing into that shape. The West was under the charge of the IInd Legion, and will have comprised the country south and west of the Cotswolds; eventually this Legion's headquarters were at Exeter. The East was under the charge of the IXth Legion, with its headquarters at Colchester: its area was the country northeast of the Thames, as far as the Cotswolds. The Central District was under the XIVth Legion, and comprised north of the Thames from the Chilterns to the Cotswolds. Southern District, with headquarters at Silchester, covered everything south of the Thames as far west as about Salisbury, and was under the XXth Legion which also constituted a general reserve.

·   ·   ·   ·   ·

No sooner had Arthur broken into revolt at Maidens Castle than Ostorius attacked him, dashing down to the place with cavalry and continental auxiliaries, and without waiting for the legions—a bold and courageous move. At Spettisbury Rings, south of Blandford, what has been described as a war cemetery probably belongs to this operation; and we can imagine the fight there having been occasioned by Ostorius summoning the Hod Hill garrison to join him on his way. Arrived at Maidens Castle, the Roman cavalry were ordered to fight dismounted; and the little force boldly assaulted Arthur's earthworks. The storming is quoted from Sir Mortimer Wheeler's reconstruction of the scene, revealed by excavation. It was directed at the eastern entrance, that consisted of an outer defended courtyard, leading to an inner crescent-shaped court, also defended and containing some huts, on to which yard two gateways opened.

The Romans began the attack with fire from some catapults (*ballistae*), which with wise foresight they had brought with them; they

put down a barrage, across the gateway, causing casualties at the outset. Following the barrage, the Roman *dismounted force* advanced up the slope, cutting its way from rampart to rampart, tower to tower. In the innermost bay of the entrance, a number of huts had recently been built; these were now set alight, and under the rising clouds of smoke the gates were stormed. But resistance had been obstinate, and the attack was pushed home with every sort of savagery. The scene became that of a massacre in which the wounded were not spared.

In the final *mêlée* 'the women had stood shoulder to shoulder with their menfolk', and the remains in general showed that

the dead had met a sometimes savagely violent end; the skulls of many had been hacked viciously at the time of death, one of them bore no less than nine deep cuts . . . whilst another had an iron arrow-head embedded deeply in a vertebra (and) this last unhappy warrior, as he lay grieviously wounded, had been finished off by a cut on the head.

That night, when the fires of the *force* shone out, as we may fairly imagine, in orderly lines across the valley, the survivors crept forth from their broken stronghold and, in the darkness, buried their dead as nearly as might be outside their tumbled gates, in that place where the ashes of their burnt huts lay warm and thick upon the ground. The task was carried out anxiously and hastily and without order; many of the dead were still contorted as they had fallen in the struggle; in any event, the living were in no condition for the niceties of ritual. Yet from few of the graves were omitted those tributes of food and drink which were the proper perquisites of the dead. . . . In two cases the dead held joints of lamb in their hands, joints chosen carefully as young and succulent. Amidst all the evidences of massacre and distraction, this final attention was not the least touching feature of the scene.

Apart from the savagery which mars their success, Ostorius and his men deserve full credit for a bravely conducted and hazardous action; to which is to be added the personal distinction of the general's son, Marcus Ostorius, being awarded the civic crown for saving a soldier's life. And, judging from his father's standard of soldiering, he will have earned it. But as Britons our sympathies lie with the other side, with our grandfathers and grandmothers who made this reckless stand and, even in their enemy's eyes, gave 'signal proofs of heroic gallantry'. They were fighting for the freedom of their own way of life, despite its faults and with all its merits; they fought to prevent themselves from being absorbed in the materialistic colossus of Rome. Looking back on history, to whom do we today owe the more —to the Roman who in the end left us only derelict roads and towns, or to our forbears who bequeathed us their ideals and resolution?

Let us turn again to Arthur, and put ourselves in his place, now an outlaw with a price on his head. What was he to do? His countrymen, for whom he had discarded any personal ambition (if he had any), had shown themselves miserably apathetic. Only a comparative few had joined him at Maidens Castle; that fortress should have been so strongly manned that nothing short of legionary armour could have attempted to cross its deep ditches and assault its palisaded scarps. Instead, his little following's attenuated line had been far too easily pierced. What had the rest of Britain been doing to let Roman horsemen and foreign mercenaries reach him so readily? They should have been camp-bound. If the voluble Wealden chiefs had raised a hand, not a man could have left Silchester; nor need they have risked fighting the Romans, merely kept them occupied until the tougher Cornishmen could arrive. His brother-in-law at Chichester was little short of a traitor, encouraging British youths to become Roman engineers and build the roads that were holding them down. He could see no vestige of hope. Even adversity would not unite the people; their petty minds were more concerned with earning foreign dollars (to use a modern analogy) than with the self-sacrifice of putting their own house in order. For himself and his queen there was nothing left but to take refuge in the West Country, where loyalty could be counted upon; thither they betook themselves, and lay hid amongst its moors.

Behind him, the Romans razed the defences and dwellings in Maidens Castle to the ground, and ordered it to be abandoned; then, building a camp at Dorchester, they caused a town to grow up there in its place. And there, sad to say, it will have been the opportunists who prospered; only a forgotten few, widowed and orphaned and fallen into destitution, remembered the derelict site and named it the Mount of Misfortune.

Ostorius' promptitude had its desired effect; all the clans in the Winchester neighbourhood laid down their arms. So, striking while the iron was hot, the Roman followed up his victory by leading an expedition against the original raiders, who indirectly had been the cause of this uprising. In the Roman annals they are called the Ceangi, located by another geographer in Cheshire; but as clans everywhere were mixed, it is likely that the Ceangi who caused the trouble were a good deal south of this, perhaps in Worcestershire. Their territory was treated with great severity; Tacitus writes that Ostorius 'laid waste the *Cangian* country. The soldiers carried off a considerable booty, the enemy never daring to make head against them; wherever they attempted to annoy the army by sudden skirmishes, they paid for their rashness.'

Faithful to a moral obligation, Arthur diverted Ostorius' attention by raising an insurrection in his rear, obliging him to fall back precipitately. Where the rebel Brigant were is not stated; but as Ostorius' next operations were in the West Country, and as the name Brigant has been left in Brent and perhaps Bristol (Brigstow), they seem to have been a Somerset people.

Ostorius hurried down through Bath, by what was later to be the Fosse Way; and Arthur met him on the Mendips, in his eleventh battle Cat Breguoin, which a marginal gloss in an old manuscript says was in Somerset. The name Bre-guocob, 'hill of caves', is appropriate; and in confirmation of the gloss, a lead plate has been dug up commemorating a Roman victory at Wookey Hole in A.D. 50, 'the year of the consulship of Antistis and Suillius'. The Roman account makes light of the operation: the Britons 'were soon reduced to subjection, such as resisted were cut to pieces, and a free pardon was granted to the rest'. But that is as it was remembered thirty years later; it applies to the local populace only; the submission of the remainder to the west was a hard process, and Ostorius died a worn-out man before it was completed.

Still able only to arouse piecemeal resistance, Arthur assembled the North Devon men behind the river Parrett, and a battle was fought at Langport. This is the Llongborth of Welsh legend; nor, according to it, was the struggle what is colloquially termed a walk-over for the enemy:

> Before Geraint, the terror of the foe,
> I saw steeds fatigued with the toil of battle,
> And after the shout was given, how dreadful was the onset.

> At Llongborth I saw the raging of slaughter,
> And an excessive carnage,
> And warriors blood-stained from the assault of Geraint.

> At Llongborth I saw the spurs
> Of men who would not flinch from the dread of the spears,
> And the drinking of wine out of the bright glass.

> At Llongborth I saw Arthur,
> And brave men who hewed down with steel,
> Emperor, and conductor of the toil.

> At Llongborth Geraint was slain,
> A valiant warrior from the woodlands of Devon,
> Slaughtering his foes as he fell.

> When Geraint was born, open were the gates of heaven,
> Christ granted what was asked,
> Beautiful the appearance of glorious Britain.

Yet it was another reverse; and after it Ostorius probably established the fort at Wiveliscombe. In Geraint, Arthur lost a relative; for the man who fell here was the Geraint ab Lud, not the Geraint ab Erbin of romance, and his wife was a 'Roman' lady related to Guenevere's mother, who also was 'Roman'—the epithet apparently referring to the institution of Amlodd.*

At this point it is interesting to note that Stewart's metrical version of Boece preserves the outline of Ostorius' campaign; he mentions the actions fought in the following order—the Tegens, Corymyn, Cornub, Cambria, Damnonia. These point to his first swift blow having been at the West Sussex Coremyn* and some folk called Tegn* in the neighbourhood of Storrington; next Maidens Castle in what was then Cornwall; next the Welsh

Ceangi, and then the Devonshire district which Geraint ruled, Cereinwg.

Arthur, whose courage was indomitable, then crossed the Bristol Channel and succeeded in enlisting the aid of the Siluri of Monmouth and Herefordshire; and with them and some Ceraint from Gloucestershire (Cirencester it will be remembered was Caer Ceri, or Cory) he brought Ostorius back to Bath. For a second time he fought the Romans on the hill above the river, but with the same ill-fortune. It seems that part of his promised force failed to live up to its undertaking; because, in the 'Dream of Rhonabwy', the tents and encampments of a mighty host were seen for a mile around the ford of Rhyd-y-groes on the Severn, and Arthur's counsellor remarks that it was a marvel for those to be there who had promised to be by midday at the battle of Badon. One wonders, with how much disappointment of this kind was he having to contend? To the chagrin of defeat was added a bitter personal blow, in the capture of his young son Gwydr* by the Romans; he was never to see him again, for the boy was sent off to Rome and died on the journey, a cruel sacrifice for conceited display. It brings home forcibly the unhappy thought that Guenevere was by custom present at many of his misfortunes, a spectator with other wives in wagons behind the fighting line, calling out to the men to stand firm for their sakes and their children's; it reminds us how nobly his resolution was being sustained by hers. On this occasion, though, she is not likely to have been present, as a daughter was being born. But truly her lot and Arthur's was a hard one, and for the sake of a people of lesser mettle.

Refusing to give way to dismay Arthur remained in the field, withdrawing with the Siluri into Herefordshire, where for six months a series of engagements was fought from the Herefordshire Beacon, Caer Essylt, to the mouth of the Usk. Caer Went was probably the furthest point reached by the Roman infantry, near where the enlarged British fort in Llan-melin Wood stands testimony to a dug-in degree of resistance. In that more difficult terrain the Britons succeeded in cutting to pieces a Roman division, and Ostorius was pulled up short in his warpath of fire and sword. In Tacitus' words: 'The Silures were not so easily quelled; neither lenity nor rigorous measures would induce them to submit.'

Tacitus continues:

To bridle the insolence of that warlike race, Ostorius judged it expedient to form a camp for the legions in the heart of their country. For this purpose a colony, supported by a strong body of veterans, was stationed at Camelodunum, on the lands conquered from the enemy. From this measure a twofold effect was expected: the garrison would be able to overawe the insurgents, and give to the allied states a specimen of law and civil policy.

But in his wording, Tacitus has slipped into a slight error in implying the camp to have been Caerleon-on-Usk: a colony called Caerleon was built at this date, but not to overawe the South-Welsh Siluri; it was built near Camelot Dun, Winchester, and was in connection with the West Sussex and Hampshire Siluri. More had happened than he relates. Concurrently with encountering stiff resistance in Monmouth, Ostorius had received news that the Itchen valley folk and Brigance men, with undoubtedly the 'Irish' of the Lake as well, were out of control, which meant that the safety of his base at Portchester was threatened. Both of Boece's translators tell this plainly; Bellenden writes that after discomfiting the west, Ostorius 'went against the east Britons, opposite the French sea, who were the principal movers of this rebellion'. (In this last remark he may be at fault in calling them the principal movers of the whole struggle, but at the same time conceivably the West Sussex Saluri took heart from their Welsh compatriots' success, and initiated this phase of the revolt.) Stewart is more specific; he says that after vanquishing the men of Devon, Ostorius caught the Icen men in a place from which they could not flee, and slew them all; after which he went to Carlisle (meaning Caerleon near Camelot) and then to Brigance, then back to Saluria, that is, in this case, South Wales.

The English romances indicate too that a Caerleon by Camelot came into prominence at about this time; so it is clear that Ostorius, having restored order in the neighbourhood, established a colony near Winchester, before going back to continue his campaign against Arthur. The name Caer Leon, 'Camp of the Legion', is the equivalent of the modern 'Cantonment'. Just as in the days of British India there have been, for example, Lahore City and Lahore Cantonment a few miles apart from each other, so did Ostorius build Camelot Cantonment (Caerleon Camelot) a few miles from Camelot Market (Venta-belgarum Camelot); and, to make the parallel even closer, just as the name Lahore Cantonment replaced an original Mian Mir, so in this case was the name changed, but conversely, from Caerleon to Clausentum.* When Tacitus wrote, the well-known Caerleon was that on Usk, in the Silures country; that near Camelot was only remembered as Clausentum; hence his mistake.

What caused the south coast rising may have been sympathy with the South Welsh, but more probably was the result of ill advice to Ostorius to reverse Plautius' policy over native rulership. When Arthur broke into revolt, Ostorius appointed his unpleasant rival Aaron Rheged of Chichester native king in his stead, evidenced by the bombastic stone at Chichester—'Cogidubnus, King and Legate of the Emperor in Britain'—which romance naïvely corroborates by saying that Arthur made the appointment himself 'before he went abroad'; and this was resented. We see the Romans falling into the same error as has sometimes happened in our own colonial administration: Arthur's strong character antagonized and driven into revolt, and Aaron's weak cupidity patronized and foisted on to an undesirous people; it raises the curious question of why is it that officialdom so often gravitates towards the colourless man? So, to give Aaron a secure residence, his Court was established at Caerleon Camelot, now Bitterne; and to prop him up in his position a strong body of old soldiers was settled there as a colony. All of this is bound to have taken time, and to have carried the date into A.D. 51; in the meantime Arthur was busily engaged in South Wales—recruiting fresh opposition against Ostorius.

·   ·   ·   ·   ·

That commander having secured his base was able to turn his attention again to his main task. Tacitus takes up the story, paying a handsome tribute to the Hereford and Monmouthshire men's constancy:

These arrangements settled, Ostorius marched against the Silures. To their natural ferocity that people added the courage which they now derived from the presence of Arthur (Caractacus). Renowned for his valour, and for various turns of good and evil fortune, that heroic chief had spread his fame through the island. His knowledge of the country, and his skill in all the wiles and stratagems of savage warfare, gave him many advantages; but he could not hope with inferior numbers to make a stand against a well-disciplined army. He therefore marched into the territory of the Ordovicians (Radnor—Shropshire). Having there drawn to his standard all who considered peace with Rome as another name for slavery, he determined to try the issue of a battle.

Before continuing with Tacitus' narrative, there is a British traditional account that deserves thought; it comes from *The Seven Champions of Christendom*. Telling of St David's deeds, it runs—'Wales was beset with a people of a savage nature ... many battles had been fought to the disparagement of Christian knighthood.' To resist them, St David gathered together a force from 'any nation whatsoever', with which he

entered the country; where they found many towns unpeopled, gallant houses subverted, monasteries defaced, cities ruined, fields of corn consumed by fire—yea, everything as much out of order as if the country had never been inhabited. . . . As they marched along at an easy pace, to prevent danger, there resorted to them people of all ages, both young and old, bitterly complaining of the wrongs thus done to their country. And when they knew him to be the champion of Wales, whom they so long had desired to see, their joy was so great that all former woes were banished, and they sought nothing but revenge. The rest of the knights . . . proposed a present onset, and to show themselves before their enemies, who lay encamped amongst the mountains with such strength and policy that it was hard to make an assault.

This description fits no invasion of Wales prior to mediaeval times, other than the Roman; the Saxon inroads were a long slow process of spasmodic and petty encroachment, spread over centuries; so the story may well refer to this campaign. Should that be accepted, then Dewi* (to give St David his proper name) was ranging himself at Arthur's side.

Once again the Roman road system appears to provide a key to Ostorius' campaign. Behind the line of the lower Wye, through the Forest of Dean, there can be seen on the Ordnance Survey map of Roman Britain the line of a road that can hardly have been planned for civil purposes; it runs from south to north,

continuing beyond the Wye valley up that of the Lugg and similarly sheltered by the river from the west. It can scarcely be other
than his militarily built line of operation, his eventual communications being slightly further east and running direct from
Gloucester. The Lugg road ends abruptly just by Leominster, and
the other by Stretton Grandison, both pointing in the same
direction and indicating that Ostorius must have been at about
Kimbolton when the operations ended. Arthur had retreated
slowly northwards to the Welsh hills, where they end in the Clees
on their eastern flank; and there he had brought Ostorius to a
standstill.

In the course of the Roman advance up the Lugg there occurred an unpleasant affair, which has been disclosed by the
archaeologist's spade; yet to call it by those moderate terms seems
almost heartless, because in it a number of patriots lost their lives,
being brutally done to death as prisoners. Their slaughter bears
the same stamp as that at Maidens Castle, doing the Romans no
credit. The scene of the engagement was Sutton Walls, a fortified
hillock on the east bank of the Lugg, nine miles short of Leominster. From the fort ditch have been recovered the remains of
more than twenty skeletons, which in Dr. Ian Cornwall's words
reveal—'the deliberate execution of a group of "last ditch" de-
fenders. Some had been decapitated, constituting what is probably the earliest documented group of *prisoners* to be despatched
in such a way.'

The word 'prisoners' has here been substituted for Dr
Cornwall's 'war criminals', surely an unthinking slip. His report
continues that they were mostly men between twenty and forty
years old, but among them was a boy of twelve. This evidence
makes the Dorset butchery no isolated occurrence, and arouses
contempt; it throws into relief the true nature of the resistance
Arthur was leading—no obstinate refusal to accept civilization,
but a strong-willed people's rejection of the sway of bullies (for
the Britons were strong-willed in everything except their self-
interested behaviour). There is no saying how much other
butchery of the kind there may not have been; the men who fell
here were aware that the Roman was seeking to intimidate them,
and they failed to be cowed by the knowledge. The pity of the
whole story of Arthur's resistance is that, had all joined their

spasmodic efforts into one combined blow, they would easily have won their cause. Conversely the evidence of Roman policy after Plautius' departure, both now and in the events shortly to come, shows a bullying nature in the conquerors; it explains how it is that, despite all the advantages of the materialistic Latin civilization, the Britons preferred their own way of life. It is interesting to recognize what our British forefathers have bequeathed us, in the spirit of our present principles of warfare: 'There is, secondly, the principle of humanity, which says that all such kinds and degrees of violence as are not necessary for the purpose of war are not permitted to a belligerent. And there is, thirdly, the principle of chivalry, which demands a certain amount of fairness in offence and defence, and a certain mutual respect between the opposing forces.' Compare that with the oath of the Round Table: 'by no means to be cruel, but to give mercy unto him that asketh mercy, upon pain of forfeiture of their worship and lordship of King Arthur for evermore'. Of that spirit were the men now gathered about Arthur in the hills beyond the river Teme.

While Ostorius was opening up his permanent communications towards Kimbolton, Arthur will have been skirmishing with the Roman outposts on a semi-circle in the hills beyond the Teme; it is inconceivable to imagine him inactive, and the enemy must have been in North Herefordshire for several months for the Gloucester–Stretton Grandison road to have been aligned and almost finished. Indeed it looks as though Ostorius had decided not to try to penetrate the Clee Hills, but to make a permanent camp in the neighbourhood of Kimbolton, as his north-west frontier station for the time being. So we can picture Arthur for several months hovering round the area, based on Knucklas, seeking to catch the Roman off his guard and lying up for foraging parties, or getting round his flank and harassing the road-builders. To counter this, Ostorius will have sent out columns constantly, to a distance of one or two days' march, striking at threatened gatherings; Arthur and he will have fenced with one another, feinting, thrusting, parrying; now stepping back, now dashing forward. Many of the British camps in the area are bound to have been scenes of stiff encounters, the Britons using them as strongholds for raiding parties, the Romans seeking to destroy them like wasps' nests; among them perhaps was the camp above Church Stretton bearing Arthur's name, Caer Caradoc. And many of the nearer ones will at times have been turned into Roman piquets, manned by legionary soldiers or auxiliaries.

The Romans were encountering what we ourselves have experienced in modern times, in hill and jungle warfare; and rightly or wrongly they were meeting the difficulties in the same way, by methodical advance, road-making and tree-clearing as they went. There will be indirect truth in the Iolo MS. boast that Arthur gave the order for—'every tree in Siluria to be felled, that the Roman might no longer allege it was the British forests, and not British valour, which baffled him'. The order for clearance along the line of communications is more likely to have been Roman; but the spirit with which it was faced was the Britons', undaunted.

In such a mood, when Dewi's aid arrived, Arthur at last saw the chance of a successful battle; so he challenged Ostorius. Collecting a force menacingly in the Leintwardine hills, he placed himself in a position about Coxall Knoll whence he would have to be dislodged: in his front was a Roman outpost on Brandon Camp, offering a target for a night assault, and which Ostorius could not leave for long in danger; while away to his right front lay the Arrow valley, the Herefordshire Llion, whose men he doubtless stirred to fresh efforts to harry the Roman road-works on the far side of the Lugg, causing Ostorious to detach more men for their protection. The situation obliged Ostorius to attack him, so Arthur took advantage of fighting a defensive battle; he chose Coxall Knoll for his position, and strengthened it by building a stone parapet wall along its foot. The Romans closed up for the attack, marching across the Leinthall hills and concentrating in the valley facing his assembly, under cover of Brandon Camp. That evening, whilst preparing for the next day's battle, a curious incident happened to the Britons: at nightfall a pack of wolves dashed out of the woods, and seizing one of the watch carried him off into the forest; yet, next morning at daybreak they brought him back again unharmed. What portent was this, the Britons asked themselves; what did it foretell?

Tacitus has left a record of what the Romans beheld facing them:

Arthur chose a spot where the approach and the retreat were difficult to the enemy, and to himself every way advantageous. He took post in a situation defended by steep and craggy hills. In some places where the mountains opened, and the acclivity afforded an easy ascent, he fortified the spot with massy stones, heaped together in the form of a rampart. A river, with fords and shallows of uncertain depth, washed the extremity of the plain. On the outside of his fortifications, a vast body of troops showed themselves in force, and in order of battle. The chieftains of the various nations were busy in every quarter. They rushed along the ranks; they exhorted their men; they roused the timid; they confirmed the brave; and, by hopes, by promises, by every generous motive, inflamed the ardour of their troops. *Arthur* was seen in every part of the field; he darted along the lines; he exclaimed aloud— 'This day, my fellow-warriors, this very day, decides the fate of Britain. The era of liberty, or eternal bondage, begins from this hour. Remember your brave and warlike ancestors, who met Julius Caesar in open combat and chased him from the coast of Britain. They were the men who freed their country from a foreign yoke, who delivered the land from taxations imposed at the will of a master, who banished from your sight the fasces and the Roman axes, and, above all, who rescued your wives and daughters from violation.' The soldiers received this speech with shouts of applause. With a spirit of enthusiastic valour, each individual bound himself by the form of oath peculiar to his nation, to brave every danger, and prefer death to slavery.

Likewise Dewi encouraged his contingent:

Now is the time, brave soldiers, to be canonized the sons of Fame; this is the day of dignity or dishonour—an enterprise to make us ever live, or to end our names in obscurity. Let not chill Fear, the coward's companion, pull us back from the golden throne where the adventurous soldier sits in glory deservedly. We are to trample on the field of death and dead men's bones, and to buckle with an enemy of great strength, a pagan power that seeks to overrun all Christian kingdoms, and to wash our Cambrian fields with innocent blood. To arms, I say, brave followers! I will be the first to give death the onset; and for my colours or ensign do I wear upon my burgonet, you see, a green leek set in gold, which shall, if we win the victory, hereafter be an honour to Wales; and on this day, being the first of March, be it for ever worn by Welshmen in remembrance thereof.

The Welsh author of the *Cambrian Biography*, writing in 1803, is scathing on the subject of the leek and on Dewi being styled a 'saint', saying that he never had heard of such a patron saint, nor of the leek as his symbol, until he came to London; and he suggests a very different origin for the emblem, in the custom of bringing leeks for the 'Neighbourly Aid' farm gatherings. Yet the tradition is not to be ignored; the Minstrels from whom it came may have been drawing on a perfectly sound source. Nor does it seem impossible, or even improbable, that the same custom of bringing leeks in common may not have been followed for that battle as for peace-time purposes. And curiously enough a family of very ancient name, Lingen, taken from a village not far from Coxall Knoll, bear a bunch of leeks as their crest. At any rate, rightly or wrongly, seeing that the leek has now come to be adopted for March 1st (though unlikely to have been the actual date of the battle), it deserves recollection as commemorating the day when Dewi, with his 'neighbourly aid', fought side by side with Arthur to preserve this country's freedom.

Returning to Tacitus:

The intrepid countenance of the Britons, and the spirit that animated their whole army, struck Ostorius with astonishment. He saw a river to be passed; a palisade to be forced; a steep hill to be surmounted; and the several posts defended by a prodigious multitude. The soldiers, notwithstanding, burned with impatience for the onset. All things give way to valour, was the general cry. The tribunes and other officers seconded the ardour of the men. Ostorius reconnoitred the ground, and having marked where the defiles were impenetrable, or easy of approach, gave the signal for the attack. The river was passed with little difficulty. The Romans advanced to the parapet. The struggle there was obstinate, and, so long as it was fought with missile weapons, the Britons had the advantage. Ostorius ordered his men to advance under a military shell, and level the pile of stones that served as a fence to the enemy. A close engagement followed. The Britons abandoned their ranks, and fled with precipitation to the ridge of the hills. The Romans pursued with eagerness. Not only the light troops, but even the legionary soldiers, forced their way to the summit of the hills, under a heavy shower of darts [and blinded by the afternoon sun in their faces as the Dewi story relates]. The Britons, having neither breastplates nor helmets, were not able to maintain the conflict. The legions, sword in hand, or with their javelins, bore down all before them. The auxiliaries, with their spears and sabres, made prodigious havoc. The victory was decisive.

·   ·   ·   ·   ·

It is impossible to tell what can have been in Arthur's mind after this appalling climax to a long series of defeats. Guenevere and her infant daughter were now prisoners in Roman hands, captured on the field of battle. Whither was he himself to turn? Kent, the Weald, Devon, Dorset, Somerset, Gloucester, Hereford, Monmouth, and now Shropshire, practically every county of his realm, or adjoining it, was smarting under the recollection of a lost cause. East Anglia remained; but sentiment there was probably only lukewarm, it was ruled by the rival branch of his family, the house of Mandubrauc. Yet it was to a member of that family, living elsewhere, that he made his way, to an old woman named Aregwedd Ffoeddawg the daughter of Avarwy (grand-)son of Llud. Her name and family appear in the table of the royal line in the Glossary, under CYMBELINE; she is the woman known to the Romans as Cartismandua of the Brigant. Her father Avarwy is usually called the son of Llud, but, as with Cymbeline, the maternal link making him a grandson has been omitted. Where she was living is uncertain. The Caledonian chronicle speaks of her as 'queen of Scots', step-mother of Caratak of Caledon; she is therefore likely to have been in the region of Caledon (Weald), and as the Caledonians after the battle of Traeth Brue returned to Brigance, it is clear that part of their territory was included in that name. For reasons given in the Glossary, under BRIGANCE, it is judged to have been East Sussex bordering the Lake. Thither it was that Arthur went.

He can have had little else in his mind than to ask her to negotiate terms for him. Reft of his family and without any purpose left in attempting to continue resistance, he must have contemplated making a peace with the enemy; but whether he had any hopes for his own life being spared is questionable. It had been in jeopardy when he surrendered to Claudius, and the extreme penalty had been remitted only at the instance of Plautius and Vespasian; but the temper at Roman headquarters now was different, revenge might be vented on him. That he should have chosen Cartismandua as an intermediary shows the straits to which he was reduced; for she was the mother of the rejected Boadicea, as is told by Boece. However, he must have concluded that the inopportune affair had by now been more or less forgiven and forgot; and it is possible that Venusius of the

Iugant,* to whom Cartismandua was now married, held out some hopes to him of her support, because the national plight was giving every Briton far greater objects for resentment than inter-family quarrels. Known to be in comparatively friendly relation-ship with the Romans, she was the best person for broaching the subject of terms.

So, in his extremity, Arthur turned to her. But he had mis-judged the woman: she put him in chains and handed him over to the Romans. The only feature of interest in this sordid story is the sidelight thrown on Arthur's character. He knew the risk he was taking, being aware of her past anger with him over her daughter, and evidently aware too of her leanings towards Rome; yet he entrusted her with his life. He can only have judged her through his own eyes, forming the opinion that faced with the country's adversity she would bury past disappointment and set its needs first. We can imagine him talking with her in that strain, begging her to overlook the personal side of what had been no more than a match for political convenience, and asking her to use all her influence for one end only—to save what was left of Britain's wreck from absolute servitude.

Disillusionment can hardly have given him acute pain, only have numbed him; he had endured too much already. He had done his best, not for himself, but for his country; and his country-men had failed him. Their soul-deadening lack of spirit left him nothing to live for: his wife and child, who might have been everything to him, were sharing his country's fate; he was power-less to help them. He was a solitary survivor among a lifeless com-munity, whose determination had been quenched and was dead, leaving him with the sense of extreme loneliness so aptly des-cribed by Coleridge:

> O wedding-guest, this soul hath been alone on a wide, wide sea;
> So lonely 'twas that God himself scarce seemed there to be.

And that was the truth of the matter: the spirit of selfless resolve for the common good, contained in the expression 'God', was absent from Britain. The people, engrossed with personal am-bitions and petty jealousies, looked on ineffectually while Arthur, without a friend by him, was led a captive to enemy headquarters.

On the Rocks

INTO the courtyard of the Governor's quarters at Silchester can
we picture Arthur being taken chained, under a heavy guard of
legionaries warned to use ruthless force at any attempt at a rescue.
Britons in the populace are being kept at a distance by other
soldiers, whence they watch the sorry spectacle; but looks differ,
some are dejected—their last hope gone—others scarcely conceal
an inward satisfaction that there is now no doubt of the house
of Rheged prospering, and with it their own fortunes. Among
the Roman soldiers there is not one who, though alert and constantly glancing right and left and over his shoulder to make sure
there is no suspicion of movement in the crowd, does not find
time to look curiously at the man who for seven years has braved
the might of Rome. Seven years takes quite a number of them
back to their first arrival in Britain as young soldiers, when they
remember their sergeant's blunt caution: 'No sleeping on piquet
here, my lad, or it'll be Arthur's knife in your throat if you do.'
    Amid such memories Arthur is brought before Ostorius, who
is seated, as Claudius was seated seven years earlier, in the centre
face of a hollow square of soldiers and officials; behind the
Governor's back stand ranged the eagles, and above the heads of
all glisten the weapons of a solid wall of spearmen, points erect
and spaced with awesome precision. But Ostorius, after a year's
stern duelling with Arthur, and having experienced the inferior
stuff of the rival he had been misled to support, feels admiration
for his opponent's courageous pertinacity, and magnanimous
towards his misfortune. The words are Boece's and typify the
tradition handed down: Ostorius greets Arthur: 'O Caratoc, this
mischance should be suffered with patience; for though you be
destitute of good fortune, yet you are not coming into our hands

naked of honour. Do not be ashamed to be in the hands of Rome, who has subdued so many rich and valiant kings, and led them in triumph.'

To which Arthur replies:

I must suffer this adversity, howbeit that it is against my will. And yet nothing is so grievous to me as Fortune, which has been so far from my control as to throw me at your feet, as an example of her instability, and has made me a prisoner more by treason than by force. While my strength endured I resisted you; but now, through the treason of my *kinswoman* Cartismandua, in whom I had the most confidence after my disaster, I am come into your hands. My part is now to obey you as victor, and to undergo the will and pleasure of my enemy; your part shall be to use the opportunity of a victorious captain, and to be merciful, so that a conquered and miserable people may have some hope of grace.

It is gratifying that Ostorius should have left a memory of this kind, and not just the traces of brutality now being unearthed; it is true that the latter may have been the work of subordinates, but should it have been possible for them to be perpetrated? Let us hope then that Arthur and the other captives were spared the sneers and coarse reminders of their coming fate, which are otherwise to be guessed as coming from an unchivalrous soldiery. After all, if even Boece's expressions are true, the mention of figuring in a triumph is tantamount to forecasting his liquidation —to use the modern gruesome parallel; but perhaps it was not said.

Arthur was now despatched to Rome, together with Guenevere and her infant daughter Gladys, also a relative of some kind whom Tacitus calls his brother. With them will have gone a train of other prisoners and vast quantities of loot, to swell the magnitude of a display at the City. There, everyone awaited his arrival eagerly; for, as Tacitus remarks, his fame was not confined to his native island, but during his seven years' heroic defiance had spread over all Italy and the European provinces. The Emperor was ready to magnify it, because the greater the defeated foe the greater his own and the national credit; so a big public spectacle was prepared, for the impressive display of prisoners and spoil. Tacitus describes the scene:

In the field before the camp the praetorian bands were drawn up under arms. The followers of the British chief walked in procession. The military accoutrements, the harness and rich collars, which he had gained in various battles, were displayed with pomp. The wife of *Arthur*, his daughter and his brother followed next; he himself closed the melancholy train.

And another Roman adds: 'Rome trembled when she saw the Briton, even though in chains.'

Tacitus continues:

The rest of the prisoners, struck with terror, descended to mean and abject supplications. Arthur alone was superior to misfortune. With a countenance still unaltered, not a symptom of fear appearing, no sorrow, no condescension, he behaved with dignity even in ruin. Being placed before the tribunal, he delivered himself in the following manner: 'If to the nobility of my birth, and the splendour of exalted station, I had united the virtues of moderation, Rome had beheld me, not in captivity, but a royal visitor and a friend. The alliance of a prince, descended from an illustrious line of ancestors; a prince whose sway extended over many nations, would not have been unworthy of your choice. A reverse of fortune is now the lot of Arthur. The event to you is glorious, and to me humiliating. I had arms, men, and horses; I had wealth in abundance: can you wonder that I was unwilling to lose them? The ambition of Rome aspires to universal dominion; and must mankind, by consequence, stretch their necks to the yoke? I stood at bay for years; had I acted otherwise, where on your part had been the glory of conquest, and where on mine the honour of a brave resistance? I am now in your power; if you are bent on vengeance, execute your purpose; the bloody scene will soon be over, and the name of Arthur will sink into oblivion. Preserve my life, and I shall be to late posterity a monument of Roman clemency.'

Claudius granted him a free pardon, and the same to his wife, his daughter and his brother. Released from their fetters, they advanced to another tribunal near at hand, where *the Empress* showed herself in state; they returned thanks to her, and paid their veneration in the same style as they had before addressed to the Emperor.

The matter-of-fact wording of this account tends to shroud the ghastly anxiety that Arthur and Guenevere must have been enduring up to this very moment, for months. For, this was the only exception ever made to the customary practice of brutally murdering captured kings and generals at a triumph, a prospect so horrible that in one instance a king went mad during the procession. And another gruesome thought is that there is no mention of clemency for the other prisoners. It is an interesting question as to what induced Claudius to make his decision. Certainly Plautius must have used what influence he had, and the Pudens mentioned at Chichester, being a wealthy young senator, may be expected to have done the same; but R. W. Morgan holds the view that they alone could not have been enough to outweigh the demands of custom. He attributes it to Providence; but he also observes that perhaps the Emperor was guided by the knowledge that, in spite of Arthur's capture, the Siluri were continuing a fierce opposition, and he judged that without tolerance worse might happen. Compare Pitt's dictum: 'Providence never interferes for the preservation of men or nations without their own exertions'—supposing the rest of Britain had shown the resolution of the Siluri?

The conditions given to Arthur were, according to R. W. Morgan, that he should never bear arms against Rome again, that he should remain for seven years at Rome in free custody, and that certain relatives should be retained as hostages; on the other hand his revenues should be forwarded to him from Britain, and his daughter would be adopted by the Emperor, who assumed accordingly his name—Claudia. In conformity with those terms Arthur took up his residence in the Palatium Britanicum, on the Mons Sacer, now the church of St Pudentiana, named after his granddaughter; and it was when first seeing the public buildings of Rome that he is said to have commented: 'It is singular a people possessed of such magnificence at home should envy me my soldier's tent in Britain.'

Here a comparison must be made with the traditions of romance. They tell of Arthur going to Rome as a conqueror, and elaborate the story with a wealth of victorious fighting, some of the sentiments expressed in which read like a recollection of what was actually said during the struggle in Britain; for example, the disgust at the Roman use of mercenaries seems certainly like a memory of the experience. However the cause for the inversion from defeat to victory is remarked in a continental comment referring to Arthur's capture of the Palug Cat;* the continental version adds to the story that in reality the Cat vanquished him and carried him off: 'but one durst not tell that tale before Britons'. There is at least some satisfaction in knowing that the country felt ashamed of its failure.

Another legend which may or may not be fantasy is Arthur's dream when embarking for Rome. Arthur's doubt as to its import suggests some conceivable foundation in fact. According to romance, when on board ship he dreamt that he saw a bear flying westwards from the east, and a dragon flying eastwards from the west; they clashed fighting, and the dragon defeated the bear. (Malory incidentally makes the creature a boar, but the Welsh is bear.) The interpretation as given in romance runs: 'The dragon that thou dreamedst of betokeneth thine own person that sailest here, and his tail which is all to-tattered signifieth the noble knights of the Round Table; and the bear that the dragon slew coming from the clouds betokeneth some tyrant that tormenteth the people, or else thou art like to fight with some giant thyself. Wherefore of this dreadful dream doubt thee nothing, but as a conqueror come forth thyself.' To which Arthur replies: 'My interpretation of the dream is other than yours. To me it typifies rather the issue of the war between myself and the Emperor. But let the Creator's will be done.' If there is any truth in it, its real significance would seem to have been a forecast of a coming struggle between a Bear of Caledon other than Arthur, and himself as Dragon of Wessex. But of necessity he could not think so far ahead when being carried as a prisoner to Rome, for maybe his death; hence his differing view. And with this story we leave Arthur with his thoughts, in Rome.

. . . . .

Ostorius was awarded great honour: 'At the next meeting of the Senate, the victory over *Arthur* was mentioned with the highest applause, as an event no way inferior to what had been seen in ancient times, when other commanders exhibited kings and princes at their chariot-wheels. Triumphal ornaments were decreed to Ostorius.' But in point of fact his difficulties were a long way from being past. Active fighting continued on the Welsh front, and throughout the province a strong underground move-

ment was smouldering; at the head of both was nominally
Modred, to whom legend tells Arthur had left 'all the governance,
save only the crown'. The crown itself is likely to have been
divided; broadly speaking, Cornwall and Albany will have been
separate now, so also East Anglia, the complete silence about
which in romance speaks for itself.

Before long Ostorius was once more in the field, and

began to experience the vicissitudes of fortune. [The account is Tacitus.] Perhaps the war, by the overthrow of *Arthur*, was thought to be
at an end and, in that belief, military discipline was relaxed; perhaps the
enemy, enraged by the loss of that gallant chief, fought with inflamed
resentment. A camp had been formed in the country of the Silures, and
a chain of forts was to be erected. The Britons in a body surrounded the
officer who commanded the legionary cohorts, and if succour had not
arrived in time from the neighbouring garrisons, the whole corps had
been cut to pieces. The praefect of the camp, with eight centurions and
the bravest of the soldiers, were killed on the spot; a foraging party and
the detachment sent to support them were soon after attacked, and put
to rout.

The site of this British success seems likely to have been in
the region of Monmouth, where an advanced post may have been
built, judging from the later pattern of roads; the usual assumption that it was near Caerleon-on-Usk is improbable, as both
archaeology and local tradition combine to indicate that the
Romans were unable to penetrate much beyond the Wye at this
time. The spade tells that the British fort in Llan-melin Wood,
already mentioned in the A.D. 50 campaign (p. 169), was not
abandoned until twenty years later; while tradition peoples the
scene of resistance in South Herefordshire. There, it is said, some
of Geraint's clan of Garawys received land from Arthur; an act
which is likely to have taken place after the Llongborth defeat,
when they may have been displaced from their home in Devon
and have crossed the Channel with Arthur into South Wales. Had
their new territory west of the Wye fallen under enemy rule
immediately, it is scarcely probable that they would have been
allowed to remain in possession of it; on the other hand if we
suppose them to have occupied it for twenty years, during which
time they headed resistance to Roman penetration beyond the

river, they may well have become looked upon as properly settled there. The Wye, therefore, is to be regarded as roughly the Roman frontier at this period.

The construction of a chain of forts, mentioned by Tacitus, is a separate matter apparently; and where they were intended is by no means certain. Boece's translator, Stewart, introduces a people named Ordel,* who correspond to the Ordovic of Shropshire and North Wales, against whom Agricola conducted an operation; the chain of forts might therefore have been connected with either the South Wales or Shropshire front; it might have been proposed as protection along the foot of the hills facing Monmouthshire and Herefordshire, or it might have been on the north of the Wenlock hills of Shropshire, to cut off malcontents there from aid from Cheshire and Staffordshire. The fighting described by Tacitus certainly seems to relate to South Wales; but it may have been a reconnaissance for the northern forts, from Leicester to Wroxeter, that brought in the Ordovic, just as it was the building of forts between the Nene and Severn which precipitated Arthur's rebellion. Fortification constituted a visible sign of encroachment; without it, people could persuade themselves that the occupation was only temporary.

The Roman account continues:

Ostorius, on the first alarm, ordered the light-armed cohorts to advance against the enemy. That reinforcement was insufficient till the legionary soldiers marched to their support. The battle was renewed, at first on equal terms, but in the end to the disadvantage of the Britons. But their loss was inconsiderable; the approach of night prevented a pursuit. From that time the Britons kept up a constant alarm; frequent battles, or rather skirmishes, were fought with their detached parties roving in quest of plunder. They met in sudden encounters, as chance directed or valour prompted, in the fens, in the woods, in the narrow defiles; the men on some occasions were led on by their chiefs, and frequently without their knowledge, as resentment or the love of booty happened to incite their fury.

This description has clearly been given to the historian at first hand; road communication must have been precarious, the legions cannot have penetrated deep into Wales.

Of all the Britons, the Silures were the most determined; they fought with obstinacy, with inveterate hatred. It seems the Roman general had declared that the very name of the Silures must be extirpated, like that of the Sigambrians, formerly driven out of Germany and transplanted into Gaul; that expression reached the Silures and roused their fiercest passions. Two auxiliary cohorts, whom the avarice of their officers sent in plunder, were intercepted by that ferocious people and all made prisoners. A fair distribution of the spoils and the captives drew the neighbouring states into the confederacy.

Ostorius at this time was worn out with anxiety; he sank under the fatigue and expired, to the great joy of the Britons, who saw a great and able commander, not indeed slain in battle, but overcome by the war.

After his death

the legion under Manlius Valens risked a battle and suffered defeat; it was the nation of the Silures (of Sussex) that struck the blow. Emboldened by success they continued their predatory war, till the arrival of Didius (Ostorius' successor) checked their operations. That officer on his arrival found the island in a state of distraction. In order to impress with terror the new commander, the Britons took care to swell the fame of their victory. Didius on his part was willing to magnify the loss; the merit of the general he knew would rise in proportion to the danger surmounted, and if he failed the difficulty would be an apology for his conduct.

That the Siluri referred to were of West Sussex is indicated by Boece, who adds that the 'Kendal'* (Kent Dale) men assisted in defeating Valens, and that the Siluri, whom he terms throughout Picts, begged the chief of Caledon to rebel. The chief's reply was typically equivocal:

Because he was confederate with the Romans he would in no way go to war with them, unless they attacked him first; for he was bound by the undertaking Arthur had given at Rome. Nevertheless he had a good presumption that they intended an attack, consequently he would come with all his strength by a certain day, more to impede the Romans than to fight them in battle.

This reply and the following narrative is a mixture of Bellenden, Stewart, and Tacitus; the two Scotsmen had evidently a good deal of native tradition to draw from, because they have not only amplified the classical story, but in one instance corrected it.

The chief of Caledon, who will now be referred to by his simple Celtic style, 'Caledon', accordingly went with a gathering into Brigance, that is to say East Sussex, where a revolt was in progress. Until recently the chieftainship had been held by one Venusius, married to Cartismandua, the woman who had betrayed Arthur, and Caledon's step-mother, his father having long since died. She, however, had now discarded Venusius in favour of her standard-bearer, and had thrown Venusius and his relatives into prison. She being a pro-Roman, and Caledon being anti-Roman with some hereditary claim to Brigance as well, the circumstances gave him an opportunity for interfering justifiably against Roman influence; he therefore made his way towards the Brigance capital, Epiak. That place is not necessarily now identifiable, it may have been on land since eaten away by the sea; Stewart describes it as standing on the bank of a river, surrounded by marsh and forest, and accessible by one approach only. The Roman governor ordered Caledon to quit the district, and sent a legionary commander, Cesius Nasica, to settle the disturbance; but Caledon arrived first, and, succeeding in releasing Venusius' relatives, punished Cartismandua by burying her alive. A party of Caledonians then suffered a reverse at Roman hands, and were beset in Epiak by cavalry while Nasica brought up the foot; Caledon himself and Venusius came to their aid, drawing off the Romans and engaging them, in which the Britons from Epiak also helped. The Britons claimed to have come to terms, inducing the Romans to believe that a rebellion was threatening in Kent; the Romans claimed a success; the Roman version is the more convincing. Two interesting points of detail occur in the Caledonian account; one is that they felt themselves indebted to Rome for the honour done to Arthur; the other that they agreed not to help the islanders of Mon, in respect of some recent misbehaviour.

Apart from keeping disturbances in check, Didius made little attempt to extend Roman territory; and, from what Tacitus was told, he only embarked upon any increase at all in order to satisfy popular opinion. Otherwise he preferred to let sleeping dogs lie, a policy which drew on him the rather scathing criticism that age and past laurels were keeping him from the field. None the less, he may well have been instructed to adopt a passive policy, because both now and later it is apparent that there were two schools of thought operating at Rome: there was the one which wanted visible results—conquest, spoil, glorious tales of slaughter—it thought in terms of material power; but there was also another, wiser and more humane, which appreciated the worth of moral gains and influence. The materialistic school certainly predominated, yet the effect of the other's advocacy is periodically recognizable. The greatest ally of the school for conquest was the Britons themselves: 'Nothing has helped us (the Romans) more than their inability to co-operate; it is but seldom that two or three states unite to repel a common danger, fighting in detail they are conquered wholesale.' As a result, Didius' successor Veranius, who arrived in A.D. 58, came with an acquisitive aim.

His first step was to tour the province, to gauge the situation; then, returning to Camelot, he made a public sacrifice to Victory and to the deceased and deified Claudius. Following on this he made a few incursions into Silurian territory, evidently not encountering much resistance, because he declared ostentatiously that he would subdue the whole island within two years. Premature death relieved him of the necessity of revising his estimate.

Before continuing with the next governor's fortunes, an internal condition in Britain needs brief mention; it is the adversity which befell the Church after Arthur's downfall. With his removal, it not only was deprived of official sponsorship, but was factiously attacked. In legend this is told of as Arthur having fallen into a 'slothful will'; it is the scene with which the Grail section of the romance opens. Partly the attack was physical: the Church's head, Pwyll Avallawch, was assaulted with the spear that formed one of the holy relics and was grievously wounded; he is thereafter known as the Maimed King, or King Fisherman 'fallen into languishment'. Partly was it influential: Lancelot deserted Elaine, the Lady of the Lake; that is to say, one of the Chichester family deserted his wife who continued to keep to her faith. Charitably he is said to have gone out of his mind; but in naked truth he abandoned her in order to suit circumstances. These had their origin in Rome, where Christianity was being persecuted; and pro-Roman Britons found it fashionable to follow suit. It was at about this time that Arthur's sister, in Rome, the wife of Aulus Plautius, was charged with embracing a foreign superstition. The procedure adopted was curious—Plautius was allowed to try her in a domestic court, consisting of her relatives; he was thus enabled to pronounce her innocent, but even so the rest of her life was passed in sadness. Yet her fortitude earned her Roman admiration—'Nothing could alleviate her sorrow [after the loss of a friend], nor was her perseverance imputed to her as a crime; in the end it was the glory of her character.' With that example by a fellow-countrywoman before them, it is unpleasant to see men in Britain employing unscrupulous obsequiousness for personal advantage. What effect the Church's set-back had on the country as a whole is difficult to assess; broadly speaking, the revival of a patriotic spirit of working for the common good, which Arthur had striven for and in which the Church aided by preaching selflessness, was being discarded for the old habit of party interests.

The next governor, Paulinus Suetonius, fully represented the school of conquest; forceful and ambitious, he set out to emulate the exploits of a fellow-general, in Armenia. For the first two years, during A.D. 59 and 60, he gained a series of successes, extending the bounds of the Roman province to Chester and York. The exact course of his operations will probably, in the course of time, be determined by archaeological dating, here it is being deduced from the lay-out of the road system. His first step seems to have been a north-west advance to Wroxeter, where he established the XIVth Legion's headquarters, and to which he extended Watling Street as its line of communication. The road followed more or less an existing British track, but with en-gineered straightness. This advance enabled the Clee Hills' resistance to be cut off from the main mass of the Welsh hills, by the opening up of a road from Wroxeter through Leintwardine to Hereford, and thence to Monmouth. The absence of Roman camps along this route is noticeable, suggesting that protection along it was provided largely by native levies; on the other hand there is a distinct frequency of temporary camps along the final stretch of Watling Street, from Wall to Wroxeter, indicating its liability to interruption from the Stafford and Cheshire Cornawys.*

In the following year Suetonius would appear to have reached Chester and York; then, in A.D. 61, he took the bold step of striking at Anglesey, a place of refuge for all Britons who wanted to continue their resistance. The boldness of his move is shown by the heavy difficulties encountered by mediaeval expeditions against North Wales; but the lack of opposition on this occasion tells that the prestige of Roman arms had numbed the people's enterprise. Yet it was not inadequate courage, it was the fatal curse of internal disunity which was undermining the country's will; it was for all the world like party strife today. So, borne to the shore of the Menai Straits by this short-sighted self-interest, Suetonius was able to set about the destruction of one of the last centres of national pride and freedom. Tacitus describes the operation:

In order to facilitate his approach to a difficult and deceitful shore, he ordered a number of flat-bottomed boats to be constructed. In these he wafted over the infantry, while the cavalry, partly by fording over the shallows and partly by swimming their horses, advanced to gain a footing on the island. On the opposite shore stood the Britons, close embodied and prepared for action. Women were seen rushing through the ranks in wild disorder, their apparel funereal, their hair loose to the wind, in their hands flaming torches, and their whole appearance resembling the frantic rage of the Furies. The druids were ranged in order, with hands uplifted, invoking the gods and pouring forth horrible imprecations. The novelty of the sight struck the Romans with awe and terror; they stood in stupid amazement as if their limbs were benumbed, riveted to one spot, a mark for the enemy. The exhortations of the general diffused new vigour through the ranks, and the men by mutual reproaches inflamed each other to deeds of valour. They felt the disgrace of yielding to a troop of women, and a band of fanatic priests; they advanced their standards and rushed on to the attack with impetuous fury. The island fell, and a garrison was established to retain it in subjection; the religious groves, dedicated to superstition and barbarous rites, were levelled to the ground.

The remark, omitted here, that the islanders perished in the flames which they themselves had kindled, can be taken as metaphoric; nor should the record of human sacrifice being practised be allowed to focus the attention too closely on what may not have been a general custom, but a relic peculiar to this isolated and perhaps antiquated community. Stewart relates the much more typical aspect of this particular college's original foundation; paraphrased, he tells of the druids that—'Not long before (it was founded) they had been at study for a long time in Greece, in the city of Athens, where they applied sundry sciences, such as music, grammar, philosophy, physic and natural arts, mathematics, moral science, and astronomy; their work was mostly to expound history and law, and to teach children, as they had seen done in Greece. From the age of seven years until twenty, kings' and lords' sons were taught under them; that was their custom for many years.' Doubtless the science was more elementary than the word sounds, and doubtless custom may have deteriorated, sensational ritual taking precedence over doctrine; but Stewart's account gives a better picture of British druidism than is done by dwelling on its decadent features.

Suetonius, having completed his task, found himself called away to Gaul, to help put down a rebellion (so Boece tells us); and in his absence the Britons around Camelot broke into revolt. Some little time elapsed before he could get back to Britain, during which the revolt spread over most, if not all, of the country; so we will now carry our thoughts to the Itchen valley, to Camelot and Camelot Colony, where the outbreak began.

.   .   .   .   .

The immediate cause of the trouble was financial; but its roots went far deeper. There had been a quantity of smouldering resentment, and much provocation, as the soldiers' behaviour recorded by Tacitus was worse than arrogant; indeed, had not the Briton chieftains been so subservient to personal expediency, the people's lot could never have been tolerated up to this juncture.

The financial measure was the Roman foreclosure on extensive loans which had been made to British chiefs, partly by the late emperor, Claudius, and partly by Seneca the philosopher—who was also a moneylender, and an avaricious one. The money was needed to meet the extravagances of the present emperor, Nero. But the method of reclaiming the money was incredibly harsh; it gives a picture of the people being regarded with complete contempt, and of soldiery allowed to get out of control; it suggests a great deal of previous high-handed insolence. All that can be said is that the people's chosen leaders' supineness deserved it. One of the persons involved was the widow of the late chief of the Iceni (Itchen valley folk), Boadicea; her husband had amassed considerable wealth, much of it evidently borrowed, which he had endeavoured to secure by leaving it in his will divided equally between his two daughters and the Emperor. However, the loan was called in, and the savage way in which this was carried out shows the Romans' sheer contempt; in their own historian's admission:

His dominions were ravaged by the centurions, the slaves pillaged his house, and his effects were seized as lawful plunder. His wife, Boadicea, was disgraced with cruel stripes; her daughters were ravished and the most illustrious of the Icenians were, by force, deprived of the possessions which had been transmitted to them by their ancestors. The whole country was considered as a legacy bequeathed to the plunderers. The relations of the deceased king were reduced to slavery.

The Britons' response was drastic: Boadicea called to arms the Iceni, from Hampshire to the Wash, and her kinsfolk the Brigance of Sussex; the Trinovant of London and Essex followed suit, and the neighbouring tribes pledged their support secretly. But although the expression 'drastic' has been used, it cannot be ignored that the response was not universally spontaneous; as will be seen, it was largely local to Camelot and London; and so, concurrently with reading about what was done, we need at the same time to infer how much was not being done, in order to reach a true perspective of the revolt. Nevertheless, locally what feeling had been smouldering now burst into rage:

What chiefly fired their indignation was the conduct of the veterans, lately planted as a colony at Camelot Dun. These men treated the Britons with cruelty and oppression; they drove the natives from their habitations, and calling them by the opprobious names of slaves and captives, added insult to their tyranny. In these acts of oppression, the veterans were supported by the common soldiers, a set of men trained to licentiousness by their habits of life, and in their turn expecting to reap the same advantages. The temple built in honour of Claudius was another cause of discontent; in the eye of the Britons it seemed the citadel of eternal slavery; the priests, appointed to officiate at the altars, with a pretended zeal for religion, devoured the whole substance of the country.

Taxation had been galling, as is told by Dio Cassius' version of Boadicea's harangue to the people:

Have we not been robbed entirely of most of our possessions, and those the greatest, while for those that remain we pay taxes? Besides pasturing and tilling for them all our possessions, do we not pay a yearly tribute for our very bodies? How much better it would be to have been sold to masters once for all than possessing empty titles of freedom, to have to ransom ourselves every year! How much better to have been slain and to have perished, than to go about with a tax on our heads! Yet why do I mention death? For even dying is not free of cost with them; nay, you know what fees we deposit even for our dead. Among the rest of mankind death frees even those who are in slavery to others; only in the case of the Romans do the very dead remain alive for their profit. Why is it that, though none of us has any money (how indeed could we, or where could we get it?), we are stripped and despoiled like a murderer's victims?

The fury aroused brought confidence. Their masters had omitted internal security defence at Camelot: 'The Roman generals attended to improvements of taste and elegance, but neglected the useful; they embellished the province, and took no care to defend it. To the incensed and angry Britons it did not appear an enterprise that threatened either danger or difficulty, to overrun a colony which lay quite naked and exposed, without a single fortification.' Portents appeared to reinforce their assurance:

The statue of Victory, erected at Camelot Dun, fell from its base for no apparent cause, and lay extended on the ground with its face averted, as if the goddess yielded to the enemies of Rome. Women in restless ecstasy rushed among the people, and with frantic screams denounced impending ruin; in the council chamber of the Romans hideous clamours were heard in a foreign accent, savage howlings filled the theatre. And near the mouth of the *Icen* the image of a colony in ruins was seen in the transparent water; the sea was purpled with blood, and at the ebb of tide the figures of human bodies were traced in the mud. By these appearances the Romans were sunk in despair, while the Britons anticipated a glorious victory.

Tacitus remarks that Suetonius was detained in the Isle of Mon while this was happening, and the Caledon version of his having sailed thence to Gaul seems a likely explanation. He continues:

In this alarming crisis the veterans sent to Catus Decianus, the procurator of the province, for a reinforcement (presumably from Silchester). Two hundred men, and those not completely armed, were all that officer could spare. The Colony had but a handful of soldiers; their temple was strongly fortified, and there they hoped to make a stand. But even for the defence of that place no measures were concerted; secret enemies mixed in all their deliberations, no fosse was made, no palisade thrown up, nor were the women and such as were disabled by age or infirmity sent out of the garrison. Unguarded and unprepared, they were taken by surprise; and in the moment of profound peace they were overpowered by the barbarians in one general assault. The Colony was laid waste with fire and sword. The temple held out, but after a siege of two days was taken by storm.

In Stewart's translation of Boece the Colony is called Ordul.*
So much is it the fashion to belaud everything Roman, impressed by the spectacle of their progress in material civilization, that attention must be drawn to the slenderness of the bubble; it was a powerful organization, overwhelming against disunited opposition, but lacking the individual and good-natured spirit of resolve that commands the admiration even of enemies, and which alone can convert military victory into friendly brotherhood. At this point the bubble was being pricked, and the hollowness of its fabric being disclosed; it is mentioned in order to point to the fallacy it reveals, which is that, no matter how magnificent the organization may be, it will collapse unless it is imbued throughout with a spirit of good-natured initiative, and that spirit is given freedom to act. In this instance the Roman structure was being tested against disjointed British ardour, and it was touch and go as to which would ultimately be the survivor.
Responsibility among the Romans now devolved upon the Procurator of the province and the several legionary commanders,

in the absence of Suetonius. The legions were of necessity scattered, in forts along the frontier and in some inland centres; no commander will have had many troops in hand, practically the whole of the disposable reserve being with Suetonius in Mon; consequently at legionary headquarters there will have been only small local reserves, and time-expired veterans. Of the four legions, the XXth seems to have been with Suetonius, and to have been mainly Italian, but perhaps of mixed troops; the IXth garrisoned the east and north of Britain, with headquarters at Colchester, and was composed mainly of Celt-Iberians from Spain; the IInd garrisoned the west, with headquarters at Gloucester, and was made up of Celto-Teutonic men from the Rhine; the XIVth was in charge of the north-west, with headquarters at Wroxeter; its composition appears mainly to have been Italian. At Silchester or London was the Procurator, Catus Decianus, the man to whom the outbreak was really due, since it was he who had advised that repayment of the loans should be exacted.

The commander of the IXth Legion courageously made an attempt to come to the Camelot Colony's assistance, but was completely defeated on the way, his infantry being cut to pieces and he himself only escaping with the cavalry to Colchester or London. The praefect at the IInd's headquarters found himself unable to risk sending aid; and the Procurator took to flight, crossing over to Gaul from Kent. Small wonder that the Britons said of the Procurator and his staff that 'in battle it was the bravest (the legions) who took spoils; but those whom they suffered to seize their houses, force away their children and exact levies, were for the most part the cowardly and effeminate, as if the only lesson of suffering of which they were ignorant was how to die for their country'.

Thus the whole Roman structure in Britain became paralysed. Everywhere local garrisons are to be pictured as camp-bound, nervous to do more than look to their own security, and anxiously awaiting each new morning's news. The Britons, possibly from a sense of honouring Arthur's bond given in Rome, but more probably from irresolution (to judge from their later behaviour around London), were largely withholding action; Boadicea's rebellion was confined to the south-east.

Two small points of geography must be remarked at this stage. One is that Tacitus has referred to the river at Camelot Colony by the name of Thames; in doing so he intended to clarify the correct name Icen,* but fell into confusing the Hampshire stream with this alternative name for the Thames (as has been explained on p. 17). Similarly in Arthurian legend, King Arthur and Guenevere are at Winchester when the Fair Maid of Astolat dies, yet her body passes them in a boat on the 'Thames'; this causes their Court to be transposed in romance to Westminster, though properly it was at Caerleon on the Icen. Another point is that Tacitus in his 'Agricola' mentions that the Colony was burnt by the Brigant* people, thus witnessing their proximity to the Camelot neighbourhood; Boece specifies them as Morays.*

.   .   .   .   .

As soon as he was able to, Suetonius took his force back from Anglesey to Chester, bringing with him the detachment he had intended leaving in the island. Stewart's claim that when the news of Camelot Colony's fall reached Mon the islanders slew all the Romans there, can be taken with a grain of salt. Suetonius marched straightway down Watling Street to London with the XXth Legion, leaving orders for the IInd and IXth to take over most of, if not all, the XIVth's duties, and for the XIVth to follow with the veterans of the XXth to London, where he would make his headquarters. How he managed to denude the frontier to this extent is surprising; it is even remarkable that he managed to get back from Anglesey without severe fighting, which suggests that he used sea transport considerably in reaching Chester. Doubtless he had terrorized the conquered area, but that does not fully explain how he could withdraw two legions from a newly occupied frontier, when behind him a quarter of the province was in turmoil. Two features are apparent: the one, that Suetonius carried with him a splendid feeling of confidence; the other, that the Britons were saturated with petty inter-clan jealousies, and unable to be unanimous even at a crisis. Suetonius had assessed the hazards of his task boldly and accurately. Accompanying him as a young staff-officer was Agricola, experiencing a severer taste of war than in the capture of Anglesey, and apparently being fired with the thrill of it.

Having reached London Suetonius reviewed the situation, and found it worse than he had hoped. The Trinovant of Middlesex and Essex were in full revolt; IXth Legion headquarters was camp-bound at Colchester, its reserve having been cut to bits; London and St Albans and several other small Romano-British settlements were holding out, but only just so, and he could not take the field with the assurance that they would not be overrun behind him. Hampshire and Sussex were in full rebellion, except around his main base at Portchester, where Cogidubnus of Chichester was studiously pursuing his loyalty to Rome. Suetonius decided to evacuate all of the small garrisons in the insurgent area, removing the civilians to the Portchester base, and leaving himself free to handle the rebellion on military lines, with all avilable force concentrated.

The decision to abandon London and its environs was a hard one to have to take; but having made up his mind, speed was the main consideration: 'Neither supplications nor the tears of the inhabitants could induce him to change his plan. The signal for the march was given; all who chose to follow his banners were taken under his protection. Of all who, on account of their advanced age, the weakness of their sex, or the attractions of the situation, thought proper to remain behind, not one escaped the rage of the barbarians; the inhabitants of Verulam (by St Albans), a municipal town, were in like manner put to the sword.' The Britons, it is regrettable to say, behaved with neither chivalry nor military nous; they 'left behind them all places of strength; wherever they expected feeble resistance and considerable booty, there they were sure to attack with the fiercest rage. The number massacred in the places which have been mentioned amounted to no less than seventy thousand, all citizens or allies of Rome.'

The force Suetonius had succeeded in collecting now consisted of the XXth Legion, the XIVth, or most of it, the veterans of the XXth, and auxiliaries from various evacuated stations, in all nearly ten thousand soldiers; but it was an unwieldy force, hampered by the huge mass of refugees that it was escorting. His first aim will surely have been to conduct these to the coast, and leave them in security at his base; in the words of Agricola— 'We had to fight for life before we could think of victory.' Tacitus' statement that he intended to bring on a decisive action

without loss of time must be interpreted in this light. Whither he
directed his march is not stated; he had the choice of two roads to
the south coast, Stane Street or the Pevensey route. He will have
chosen the one on which he would expect to encounter the less
hostility from the surrounding populace; so we can imagine him
setting off in the direction of Chichester, down Stane Street, a
long column of wagons and pack animals, but mostly civilians
on foot, flanking parties of infantry at close intervals marching
with it on either side, a strong advance guard, and an equally
strong rearguard hurrying up the stragglers, and cavalry further
out in all directions reconnoitring.

The general cannot but have marched anxiously through the
wooded Thames valley, towards the North Downs; no more
awkward a formation for heavy fighting could have been imposed on him—he had to be guarded at every point, thus rendering his troops strung out and weak everywhere; while the length
of the column meant that his small reserve was unable to reach
readily any spot that might suddenly be assailed. For the first
twenty miles, however, he met with no serious opposition. Then,
when he approached the cleft in the downs, where now stands
the town of Dorking, he found the Britons in full force barring
his passage. He will have camped for the night near the foot of
the hills, ready to force his way through early the following day.
Tacitus is scarcely right in giving Suetonius the initiative; the
choice of ground lay with the Britons; the Roman had deliberately
abandoned everything in his rear, and now had no alternative but
to cut his way through to his base. Next morning, momentarily,
he stood on the defensive, a tactical move which induced the
enemy to open the attack.

He chose a spot encircled with woods, narrow at the entrance and
sheltered in the rear by a thick forest. In that situation he had no fear
of an ambuscade. The enemy, he knew, had no approach but in front.
An open plain lay before him. He drew up his men in the following
order: the legions in close array formed the centre; the light-armed
troops were stationed at hand to serve as occasion might require; the
cavalry took post on the wings.

The Britons brought into the field an incredible multitude. They
formed no regular line of battle. Detached parties and loose battalions
displayed their numbers, in frantic transport bounding with exultation,

and so sure of victory that they placed their wives in wagons at the extremity of the plain, where they might survey the scene of action, and behold the wonders of British valour. Boadicea in a warlike car, with her two daughters before her, drove through the ranks; she harangued the different nations in their turn: 'This is not the first time that the Britons have been led to battle by a woman. But now she did not come to boast the pride of a long line of ancestry, nor even to recover her kingdom and the plundered wealth of her family: she took the field, like the meanest among them, to assert the cause of public liberty and to seek revenge for her body seamed with ignominious stripes, and her two daughters infamously ravished. From the pride and arrogance of the Romans nothing is sacred; all are subject to violation; the old endure the scourge, the virgins are deflowered. But the vindictive gods are now at hand. A Roman legion dared to face the warlike Britons: with their lives they paid for their rashness; those who survived the carnage of that day lie poorly hid behind their intrenchments, meditating nothing but how to save themselves by an ignominious flight. From the din of preparation and the shouts of the British army, the Romans even now shrink back with terror. What will be their case when the assault begins? Look round, and view your numbers. Behold the proud display of warlike spirits, and consider the motives for which we draw the avenging sword. On this spot we must either conquer or die with glory; there is no alternative. Though a woman, my resolution is fixed; the men, if they please, may survive with infamy and live in bondage.'

Suetonius, in a moment of such importance, did not remain silent. He expected everything from the valour of his men, and yet urged every topic that could inspire and animate them to the attack: 'Despise the savage uproar, the yells and shouts of undisciplined barbarians. In that mixed multitude, the women outnumber the men. Void of spirit, unprovided with arms, they are not soldiers who come to offer battle; they are dastards, runaways, the refuse of your swords, who have often fled before you, and will again betake themselves to flight when they see the conqueror flaming in the ranks of war. In all engagements it is the valour of a few that turns the fortune of the day; it will be your immortal glory that with a scanty number you can equal the exploits of a great and powerful army. Keep your ranks; discharge your javelins; rush forward to a close attack; bear down all with your bucklers, and hew a passage with your swords. Pursue the vanquished, and never think of spoil and plunder. Conquer, and victory gives you everything.'

This speech was received with warlike acclamations. The soldiers burned with impatience for the onset, the veterans brandished their javelins, and the ranks displayed such an intrepid countenance that Suetonius, anticipating victory, gave the signal for the charge.

The engagement began. The Roman legions presented a close-embodied line; the narrow defile gave them the shelter of a rampart. The Britons advanced with ferocity, and discharged their darts at random. In that instant, the Romans rushed forward in the form of a wedge; the auxiliaries followed with equal ardour; the cavalry, at the same time, bore down upon the enemy, and with their pikes over-powered all who dared to make a stand. The Britons betook themselves to flight; but their wagons in the rear obstructed their passage. A dreadful slaughter followed; neither sex nor age was spared; the cattle, falling in one promiscuous carnage, added to the heaps of slain. The glory of the day was equal to the most splendid victory of ancient times.

.   .   .   .   .

The consequences of the defeat were terrible to the Britons: the slaughter had been ghastly, and it was followed by famine, while, as can be imagined, the Romans returned to their domineering with a heavier hand than ever. Boadicea took her own life. The men of Mureif left their lands by the Lake, and eventually settled by the Moray* Firth in Scotland, which bears their name. Suetonius directly after the battle, as befell a good commander, got his troops in hand and prepared to strike again; a reinforcement was received from Germany, consisting of two thousand legionary soldiers, eight auxiliary cohorts, and a thousand horse. With these he brought the IXth Legion up to strength again, and established some new stations. Wherever there had been hostility the land was laid waste with fire and sword. The inactivity of the IInd Legion's headquarters praefect punished itself: feeling himself disgraced at not having taken part in the victory, he ran himself through with his sword.

What, it may be asked, was Cogidubnus of Chichester doing during this uprising? The answer is—maintaining his policy of loyalty to Rome. It is true that he may have claimed to feel himself bound by Arthur's undertaking; but even so, what would the reader, himself or herself, have done? It was women and girls of his own kindred who had been flogged and raped. We think a formula would have been found. But perhaps the reader would not have surrendered his allegiance in the first place.

Suetonius now encountered trouble of another kind. There had always been a certain degree of conflict between the Procurator's office and the military command, and at this stage, under Decianus' successor Julius Classicanus, it became acute. To quote Tacitus:

Classicanus, being at variance with Suetonius, did not scruple to sacrifice the public good to private animosity. He spread a report that another commander-in-chief might be soon expected, and in him the Britons would find a man who would bring with him neither ill-will to the natives nor the pride of victory; the vanquished would, by consequence, meet with moderation and humanity. Classicanus did not stop here: in his despatches to Rome, he pressed the necessity of recalling Suetonius. The war would otherwise never be brought to a conclusion by an officer who owed all his disasters to his own want of conduct, and his success to the good fortune of the empire.

In consequence of these complaints, Polycletus, one of the Emperor's freedmen, was sent from Rome to inquire into the state of Britain. The weight and authority of such a messenger, Nero flattered himself, would produce a reconciliation between the hostile generals, and dispose the Britons to a more pacific temper. Polycletus set out with a large retinue, and, on his journey through Italy and Gaul, made his grandeur a burden to the people. On his arrival in Britain he overawed the Roman soldiers; but his magnificent airs and assumed importance met with nothing from the Britons but contempt and derision. Notwithstanding the misfortunes of the natives, the flame of liberty was not extinguished. The exorbitant power of a manumitted slave was a novelty which those ferocious islanders could not digest. They saw an army that fought with valour, and a general who led them on to victory; but both were obliged to wait the nod of a wretched bondsman. In the report made by this man, the state of affairs was such as gave no jealousy to Nero; Suetonius therefore was continued in his government. But it happened, a short time afterwards, that a few ships were wrecked on the coast, and all on board perished in the waves; this was considered as a calamity of war, and on that account Suetonius was recalled. Petronius Turpilianus, whose consulship had just then expired, succeeded to the command.

The reason for Suetonius' recall provides an interesting object-lesson in character. The circumstances were that—'Many guilty rebels refused to lay down their arms, out of a peculiar dread of the legate; fine officer though he was, he seemed likely to abuse their unconditional surrender, and punish with undue severity wrongs which he insisted on making personal.' To their credit the authorities at Rome recognized this: 'The government therefore replaced him by Petronius Turpilianus; they hoped that he would be more merciful and readier to forgive offences to which he was a stranger.'

As the result of a kindlier approach, Turpilianus succeeded in settling the country's troubles during his governship from A.D. 62-4, though not without disparagement from Roman 'realist' critics; the half-tones they voiced run—'A languid state of tranquillity followed; the general saw the passive disposition of the Britons, and not to provoke hostilities was the rule of his conduct; he remained inactive, content to decorate his want of enterprise with the name of peace.' But the plausible term 'enterprise' was not used with generous welfare in mind; they were demanding material results for themselves, in other words conquest; they were craving for impressive physical government *by*, instead of unspectacular moral aid *to*.

Classicanus has been done an injustice; and as he is a man to whom this country is deeply indebted, the slight on his name deserves removal. The charge that he did not scruple to sacrifice public good to private animosity does not ring true; the event proves the contrary. Tacitus' father-in-law's admiration for Suetonius, under whom he had served through the crisis, seems to have led him to pass falsely harsh imputations against the man who had to press for his replacement. Yet in the light of after events we can see that Classicanus was not only right in advocating leniency, but remarkably courageous in pursuing his opinion. He was risking his own career in recommending his superior's recall; popular sentiment at Rome favoured arrogance, and Nero was hardly the type of emperor to sympathize with an unusually humane policy. Yet he pressed for it, and possibly for even more; because, in point of fact, more was done. Not only was a lenient governor appointed, but the Britons' injured pride was assuaged and their cherished wish fulfilled: Arthur was restored as native King.

The country now entered into its heyday of national spirit, very different from the 'languid state of tranquillity' of prejudiced perspective. What has been deemed uncharitably 'inaction' and

204   GUARDIAN OF THE GRAIL

'want of enterprise' was in reality the wise policy of conqueror and conquered working hand in hand; better perhaps are they regarded as external and internal authority, the one foreign, the other native. Much of this must be owed to Classicanus, probably a romanized continental Celt. We know at least that it was from his initial endeavour that the eventual outcome materialized; must he not have been a man of fine qualities? He died in London; and the remains of his tomb stand in the British Museum. Let us remember kindly the ashes it once contained, those of a man whose generous nature and moral courage now open one of the happier chapters in our national history.

12

Safe Home to Port

GREAT was the joy at Arthur's return. When he landed:

People rejoiced to see him with their own eyes; and soon they began to sing songs about Arthur the king, and the great honour he had won. Fathers kissed their sons and bid them welcome, daughters their mothers, and brothers one another; sisters kissed sisters, so happy were they in heart. And as Arthur and his household journeyed home, folk stood by the wayside in hundreds of places asking them questions of all kinds; and the Britons told them of their fortune, and boasted of what they had brought back. It is beyond man's pen to describe half the pleasure felt by the people. His men could fare over the kingdom at their will, from town to town being entertained everywhere; and thus it continued for some time—Britain revelled in her brave king.

The words are a free paraphrase from Layamon; and the same method has been followed throughout this chapter. The narrative and descriptions are taken from the romancers—Layamon, Wace, and the unknown writer for Johan de Neele—but their mediaeval wording has been adapted, because otherwise their sentences read tediously, through the constant effort to decipher the meaning of obsolete phrases. As great care as possible has been taken, though, to preserve their sense and form, so that on the one hand nothing genuinely traditional may be lost, while on the other that nothing of personal imagination may be put in. The problem has been the same as has faced the story-tellers all down the ages, how to translate from one dialect to another without tampering with accuracy. What is written here, accordingly, is for the ordinary person reading for pleasure, yet with the satisfaction of knowing that it is faithful tradition; for critical study a comparison should naturally be made with the originals; not that, it is hoped, the process will reveal any discrepancy in substance.

The need for adhering as closely as possible to the romancers comes from there being definite signs of original material being preserved in their work. For example, there is the custom of men and women eating apart from one another, especially remarked as inherited from Trojan days; there are the chieftains who took part in the coronation—Cornwall, Gloucester, Winchester, Salisbury, Canterbury, Silchester, and Leicester—all from within the limits of Roman Britain before A.D. 70; and there is the threat of war from Rome, when previously the enemy had been Saxon. All of these have the appearance of genuine tradition. On the other hand much of the coronation scene is mediaeval, and the prosperity of Caerleon within three years of its sack is impossible; to attempt to amend such description would not be feasible, though, without inserting ideas of personal invention, so it has been thought best to retain the romancers' colouring, no matter if illusory.

Actually Arthur's home-coming must have been marred by many a painful sight and thought: the scars of Boadicea's calamitous rising yet saddened the face of the land, while the Roman soldier stalked across it arrogantly, wreaking his will on a broken-spirited populace. Some slight check on overbearing behaviour may have been exercised by the Roman governor, but idleness and lax discipline were taking a hold on the legions, and, especially at a distance from headquarters, much petty offensiveness will have brought home to the people the contempt in which they were being held.

Consequently the pride and relief felt by all loyal hearts at Arthur's restoration to the kingdom were intense; and if those who had obsequiously sided with the enemy felt chagrin, they could only conceal their discomfiture and await events. For his part, Arthur's first concern was to restore confidence; and for this he had two principal agencies—the Round Table and the Church. Both of them he revived, preparatory to his coronation.

Romance makes Queen Guenevere the inspiration of his endeavours, because for some curious reason his captivity at Rome is spoken of as a 'slothful will' having fallen upon him.

Doubtless her encouragement helped and stayed him over many
an obstruction and through frequent misgivings, so, save that it
must not be imagined that Arthur was really lacking in will, the
story as handed down paints a charming domestic picture of King
and Queen together facing the task of resuscitating the country.
The scene is Caerleon Camelot, in the spring of the year.

Arthur had risen from his meal and went to the far end of the
hall, where he saw the Queen seated at a window. He went to sit
beside her, and looking at her noticed that tears were falling from
her eyes. 'Lady,' said the King, 'what aileth you, and why do you
weep?'

'Sir,' said she, 'I used to see on Ascension Day, and on other
great festivals, such a throng of knights at your Court that no
one could count them; now there are so few in it that I feel greatly
ashamed. I feel much afraid that you have forgotten your chivalry.'

'Truly, Lady,' replied the King, 'I know well that I have lost
my knights and the love of my friends.'

'Sir,' said the Queen, 'if you were to go to the chapel in
the White Forest, which will only be found after a test of en-
durance, I am sure that on your return you will regain your
desire for knightly achievement; never yet did anyone in doubt
ask counsel of God but received it, so long as he asked whole-
heartedly.'

'Lady,' answered the King, 'willingly will I go.'

There follow some remarkable adventures; and not the
least among the attractions of the story is the description of
Arthur mounting his horse, a scene plainly written by someone
familiar with the sight of a mail-clad knight doing so: In the
make of his body and in his bearing the King impressed onlookers
as being a man 'of great pith and hardiment'. He sprang into the
saddle with such vigour that the saddlebows creaked and the
horse, although a powerful beast, staggered beneath him; then
Arthur struck his spurs into his flanks, and the horse responded
with a great leap—'Lords,' said the Queen to those around her,
'seemeth he not a goodly man?' The picture is reminiscent of
a mountain battery limbering up, and of the gun-carriage mule
staggering as the load comes down on to its back; without
sympathy for the mule, but in admiration for the speed of the
work, the onlookers say—'Fine fellows, those!'

The long and short of the adventures is that Arthur is bidden by the hermit of the chapel to restore the new faith in Britain; and in token of his acceptance of the charge, Arthur overcomes a representative of the old creed, a Black Knight. As a figure of speech for the old creed of Britain, this is one of the subjects in the next chapter. The outcome of the adventures was the happy event to which everyone had been looking forward; in legend it is told of as that, while Arthur is riding back to Caerleon, he hears a voice from the thick of the forest—'King Arthur of Britain, right glad at heart mayst thou be of this that God hath sent me hither unto thee. And so he biddeth thee that thou hold Court at the earliest thou mayst, for the world shall thereof be greatly amended.'

Accordingly, having returned to Caerleon, Arthur sent out notice that he would hold Court after Whitsuntide, at Pannenoisance on the feast of St John: He decided to put it off until that day because Whitsuntide was already too near, and it might not be possible for all who ought to do so to be present by the earlier date. The knights of the Round Table, who were scattered all over the country, some in forest dwellings, heard the news with extreme pleasure, and came to the Court without delay. But neither Sir Gawain nor Lancelot attended it. Otherwise all who were still alive did so.

The knights when they arrived for St John's Day expressed surprise that the Court should not have been held at Whitsuntide, but did not know the reason for the change. St John's Day dawned fresh and clear; and within the hall, which was wide and high, was a great array of knights, with tables made ready for them spread with cloths. The King and the Queen entered the hall, washed their hands, and went to the head of one of the tables; the knights then sat down, a full five score and five of them. Kay the Seneschal and Sir Owein, the son of King Urien, with twenty-five knights beside, served the food; and Lucan the Butler served the golden cup to the King. Sunshine streamed through the windows; and the sweet herbs and flowers strewn over the rushes on the hall floor gave a scent as of balm.

Then, as happens in the accommodating circumstances of romance, no sooner had the first course been eaten and the second was being awaited than a strange procedure was beheld: a lady accompanied by a damsel entered, the damsel carrying a shield of blue and white bands charged with a red cross, which she hung against one of the hall pillars; and the lady spoke to Arthur— 'Sir, will you do me the favour of hearing the errand upon which I have come? The shield that this damsel bears belonged to Joseph, the good soldier knight who took down our Lord from the Cross. I am presenting it to you with this behest—that you shall keep the shield for a certain knight who will come here for it; you shall keep it hanging on this pillar in the hall, and guard it in such a way as that no one may take it and hang it at his neck, save only the knight for whom it is destined. That knight is the one who, with this shield, shall achieve the Grail; you will know him by his leaving in its stead another shield, red charged with a white hart.'

Fantastically though the rest of the story reads, this incident is the kernel of the whole legend of the quest of the Grail; because the White Hart is the name and symbol of the old British religion, or preferably social philosophy, for it contained nothing mystic but simply common-sense principles for a happy life. It had however become corrupt, and needed setting right; and it is the change from that old philosophy to the new faith, from the creed of the White Hart to that of the Cross, which constitutes the tale of knightly adventures in the romantic legend of the Grail. The meaning of much of the romances' peculiarly veiled language has been lost; but here and there pieces of it can be comprehended, providing between them enough for the main outline to be determined. The adventures fall into two categories: one consists of the Round Table knights' famous endeavours to prove themselves worthy of appointment to the new Church's headship; the other poetically conceals some concurrent infamous efforts, in what was merely a sordid struggle for political power.

First of all, however, let us scan the nobler features of this sadly human picture; for sad it is, despite the gaiety of courtly gatherings and the sheen of knight-errantry in tournaments. Just as in the early years of the present century, the brilliance of social London,

The lights that burn and glitter in the exile's lonely dream,
The lights of Piccadilly, and those that used to gleam
Down Regent Street and Kingsway,

was only the prelude to—'But other lights keep burning . . . when little homes lie broken and death descends from the skies,' so too the imaginative glory of knights clashing in arms for a lady-love, or punishing miscreants in righteous wrath, leads only to the final tragedy of Arthur's death; and that came to him with the full knowledge that his task was unaccomplished, and his life's work undone. The glamour and bravado were only a veneer; beneath the shimmering tinsel the spirit had tawdry streaks, the gallant would weigh his chances of personal profit, coldly calculating before drawing his sword for the faith or for love. But, like the chivalrous strain which also ran through social London, Arthur was not a man to dwell upon shortcomings; he knew his aim, he could but try, and if men failed him—'sufficient unto the day'. It was in this spirit that he held his Court; so in it let us turn to the famous quest of the Grail.

On arrival back in Britain, after his nine years' captivity at Rome, Arthur found the whole Church in languishment, in fact stricken to the point of collapse. Pwyll Avallawch lay, a bedridden cripple, in his island of Avalon; the blame for his impotence was laid on his nephew Perceval, to whom the Grail had been shown but who had delayed to speak a certain word, in plainer terms who had declined the responsibility. Not that the step to be taken required a *volte-face* in belief; on the contrary the issue was narrow, calling for wise magnanimity over a subject too often shrouded by popular prejudice. Indeed, so close were the two creeds in essence, that the Britons regarded the White Hart as the equivalent of the Old Testament; in the words of Taliesin the bard —'Christ, the Word from the beginning, was our teacher; Christianity may have been a new thing in Asia, but there was never a time when the druids of Britain held not its doctrines.' This outlook is illustrated by the following story from the quest, which will be quoted as an example of the way in which druidism could slide quietly into Christianity. It was enacted under the firm-hearted lead of Galahad.

The story as told by Malory is that Galahad, Perceval and Bors, and Perceval's sister with them, came to some wild country, and saw before them a white hart led by four lions. They agreed to follow them, and reached a valley where was a hermitage, in which a good man dwelt. The hart and the lions entered the hermitage; so they all of them turned and went into the chapel, where they saw the hermit clad in vestments. At the sacring of the mass they beheld a spectacle that made them marvel—the hart became a man, and sat himself on the altar in a fine seat. And they saw the four lions change, one to the form of a man, another to an ox, the third to an eagle, and one remained as a lion; these also sat by the hart. Then all disappeared through a glass window, without causing it any break or damage, and they heard a voice say: 'In such a manner entered the Son of God into the womb of a maid, Mary, whose virginity was untouched.'

They went to the good man, and, telling him of what they had seen, begged him to declare its meaning. 'Ah lords,' he said, 'you are welcome; now do I know that you are the good knights who will achieve the quest of the Sangreal, and to whom our Lord will show great secrets. Rightly ought our Lord to be signified by a hart, because . . . And the four creatures that were with Him are to be understood as the four evangelists, who set down in writing a part of Jesus Christ's deeds, done when He was an earthly man among men. Know this too: that never before now was the Truth known, for often in the past our Lord used to show Himself to good men in the likeness of a hart; but I suppose that from henceforth He will no more do so.'

The hermit's explanation has been omitted here, because it seems to be embellishment, except in its indirect reference to the ancient creed of 'perpetual youth'. And there are other curious occurrences with stags in romance which are to be interpreted similarly as examples of the White Hart creed, that was so deeply embedded in British life. Today traces of it are still to be found in a few distorted remnants. One of them is the Horns Dance at Abbots Bromley; there the five principal dancers are just discernible as personifying the five old principles of happiness, which constitute the Old Testament book of *Ecclesiastes*.* Further back in Elizabethan times there were 'the playing of the stag' at church doors, and the annual procession with harts' horns to St Pauls; while earlier still is to be found the shadowy figure of Herne the Hunter, the anglicized designation of the Cerne druid of the stag-headed deity Cernunnos. Descendants of the people who held that creed form much of present-day Britain.

Their name, Cerne-wy or Corna-wy,* appears on the map of
Roman Britain in Shropshire and Cheshire and the Scottish
Highlands, also near Cirencester, while it is the very root of
Corn-wall. The popular Scottish ornament of a stag's head with
a jewel between the antlers is the original symbol of their creed;
its counterpart, as the sign of Herne the Hunter, distinguishes
the arms of Windsor borough, through which we can visualize
the sign of the White Hart borne on Perceval's shield. So deeply
was its tradition engrained in the country that for Arthur to have
condemned it would have been foolish, he could only aim at its
gradual transformation. Some men would have been timorous of
experimenting with a change at a time when stability of all kinds
appeared so essential; Arthur nevertheless was resolute in his
purpose, and, just as he had taken the bold step of sponsoring the
new faith at the crisis of the Roman invasion, so now was he
renewing his endeavour.

.   .   .   .   .

The quest of the Grail is recounted chiefly in Malory's
seventeenth book, which bears the heading 'The Book of Sir
Galahad', and in a French work carrying at the end the sub-title
'The Romance of Perceval'. In them the principal actors are
Lancelot, Gawain, Perceval and Galahad, though Galahad does
not figure in the French story. On the quest, the first to repair
to the castle where the crippled Avallawch, 'King Fisherman',
lay is Gawain. He had succeeded in recovering one of the holy
relics, the sword with which John the Baptist had been beheaded,
and he brings it to hand back to Avallawch as earnest of his
sincerity. The bedroom scene, it need hardly be remarked, is
mediaeval rather than Romano-British. None the less it provides
the old-world touch; and among such details, revealing an earlier
mode of life and serving as a practical reminder of shortcomings
in cleanliness, are the several references to the pleasurable scent
of balm.

He is led into King Fisherman's chamber; it is strewn with
reeds and green herbs, so that it seems to him as though it were
strewn and sprinkled with balm. King Fisherman lies on a bed
hung on cords from ivory stays, on a straw mattress and with

a coverlet of sable fur lined with rich cloth; on his head is a cap of sable covered with red samite silk, embroidered with a golden cross, and his head rests on a pillow with four jewels at the corners, scented with balm. Facing him is a copper pedestal, on which is an eagle holding a cross of gold, within it set a piece of the True Cross which the good man adores. About him are four tall golden candlesticks, with wax tapers in them, renewed whenever required.

Gawain is then taken to the hall and feasted; and while this is happening the holy Grail appears. He sees two damsels come out of a chapel and enter the hall side by side, one bearing the Grail, and the other the Lance from the point of which blood drops into it; and this is accompanied by so sweet a scent that Gawain and the knights stop eating. Sir Gawain looks at the Grail, which seems to have a chalice within it (yet that was not so at this time), and he sees the point of the Lance from which the blood runs into it; and he thinks he sees two angels bearing candles in golden candlesticks. The damsels pass before him, and go into another chapel. Sir Gawain is thoughtful, and feels so great a joy that he thinks of nothing else but of God; the knights, though, are all disappointed and sorrowful, they look at him, and the Master of the knights beckons to him to act. Sir Gawain gazes in front of him, and sees three drops of blood fall upon the table; he is abashed, and speaks never a word. At that the two damsels again come before the table; and it appears to him that there are now three persons, and that the third is the Grail which has become flesh, in the form of a crowned King above it, but nailed to a cross and with a spear fast in his side. Sir Gawain sees this with great sorrow, and thinks of naught else but the pain that the King is suffering. The Master of the knights then speaks to him, telling him that if he delays longer he will be given no further chance; but Sir Gawain is silent, as though he did not hear him, his eyes cast upwards. The damsels withdraw to the chapel, taking with them the most holy Grail and the Lance; the knights rise from the tables, order the cloths to be cleared away, and go into another hall. Sir Gawain is left alone. His silence has been fatal; he has failed in the test.

Following upon this Lancelot rashly attempts, a little time afterwards, to force his way into the Grail chapel, for which he is struck unconscious and lies in a stupor for twenty-four days. The chapel is 'Carbonek'.* When he has recovered, he is told that his wife Elaine has died; he returns to Arthur's Court at Camelot. A few remarks must now be made about Lancelot's attitude towards the Church: from the outset it suggests self-interest, not moral zeal. For, when the Round Table was instituted, twenty years earlier, the chief seat in it—the Siege Perilous—had been left vacant, with the declaration that only the man should sit in it who would achieve the Sangreal; Lancelot thereupon rode off on an adventure, which took him to the place where it was kept, and there, after being shown it, he married Pwyll Avallawch's daughter Elaine. By her he had a son Galahad. His behaviour to Elaine, though, rings hollow; in the generous wording of romance he went out of his mind and left her (which, although the tale makes it take place just after Arthur's return from Rome, must have happened a few years before that), but the truth seems to be that he deserted Elaine at the time of Boadicea's national rising, when he saw no more value in the Church. Then, after Arthur's restoration, he once more patronized it; as the romance puts it, he was made sound again by Elaine, healed through the virtue of the Grail. But he tried to gain its headship forcibly; and he was denied it.

Finally the supreme test is accomplished by Galahad, or, according to the French version, by Perceval. The discrepancy is a matter for critical analysis, but does not affect the present subject; it is sufficient to know that in either case there is great rejoicing. At Caerleon the extraordinary occurrence is seen of two suns shining simultaneously, one from the east and another from the west, while a voice speaks to Arthur—'King, marvel not that two suns should appear in the sky, for our Lord God hath well the power to do this. Understand that it is a sign of joy for the conquest which the Good Knight hath made; he hath regained the land belonging to good King Fisherman from the evil king who had abolished the new faith, for which reason the Grail had been hidden. Now God desires you to go thither, with the best knights of your Court; for a better pilgrimage could not be made. And when you return hither, your faith will be doubled; and the people of Britain will be better disposed and better taught to maintain the service of the Saviour.'

The Grail, however, does not remain in Britain. In the romance of Perceval, the knight hears a voice say—'Perceval, you shall not long abide here; wherefore it is God's will that you distribute the holy relics amongst the hermits of the forest. The most holy Grail shall no more appear here, but within a brief space of time you shall learn of the place where it will be.' Shortly afterwards a ship comes to the shore; and in it Perceval sails away, none know whither.

In the romance of Galahad, the figure of Christ appears from out of the Grail, and Christ himself takes the holy vessel and approaches Galahad. The knight and his fellows kneel down; and the Grail is served to them by Christ, who says to Galahad—'My son, do you know what it is that I hold in my hands?' Galahad replies: 'No. But tell me, if you will.' 'This is,' says Christ, 'the holy dish on which I ate the lamb on Sher-Thursday. Now you have seen what you had most desired to see; but yet have you not seen it so openly as you shall in the city of Sarras, in the spiritual place. Therefore you must leave here, and take with you this holy vessel; for tonight it shall leave the realm of England, nor will it ever be seen here again. Knowest thou why? Because I am not served nor worshipped aright by the people of this land, who have turned to evil ways; for this I shall disinherit them of the honour which I had done them.' So Galahad, Perceval and Bors ride to the seashore, where they find a ship awaiting them; and in it they sail to the city of Sarras.* There, one day a hand is seen to reach down from heaven; it comes right to the Sangreal, and takes it and the spear and bears it up to heaven. Nor after this is any man so bold as to say that he has seen the Sangreal.

Such is the legend. It tells us that all was not well in Avalon. On that account, when Pwyll Avallawch died, not long after the quest of the Grail had been achieved, Arthur probably took the opportunity of transferring the seat of the Church to Glastonbury. He moved it from the Isle of Avalon, that is to say Wight, to the little hill in the Somerset valley of the Brue, where in A.D. 63 or 64 he granted it twelve hides of land free of all tax in perpetuity. Remarkably enough part of the hides today carry the name Ynis Witrin, Isle of Wight. Glastonbury lay in Joseph of Arimathea's own country, and Joseph himself was to be buried there some ten years later, in A.D. 72; but chiefly what drew the Church to the site was the great tradition which lived in the neighbourhood and still does:

> And did those feet in ancient time
>   Walk upon England's mountains green?
> And was the Holy Lamb of God
>   In England's pleasant pastures seen?

It would seem that Arthur realized that conditions in Wight were not such as to enable the Church to withstand the popular appeal of the old creed, by which it had already been assailed; so he transferred the seat of his fresh effort to the West Country. Thither it was that he directed the pilgrimage he had been bidden to make.

.   .   .   .   .

At Whitsuntide of the year after his return from captivity, Arthur's coronation was celebrated with great ceremony. In Wace's chronicle this took place at Caerleon on Usk, after his return from France; but it is clear that the locality must have been Caerleon on Itchen, and the event to have happened after his return from Rome, because prior to then the town had not existed. With those modifications in Wace's story, and with some allowance for gilding at the hand of Time, let us look on the picture of the scene:

Arthur took counsel with his lords, and decided that in order for his position and authority to be proclaimed the more clearly, he would be crowned in the presence of all the leading men in the realm. The festival would be held at the beginning of summer, at Pentecost. Accordingly he commanded all the notables who owed him allegiance to attend at Caerleon; he chose that city because it was the finest in the kingdom, and a wonderfully pleasant one. . . .

On the morning of the coronation itself, first of all a dignified procession of bishops and abbots, headed by the archbishop, made its way to the King's palace, to place the crown on his head and escort him to the church. Then from the palace four princes led the way, each bearing a sword in his hands, pommel and hilt and scabbard of wrought gold. First of the four was Albany, next came Gower, then Gwynedd, and then Cador of Cornwall; this was the customary procedure when Arthur held his Court in state. And all of these great princes were at unity with one another, with one purpose: the crowning of Arthur as King. Then came King Arthur, supported by two bishops; they walked on either side of him through the streets, and, when the church was reached, placing a hand under either arm, carried him to the throne. The church service and ceremony were performed by the Archbishop Dubric, as prelate of Caerleon.

In order that the Queen might be equally honoured, she was crowned separately. She had bidden to her Court the great ladies of the realm, wives of her friends, ladies of her kindred, others of her choice, and many comely maidens whom she wished to attend her at the festival. The presence of this gay company of ladies when the Queen was crowned in her chamber, and when she was brought to the church of the convent for the conclusion of the rites, made the ceremonial even more brilliant. The streets were so tightly packed with people that there was scarcely room for the Queen's procession to pass along them. She was preceded by four ladies, carrying four white doves in their hands; they were the consorts of the four princes who bore the golden swords before the King. Behind the Queen followed a beautiful train of damsels, singing and making merry; they came of the noblest families in the land, and were marvellously dainty, wearing rich mantles over silken dresses, and with their heads attired in the brightest of wimples. Never were to be seen so many splendid dresses of different colours, such costly mantles, so precious jewels and rings, nor such furs and embroidery; never was known so gay and noble a procession. Men gazed at it in delight, for in that retinue of beauty none was fairer than another. And they pressed forward to the church, lest they should miss taking part in the ceremony.

The processions having reached their respective churches, and the King and Queen having taken their places, Mass was celebrated with due pomp and reverence. In each church the organ's notes echoed through the building, and the clergy in the choir sang melodiously, their voices swelling or falling accordingly with the chant's rising in praise or fading away in supplication. The knights passed from one church to the other; now they would be at the convent of St Julius, now at the cathedral church of

St Aaron; this they did in order to compare the singing of the choirs, and to enjoy the loveliness of the damsels. They came and went from church to church frequently, nor was it possible to say at which they remained the longer; so sweet was the music that they could not listen to it enough; truly, had the singing continued the whole day through, it is doubtful whether the knights would have wearied of it.

The ceremony having drawn to its appointed end and the last words chanted, the King took off the crown which he had worn for the service, and put on a lighter one; so did the Queen. Likewise they changed from the heavy robes and jewels of state, into less tiring clothes. The King left St Aaron's church and returned to his palace for the banquet; and the Queen for her part went back to her own hall, accompanied by that beautiful and lively train of ladies, still rejoicing. For the Britons still kept the custom, brought by their sires from Troy, that men and women should dine separately; and the only men present in the ladies' hall were the servants. Their banquet was as stately as the King's. . . .

When the fourth day of the week was come, on a certain Wednesday, the King bestowed various honours. He dubbed knight some of the youths then serving under his knights' banners, granting them lands in support of their duties; and he rewarded those lords of his household who held land from him for their service. Such clerics as had been diligent in their Master's business he made abbots and bishops; and on his own counsellors and friends he awarded castles and towns. To everyone Arthur gave most bountifully.

.   .   .   .   .

While yet this was happening, the rejoicing and merriment of the occasion were rudely broken, so Wace tells us, by an astounding message from the Romans, threatening war. On the face of what classical evidence there is, this would appear to be complete fiction: Petronius Turpilianus was Governor, and of him Tacitus records explicitly that he 'risked no further move before handing over his province to Trebellius Maximus', which he did not do until the year after this event. Though of his successor he writes that he 'was deficient in energy and without military experience, but he governed his province like a gentleman. . . . There was, however, a serious outbreak of mutiny; for the troops, accustomed to campaigns, ran riot in peace. Trebellius fled and hid to escape his angry army; . . . by a kind of tacit bargain the troops kept their licence, the general his life, and the mutiny stopped short of bloodshed.' Reading between the lines, therefore, there seems the possibility of real foundation for Wace's story.

The Roman government may have been conciliatory, but the soldiery were spoiling for aggression, which for them meant plunder; peace-time idleness, with looting forbidden, made discipline in camp galling and tended to induce disorderliness. For some little time before this had reached the stage of mutiny, therefore, some of the commanders must have noticed that there was trouble brewing, and have suggested to the Governor that a small campaign would help them to restore discipline. Tacitus' phrase, that the Governor 'risked no further move', certainly allows the inference that some further move was proposed to him. So let us suppose that the suggestion was made, and that the Governor approached Arthur confidentially—What would be southern Britain's attitude if the northern Roman boundary were advanced from Wroxeter and Lincoln to the Mersey–Humber line, making a more practicable frontier? This unexpected blow to hopes of mutual co-operation came to Arthur just at the close of his coronation festival. Consulting his two leading chiefs, Cador of Cornwall whose province had escaped the ravages of Boadicea's revolt, and Gawain of Albany whose lands had suffered the full weight of the disaster, he received replies much in the tenor of Wace's picturesque wording:

As they mounted the *steps*, earl and prince, pell-mell together, Cador, who was a merry man, saw the king before him: 'Fair king,' said the early gaily, 'for a great while the thought has disturbed me, that peace and soft living are rotting away the British bone. Idleness is the stepdame of virtue, as our preachers have often told us. Soft living makes a sluggard of the hardiest knight, and steals away his strength. She cradles him with dreams of woman, and is the mother of chambering and wantonness. Folded hands and idleness cause our young lads (damoiseaux) to waste their days over merry tales and dice, raiment to catch a lady's fancy, and things that are worse. Rest and assurance of safety will in the end do Britain more harm than force or guile.

May the Lord God be praised who has jogged our elbow. To my mind he has persuaded these Romans to challenge our country that we may get us from sleep. If the Romans trust so greatly in their might that they do according to their letters, be assured the Briton has not yet lost his birthright of courage and hardiness. I am a soldier and have never loved a peace that lasts over long, since there are uglier things than war.'

Gawain overheard these words. 'Lord earl,' said he, 'by my faith be not fearful because of the young men. Peace is very grateful after war. The grass grows greener, and the harvest is more plenteous. Merry tales and songs, and ladies' love, are delectable to youth; by reason of the bright eyes and the worship of his (lady) friend, the bachelor becomes knight and learns chivalry.'

Cador's cheery stout-heartedness decided Arthur. He answered the Governor that it would be unwise for him to incur the risk of a sympathetic rising in the South. The threatening cloud vanished; and once more there spread over Caerleon the sunshine of a strong man's peace.

13

The Haven under the Hill

THE gaiety of the coronation ended, and its concourse's splendour dispersed into jewel casket and chest, Arthur and his Court returned to their serious task of repairing the country's damaged state; this, if momentarily put out of mind in the thankfulness and pageantry of his restoration, lay very close to the surface. For the last fourteen years, ever since his revolt against Ostorius, the people had felt the weight of alien rule, unmitigated by the sympathy which he as native king could have interposed. Forced supplies to feed troops, followers and animals, forced labour to build camps and roads, these had been their lot; they had learned that—'We gain nothing by submission except heavier burdens for willing shoulders . . . the legate to wreak his fury on our lives, the procurator on our property.' Revolt had brought worse—pillage, sack and famine, the people were impotent and being trampled upon, there were many sores to heal.

These sores were not only physical but of the soul. The physical ones needed stable conditions and time, they would then mend of their own accord; those of the soul wanted national contentment and pride to be restored. And so the factor common to both, to stability and to contentment, was the first requisite. Looking back over the past fourteen years, the unstabilizing influence had been discontent with any form of rule: Roman rule had rankled, native rule had irked; each province had desired to be independent, while even within provinces were dissentient factions; disintegration was a national obsession. There was no public spirit. Fundamentally the lack was due to sheer selfishness; so, to combat this and to produce the co-operative will that would give internal peace and allow the country's prosperity to recover, a sounder moral sense had to be inculcated. The first step towards it, the choice of a man to head the movement, has already been narrated under its legendary name, the Quest of the Holy Grail; but that was only a preparatory measure, for practical accomplishment popular opinion had to be captured. Thus there is material interest in appreciating the reasons which led Arthur to adopt his particular method of restoring the country's soul.

Two agencies lay at his hand for stimulating a healthier patriotism, and the sense of public spirit that would put duty to others before self-interest—there were the druids, who taught the old national creed, and the Church, with its new faith. Both preached the same principle. Druidic doctrine pronounced that man's affairs should be governed by reason, and that one of the prerequisites for sound reasoning was a selfless character, so that opinion should be unbiased by any personal consideration; it taught that man was endowed for the purpose with the faculties of acquiring knowledge and of making moral choice, and that over selflessness he must train himself to be prepared to go to the extreme, readiness to lay down his life for his fellows:

'Three duties of every man: worship God, be Just to all men, die for your Country.'

But in practice druidism had failed to evoke that character. When it came to the point, men would quibble over what was their country, narrowing it down to something closely akin to their local interests; Britain as an island had not been welded into a single people with a common purpose. Was druidism capable of doing that? Arthur must have asked himself the question, and apparently concluded otherwise. Nor is it conceivable, from the evidence which has come down to us, that an Albany druid would ever have preached the unpopular theme of amending cherished habits in order to strengthen the position of a Cornish king, the main source of resentment.

The new Church, however, founded as it was on the supreme example of self-sacrifice, preached unselfishness conspicuously; and it taught it as a divine behest, from a Power above human comprehension. It appealed to minds mistrustful of human reasoning, but which wanted to feel none the less that right behaviour was assured. It was faith in the practical need for morality, though with its reasons for the morals placed beyond the scope of argument. But the Church had not, colloquially speaking, caught on; it had been smothered forcibly, and even though it was now being resuscitated, something was amiss. The actual event had not yet happened, but the circumstances were taking shape that were to cause the Good Knight at its head to remove the hallowed relics elsewhere. It was powerless to influence public ways. Furthermore there had been a rift between it and druidism; the two were not acting in concert to preach a better morality. Merlin had desired that they should, the one teaching it as divine behest, the other on the grounds of reason; but Merlin was no more. Arthur must have remembered his warning that he would miss him—'Ye had lever than all your lands to have me again'—and it was he who had broadmindedly advised Arthur to take to himself the Church's sword. Now indeed the time had come: the lands were Arthur's, in name but not wholly in spirit; he was facing the feebleness of a people whose hearts were not at one amongst themselves.

Casting his mind back over the circumstances which had produced the country's fallen fortunes, Arthur must have reflected that when he had called for united endeavour he had received mistrust; the withholding of support had not only been negative action in manœuvres of rivalry, but also was positive distrust from minds steeped in it. The same mutual distrust was keeping the new and old faiths from acting in concert. He had no cause to doubt his own integrity; the enemy whom he had thrice flouted had none the less deemed him trustworthy and fit to govern both loyal adherents and jealous rivals; the latters' suspicion that he would not do so fairly was not upheld by an outside opinion. There must, though, have been some reason in the national character for rulers' impartiality always to be suspect; stripped of exoneration the plain truth was that goodwill was lacking, there was not the generous frame of mind that could see fellow-men in a broad-minded light and would co-operate. His countrymen were generous in matters material, but not in those of opinion; and it was over opinion that tolerance was so greatly wanted, in order that priest and druid might combine to generate moral uplift and contentment, and that the land might recognize sincerity in a ruler when it stood before them. The source of goodwill lay in the same teaching as selflessness; both moral agencies needed encouragement.

A factor in favour of the new faith's acceptability, which might weigh with a people proud of itself, was its intimate personal connection with Britain. A number of leading persons in the land were closely related to the Holy Family. In the words of tradition, King Arthur was but eight degrees removed from Jesus Christ; Pwyll Avallawch and his daughter Elaine and her son Galahad were in a similar degree of kinship, and so also were St David (said to be Arthur's kinsman) and the children of Arthur's sister Anna, with many others. It was a prized tradition—'and Sir Galahad is of the ninth degree from our Lord Jesu Christ, therefore I dare say they be the greatest gentlemen of the world,' thus speaks Guenevere in Malory's story; while the Grail romance opens—'Good knight was *Perceval* of right, for he was of the lineage of Joseph of Abarimacie' (the Virgin Mary's uncle); and several Welsh pedigrees mention Anna,* whose name has become displaced but seems originally to have implied 'of the family of Amlodd':* 'his mother was Anna, who is said to have been cousin to the Virgin Mary, mother of our Lord Jesus Christ.'

This honoured relationship came through the family of Amlodd, as is shown in the table below; in it the numerals indicate how the expression that Galahad was of the 'ninth degree' was reached:

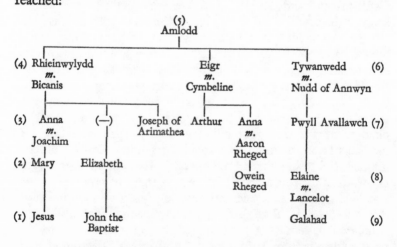

There are the inevitable slips of oral tradition. Thus Arthur being of the 'eighth degree' is not correct unless there has been another generation between Eigr and Amlodd; this though, judging from the relative ages of Arthur and Avallawch, would appear actually to have been the case. So also Avallawch, as King Fisherman, when speaking of Galahad as being of 'my' blood of the ninth degree, means obviously that of the family to which he was kins-man; and when Lancelot is said to be of the eighth degree from Christ, he is being mistaken for his wife Elaine. Descent from Amlodd introduces a great number of other well-known names not entered above, mainly belonging to the West Country; and this table demonstrates why the sword with which John the Baptist was beheaded should have been among the holy relics, showing as it does the family nature of his position.

Accordingly Arthur renewed his encouragement of the Church, particularly in the West Country, where, besides endow-ing Glastonbury with twelve hides of land, he helped establish other churches. Several tales seem to belong to this period, which presumably represents the 'pilgrimage' he was told to make. Among them is a story from the *Life of St Carannog*, which remarkably enough hints at Arthur's unwillingness to supplant whatever was good in druidism. It runs that Arthur and Cador were together ruling in the West, at Dindraethwy (which A. Wade-Evans takes to be Dundry near Bristol), when Arthur came to Carhampton in Somerset where Carannog was in search of a formidable serpent—by which is implied a 'dragon' druid. The saint wished to learn from Arthur where his altar had landed, for he had cast it into the sea from the Welsh coast; the conversation ended in a bargain being struck that, should the saint deal with the serpent, Arthur would find the altar. Previously Arthur had cogitated turning the altar into a table, but he had found that it tossed off everything placed upon it. In the end the King gives Carhampton to Carannog, who builds a church there. Then a voice from heaven bids Carannog cast his altar again into the sea, and the saint calls upon Arthur and Cador to enquire where it has landed; this proves to be at the Gannal estuary in Cornwall, and there Arthur gives him land to build a church at Crantock.

Another incident of the same kind is the encounter between Ederyn or 'Ider', the son of Nudd, and the giants of Brent Knoll, at the mouth of the Brue in Somerset. Ederyn having joined the new faith, Arthur took him there and bade him defeat the giants in order to prove himself. The fight was won, but it almost brought about the death of Ederyn; which caused Arthur to endow twenty-four monks to say mass for his soul, in remorse for having come late to his aid. Ederyn's brother Gwyn ab Nudd was a celebrated astronomer, said to be able to predict whatever was wished to be known to the end of the world; their home was Annwyn, the vale of the Ann or Test, consequently it is of interest that Wace should have mentioned, when describing the coronation, that the Caerleon priests were astronomers who 'often enough prophesied to Arthur what the future would bring'. The astrologers of Nudd had been absorbed into the Church. Their memory is with us still, in the nursery name for the sky, the 'land of Nod'.

Gwyn however did not become a churchman, but retained his position as King of the Fairies. For this he had a flask of holy water poured on to his head by a later Abbot of Glastonbury—but that is another story.

The curious tale of Gwyn ab Nudd and Cordelia the daughter of Lear would also seem to belong to this period, and to refer to the land round Silchester.* It will be remembered that Cordelia had married a chieftain of the Pas de Calais; while from subsequent events it appears that he was given as a dowry the Silchester district (evidently a conquest by Lear south of the Thames), accounting for the fact that in Julius Caesar's day there were Atrebates from Arras ruling it. After Lear's death both Cornwall and Albany contested its ownership, as is related by Geoffrey of Monmouth; and the dispute evidently lasted until Arthur's day, when Gwythur* mab Greidiawl and Gwyn ab Nudd strove for the land, personified as Cordelia. Arthur's settlement for the dispute was that the district should be independent, but that the subject should be raised for reconsideration every May-day—which was the beginning of the legislative year, to judge from the annual congregation of the Eagle druids of the Lake on that day.

But there was more in Arthur's settlement than that, as is told by the French story of the Grail, in the interpretation put forward by Sir John Rhys. Gwyn ab Nudd was a hater of Christians, and threw into prison two of the men he had captured. Both were rescued, though, one of them by a hand which appeared from a cloud, and which struck off his fetters; and in this we can recognize the hand grasping a sword pictured on page 106, Arthur's

Caliburn. Gwyn ab Nudd was evidently a confirmed adherent of the old faith; but Arthur was equally resolute for the new, so, once a year the two faiths met competitively.

Nevertheless all was by no means well between Arthur and the Church; as, from a tale of St Cadog, it seems that the Church were attempting to arrogate to itself the right of sanctuary for wrongdoers, against his will. The site of the event is commonly taken to be the Usk valley, in Monmouthshire; but taking into account Cadog's birthplace, and the location of the college where he studied, and the identities of his associates, it seems more likely to have been that hot-bed of unrest, the border-land between Cornwall and Albany fringing upon the Lake. As Usk simply means 'water', any river may have been intended. Without however insisting upon any particular quarter of Britain to have been the scene, Arthur was certainly at issue with the Church over a matter of principle.

The dispute began with Cadog, who was born in the Gwyn* valley, giving refuge to a Briton who had killed three of Arthur's soldiers. Arthur came to the district and demanded the man for trial; Cadog faced him on the opposite bank of a river, supported by St David of the Mynyw, St Teilo of the Gwyn valley, and Dochau of the West Country, together with clerics from all over the land. Feeling ran strong, and the argument was conducted across the water from either bank. Arthur claimed one hundred cattle as a fine; the most that Cadog would concede for his ward was three 'best oxen' for each man slain, nine in all. Arthur eventually accepted this, except for stipulating that they must be cows, red afore and white aft—a difficult proviso. Cadog told his followers to produce any nine heifers, which was done; and straightway they were changed by God to the right colouring. The situation remained however very delicate; for doubts were held about the method of delivery of the kine, and Cadog typified the Church militant, being remembered as one of the country's 'protectors of innocence—through church law, common law, and the law of arms'. However, agreement was reached, that Cadog should drive the cattle to the centre of the ford, where Arthur, Kay and Bedivere should receive them, everyone else remaining seated on the banks. Even so, when Kay and Bedivere took the animals by the horns they were miraculously transformed into bundles of fern—the Church had had the last word! And so, in the end, Arthur granted Cadog the right of sanctuary.

Philosopher as he was, we can picture Arthur returning with Kay and Bedivere to a hill-top camp, where they play dice together; which is how they figure in another tale. And, although the story does not say so, if during the game Arthur remarked ruminatively—'That turbulent priest is going to come to a sticky end,' we can appreciate that he was speaking prophetically, not voicing a wishful thought.

.   .   .   .   .

Scenes from the adventures of Arthur's knights, when bound on proselytizing quests, are described in several of the stories from Lady Charlotte Guest's *Mabinogion;* these are The Lady of the Fountain, Peredur the son of Evrawc, and Geraint the son of Erbin. The first of them is particularly interesting, and is paralleled by the VIIIth part of Malory's *Morte d'Arthur*, the part about Sir Gareth. It tells of what was more or less the social code of thought of a considerable proportion of the populace; so, as this exercised a good deal of indirect influence on events of the time, it will be narrated in some detail. The code of thought is cloaked in the form of a custom; and it is the prevalence of that custom rather than its nature which is the important point, for the moment, as the frequency with which it occurs in Arthurian legends indicates the extent of the influence.

The leading figure in the custom is a 'black man' or black knight, so called from the garments worn, and from the tabard over the knight's armour and the caparisons of his horse. He guards a stone slab near a spring of water (called a 'fountain'), and he is associated with other men clad in green, red, and blue; to these colours a fifth is to be added by inference, white, as it figures in the magic agency of a ring. The five have a significance, each one standing for an article of the creed which the whole group represents; but the five are properly black, green, red, gold, and white. Blue has been an inversion for gold; the reason for the inversion is immaterial to the present story, but it is worth remarking that Malory was aware of some mistake, for he does not speak of blue by its direct name, but calls it obliquely

the 'colour of Ind', an expression that might equally well apply
to gold.

Black was the chief colour; and up to a point it represents the
group. It was the people's 'lucky' colour, derived from the
thunder-cloud which brings rain and prosperity—for the custom
had come with the people from the East, where good luck or the
reverse over rain was a serious concern. The Black Man was
originally a rain-maker; in Britain, though, his professional
services were scarcely in demand, and he was more realistically
a wise-man, whose title has since degenerated into wizard. Yet it
should be appreciated that rain-making was more than mere
indulgence in magic; it was early meteorology, and the wise-men
were or had been advanced astronomers, who kept the calendar
and who studied the sky. Among some the science had become
charlatanism, but amongst the genuine it had developed into
remarkably accurate powers of observation. The ritual evidences,
however, that corruption had taken hold of the institution, and
that the rain-maker's privileges were dependent on strength,
wisdom having given place to force. Consequently, if anyone
wished to challenge the ownership of the position, he would make
his way to the fountain, where the slab stood beneath a tree, and
dash a bowl of water on to the slab; a terrific thunder-storm would
follow, after which he would have to fight the Black Knight, and,
as described in Sir James Frazer's *Golden Bough*, it would be a case
of the survival of the fittest. The victor married the Lady of the
Fountain, to whom were attached land and handmaidens.

It is easy to visualize the corrupt aspect of the institution, and
perhaps too easy, as it blinds the eye to the fact that a distinctly
moral doctrine was perpetuated by it. That could have been
transmitted from wizard to wizard in either of two ways. If the
legends are to be taken literally, the outgoing Black Man was
killed by his rival and could pass on nothing; but it is by no
means impossible that, as with other adventures in romance, the
idiom of physical combat may in reality have been only a battle of
wits, with a peaceable transfer of duties. More probably, though,
the continuity of doctrine came through the Lady of the Fountain
and her handmaidens, who stood in relation to the Black Man as
did the ladies of the Lake to the knight achieving the Grail;
indeed the prominence with which women were associated with

druidism, such as in the many 'Nine Maidens' stone circles and in the many witch survivals, indicates that women customarily held responsible positions in religious practice.

The nature of the 'Black' doctrine, like that of the White Hart, can be summarized as the equivalent of the Old Testament book of *Ecclesiastes;** it was a widespread ancient faith, and a distinctly moral one, its philosophical enquiries leading to the conclusion: 'This is the end of the matter, all hath been heard: fear God and keep his commandments, for this is the whole duty of man.' Thus the Black Man and his acolytes occupied a strong place in popular affection; they were venerated for their inherent goodness, for their extreme antiquity, for the surreptitious feeling that perhaps they really did bring luck, and for all the ties belonging to old established ways. But they had failed to inculcate the unselfishness needed for a healthy public spirit, in point of fact the competitive nature of the institution's headship practically precluded its doing so; consequently, as we have seen, Arthur found it necessary to replace it with a creed that preached disinterested goodness. In his doing so, the friction with vested interests and prejudices can well be imagined; the Round Table knights' combats with 'black knights' are likely accordingly to have consisted more of tact and compromise than of blows, into which commonplace texture Time has woven a romantic thread of gallantry.

The scene of Owain's encounter with one of these offers a realistic picture of the site. At the head of a valley the ground sloped upwards to a plateau, where beneath a tree rose a spring, and beside the spring lay the ritual slab with its bowl. The tree in the story of Sir Gareth is a blackthorn; and, although the resemblance of the ground is perhaps too remote for the site to be suggested as Glastonbury itself, yet the picture certainly gives a vivid idea of what used to take place by Chalice Well in pre-Christian days. Another realistic scene is also described later, in the story of *The Lady of the Fountain.* After having vanquished the Black Knight, Owain eventually came to a craggy mound in the middle of a wood, where a serpent resided; he saw the serpent attack a lion, to whose rescue he went and slew the serpent, causing the lion to become his devoted companion. Like the serpent, the lion can be understood as being a druid, and one that is to be identified with the name Catherine given to many hills in southern

England; the lady was once the deity of the Lion people, more familiar in Britain through their diminutive emblem the Cat, before she became a Christian 'saint'. It is curious that one of the St Catherine hills, the one near Guildford, used to bear the earlier name of Drake-low, that is to say Dragon or Serpent's Hill; these names in themselves tell us that originally the hill was tenanted by a Serpent druid, who later gave way to a Lion one, who in turn was replaced by the Church—and canonized. It is not necessarily to be assumed that the Guildford hill is the site of Owain's encounter; all that can be said is that the story of Owain draws a vivid picture of a similar event which took place there. However faint may be the resemblances with romance of sites such as Glastonbury and Guildford, knowing them enables a livelier mental view to be gained of what took place in Arthurian days; it brings us into closer contact with the rather fantastically written legendary deeds, otherwise so far removed from us in time.

Even more tangibly the Black Man's descendants can be recognized as living amongst us today, in the shape of persons bearing one or other of several well-known surnames. In the Breton version of *The Lady of the Fountain* the Black Knight is called Le Rous, anglicized in the English translation to The Rouse; this name has come down to modern times as Rous, Roos, or Ros, and sometimes mistakenly even as Rose and Ross, the error in the latter and their true Le Rous origin being indicated by the water-bags borne on their shields of arms, with, in at least one instance, a black-haired man's head as crest. The water-bag in particular denotes the rain-maker; it represents the stock-in-trade of the heavenly rain-maker Aquarius, the *mussack* or skin-bag from which he waters the earth. So too the water-bags and black-haired man's head of the Bourchiers or Bouchers point to the same origin, the surname referring to the emblem instead of the reverse as is often supposed.

Much of the strangeness in the romances can thus be rendered comprehensible as real occurrences, among persons and places such as we know in everyday life; not all of course can be disentangled, some incidents have become too garbled, but there is enough to illustrate the general trend of what was happening. We see Arthur carefully but determinedly setting his knights to the task of clearing the land of insincerity. The common good was to be everyone's aim; self-interest was to be abandoned. Old faiths were to be retained, as foundations for a better edifice than had been raised upon them in the past. The White Hart was recognized as the forerunner of Christianity; Herne the Hunter was bracketed with the archangel Gabriel; the deity Beli Mawr was metamorphosed into St. George; likewise the deity of the Khatti Eireann became St Catherine, as did that of the Yew-tree Iubor become St Hubert. The charity which accompanied the Black Man of the Fountain's position was taken over by the Church; it is illustrated by the sequel to the Church's disablement when Arthur was at Rome:

In the wells and springs of *England* harboured damsels who fed the wayfarer with meat and pasties and bread. But *Aaron* did wrong to one and carried off her golden cup, so that never more came damsels out of the springs to comfort the wanderer. And the men of *Aaron* followed his evil example. Therefore the springs dried up, and the grass withered, and the land became waste, and no more might be found the court of the Rich Fisher, which had filled the land with plenty and splendour.

Not all of the transformation is to be attributed to Arthur; but it was he who started it off on a right course, and that was his main concern at this juncture. To repeat what has already been observed, the legendary tales of dragons being slaughtered, wrongdoers put wholesale to the sword, and evil customs abolished ruthlessly, must be interpreted with latitude; the customs may have been bad but they were much liked, and the dragons may have behaved scandalously yet they gave a lot of benefit; while as for the knights themselves, having rid the sacred places of the men who conducted them so disgracefully, they usually found it fit to marry the lady of the place themselves and continue the practices, though on a higher level. The principle of the change was evolutionary not revolutionary; a *modus vivendi* was found for old and new together, which is why some of the greatly valued remnants of the past are with us still; even the lion could lie down with the lamb, provided that (as the apocryphal story tells) the lamb were replaced sufficiently often! Behind the almost happy-go-lucky method of change, though, was an inflexible social purpose—the common good; and with this as his aim, and with good nature as the way, Arthur set about rebuilding Merry England.

14

Only to Founder

IT WILL have been at the Whitsuntide following Arthur's coronation that the quest of the Grail was achieved. But with it, quarrels which already had been festering came to a head. Scarcely had Arthur seen the two suns and heard the voice bidding him make his pilgrimage, than he became involved in a feud with Kay the Seneschal, previously one of his most trusted knights and his foster-brother. As the tale stands, Kay had killed Arthur's son, without the King having been aware of it until now; needless to say, such a circumstance is inconceivable and the story may have arisen through a confusion of Arthur's son Gwydr with another Gwydr, grandson of Kaw, whose death similarly occasioned enmity between Arthur and the sons of Kaw. Kay* and Kaw* are not the same person; but they came from the same district, the Pictland lying between the mouth of the Meon (Mynyw) river and Alclud (Butser Hill), and without enquiring into their families it is sufficient to know that Arthur was encountering trouble in that area.

The exact nature of the trouble is concealed in the customary picturesque language of personification; so the story will be told in the form in which it has been handed down, without attempt at disentangling the allusions. The enmity with the sons of Kaw began, so it is said, through Howel son of Kaw having stabbed Gwydr, his own nephew, son of his sister Gwenabwy; which, for some unstated reason, aroused Arthur's anger. To this was added rivalry between Arthur and Howel over a lady whom both were courting; it led to a fight, in which Arthur was worsted, receiving a wound in the thigh that left him with a limp. Some time later the King fell in love with another lady, and, in order that he might enjoy her company the more often, he used to dress himself up in women's clothes; one day, however, when he was dancing with her, Howel recognized him because of his lameness, and observed—'This dancing might do very well, but for the thigh.' Arthur overheard his remark, and was so incensed that he had Howel executed.

Whatever these tales may mean, the sons of Kaw left the district. Not unconnected with their dissatisfaction may have been the circumstance that Arthur had given the primacy at Caerleon—termed 'the abbacy of the island of Britain'—to Dewi in preference to one of the sons of Kaw, Gildas. Nor was this necessarily nepotism; for Dewi (St David), besides being a definite person and kinsman of Arthur, represents also the absorption into the Church of the Black fraternity. His distinctive colour black, recorded in *The Seven Champions of Christendom*, and his Watermen render the identity unmistakable. And black, for the revised principles of *Ecclesiastes*,* was allotted to Selflessness, the very school of thought that Arthur wished to encourage. May it not be that Arthur was now appreciating the wisdom of Merlin's advice, and introducing the new through the agency of the old? Gildas' school perhaps tended to be laxer, for he accuses Dewi's of over-asceticsm—of neglecting charity for fasting, justice for vigils, and concord for their own concepts. It is impossible to tell which view was being exaggerated.

Kay the Seneschal left the land too; he was given forty days grace to make himself scarce, and he betook him to Brynach* the Gael, of the Lake, known in romance as 'Briant of the Isles'. He wielded considerable power, and at this period was hostile to Arthur; so, as soon as Arthur had set out on his pilgrimage, which seemed likely to entail his spending some time in the West Country, Brynach attacked the royal lands in the Camelot neighbourhood.

The unedifying story, to which this dressing of Arthur as an amorous gallant is the prelude, is in reality a sidelight on the mutinous state of affairs at Roman headquarters, already mentioned. Like master, like man: but Arthur, though nominally king, was not master in Britain; the Roman governor ruled it, yet was failing to rule his own soldiers, and the people were taking their cue from his shortcomings. The legions were licentious; the Britons copied them, in a shameful political contest of catch-as-catch-can. Steadfastly though Arthur was endeavouring to build a worthy structure, the cracks appearing in its walls all point to a foundation of clay at Roman headquarters; his position lacked the firm backing of authority.

Accordingly we see Lancelot returning to his old love of the 'queen', which as has been pointed out was the crown, not Guenevere. This particular disaffection though was multi-sided, as can be told from the French romance of Perceval. For, Brynach was not only at enmity with Arthur but was jealous of Lancelot; and he was ready to sell his allegiance in whichever direction would enable him to gain an advantage over either. Lancelot at heart wanted the crown, but for the time being was finding it more expedient to appear loyal to Arthur; he was in ill-favour with the Roman authorities, with whom Brynach had characteristically ingratiated himself. Gawain generally speaking was in concert with Lancelot, though not actively disloyal to Arthur. Another Albany chieftain, Meliagrance, was also about to show hostility; while Modred, although not mentioned in the romances at this stage, cannot but have been waiting his opportunity. Thus the old antagonism between Albany and Cornwall, between Gael and Briton, was as bitter as ever; it was compromised, though, by at least one internal feud in Albany, between Brynach and Lancelot, which was further complicated by Roman intervention on behalf of the one. Arthur's position at this point, consequently, was far from a happy one; some of the ill-feeling may not yet have fully disclosed itself, in the first flush of enthusiasm or caution over the new native sovereignty; but he is bound to have sensed its presence, and it can only be imagined that he viewed the future with disquiet.

For this reason he adopted the measures already described to remedy the canker, a plan which must have been evolving in his mind gradually during the two years following his return, and before Kay's disloyalty had manifested itself. We will now hark back to his first arrival, and trace the troubles as they concurrently developed. The earliest sign that all would not be smooth came at the outset, in the response to his summons for the old knights of the Round Table to reassemble; Lancelot and Gawain kept away, Lancelot being figuratively 'out of his mind', while Gawain was brooding over a grievance which it will be remembered went back to the first founding of the Round Table, when King Pelles' son was knighted before him. The jealousy still rankled; Gawain was a vengeful man, his own brother had said.

However, by the time of the second Whitsuntide, when Arthur was crowned, both had returned to the Round Table. Yet, we must ask, was it not with ulterior motives? For, when Galahad was chosen for the Siege Perilous, the post of honour in the quest for the Grail, Gawain's jealousy again burst out. Malory tells the story: Galahad had demonstrated his fitness for the honour by drawing a sword from a stone, which no one else had been able to do; the Grail then appeared, but covered, a reflection on the unfitness of the other knights. Gawain thereupon announced that he would leave the Court, and not return until he had seen the Grail openly; and Lancelot made ready to go with him. The discontent spread, for:

When they of the Table Round heard Sir Gawain say so, they arose up the most part and made such avows as Sir Gawain had made. Anon as King Arthur heard this he was greatly displeased, for he wist well they might not again say their avows. Alas, said King Arthur unto Sir Gawain, ye have nigh slain me with the avow and promise that ye have made; for through you ye have bereft me the fairest fellowship and the truest of knighthood that ever were seen together in any realm of the world; for when they depart from hence I am sure they all shall never meet more in this world, for they shall die many in the quest. . . . Gawain, Gawain, ye have set me in great sorrow, for I have great doubt that my true fellowship shall never meet here more again.

The quest of the Grail that follows is a picturesque rendering of mixed motives; and even though it is not always easy to correlate the events in the French romance of Perceval with Malory's narrative, it can be done on general lines. It seems that while on this quest Lancelot decided to renounce his hopes for the crown, and to aim for the achievement of the Grail, in other words the headship of the Church, in its stead; for he confessed to a hermit of his wrong in craving 'the queen', but he followed up this repentance with a forcible attempt to see the Grail, for which he was struck unconscious and lay so for twenty-four days. Not long afterwards the quest was accomplished successfully by either Perceval or Galahad; and it was when this news reached Arthur's

Court that Lancelot returned to his old hankering after 'the queen', and Kay's treachery came to light.

Kay left the Court and joined Brynach the Gael, known to be hostile; while Arthur, evidently aware that the Lake was plotting rebellion, removed the Church's centre to Glastonbury, spending some time in the West Country, on such enterprises as the ones related about St Carannog and Edeyrn. A small incident in one of the romances discloses a typical item to be deduced from the veiled language in which it has been couched. While Arthur is at Tintagel, he is told by a priest the story of his birth out of wedlock, which shames him because of its being spoken in front of Lancelot and Gawain; on the face of it the incident is pointless, because Arthur and the whole country had known about the circumstances of his birth (whatever they were) for the last forty years. On the other hand it may well indicate that at this time it was deliberately being bandied about, coupled with the slur against him contained in Boece—'the ane was a bastard'—for the purpose of discrediting his right to the throne. Disaffection was now coming to a head. Taking advantage of Arthur's absence in the West, Brynach attacked the country round Caerleon; and the rumour went around that Arthur was 'dead' and that the crown was for anyone to win. Lancelot, who had accompanied Arthur to the West Country, then returned to safeguard the Caerleon neighbourhood; and it seems to have been at this juncture that he became entangled with the Fair Maid of Astolat.

Romance has been kind to Lancelot, in the way that history always seems inclined to sympathize with the Napoleons of life, rather than with the Wellingtons, attracted by colourful glamour and chilled by plain duty. Lancelot at this time was courting glamour in the form of 'the queen', not the lady but the poetic presentation of Arthur's other affection, the people. So when romance pictures him as longed for by a fair maid, but immune to her charms, the doubt justifiably arises as to whether Elaine of Astolat was in truth a woman or something more in the nature of a profitable transaction; we find ourselves wondering whether she may not have been the land around Guildford, and whether there may not have been some bargaining over its governorship, Lancelot deciding though to play for a higher stake. Some scepticism over his actions is deservedly entertained, because however

attractively they read, we know that when they came to the final
test, when Arthur needed every man at his side, Lancelot was
absent in revolt. After Arthur's death he became a high Roman
official (p. 320); but Lancelot in the flesh must have been a
lesser man than the Lancelot of story. So when the romancer
tells us at this point that—'Sir Lancelot would not ride with
the King, for he said that he was not whole of the wound the
which Sir Mador had given him, wherefore the King was heavy
and passing wroth;' and 'Wit you well, said Sir Lancelot, that at
that jousts I will be against the King, and against all his fellowship;' we can appreciate that he was failing to support Arthur at
a time when the Isles of the Lake were actively seditious.

Arthur himself returned to Caerleon, where he held a great
meeting of his Court in the early spring, at Candlemas. The place
is called by Malory 'Westminster', implying the minster near the
capital on the Icen, but confusing the Icen of London with that
of Hampshire, and London the mediaeval capital with Winchester
the British one. The next occurrence is prefaced in Malory with
a delightful reverie on May-time and true love, most apposite
and perhaps recited by bards and minstrels purposefully, in order
to stir patriotism by alluding to it lightheartedly in terms of love
between man and maiden (XVIII, xxv). Set down by him at the
end of the Wars of the Roses, does it not seem that, whatever the
contemporary laxity of morals, it was lax patriotism which was
really meant? The closing words about Queen Guenevere are
singular—'that while she lived was a true lover, and therefore she
had a good end'—yet throughout the romance she has been
painted as toying with Lancelot; they seem to confirm that the
reverie's composer was aware that the 'queen' of Lancelot's
desire had never been her.

·   ·   ·   ·   ·

The occurrence introduced by this discourse was the seizure
of 'the queen' by a chieftain called Meliagrance,* living some
seven miles from Caerleon; he is Meliant of the Waste Manor in
the French romance. The expression 'seizure of the queen' is
evidently a slight exaggeration, for in the French story he does
no more than join Brynach the Gael in his harrying of the

country round Caerleon; even this though represents a nasty state of affairs, because it shows rebellion to have been taking place at the very gates of Arthur's palace. Fortune fluctuated; at one point Kay captured a loyalist, Ywain li Aoutres, but not long afterwards Lancelot defeated Kay and rescued Ywain, causing Kay ultimately to retire across the Channel to Brittany. Yet another malcontent then entered the lists, by name Magdelant of Oriande, brother of an Albany chieftainess Landyr ('Jandree' in the French tale); he was challenging Arthur on behalf of his sister for the possession of the Round Table. This can only mean that Arthur's power in the district, which was the border-land between Cornwall and Albany, had become weak, and that Albany was demanding the extension of her boundary westwards. However some success came in Arthur's way when, as the result of a raid by Brynach and Meliagrance on the coastal castle of Pannenoisance, Lancelot joined the King and slew Meliagrance. But the antagonism was three-cornered, for Lancelot was not so much fighting on Arthur's behalf as from personal enmity with Brynach.

The next turn of events comes as a surprise: Brynach gave Arthur his allegiance, and was made Seneschal in the place left vacant by Kay. Arthur's position was temporarily strengthened; once more he was

safely stablished, and redoubted and dreaded of all lands and of his own land like as he wont to be. Briant hath forgotten all that is past, and is obedient to the King's commands, and more privy is he of his counsel than ever another of the knights, insomuch that he put the others somewhat back, whereof had they much misliking. The felony of Kay lay very nigh the King's heart. . . . Briant was feared and re-doubted throughout all Britain; King Arthur had told them that they were all to be at his commandment.

But in view of Lancelot's feud with Brynach, it is easy to visualize what tangled interests came into collison amongst their respective adherents.

The Albany claim to the Round Table then began to materi-alize, Magdelant bringing a force from overseas in its support. Lancelot was deemed the best placed man to counter this, as he was himself an Albany chieftain, with, as we have seen, interests in the Guildford district; he repelled Magdelant successfully, but afterwards found it opportune to remain in possession of the land he had liberated—as is apt to happen. An awkward complication ensued: Arthur received an abrupt summons from the Romans (from 'King Claudas' in the nomenclature of romance, referring to the late invader, Emperor Claudius) to cease abetting Lancelot, whose killing of Meliagrance had displeased them. Arthur answered justifying Lancelot, perhaps somewhat prevaricatingly; and he put the matter before Brynach the Seneschal and other knights. At once a storm arose: Brynach criticized Lancelot, drawing a caustic rejoinder from Gawain that he was accusing an absent person unable to defend himself, and moreover one who was away on the King's business. Brynach then advised Arthur to disown Lancelot for a year, and keep out of the dispute; to which the other knights retorted that to do so would be sheer cowardice—Lancelot had served the King well, nor was there any reason to fear resisting the Roman demand, seeing that the Court was resolute. The words were perhaps braver than the speakers, Arthur had after all tested his countrymen's firmness several times against the Romans; he decided to recall Lancelot from the territory he had occupied.

The sequel was not long in appearing: Magdelant returned with fresh forces. This time Arthur sent Brynach against him; but the Gael made only a pretence of fighting, and, disloyal at heart, let himself be beaten. Arthur then contemplated allotting the task once more to Lancelot, but Brynach dissuaded him, hinting that Lancelot was seeking independence. The unrest fomented by Magdelant spread, in the absence of effective measures; and Lancelot's friends, Gawain and others, left the Court angered at the confidence Arthur was reposing in Brynach. Ultimately the King entrusted Lancelot again with the mission; and, as before, he accomplished it with complete success. At this the Romans incited Brynach to engineer a breach between Arthur and Lancelot, which the Seneschal did by concocting a rumour that the land Lancelot had occupied was plotting to secede from Arthur, in his favour; with the result that the King was misled into having Lancelot waylaid and imprisoned. But Brynach went further, and induced the Romans to send troops against Albany, presumably on account of some disobedience; this dispelled any further illusion by Arthur, who released Lancelot and accepted Brynach's consequent opposition.

At first thoughts, Arthur's behaviour appears disloyal to his Roman masters; they will have had their own sources of information and their own reasons for bidding him break with Lancelot, and for regarding Brynach as trustworthy. But the circumstances of the time were not straightforward; the Romans were not at one amongst themselves, the central authority was losing control and the legions were becoming mutinous. This dissension was confined to the small area of Sussex with the islands off its coast; it is by no means improbable that the underhand Roman connivance with Brynach came from the local legionary commander, not from the central authority, while Arthur on the other hand was definitely the central authority's agent. The Roman behaviour smacks of intrigue; Arthur's character conversely was loyal. The Roman messenger's demeanour to Arthur suggests contempt of the central authority; and Brynach boasts as though sure of his position. The Gael's parting words to Arthur illustrate the uncompromising jealousy with which the King was having to contend; rather than play for the side, he insists on playing for himself, and says to his captain:

'Sir, you are my lord, and I am one you are bound to protect. You know well that so rich am I in lands and so puissant in friends that I may well despise mine enemy, nor will I not remain at your court so long as Lancelot is therein. Say not that I depart thence with any shame as toward myself. Rather thus go I hence as one that will gladly avenge me, so I have place and freedom; and I see plainly and know that you and your court love him far better than you love me, wherefore behoveth me take thought thereof.'

(Arthur none the less is patient, and replies): 'Briant, remain as yet, and I will make amends for you to Lancelot, and I myself will make amends for him to you.'

'Sir,' saith Briant, 'By the faith that I owe to you, none amends will I have of him nor other until such time as I have drawn as much blood of his body as he did of mine, and I will well that he know it.' With that Briant departeth from the court all wrathful . . . into the land of King Claudas, and saith that now at last hath he need of his aid, for Lancelot is issued forth of the King's prison and is better loved at court than all other, so that the King believeth in no counsel save his only. King Claudas sweareth unto him and maketh pledge that never will he fail him, and Briant to him again.

·   ·   ·   ·   ·

Lancelot had not long been back in favour before two other chieftains came to Arthur with a similar report that he was plotting for the crown, personified as 'the queen'. This time it was Agravaine and Modred, who did so in spite of Gawain's plea to them to keep silent, because the accusation would bring about general strife, on account of Lancelot's considerable following. Nevertheless they proceeded with their purpose, which caused Lancelot to withdraw himself to his stronghold of Joyous Garde, in open rebellion; there he was beset by Arthur and Gawain, his two accusers having been worsted in a previous encounter. The punitive action obliged Lancelot to relinquish 'the queen'; but he crossed the sea to another possession of his, 'Benwick,'* together with his followers. His intention must have been ominous, because Arthur and Gawain thought it well to follow him there with an armed force, leaving, so the story says, Modred in charge of Britain.

Benwick in the romance is mistaken for Bayonne, probably on account of the contemporary mediaeval importance of that place; actually it would appear to have been either in the Isle of Wight or in one of the neighbouring since-eroded islands. The reason for this view is that Benwick had belonged to Lancelot's father, and had been wrested from him by the Romans; it was therefore close at hand to Britain; Sir John Rhys considers it likely to have been the Welsh word Bannawc, drawing the conclusion that it was a four-cornered 'castle', that is to say earthwork, in fact later a Roman camp. As Pwyll Avallawch had been in dispute with Lancelot's father over its possession, it might well have been an earthwork on either the Isle of Wight or an adjacent island.

While Arthur was thus engaged the whole of Albany declared its independence; in the terminology of romance, Modred tried 'to seize the queen'. What was the cause for this revolt may well be as is claimed in Boece—that Arthur declined to designate Modred as his heir. Such an agreement had evidently once been

made with Modred's father, in the days when Arthur was unmarried and before the Romans had brought Britain under their
sway; but circumstances since had changed, and, without dwelling
upon an invidious subject, Albany's chieftains had proved themselves impossible bed-fellows, unreliable and ineffectual. Cornwall
refused to accept the chief of Albany as heir to the kingdom, so
Arthur had nominated the Cornishman, Constantine. Judging
from after events, as well as from a common-sense point of view,
this does not mean that he proposed Constantine for rulership
over the whole kingdom; more probably he recommended to the
Romans that, after his own death, it would be better for Cornwall
and Albany to be separate, the one under Constantine, the other
under Modred. This would equally well explain Modred's precipitation, angered at not being left the whole. But the speculation
arises as to how the matter should have come to be known at this
particular moment. Presumably Arthur's recommendation was
made to the Roman governor in confidence, and, like a will, not
to be disclosed until after his death; if so, then it would seem that
some trouble-maker had chosen this inopportune time to let the
knowledge leak out.

Modred vented his wrath by immediate retaliation. In his
capacity as Arthur's lieutenant he went to Gelliwic in Cornwall
(perhaps Callington), one of the King's courts, and there a Triad
tells us he left neither meat nor drink, not even so much as would
feed a fly, but consumed and wasted all. Then he and Caledon
assembled a rebel force on the Arun. This obliged Arthur to
relinquish his business with Lancelot at Benwick, and make ready
to come back to the mainland, a far from easy operation, which
would entail crossing an unfordable tidal estuary in the face of
strong opposition. Welsh tradition places the crossing at Hamwnt
(Southampton); but that must be regarded as its nominal site only,
its actual one will have been some distance away, opposite to it in
the marshes which are now the Solent. There the sunken river
bed was still known as the Dyfi, hence Malory's mistaken name
Dover for the place; for the one is the British word *Dubo* 'Black',
and the other the British *Dubra* 'waters', an easy confusion when
the Dyfi had been completely forgotten. Other romance variations
of the site are explained in the Glossary under their respective
names.

The awkwardness of the problem facing Arthur is worth visualizing: he had to force his way across a wide estuary with perhaps two tides, with mud flats intersected by channels like the Essex marshes, and with a practically unfordable river at the centre; and this had to be done against a confident enemy, meaning one stronger than himself. A foothold on the far bank would have to be gained at high tide by men landing from coracles, who would cover the crossing of the remainder at low tide and mostly on foot. The safety of the first party would be very precarious until reinforced. In his favour, though, will have been the fact that Modred would not be able to tell whether his force, assembled about where the Calshot lightship is now moored, was aiming for the east or west bank of Southampton Water; so that if Modred kept his men on the wrong side they would have a similar estuary to cross, and Arthur could get ashore first. It is impossible to guess which will have been the easier line for Arthur to take, all we can know is that the advantage over choice lay with him.

Wace paints a colourful picture of the landing; but his haven has to be altered into the marshy shore of an estuary, and his galleys into coracles. However, his outcome of the fight is what matters—'When Arthur's sergeants won forth from the boats, and arrayed them in open country, Modred's meinie might not endure them.' This happened on a 10th of May, the year being either A.D. 66 or 67. For three days Arthur consolidated his position, burying his dead, a rite carefully to be observed as happened at Maidens Castle, and rallying all loyalists within reach. Then he advanced on Winchester, where Modred made another stand, and where he attacked him. Again Wace tells the story:

Arthur drew near the city, and lodged his host without the walls. Modred regarded the host which shut him fast. Fight he must, and fight he would, for the army might never rise up till he was taken. Once Arthur had him in his grip well he knew he was but a dead man. Modred gathered his sergeants together, and bade them get quickly *to their arms*. He arrayed them in companies, and came out through the gates to give battle to his pursuers. Immediately he issued from the barriers the host ran to meet him. The contention was very grievous, for many were smitten and many overthrown. It proved but an ill adventure to Modred, since his men were not able to stay against their adversaries. Modred was persuaded that for him there was only one hope of safety; for his trespass was beyond forgiveness, and much he feared the king. He assembled privily the folk of his household, his familiar friends, and those who cherished against Arthur the deepest grudge. With these he fled over by-ways to *the Camel*, leaving the rest of his people to endure as they could.

The Camel* is the Upper Wiltshire Avon, its name preserved in an old Camelham near Amesbury; in Malory's words, it was to —'a down beside Salisbury' that he fled. The usual supposition that it was on the Cornish Camel that he took his stand is easily explained, in that the 'Cornwall'* of romance included Wiltshire; the impossibility of the remote present county needs little comment. On the other hand, the reason for his having withdrawn to Wiltshire, to almost the heart of Arthur's Wessex, certainly needs a thought. He was a beaten man; twice he had fought Arthur, and twice had been routed. Arthur had 'sent after his men to the very Arun ("Humber")'; Caledon had abandoned him and made its submission; and, as Malory naïvely observes: 'Much people drew unto King Arthur, and then they said that Sir Modred warred upon King Arthur with wrong.' He was evidently making his way to Wales, to the nearest folk not under Roman sway; for Arthur was part of the Roman rule in Britain. Modred's rebellion had been a 'fascist' one; he had been supported by the ultra-nationalists, but had failed because at heart their ends were self-centred; now, the only sympathy he would find would be from free Britons beyond the border.

So, the situation which Arthur saw before himself was: an attempted rising by Caldeon and the extremists had been quelled; Lancelot in the Isle of Wight had still to be brought to order; and further trouble from his renegade nephew, who was making for Wales, had to be circumvented. Accordingly he set out after Modred.

Should there remain any lingering doubt over the geography of romance, it is surely dispelled by Wace's record of tradition, that: 'King Arthur besieged Winchester strictly; at the end he took burgesses and castle. To Owein son of Urien, a baron beloved of the court, Arthur granted Scotland as a heritage.' Scotland is Caledon, and Caledon is the Weald of Sussex adjoining Winchester and Chichester; it had joined in the revolt, and now in punishment was being placed under the jurisdiction of Owein of Chichester.

Thus Modred was in retreat towards Wales, accompanied by only a small caucus of adherents; while Arthur's intention was to prevent their escape and their stirring up fresh trouble. For this he had two alternatives: either he could kill them, or else he could endeavour to dissuade them. The latter was his preference; but he had to see the other as a possible grim necessity, grim because the legacy of a blood feud was no way to engender goodwill. Arthur came up with the rebels on Salisbury Plain, where he found them in recuperated strength. It would seem that where the Ridgeway, the continuation of Icknield Way from East Anglia, meets the Plain, Modred must have received some support; probably it was from East Anglian malcontents, nationalist extremists, or from an internal feud against Arthur. So, it will have been in the region of Upavon (Upper Camel Avon, to give it its full name) that Arthur encountered Modred standing his ground, and ready to challenge him with battle.

True to his purpose, Arthur's first endeavour was to come to terms. What was offered can only be guessed: the surrender of sovereignty which is Malory's version cannot be entertained, it conflicts entirely with his position as the pursuer of a defeated rebel; but that he was ready to concede generously in order to achieve peace can well be supposed. As he had already placed Caledon under the rule of Modred's half-brother, Owein, territory in Albany was not available for disposal; let us imagine therefore that what Arthur offered him, as a so-to-speak prince of the blood-royal, was some nominal all-Britain dignity that would satisfy appearances, and some provisional condition over heirship to the kingdom (to which his own children had naturally the prior right). More than this he can scarcely have offered; but that he was ready to make a conciliatory settlement is evidenced from both sides, for Modred's protagonist Boece corroborates that Arthur was willing to come to terms.

Mistrust, however, was afoot, more so than treachery. Iddawc the Gael, a well-known druid, apparently from the Meon valley, when charged with a conciliatory message from Arthur is said to have delivered it to Modred harshly; this we are told of in the *Dream of Rhonabwy*, and in Iddawc is to be visualized the leader of Boece's 'bishops and famous men of religion' who went between the armies. The Scot's account, on the other hand, alleges that it

was the Cornishmen who would not let Arthur make terms.
Neither of these tales reads convincingly; and Malory's story
seems the nearest to likelihood—briefly, neither side trusted the
other; it was touch and go whether agreement could be reached,
when chance set the powder alight.

This is his description of the scene. In endeavour to avoid
bloodshed, Arthur sent Lucan the Butler and his brother Bedivere
to try to come to a compromise with the rebels; and after much
negotiation they obtained a settlement—that Modred should hold
Albany in independence, and that after Arthur's death he should
succeed to Cornwall and the rest of Cymbeline's kingdom. These
conditions differ slightly from those given by him, but accord
with the tenor of Boece's account; and although for the reasons
already given they cannot be accepted literally, they can be taken
as an earnest that Arthur in actual fact was ready to concede much
for concord. As a result it was

condescended that King Arthur and Sir Modred should meet betwixt
their hosts, and every each of them should bring fourteen persons; and
they came with this word unto Arthur. Then said he: I am glad that
this is done; and so he went into the field.

And when Arthur should depart, he warned all his host that an
they see any sword drawn: Look ye come on fiercely, and slay that
traitor Sir Modred, for I in no wise trust him. In likewise Sir Modred
warned his host that: An ye see any sword drawn, look that ye come on
fiercely, and so slay all that ever before you standeth; for in no wise I
will not trust for this treaty, for I know well my father will be avenged
on me. And so they met as their appointment was, and so they were
agreed and accorded thoroughly; and wine was fetched, and they
drank. Right soon came an adder out of a little heath bush, and it stung
a knight on the foot. And when the knight felt him stung, he looked
down and saw the adder, and then he drew his sword to slay the adder,
and thought of none other harm. And when the host on both parties
saw that sword drawn, then they blew beamous, trumpets and horns,
and shouted grimly. And so both hosts dressed them together. And
King Arthur took his horse, and said: Alas this unhappy day! and so
rode to his party. And Sir Modred in likewise.

For the sake of realism let us assess the numbers actually
likely to have been assembled; because the word 'hosts' gives an
impression of multitude that may be faulty, while Geoffrey of

Monmouth's 'sixty thousand' is fantastic. Two or three thousand on either side seems to be the most which can be considered. Modred had left Winchester with a handful only; he was in Cornish loyal country, and the insurgents who had joined him must have come from a distance; nor would the Romans have been likely to allow any large band to gather and come to his assistance. The numbers must have been on a small scale.

Neither do we know much about the fight. Arthur had suffered at least one defection beforehand: Alan Fyrgan's household had absconded stealthily by night on the way to the field, though their chieftain remained gallantly at Arthur's side—only to lose his life. The rest is fragmentary. Geoffrey of Monmouth tells us that Arthur had drawn up his force in nine battalions, forming them each in square, and with a right and left wing; and from elsewhere we learn that there was probably a reserve under Gwynnhyvar, Mayor of Cornwall and Devon. Boece says that the Cornishmen were in the vanguard, facing the Ordul Picts. But it is impossible to glean a clear picture of the field. While of the battle's course, all that is known is that it was fought to practically a drawn issue, Modred being killed and Arthur, in the moment of victory, mortally wounded. Gwynnhyvar rallied the battle; but beyond that we only hear the names of those who escaped, giving the impression that with the leaders' deaths the remnants of their forces melted away. Last to leave Arthur was Kynwyl Sant, save for the two knights of his household who bore him from the field—Lucan the Butler and Bedivere the Cupbearer.

Then comes the final scene of all, so beautifully told by Malory, to which here has been added the immortal trust mentioned by him but penned by Layamon. Arthur had been taken to a little chapel near the shore of the Lake, borne it may have been down the river Avon, then a big enough stream for the blue stones of Stonehenge to have been floated down it in caissons. There Sir Lucan, himself hard hit, died; and Arthur was left alone with Sir Bedivere, whom he bade carry out his last wish:

My time hieth fast; therefore take thou Excalibur, my good sword, and go with it to yonder water side, and when thou comest there I charge thee throw my sword in that water, and come again and tell me what thou there seest.

My lord, said Bedivere, your commandment shall be done, and lightly bring you word again. So Sir Bedivere departed, and by the way he beheld that noble sword, that the pommel and the haft was all of precious stones; and then he said to himself: If I throw this rich sword in the water, thereof shall never come good but harm and loss. And then Sir Bedivere hid Excalibur under a tree. And so, as soon as he might, he came again unto the king, and said he had been at the water, and had thrown the sword in the water.

What saw thou there? said the king.

Sir, he said, I saw nothing but waves and winds.

That is untruly said of thee, said the king, therefore go thou lightly again, and do my commandment; as thou art to me lief and dear, spare not, but throw it in.

Then Sir Bedivere returned again, and took the sword in his hand; and then him thought sin and shame to throw away that noble sword, and so efte he hid the sword, and returned again, and told to the king that he had been at the water, and done his commandant.

What saw thou there? said the king.

Sir, he said, I saw nothing but the waters wappe and waves wanne.

Ah, traitor untrue, said King Arthur, now hast thou betrayed me twice. Who would have weened that, thou that hast been to me so lief and dear? and thou art named a noble knight, and would betray me for the richness of the sword. But now go again lightly, for thy long tarrying putteth me in great jeopardy of my life, for I have taken cold. And but if thou do now as I bid thee, if ever I may see thee, I shall slay thee with mine own hands; for thou wouldst for my rich sword see me dead.

Then Sir Bedivere departed, and went to the sword, and lightly took it up, and went to the water side; and there he bound the girdle about the hilts, and then he threw the sword as far into the water as he might; and there came an arm and an hand above the water and met it, and caught it, and so shook it thrice and brandished, and then vanished away the hand with the sword in the water. So Sir Bedivere came again to the king, and told him what he saw.

Alas, said the king, help me hence, for I dread me I have tarried over long.

Then Sir Bedivere took the king upon his back, and so went with him to that water side. And when they were at the water side, even fast by the bank hoved a little barge with many fair ladies in it, and among them all was a queen; and all they had black hoods, and all they wept and shrieked when they saw King Arthur.

Now put me into the barge, said the king.

And he did so softly; and there received him three queens with great mourning; and so they set them down, and in one of their laps King Arthur laid his head. And then that queen said: Ah, dear brother, why have ye tarried so long from me? alas, this wound on your head hath caught over-much cold. And so then they rowed from the land.

And Sir Bedivere beheld all those ladies go from him; then Sir Bedivere cried: Ah, my lord Arthur, what shall become of me, now ye go from me and leave me here alone among mine enemies?

Comfort thyself, said the king, and do as well as thou mayest, for in me is no trust for to trust in. For I will fare to Avalon, to the fairest of all maidens, to Argante the queen, an elf most fair; and she shall make my wounds all sound, make me all whole with healing draughts. And afterwards I will come again to my kingdom, and dwell with the Britons with mickle joy.

.   .   .   .   .

Then was it accomplished that Merlin said in times gone by, that much sorrow should be of Arthur's departure. The Britons believe yet that he is alive, and dwelleth in Avalon with the fairest of all elves; and the Britons ever yet expect when Arthur shall return. Was never the man born, of ever any lady chosen, that knoweth of the truth to say more of Arthur. But formerly was a sage hight Merlin; he said with words—his sayings were true—that an Arthur should yet come to help the English.

15

Flotsam and Jetsam

As Arthur's barge faded slowly into the mists of the Lake, Bedivere turned away and set his footsteps towards the wreckage of what had been Britain. For indeed it was 'had been'; in future the land would be Britannia, a Roman province without hope of ever again becoming a state in partnership with Rome, instead of ruled by her. And had he been a prophet he would have seen that for the next thousand years this country was never to be governed by a Briton, until Henry Tudor took hold of the broken and warped timbers and started working them back into shape. Other castaways besides Bedivere surveyed the wreckage, stung with remorse at the neglect which had let the ship founder, when within a stone's throw of safety and contentment on the shore they were seeking; it was they who conceived the thought, which was in itself a prayer, that Arthur should come again and they would be given another chance. There were many among them who could have rallied to Arthur's side before the battle, but who had casually held aloof, following fashion and comfortably deluding themselves that he was too forceful, and that matters would straighten without their effort. Malory's words bear imprint of the same inconsistency having been manifest in their descendants during his day, when the wars of the Roses were being fought, and people were drifting with the tide. He describes, in terms of what he was seeing with his own eyes, the wreckage that Bedivere was left to face, the heedlessness and abandonment to pleasure as they had appeared on the eve of the disaster:

For then was the common voice among (the people), that with Arthur was none other life but war and strife, and with Sir Modred was great joy and bliss; thus was Sir Arthur depraved, and evil said of. And many there were that King Arthur had made up of nought, and given them lands, might not then say him a good word. Lo ye all Englishmen, see ye not what a mischief here was! for he that was the most king and knight of the world, and most loved the fellowship of noble knights, and by him they were all upholden, now might not these Englishmen hold them content with him. Lo thus was the old custom and usage of this land; and also men say that we of this land have not yet lost nor forgotten that custom and usage. Alas, this is a great default of us Englishmen, for there may no thing please us no term; and so fared the people at that time . . . (they) were so new fangle.

But by the time that Bedivere had joined the castaways, sorrow had smitten them at the calamity their new-fangled ideas had caused; and they were trying to make amends for it by per-suading themselves that Arthur's loss was not final, and that he would return. They now realized that he had represented all which was good in the country's character, the ideals which they themselves wanted but fell short of; hence it was with affection, even more than with pride, that they were telling one another tales of his life, to be passed down and treasured by succeeding generations. For the keynote in the legends is affection; and it is for his aims and endeavours. Conversely, pride in his achieve-ments had been forfeited; because, when all has been reckoned— what did he accomplish? For all practical purposes, nothing. The fault was his countrymen's, and they tacitly acknowledged it; but the credit for his aim and for the steadfastness with which he pursued it were his alone, and it was for these that he was loved.

To Roman eyes his death was of small account; the machine would continue to work without him. They had tried to integrate the kingdom, but the natives were incapable of unanimity, so they would leave the matter alone; the concord which Britain had refused to adopt of her own free will could be imposed upon her instead by the legions, the *pax Romana*. Consequently the Roman historian's only mention of these years, and of the events filling so many chapters of Geoffrey's and Malory's histories, is that— 'Under (Turpilianus) a languid state of tranquillity followed.' This is a humiliating commentary on what our forefathers were looking upon as heroic. The outside world could see other short-comings too, in the Britons succumbing to the line of least resistance; and the same historian continues about later governorship—'The barbarians now learned, like any Romans, to condone seductive vices.' 'The Britons were gradually led on to the amenities that made vice agreeable, arcades, baths, and sumptuous banquets; they spoke of such novelties as "civilization", when really they were only a feature of enslavement.'

Such was the wrack left floating on the tide, after the loss of Arthur's statecraft.

.   .   .   .   .

Since then, however, vicissitudes have seasoned the irresolute material; so that with the flotsam, which has been carried all over the seven seas, have been borne Arthur's ideals for shaping nationhood and his enterprise for grappling with adversity. Wherever the driftwood has come ashore his tradition has travelled with it; and who is to say that it may not be to Britons overseas that he will return, just as probably as it may be to England? Each of us will trust that it may be his own land which will be favoured, and his own land that will see Arthur gather together a new Round Table fellowship, and hear him bind it with the oath always to uphold a Commonwealth cause, never being diverted by expediency or worldly aims. And whatever country it may be, its Bediveres and Galahads are to be pictured as reappearing too, sprung from the same stock as the bygone knights of romance.

There will be few people with British blood in their veins who have not some personal connection with the men and women of King Arthur's day, whose parents on one side of their family or the other, in the not so very distant past, have not hailed from that part of England over which he ruled and fought. So great has been the tendency, until recent years, for people to cling to their birthplaces, that it is probable that a strain of the same blood is to be found today flowing in any village where it flowed in Arthur's day—mixed with much else besides, but none the less still a live strain. The thought gives an added interest to names which have been taken overseas from places linked with Arthur's England. Winchester, for example, whether beneath the Alleghanies or on the uplands of the Ottawa, must have been named by men whose

forefathers may have fought against Claudius' elephants on the
banks of the Itchen, and have seen Guenevere gracing the court
overlooked by the Bryn Gwyn where Cymbeline's head lay
buried. Or the Murray folk of Australia, the Cape, and Kentucky,
their forbears must surely have taken up arms under Boadicea,
and suffered through the retribution following her defeat? Or
Boston, Massachusetts, will it not have been named by men
whose ancestors at Icen-ho knew King Lear? So also Bath carries
with it to New York and Maine, to New Brunswick and Ontario,
memories of the men who twice faced the invader on the slopes
above the Avon, and who laughed to see the steel fish lying where
they had struck them down, in the river-bed below. While
Plymouth, New Zealand, conjures up remembrance of that
irrepressible and cheery warrior Cador. The whole earth is strewn
with jetsam from the battle of Camlan.

·   ·   ·   ·   ·

Let us now follow the fortunes of some of the persons and
people after that hapless fight. First to be scanned is Cornwall,
with its chieftain the young Constantine, Arthur's heir. He continued the feud with Albany, killing the two sons of Modred, and
then himself falling at the hand of his own nephew. Thereafter
the provincial antagonism continued, down to the days of Coel of
Colchester, an internal bickering accompanied by intrigues with
outside marauders which finally exasperated the Romans—'Will
ye always set your hopes upon being safeguarded by the foreigner?
Will ye even yet not teach your hands to fight with shield and
sword and spear against these thieves and robbers, no whit
stronger than ye be yourselves, save for your own listlessness and
lethargy?' The words are put into a Roman mouth by Geoffrey of
Monmouth.

Beyond the Sussex Humber the Romans embarked on a new
venture: Boadicea's elder daughter, who had been raped by
a Roman, Marius, had since been recompensed by his marrying
her; she was of the royal house of Lear and of Brigance, so
Marius* was appointed in her right as native king of Albany. This
was accepted by the people; and from that fortunate and wise
amende has come down in historical tradition a link with innu-

merable British families; because, from her sprang two Welsh
names that have spread all over England, and permeated the whole
Welsh people—the lines of Cunedda and Cadwaladr the Blessed.
This is shown in outline on the table overleaf. It is one of the
pieces of flotsam that brings us close to Arthur himself.

Even the satisfaction brought about by this measure was
marred, though, by partisan strife. The Queen's younger sister,
Vodicia, chose to lead a refractory party, for which she was exiled
by her brother-in-law, Marius; she then raised a revolt in East
Sussex (Brigance), directed against a Roman force encamped near
its capital, Epiak. She enlisted the aid of men from the island of
Mon as well. At first she had some success, in that she gained an
entry to the camp by a surprise assault, and was only thrown out
after severe fighting; after which she passed on to Epiak, where
she burnt the town and slew in it time-expired Roman soldiers and
Britons in Roman pay. At this point her good luck ended; a force
went in pursuit of her and she was captured, then unchivalrously
she was put to death by the Romans.

The particular reason for relating her revolt is that, accidentally, Tacitus has given her name to her mother in his account
of that lady's great rebellion, in A.D. 61. His mistake has not been
corrected in the preceding pages, his Romanized version of
Vodicia 'Boadicea' having been retained because of its familiarity;
but the moment is now opportune for it to be mentioned. Boece,
who had Tacitus in front of him when he wrote, deliberately
corrects her name; she was Voada or Vo'ouda, it was her daughter
who was Vodicia or Vo'oudicia. The 'B' in the Roman version of
either name is the Gaelic 'Bh', pronounced 'V'. Tacitus was
writing twenty years after the daughter's revolt, and evidently
confused the two names; it would be only right, now, to remember
the mother by her proper one, for she at least deserves that tribute.

We next come to Voada's grandson, Coel, the Old King Cole
of happy memory. Of him Geoffrey of Monmouth writes:

Coel from childhood had been brought up at Rome, and having
been taught Roman ways, had conceived a mighty liking for the
Romans. Wherefore he also paid them the tribute and eschewed all
wrangling about it, for that he saw the whole world was subject unto
them, and that their power did surpass the power of any one province

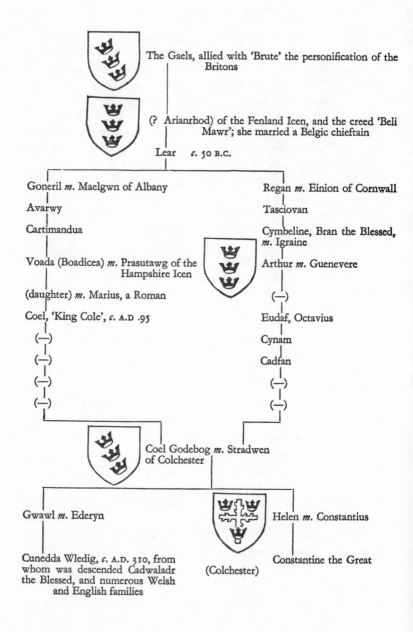

The Gaels, allied with 'Brute' the personification of the Britons

(? Arianrhod) of the Fenland Icen, and the creed 'Beli Mawr'; she married a Belgic chieftain

Lear   *c.* 50 B.C.

Goneril *m.* Maelgwn of Albany

Avarwy

Cartimandua

Voada (Boadicea) *m.* Prasutawg of the Hampshire Icen

(daughter) *m.* Marius, a Roman

Coel, 'King Cole', *c.* A.D .95

(—)

(—)

(—)

(—)

Regan *m.* Einion of Cornwall

Tasciovan

Cymbeline, Bran the Blessed, *m.* Igraine

Arthur *m.* Guenevere

(—)

Eudaf, Octavius

Cynam

Cadfan

(—)

(—)

Coel Godebog *m.* Stradwen of Colchester

Gwawl *m.* Ederyn

Cunedda Wledig, *c.* A.D. 310, from whom was descended Cadwaladr the Blessed, and numerous Welsh and English families

(Colchester)

Helen *m.* Constantius

Constantine the Great

or of any alliance among the smaller nations. He paid therefore that which was demanded, and in peace held that which was his own. None of all the kings ever showed greater honour unto his nobility, for them that were rich did he allow to live in peace, and them that were poor did he maintain with unfailing bounty.

Which shows the advantage of a classical education!

Five generations later we reach another Coel, of Colchester. His first recorded achievement is, as usual, a battle with Cornwall, in which he was successful, causing Rome to despatch a special senator Constantius to settle the conflict. Constantius' method was masculine: he married the disturbance's daughter; and she presented him with the renowned son known to history as Constantine the Great. From Coel's other daughter, Gwawl, came the famed British figure Cunedda, whose blood runs in a multitude of British folk. But it is the first-mentioned daughter, Helen, wife of the senator who became Emperor Constantius, who is so indelibly inscribed in British tradition. Her accomplishments are only known vaguely as yet, in the half-figurative terms of having retrieved the Three Wise Men's relics, and of having discovered the True Cross; but it is possible that some day their full meaning and import will be understood, and that she will be ascribed the honour which she received during the Middle Ages.

Visible evidence of her influence is contained in the quantity of East Anglian and other localities' shields of arms distinguished by Three Crowns, referring to her successful search for the Wise Men's remains; but their primary significance is her East Anglian stock, and it is that which gives town names which bear those arms, such as Colchester, Boston, Ely, Nottingham, Oxford, Bristol, Hull and Tynemouth, their special interest. The arms betoken the ancient Celtic stock of those places; their distribution is illustrated in the map facing page 260, and there is more about them in the next chapter and the Glossary, under THREE CROWNS. For, the Britons remained everywhere in England, despite the the Saxon conquest, in serfdom maybe and as the ill-considered mothers of half-breed children, but so numerously as to inspire mediaeval England with its wholly Celtic national tradition and folk-lore. In fact the colourful heraldry kindly conceals a harrowing story of how it came into being; but nevertheless it is through these arms and the town names belonging to them that links with Arthurian Britain are to be found all the world over. They furnish an ancient foundation on which modern accomplishment can be built. A passing thought, too, is that, ineffectual though the bulk of the population showed itself to be, yet from time to time fine characters have repeatedly sprung to life from it; it seems as though the germ of greatness has run in its veins and has been transmitted down the ages, but that some chance or even mischance were needed to make it sprout.

Next is the provoking question of whether the very blood of Arthur may not be found running in some British veins. It may well be that it does. The fact that he nominated a kinsman as his successor does not necessarily mean that he died childless; contrarily the evidence is that he had several daughters, but they were young and unmarried when he fell, nor could the crown have been left to a problematic future. Welsh pedigrees unhesitatingly assign children and descendants to Caradoc ab Bran, his usual name in Welsh tradition; some of these are men, probably meaning that they were his grandsons, with the mother's name omitted, as we have seen happened in the case of Bran ab Llyr. Two men in particular seem undoubtedly to have been of his lineage—Eudav ab Caradoc ab Bran, and Cyllin ab Caradoc ab Bran. The first of these, whose name is the native pronunciation of the Latin Octavius, figures in the table on page 256; of him the *Cambrian Biography* relates that he was a chieftain of Archenfield, South Herefordshire, at the close of the first century. Land had been possessed there by Arthur's uncles, brothers of his mother Eigr; they came from the Devonshire or Somerset coastal district of Llydaw, and evidently must have moved to the South Welsh border at the same time as Geraint Garwy did so, after the defeat of Llongborth. Cyllin is more difficult to place, because of uncertainty as to which of several Coels was his son; there is interest in knowing that his son introduced to Britain a new pattern of grinding mill with wheels, and this the *Biography* suggests was brought by him from Rome. Nothing more precise than the foregoing can be attempted; nor does it appear needed, it is enough to accept the belief as reasonable that Arthur's and Guenevere's line did not die out but continued through at least those two persons —in Merlin's words (quoted on page 86): 'The other ray betokens a daughter, whose sons and grandsons shall hold the kingdom of Britain in succession.'

Of their daughters, the eldest married a Roman, Rufus Pudens, by whom she had five children, all martyrs, one of whose names is perpetuated by the church of St Pudentiana in Rome, where the family had lived. Another daughter, Eigen, also a Saint, married the lord of Old Sarum, Sarllog; no children of them are mentioned, but the two founded the monastery of Llan Illtud in Glamorgan (Lantwit Major), which became one of the most famous early colleges. Although doubt is sometimes cast on the legend of its origin, there is perhaps no justification for scepticism; logically it would have been planted there at this period, to aid in the pacification of South Wales. So, there is satisfaction in being able to think that Arthur's work did not come to an end with his death, but was continued by his daughters.

The word 'death' was written inadvertently. All three branches of contemporary belief were at one in telling that he yet lived; and without trying to suppose that his body survived, let us not think too lightly of Celtic metaphor as regards his spirit. Phraseology varied: to the Church, Arthur rested in Avalon; to the Cornishmen he became a Chough, and to their Gaelic element a Raven. So strongly did this latter belief obtain that it is mentioned in *Don Quixote*; while even so late as the year 1800 a Cornishman reproved a man for shooting at a raven, lest it might have been King Arthur. Clansmen used to be known by their emblems, like the 'shaggy horses' of Glassary in Argyll, or 'Falcon' herald; and when hearing the word spoken, it was but a short step in imagination to conceive the man as a bird. The Scottish belief that to harm a robin is a sin, because the bird has a drop of Christ's blood in its veins, is an exact parallel. The Raven Britons had Arthur's blood in theirs; and where the blood ran the spirit might return. Few men have left in their fellow-countrymen's minds so affectionate a trust.

16

The Shipwrights

THERE remains to be considered the banner assigned to King
Arthur by mediaeval heralds, the frontispiece to this book. It
tells a good deal about the people over whom he ruled, and their
nature, which throws into relief his own character. Commonly
this and similar armorial drawings are classed as fabulous; but the
term is misleading. True enough it is that they were never borne
by the Britons, yet they portray genuine folk-lore, reproducing
pictorially traditions handed down from those times; they are
a form of picture-script, which fortunately has preserved much
that would otherwise have been lost. Before the days of printing,
these signs were well understood; it is but comparatively recently,
since education became fashionable and illiteracy looked down
upon, that their language has been disdained and forgotten.

The manuscripts from which this banner has been taken, as
well as several shields of arms referred to later, are described in
the Glossary under HERALDRY.* There is it explained why the
Scottish version of blue, for the field of the three crowns quarter,
has been preferred to the usual English version of red.

The first quarter of the banner, a cross with the Virgin Mary
in the canton, is personal to King Arthur, recalling his having
borne her image on his shield at the battle near Winchester. The
second quarter, charged with three crowns, is both family and
national. The Three Crowns, arranged in various ways, constitute
a device in themselves; it became remarkably popular during the
Middle Ages, for a reason that can only be explained as having
been a much treasured tradition of one section of the people.
Opposite is a map illustrating the principal locations of the device;
from it will be noticed that it was mainly centred in East Anglia,
with a distinct group around the Moray Firth which must relate

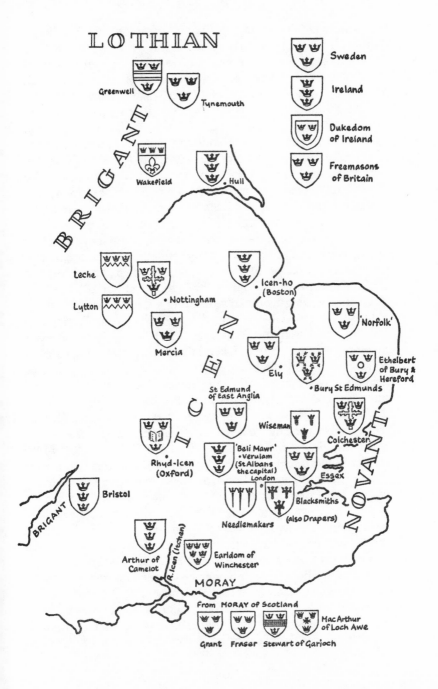

LOTHIAN

Sweden

Ireland

Dukedom
of Ireland

Freemasons
of Britain

Greenwell

Tynemouth

Wakefield

Hull

BRIGANT

Leche

Lytton

• Nottingham

Mercia

Icen-ho
(Boston)

'Norfolk'

Ely

Ethelbert
of Bury &
Hereford

• Bury St Edmunds

St Edmund
of East Anglia

Wiseman

Colchester

Rhyd-Icen
(Oxford)

ICEN

'Beli Mawr'
• Verulam
(St Albans
the capital)
London

Essex

Bristol

BRIGANT

Needlemakers

Blacksmiths

(also Drapers)

NOVANT

Arthur of
Camelot

R. Icen (Ichnan)

Earldom of
Winchester

MORAY

From MORAY of Scotland

Grant   Fraser   Stewart of Garioch

MacArthur
of Loch Awe

to the men of Mureif having migrated thither after Boadicea's disaster. There are some conspicuous foreign arms, that will be discussed later; and there are two so-called fabulous ones of British notables—Brute the personification of Britain, and Beli Mawr, nominally King Lear's father but in reality the deity.

The origin of the Three Crowns lay in Helen of Colchester's recovery of the Three Wise Men's remains, in the fourth century. They were first enshrined at Constantinople, then were removed from there before it fell to the Turks, and eventually in the twelfth century brought to Cologne, where they still are. The Wise Men thus became known as the Three Kings of Cologne, and ostensibly the three crowns represent them; but that interpretation does not convey the whole of their significance.

The relics' arrival in northern Europe, from Italy, seems to have caused an immense stir: numbers of towns, counties, private persons, and London livery companies adopted the device; and mediaeval herals assigned it to the Celtic royal house, and to the East Anglian kings (probably denoting a Celtic marriage), while Edward III especially dedicated one of his sons, Edmund of Langley, to its tradition. Why so great a pride in the Wise Men's memory should have been taken in Britain is a problem yet to be solved; so far as this history is concerned, it can be accepted primarily as the recollection of Helen of Colchester's zeal and initiative, and a symbol of her racial stock.

What that stock was, the map indicates. Foremost comes the name Icen, stretching from Icen-ho (Boston), through the Icen of the Fens, down the Icen-hyllt (Icknield Way), to Rhyd-Icen (Oxford) and the Hampshire Icen (Itchen). A second people are the Novant of Essex and London, where, in addition to the livery companies, Coutts Bank preserves the memory of 'The Sign of the Three Crowns, in the Strand'. A third tribe are the Moravians, of Mureif, now represented by the names Moray and Murray, whose history is international; Boece mentions their having come to southern England from the Rhine (though his date is inaccurate), whence they can be traced in the Merovingan dynasty of France and in the Moravians of the Danube. But their name is far more ancient than that, and far more widely spread. Note should be taken that in the arms of Murray three stars replace the three crowns; the implication is the same, however, as will become apparent later. As regards the Tynemouth instance of the Three Crowns, they originated from a North Anglian chieftain who may have been related to the East Anglian house; another distant occurrence is in Hereford see, but as its founder came from Bury St Edmunds its arms have been placed there. From this survey the conclusion to be drawn would seem to be that the Three Crowns stand for the race to which the Icen, Novant, and Morays belonged; but to identify that race we have to look further afield.

There are two oversea occurrences of the arms which furnish a clue to the people; they are those of Sweden and of mediaeval Ireland. As regards the latter, a commission under Edward IV decided upon a form of arms which happens to coincide with those of King Arthur, a measure which must surely have been intended to affirm the two islands' oneness of race? Other Irish variations are those granted to the dukedom, which are similar to Sweden or St Edmund's within a white border, and those of the province of Munster, also similar but rayed and without the border. The common denominator to these and Britain is the race known in Ireland as the Danaan, and in Britain as the Children of Don; better are they called the Gaelic Picts, the Gwyddel Ffichti of Welsh tales. They are said to have come to Ireland from Scandinavia, possibly on a return migration like the later Danes; in fact, Dane is the simplest name for them, nor should the nickname East-men for the Danes be forgotten. Thus it seems clear that the Three Crowns stand for the Gaelic substratum of what is now England, which had retained its identity more in East Anglia than elsewhere.

Turning to Arthur's parental connection with this mediaeval device, the particular form of it assigned to him will be seen to be identical with that of Beli Mawr; and Beli is traditionally said to have been King Lear's father, Arthur's great-great-great-grandfather. However, as was remarked in Chapter 2, Lear's father seems to have been a Belgic Celt; so these arms are more likely to represent his right to the East Anglian kingdom through his mother, whose daughter, Lear's sister, was named after one of the Children of Don.

The other parental coat of arms is that of Brute, the traditional father of England (Loegria), Albany, and Wales. Two quarters are assigned to him: in the first a lion, and in the second three crowns, slantwise. The first quarter evidently stands for Britain itself; the second would seem intended for Brute's wife Ignoge.* According to tradition she was by birth Grecian; but as the alternative word Danai for Greeks is also used, the legend could be interpreted that she was Danaian, which is to say of the race of Don, and which had become mistaken for Greek. The discrepancy is the less when account is taken of the fact that both Cromarty and London legend carry our race back to Greece and Syria. Indeed the adoption of the Three Crowns device for such otherwise diverse entities as Ireland, Sweden, East Anglia, and Ignoge of Greece indicate that the legend was very much to the fore in people's minds—which the Elizabethan folk-tale *The Seven Champions of Christendom* confirms.

A small corroboratory point, in case the name Ignoge is puzzling, is that its first syllable Ign- corresponds with the name Ing of the Swedish royal stock; and a rhyme on the rune Ing* or Ign (the letter 'ñ') runs—'Ing was first among the East Danes seen.' This brings us back to the Danish East-men.

Thus the Three Crowns in Arthur's banner characterize him as claimed by the Children of Don, the Gaelic Picts of England, to have been one of themselves. Yet the device does not signalize one of his deeds, it commemorates Helen of Colchester's recovery of the Three Wise Men's remains. Why that act should have been chosen for King Arthur, and for an almost national device, warrants some further investigation.

·   ·   ·   ·   ·

On the face of the story, the Three Crowns indicate the three Kings of Cologne, as the Wise Men were called familiarly. But each of them also happens to have been assigned personal arms by the mediaeval heralds; and these, remarkably enough, denote three slightly differing codes of wisdom, of world-wide usage and current in Britain. The Three Crowns stand for the combined schools of thought. Should the idea of codified wisdom sound incongruous for ancient Britain, the remark must be repeated that the people's crude mode of material life is not to be mistaken for their intellectual capacity. Much of past simplicity was of deliberate choice, on the lines of a Chinese peasant's reply to a disciple of Confucius: 'I have heard from my teacher that those who have cunning implements are cunning in their dealings, and have cunning in their hearts; it is not that I do not know of these things, I should be ashamed to use them.' The Britons of Arthur's day were in some ways particularly advanced in intellect: they may be said to have loved reason to the extent of worshipping the right of freedom to exercise it; though in practice, perversity intruded.

The codes of wisdom denoted by the respective arms are the equivalent of modern reasoning as applied to justice, education, and trade. The arms are to be seen in Harleian MS. 2169 in the British Museum.

Caspar's device has been illustrated on page 28; it is the 'Light' which Megasthenes recorded as light of mind, or reason (page 105). It is repeated in the name Caspar itself, 'the White One', which like the Greek 'white browed one' and the English 'fair of face' alludes to the white tint of moonlight; for, the moon represented knowledge, in that its calendar was the earliest application of scientific observation, and its monthly phase was believed to affect people's minds. Thus his code of wisdom typified science, or education.

Melchior, whose name means 'King of Light', with the same implication, was assigned arms of seven stars. These are the Pleiades or Western Maids, the Hesperides, who according to Greek legend used to guard an apple grove in the isle of the Hyperboreans,* which lay somewhere near Britain. This Land of Seven Stars is mentioned in Welsh tradition as having been that of Lucifer, the Light-bringer, once an angel but fallen: 'Lucifer the corrupter, like his destitute country Seven Stars there are.' In that island near Britain his creed had survived, as Greek legend corroborates, calling it Saturn (Cronos) and telling that he lies sleeping in an isle of the West; it tells too that his reign was the Golden Age, and that his wife was Justice, 'the Starry One', whose name also was given to the Golden Age. In the East Lucifer may have become corrupt, but here in the West there is no cause to suppose that he had not retained his original pure form.

Balthazar's arms, in Sir David Lindsay's Scottish manuscript, are painted as a Moorish youth bearing a pennon. This is the

Black Man of Chapter 13 above; and his name 'Lord of Treasures' points to the interpretation of his wisdom taken here, as trade prosperity.

The three colleges* of thought are combined in the arms of Three Crowns; they stand for the virtue of reasoning, and are a reminder of three requirements in social life to which it needs to be applied—justice, education, and welfare. It is plain common sense. It is the reasoning, or 'light', or 'word', of page 105 above, that used to be pictured as a sword (as in *Ephesians*, vi, 17, and common to the whole ancient world) coming from a man's mouth; which in Britain was betokened by the figure Prester John.* Hence the note in Harleian MS. 619 that he was one of the Magi, and the triple crown surmounting his arms. Studied common sense is what the three crowns in Arthur's banner denote; and it was the banner of Britain.

·   ·   ·   ·   ·

It is impossible, though, to appreciate the extent to which these ideas permeated British thought, until the actual principles comprising their code of common sense have been written down; then it will be recognized that they recur frequently in folk-lore, that is to say in what were the everyday reflections of ordinary people, and are part of our inherited nature. The bare fact of their survival, cherished in romance, through twenty centuries of disaster and discouragement—Roman conquest, Saxon conquest, Norse conquest, ecclesiastical disapproval, scholarship's disdain —speaks of a natural love for it.

The old code and its principles ran as follows:

Happiness is the sign of a healthy mind, which means a contented one, for which also is needed a healthy body (*mens sana in corpore sano*); contentment comes from the guidance of reason, and this has five components:

Ideal Aims
Knowledge
Wise Judgement (for making use of knowledge; it includes justice)
Selflessness   (so that judgement will be unbiased)
Goodwill   (which is generosity over conflicting opinion as
                 much as it is over material things; it includes love).

To these are to be added two principles of physical life—that Health and Strength are necessary, as is Prosperity. Lastly came a principle of Determination, enjoining strength of will to accomplish each one of these.

Probably the earliest reminder for this code of life was the assignment of a day of the week to each of the five moral and two physical principles, the eighth—determination—being understood as implicit in all. To each also was assigned the name of one of the planets, or heavenly bodies, with an accompanying colour. Since the reminder was first formed some small changes have crept in, which will be explained; the shape in which it has come down to the present day is as follows:

Ideal Aims	*Thursday*, Jeudi	Jove, Jupiter	Blue
Knowledge	Monday	Moon	White
Wise Judgement	*Tuesday*, Mardi	Mars	Red
Selflessness (Luck)	*Friday*, Vendredi	Venus	Green
Goodwill	*Wednesday*, Mercredi	Mercury	Purple
Health & Strength	Saturday	Saturn	Black
Prosperity	Sunday	Sun	Gold

The planetary names for colours are still instanced in an obsolete heraldic nomenclature; the principles have survived in a nursery rhyme, slightly distorted but recognizable:

> Monday's child is fair of face,
> Tuesday's child is a child of grace;
> Wednesday's child is loving and giving,
> Thursday's child has to work for its living;
> Friday's child is a child of woe,
> Saturday's child has far to go;
> But the child that is born on the Sabbath day
> Is bonny and blythe, and good and gay.

These entail some comment. The ideal aims of Thursday have been interchanged with the prosperity of Sunday, presumably at the Church's instigation; gold however certainly stood for wealth (whether in coin or corn), and Jupiter's blue certainly represented ideal aims, spoken of as 'the sky-way to happiness'. Accordingly prosperity is Thursday, with the observation that it comes from hard work. The kind of prosperity taught, though, was content-ment with a simple sufficiency; so much so, that the idea of wealth was almost lost in one of simplicity.

In Monday, the moon's association with knowledge and the colour white have already been remarked. Tuesday's 'grace' apparently refers to *Proverbs* iv, 9—'(Wisdom) shall give to thine head a chaplet of grace'; it dispels Mars' illusory character of warfare. Mars, like his British counterpart Camelos, whose name 'crooked' alludes to the crooked water-line of Aquarius the heavenly rain-bringer, was one of the five-colours quintet of wisdom (the Black Man's fraternity): his misrepresentation as a man of war is no more than a slander against his armed deter-mination to secure justice. In Wednesday's Mercury is to be seen the herald of goodwill and peace; while in his colour purple is the glow of the wine that stimulates generous sentiment.

These are amplified in the Glossary, under ECCLESIASTES,* where Friday's Venus as selflessness is shown as a transformation from the earlier worldly-wise code, in which one of the consti-tuents of happiness was luck. What is so remarkable is that at some very early date it became realized that luck comes more from unselfish behaviour than sheer chance; consequently 'The Woman's' day (for Luck is the Strange Woman of Hebrew literature) and its colour green were pronounced as unlucky, and it was ordained as a fast day on which the control of self-indul-gence was supposed to be practised.

Over the colour green a curious transformation has crept in: the proper colour for luck was black (the rain-cloud), while green stood for 'Youth', the colloquial term for health and strength, derived from the springtime, the youth of the year. Venus' and Saturn's colours have become interchanged; it was Saturn to whom 'Youth' was dedicated, whose child had 'far to go' through the vale of life, because it was yet young—a practical reminder for cultivating health and strength. Nor did this refer to personal life only; it was just as applicable to national military security. Thus Saturn has mistakenly become black, he should correctly be green; and it is Saturn the cavalier, not Saturn the puritan, who is said to have gone to rest contentedly in an isle of the West. Where perhaps he still is.

This glimpse of ancient British mentality may have made clear the nature characterizing Arthur's people. They were thoughtful, courageous, and high-minded—but up to a point only; even at a crisis they would be readier to trust in 'muddling through' rather than forgo self-interest. The shipwrights who built his Britain could draw excellent designs, fashioned wholeheartedly from ideals, but the craftsmen who shaped the timbers and pinned them together stinted their work. So, instead of his being a living figure amongst us, we have only a fusty picture of his banner, tucked away in a forgotten manuscript.

Yet the trust that he will once again come to raise it in this realm has ever since remained. Is it not conceivable that, if given the will, the hope could materialize into reality? To quote an analogy from Indian wisdom—We see many stars at night in the sky, but not after sunrise; are we to say that there are no stars in the heaven of day? So, because we see not Arthur in the days of our ignorance, it is not for us to say that there is no Arthur.

17

Arthur Shall Come Again

LET us accordingly look forward hopefully to his return. Already once has this nearly happened, in the Middle Ages when there took place that great outburst of national spirit, the remains of which still inspire our admiration with their beauty and discernment. The magnificence of perpendicular architecture, the magnanimous parliamentary principle that 'What touches all should receive the consent of all', the gentle chivalry of the Knighthood of the Garter—founded as a revival of the Round Table—the lofty ideal voiced by Piers Plowman 'Reason shall reign said the King', and the fearless morale of an army that was the finest in Europe, these are some of its memories and remains. It was a spirit which all but produced an Arthur; so the course of its rise and fall is worth following.

The revival of national spirit began with William the Conqueror, who, when he replaced the Saxon rulership of England, found a large serf population that was not Saxon, but Briton or half-breed, the survivors of those who had yielded themselves to the invaders through force of hunger (Gildas records their plight), and the hapless progeny of rape. All of these were mostly Briton in sentiment. And there were also the descendants of deliberate Saxon-British marriages, as were encouraged under King Iñe. To such an extent did the numbers or influence of all these spread, that practically the whole of our national tradition has come from them; it is Celtic, not Saxon. The new Norman rule identified its interests with this radically Briton stock, thus gaining a popular standing; it gave its sympathy to a sentiment which was not Angle-land but Ynge-land, Iñe's fusion of Celt and Saxon, and reminiscent of the names Ignoge and the Swedish Ynglingar.

From the very outset we see the Norman kings using the prided Briton standard—'Then caused he the Dragon to be set up, the matchless standard'. Barons and lesser lords did likewise; and many feudal armorial bearings can be traced to the folk-emblems of their particular tenants.

As a result, very shortly after the Conquest a resurrected British spirit is to be seen manifesting itself. In 1090 stories of King Arthur are reaching Italy, and are popular there; in 1113 when a foreigner in Cornwall questions the truth of a statement that Arthur is still alive, the doubted man hits him and a riot is started; and in 1139 Geoffrey of Monmouth is being pressed by the Archdeacon of Oxford and the Bishop of Lincoln to translate a Welsh manuscript, and to collect current oral tradition into a comprehensive history of the old British kings, especially that of King Arthur. All of this is within a lifetime of the Conquest; and it is significant that the inducement should come largely from the Church, since that body was the most closely in touch with the submerged folk; its action seems to reflect their popular want. Other romancers follow, among them Wace, who writes in Norman-French; then Layamon in 1204, who writes in English, by which date the tradition has ceased to be a Celtic legend, and has become an English epic common to the blended blood. National pride is getting into full swing; and in response to the sentiment one of the royal princes is christened Arthur.

It is at this period that the Three Crowns tradition blazons itself all over eastern England, betokening both remembrance of Arthur's deeds and the social creed it portrays; very much did it comprehend the latter, it was the forerunner of the next century's call—'Reason shall reign'. That was the common man's craving, a rule of reasoned good in place of the avaricious strife that was sucking the country's blood. Conceivably also at this date the ideal of the Common Weal was being mooted verbally, even though it does not appear in writing for another three centuries; for, when it does appear it has the same moral framework as the old social philosophy. Below are Edmund Dudley's 'Five roots of the tree of Common Weal', in italics, with their equivalents against them. His actual term 'Commonwealth' has here been altered to Common Weal, because it better expresses the meaning intended.

Fear of God	An aim of Reason (cf. God—the Word—Reason. And, 'In the fear of God is the beginning of wisdom.')	
Truth	Knowledge	(Education, Justice)
Justice	Wise Judgement	
Unity	Selflessness (which enables unity)	
Tranquillity	Goodwill (the way to peace and tranquillity)	

With Edward I's accession national sentiment received splendid leadership from the crown, the young king declaring himself ever to be true to 'the commonalty of England', and the cross of St George (a purely Celtic figure) being adopted as the national ensign; while the royal family took for their badge a rose, the flower which in popular understanding stood for goodwill. These actions show that the sentiments of the humbler people of the realm were reaching royal ears. How they did so is a matter of no small interest; two possible channels suggest themselves, the clerics and the heralds. The former as already remarked were a link between the higher and lower in the land, and may well have spoken for the humble; but it is impossible, when noticing the artistry and poetic allusion in the chosen devices, not to believe that the latter were the King's main source of inspiration, which, in their role of custodians of tradition, would be but natural. Especially is their artistry conspicuous under the King's grandson, Edward III.

Of the nobles, some responded to the King's lead, but in general their opposition was obstinate; it is noticeable that under a strong crown they would fulfil their feudal obligations, but under a weak one would become self-seeking. The King's task lay in inducing the baronage to serve the country's good. The practice adopted based its appeal on moral issues: he set the example, and required the nobles to follow it, of making the native English social code fashionable; that is to say, he required them to have ideals as their aims, and to acknowledge that privileges entailed obligations, that the lord owed a duty to his people.

It was in response to a lead of this kind that in 1283, only eight years after Edward I's accession, Roger de Mortimer established a Round Table at Kenilworth, for 'the encouragement of military pastimes'; then, almost seventy years later, in 1348, the

King himself revived Arthur's Round Table in the Order of the Garter. The fable of a lady's garter being dropped was no more than disparagement by the very persons whose ways the King was endeavouring to amend; but even if the concocted slight caused any cheap sniggers at Court, it certainly carried no credence among the people, in whose tongue the King was speaking, the language of folk-lore. To the country at large the message was clear: the King was calling upon his nobles to wed themselves to their country's good; and he was warning them against thinking of it derogatorily—'Ill luck to him who scorns it'. The garter was the well-known emblem of married love, and a charm for gaining it:

The Spell

> I twitch'd the dangling garter from his knee;
> Now mine I quickly doff of inkle blue;
> Together fast I tie the garters twain,
> And, while I knit the knot, repeat this strain—
>> Three times a true-love's knot I tie secure;
>> Firm be the knot, firm may his love endure.

So, garters and true-love's knots and roses were linked together, to form the insignia of what represented its knighthood's marriage to their country's welfare. The patron figure for this was none other than the old British deity, familiarly known as Gôg, anglicized to George. In the British tongue, Gôg was the cuckoo —the herald of the new year and of good times to come; he is depicted teaching the British dragon to appreciate the merits of wisdom, by thrusting a shaft of it (metaphoric 'light') literally down his throat. But that was in the days of an older system of education. The whole sentiment, be it repeated, is Briton, cemented by the Saxon capacity for united effort.

This institution of the Garter came as the culmination of some twenty years' prior inculcation of ideals; its recipients were men who had been brought up from childhood to think in such terms, broadcast by various devices in royal heraldry. For example, the King's shield of three feathers on a black field: its significance lay in its designation, the 'Shield of Peace', and in the motto on each feather, 'I serve'. They proclaim the King's aim to be the service of his people; under his royal arms he would lead them in war, but under the Three Feathers he would serve them in peace; his power would be used like that of Thor's hammer: 'In war to shatter, but in peace to bless'. And he was speaking to descendants of the Warriors of the Hammer, the Ordovic of the Welsh Border and of Winchester, in their own tongue. Once more we meet black, their lucky colour and a reminder for unselfishness; and there seems more than chance coincidence between its use for the field of that shield and the verse from *Ecclesiastes*—'The profit of a land every way is a king that maketh himself servant to the field', the correct rendering of what the Authorized Version has inverted.

Of like implication are the collars of knighthood and high office, and the collars and chains with which heraldic creatures were customarily fettered. They portray the individual, represented in heraldry by the creature, as being 'bound by the unseen chains of divine love', that is to say of selflessness, duty. They were borne proudly; men were learning to acknowledge that, to all alike, privileges carried with them obligations. Among the royal badges, particularly conspicuous are those relating to 'light', such as rays from a cloud, the sun in splendour, and later a rayed rose; these all relate to the philosophy of wisdom described in the last chapter. Their prominence evidences the degree of regard held for it.

All of this in mediaeval times was popular tradition. And for its encouragement, Edward III dedicated his son Edmund to it, assigning him the armorial bearings of the Three Crowns (its epitome) to carry in its honour, and naming him after the East Anglian king with whose memory they had come to be associated. The whole tenor of his rule was a call to the country, from highest to lowest, to live up to the people's old ideals; he offered reasoned law, and he required mutual obedience in return, with unselfishness and goodwill in binding themselves to their country's service. It was practical 'light of mind', and was the King's reply to the people's yearning, put plainly on parchment by Piers Plowman—'Reason shall reign, said the King'.

The result was astonishing in its military effect: A. H. Burne has brought to notice recently the remarkable standard of prowess attained by the Anglo-Welsh army during the French wars;

Edward III demonstrated that the spirit this social tradition generated gave his men irresistible force, because fundamentally it was honoured. Under it and its royal lead, the Britain of King Arthur was being born again.

.   .   .   .   .

Yet it died in infancy. Instead of growing from strength to strength, England sank ignominiously into a hundred years of civil war. When death removed the strong hands of King Edward and his like-minded son, the Black Prince, the smouldering jealousy of avarice burst into flame; and rule of the country passed from those who would have led it high-mindedly to those who made it the prize of grasping strife. But the struggle was among the would-be rulers, the common people were scarcely affected; so when the crown came back into strong hands, in the person of Henry Tudor, the spirit of Arthur once again began to manifest itself. This was round about the year 1500. Shortly before then we find Caxton printing Malory's romance, to serve what must have been a popular demand; Edmund Dudley is writing his plea for the common weal; and in the next year the King christens his eldest son Arthur. It is plain as to the direction in which national thought was trending.

Sternly though the two Henry Tudors controlled the people, however, they were unable to stop the self-centred fashion of ostentation and of accumulating wealth that had set in; consequently among their officers of state personal motives supplanted disinterested service. Possibly the Tudors' own motives in their forceful acquisition of the crown, and endeavour to maintain their line, beneficial though they proved to be, were not so completely disinterested as to enable them to preach selflessness convincingly. But when Elizabeth succeeded to the throne in her own right and with her country's will, her example could not be disparaged by sneers; so under her the spirit of Arthur regained fresh life. We see Spenser modelling his *Faerie Queene* on the legend, and Shakespeare fashioning patriotic plays from themes of British tradition, while the last remnants of mediaeval minstrelsy to survive the printing press' greater attraction repeat the tales of *The Seven Champions of Christendom*. Even so, the country's spirit was not untainted; and Wingfield-Stratford writes that Shakespeare, in four of his plays, has weighed the individualism of his time in the balance and has found it wanting. The nature of the flaw deserves notice. Arthur did not return.

Once again with the death of a strong ruler, and with government falling into weak hands, prone to prejudice, self-interest came to the fore: in the next reign, to quote the same historian, 'the men who held the reins of power, and enjoyed its sweets, had got out of touch with what was best in the nation, they ceased even to understand in what direction their duty lay'. Their example spread through the land; national spirit was smothered. A utilitarian outlook was now abroad, rendered impressive and alluring by the visible profits of commerce.

For the ensuing two and a half centuries wealth flourished, with the industrial revolution opening new and enormous avenues for fortune. The lot of the common people was at the least neglected, at the worst exploited. It was not a change of character but of fashion; the country was embarked upon a false aim, deeming that happiness was to be found in opulence rather than in the contentment which comes from the mind. The influence of public spirit, that should have kept fashion along generous lines, and have heeded their fellow-creatures' welfare, was lacking. It was unchivalrous, as is evidenced from the sweated labour of industry, to the heartless eviction of Highland crofters, and to the exploitation or parsimonious neglect of colonial planters. Seen in retrospect it was not only devoid of sentiment but of reason; and it met its punishment in the separation of the American colonies from the Motherland, leaving a slur on the nation's character which time may never efface. Can it be wondered at that for two hundred and fifty years Arthur's spirit remained in oblivion?

In the end, as was but natural, reason revolted. Britain, thanks to a tolerant-natured people's sense of balance, was spared the ghastly scenes which accompanied the French revolution (against far worse conditions); and among the better-thinking section of the public a genuine desire for ideal aims helped overcome the privileged persons' reluctance to rationalize their position. The change was gradual; but by the Victorian era a change had certainly set in. The kindlier atmosphere allowed idealism to start

to blossom, and fired with hope Tennyson penned his beautiful
lines foretelling Arthur's return, and taking up the theme from
where Sir Bedivere had borne Arthur to the barge that sailed with
him across the Lake to Avalon:

> Long stood Sir Bedivere
> Revolving many memories, till the hull
> Look'd one black dot against the verge of dawn.

> Yet in sleep I seem'd
> To sail with Arthur under looming shores,
> Point after point; till on to dawn, when dreams
> Begin to feel the truth and stir of day.
> To me, methought, who waited with a crowd,
> There came a barque that, blowing forward, bore
> King Arthur, like a modern gentleman.
> And all the people cried,
> 'Arthur is come again: he cannot die.'

> Then those that stood upon the hills behind
> Repeated—'Come again, and thrice as fair;'
> And, further inland, voices echo'd—'Come
> With all good things, and wars shall be no more.'
> At this a hundred bells began to peal,
> That with the sound I woke, and heard indeed
> The clear church-bells ring in the Christmas-morn.

> Ring out the old, ring in the new,
> Ring, happy bells, across the snow:
> The year is going, let him go;
> Ring out the false, ring in the true.

> Ring out the grief that saps the mind,
> For those that here we see no more;
> Ring out the feud of rich and poor,
> Ring in redress to all mankind.

> Ring out a slowly dying cause,
> And ancient forms of party strife;
> Ring in the nobler modes of life,
> With sweeter manners, purer laws.

> Ring out false pride in place and blood,
>   The civic slander and the spite;
>   Ring in the love of truth and right,
> Ring in the common love of good.

.   .   .   .   .

How unhappily different has been the reality. A hundred years have passed by, and although we can be thankful that poverty has well-nigh gone, yet the feud between classes is almost more vicious than ever; and party strife, so far from ceasing, acclaims its Modreds as heroes. Instead of an Arthurian pride in accomplishing what is right, we see good being subordinated to what is profitable factiously. The country looks on acquiescently, not the whole of it perhaps, but the majority; it has been no land for Arthur.

Yet this country breeds men capable of wielding power justly and wisely. Under our much maligned colonial administration, we find constantly that, given freedom to act and trust in their integrity, we produce men who devote their authority generously and selflessly to the welfare of the peoples under them; it is at home that we find mistrust and a liking for demagogic leadership. Why is it that the Modreds and Lancelots are chosen in place of an Arthur?

May it not be that the nation's vision is coloured: men are suspicious of their fellows, afraid they will use power for selfish ends; and accordingly they fetter their authority? And through the same coloured spectacles they choose Modreds and Lancelots, popular through imputing an Arthur falsely with the motives the people fear. This habitual scepticism is unhealthy; it is unchivalrous at its root. The following words of one of our imperial officials are typical of the rule we have given, and of the men who are available in plenty for public life, were they but chosen, and allowed scope—'I have never sought to influence any man's mind, save by impressing on him the advantages of forming his own thoughts, rather than blindly adopting those of myself or of others; I have endeavoured to impress on all the grand and simple truth, that real nobility of mind consists in doing good and right, for good and right's sake only. These principles have in practice never failed; they give a force which nothing can overthrow; and under their influence I have been permitted to witness a (people) being raised from a state of violence, misery, and cruelty, to one of peace, comfort, social order, and happiness.' From men of this kind a magnificent Round Table could be formed; and then with a knighthood in readiness for his command, King Arthur could be expected to return.

Chivalrous trust in fellow-men, an unselfish sense of public duty, and a common purpose of doing good and right for good and right's sake only, these qualities seem needed in the land beforehand. Yet it can scarcely be said they form part of our General Certificate of Education, else they would already be the vogue. A familiar presidential figure is absent from the Board. Merlin still lies beneath the stone where the damsel of the Lake imprisoned him. Merlin who was formerly called Myrddin—'Reason'. 'John the Divine called me Myrddin' wrote Taliesin, referring to the Word that was the discourse of Reason (page 105), and the guiding hand in life. Merlin, who built the first Round Table, where party strife was surrendered to goodwill, and from whom this island gained its earliest name—Clas Myrddin, 'the Green Isle of Reason'.

King Arthur's banner bears the tokens of Merlin's and the Lady of the Lake's Britain blazoned in unison, the cross as the Church's doctrine of the Word, the three crowns as Merlin's teaching of Reason; they are for men to choose at will, and without disparagement when choice differs. So, let us picture that Merlin has been set free, and together with the damsel of the Lake is bidding us refashion our moral arms needed in preparation for Arthur. Then will be heard the sound of hammers ringing upon the anvils throughout the kingdom, in every smithy where public opinion is forged or tempered—in schools, colleges, printing presses, broadcast stations, theatres, cinemas, and churches. Sword blades will be sharpened, dinted helms made true, burnies hardened, and all the various means for keeping firm our will to sustain the banner of Arthur will be hammered into shape. And when the echoes reach Argante in Avalon, she will know that the time has come to give Arthur the ring that will restore him to health and strength, the sapphire ring of Adam that weds men to ideals. Then will we see, approaching our shores from across the far horizon, the sails of his ship *White Wings*, heralding a new era of peace and prosperity; and in it, girt with Caliburn as of old, Arthur will come again.

The Hard Cleaver, the 'sword of the spirit which is the word of God', 'quick and powerful, sharper than any two-edged sword, piercing even to the dividing asunder of soul and spirit, and of the joints and marrow, and a discerner of the thoughts and intents of the heart'. 'The similitude of two serpents was on the hilt in gold; and when the sword was drawn from its scabbard it seemed as if two flames of fire burst forth from the jaws of the serpents, and then so wonderful was the blade that it was hard for anyone to look upon it.' The two intertwined snakes are Harmony, which is 'as a man drawing inspiration from God; it is the harmony of contraries lighted by the glory of wisdom'

Index of Dates*

† stands for 'approximately'

A.D.

37   Tiberius Caesar died; Caligula became emperor. Joseph of Arimathea arrived in Britain.

38   † Adminius rebelled against Cymbeline.

39   † Cymbeline died; Gwydr succeeded him as king.

40   † Caligula's farcical assembly at Boulogne; Beric's defection.

41   Caligula murdered; Claudius became emperor.

42   Gwydr's demand for the Briton rebels, and his refusal to pay tribute.

43   Aulus Plautius' invasion; the south-east captured. Gwydr killed; Arthur became king.

44   Claudius arrived; Arthur submitted and was appointed king; revolted and fought at Exeter, the Brue, and Bath; re-appointed king; Plautius appointed governor.

45 ⎫
46 ⎪
47 ⎬ Arthur's reign
48 ⎪
49 ⎭

45   † Arthur married Guenevere. The Round Table formed.

49   Plautius recalled; Ostorius appointed governor. Ostorius subdued the Ceangi.

50   Arthur revolted; fought at Maidens Castle, Langport, Wookey Hole, and Bath.

51   Arthur continued resistance in South Wales; Ostorius established Caerleon-on-Itchen.

52   Arthur's campaign in Herefordshire; captured and sent to Rome.

53 ⎫
54 ⎪
55 ⎪
56 ⎬ Arthur at Rome
57 ⎪
58 ⎪
59 ⎪
60 ⎪
61 ⎭

53   Silurian resistance continued; † Ostorius died; Didius appointed governor. Venusius revolted.

54   Claudius murdered; Nero became emperor.

58   Veranius appointed governor in place of Didius.

59   Veranius died; Suetonius appointed governor.

61   Suetonius' campaign against Mon; Boadicea's revolt.

281

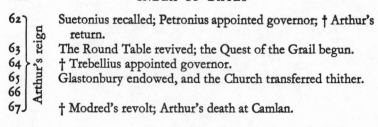

Glossary

ABBREVIATIONS

A.S.	. .	Anglo-Saxon
Br. Mus.	. .	British Museum
Boece Bel.	. .	Hector Boece, Bellenden's translation
Boece St.	. .	Hector Boece, Stewart's version
C/A	. .	College of Arms
C.B.	. .	*Cambrian Biography*
Dio	. .	Dio Cassius' *Roman History*
Eck.	. .	Eckwall's *English River Names*
G/M	. .	Geoffrey of Monmouth
Guest	.	*Origines Celticae*
Graal	. .	*Perceval le Gallois*
Iolo	. .	MS. quoted in Guest, II, 48
Loomis	.	*Wales and the Arthurian Legend*
Mab.	. .	Lady Charlotte Guest's *Mabinogion*
Mal.	. .	Malory's *Morte d'Arthur*
McClure	.	*British Place Names*
Morgan	.	*Origin of British Christianity*
Rhys	. .	Sir John Rhys' *Arthurian Legend*
Skene	. .	*Four Ancient Books of Wales*
Tr.	. .	Triads, Welsh

ABER-FFRAW:

Frome estuary (pp. 45, 55, 63, 70).

Belonged to Matholwch the Gael (Mab. *Branwen*).

Geographic: *see* SOLENT;* reached by sea from the Meon, Aber Menai; and close to the Lake of the Cauldron, presumably that of Gwyddno Garanhir of the Lake (Mab. *Branwen*).

ADARWEINIDOG: *see* GWEIRYDD.*

AFFARAON:

The original name of Dinas Emrys, *see* AMBROSE.*

It cannot be Stonehenge, because it was the seat of Brynach the Gael near the sea coast of Arllechwedd, *see* CAT PALUG, i.e. off West Sussex, the Lake. Thus the Eagles' home, Eryri, the Lake was mistaken for that of Salisbury Plain. The 'Oxford'* near where it lay will have been Icen-ford, on the lower Itchen.

ALBANY (*see also* CORNWALL*):

The traditional origin of the Albanys is told by Boece; it is that of the Gaels of England, Scotland, and Ireland.

Boece's place names have to be viewed from the revised geographical outlook given in this book; they centre largely round BRIGANCE,* Sussex. Other names closely associated are Ireland* and the Isles, *see* LAKE.* A misleading name is Argathill, which is not Argyll of Scotland but properly means the Gathill or Goidel Border—*Margo Hibernensium* in mediaeval Latin, the 'Irish' March, a term applicable to any local Gaelic border, in this case between Sussex and the 'Irish' Isles.

The Albanys' history is interwoven with that of the Picts, who, although given a separate identity, must in fact have been to all intents and purposes the same. They were the combined peoples known in Welsh tradition as the Gwyddel Ffichti, the Gaelic Picts; in the romances the Gaels are called 'Irish' (p. 24) and the Picts retain a separate name, but the difference seems no more than between modern Highland clans. Boece's account of the quarrel between Caswallon and the Trinovant of London shows the Albanys of the Weald supporting the Trinovant; hence, cf. the period of this book, their alliance with the Trinovant chief's family. Consequently the Trinovant can be considered one of their clans. Likewise the Catuuellaun of the Chilterns and the Iceni of the Fens; although hostile to one another the enmity was clannish, racially they were one. This racial tradition lasted down to the Middle Ages, and is the substance of the heraldic Three Crowns (*see* Chapter 16).

The ruling feature in Geoffrey's and Boece's histories is the antipathy between Albany and Cornwall, called Pict and Briton in the latter. Typical is G/M II, xv—'foul shame it was that he, the eldest born (and chief of Albany), should not have dominion over the whole island'. For the mixture of Albany and Cornish narrative in G/M, and for his Book IV being Albany, *see* p. 29 above.

A diagram of the claims for chieftainship in Albany is under Caledon.* The title Dubno* seems to have been an Albany one.

ALCLUD (pp. 135, 137, 153, 233):

Founded by Ebrauc of Maidens Castle, 'towards Albany' at the same period as 'York'—beyond the Humber (G/M II, vii). Seeing that he was enlarging his realm, both are likely to have been by his eastern boundary, the Arun. 'York'* has been identified as Bow Hill, above Chichester; Alclud seems probably to have been Butser Hill, with the river Rother below also bearing the name Alclud.

That it lay on the South Downs towards Hampshire/West Sussex is indicated in Taliesin's poem about a cattle raid from the Chilterns (Calchvynyd) into the Lowland* Hundred, 'the land of Gwyddno' (Skene, xlvi); it was resisted by Owein Rheged (of Chichester), and fighting took place at the ford of the Alclud and on the Gwen. These will have been the Rother and Gwyn of Winchester, the Itchen.

See also under PELLINORE.*

AMBROSE (p. 144), in Welsh *Emrys*, is applied to several places and persons:

Affaraon* (Mab. *Lludd & Llevelys*), Stonehenge (*Camb. Biog.* and cf. G/M viii, ix and xii), Merlin, Uther's brother Aurelie, and Owain who buried the head of Vran (Tr. liii). Amesbury is ? Ambrose-bury. The name evidently relates to the brewing of mead, for the cup of goodwill that harmonizes disputes. Like the Greek *ambrosia* it is connected with honey; its survival is to be found in the figure of St Ambrose, distinguished by a beehive. Presumably therefore it was the style of certain druids, cf. Aeddan Foeddog son of Kaw.*

AMLODD (pp. 37–8, 47–9, 103–4, 168, 224–5):

The known 'daughters' of Amlodd are:

Eigr (Ygerne) – *m.* Cymbeline; children, Arthur and Anna.

Rhieinwylydd – *m.* Bicanys; children, Anna and Joseph (of Arimathea).

Tywanwedd – *m.* Awstl; children, five saints (but a generation must have intervened).
  m. Tudfwlch; child, Huallu.
  m. Nudd; children, Evrawc, Pwyll Avallawch, and the widow Lady of Camelot.

Goleuddydd – *m.* Kilydd of Caledon; son, Kilhwch.

The expression 'Roman lady', by which the daughters were sometimes known, may possibly be explained by the Institution of Amlodd (*see* pp. 37–8), having been adopted by the Romans as a local authority, at a later date (*see* Wade-Evans *Welsh Christian Origins*, v, §14). The number of saints its daughters produced is noticeable; it was a definite influence in the early Church.

Another apparent 'daughter of Amlodd' is Anna the grandmother of Dewi.* Her father Vortimer 'the Blessed' is regarded by Rees (*Welsh Saints*, p. 134) as son of Vortigern. The names represent Gwrth Ymer, Gwrth Igern; Gwrth the equivalent of Count. Igern is reminiscent of Ygerne, daughter of Amlodd; and Ymer was Danaan, the Creator in Scandinavian myth. The name 'Hamlet' of Denmark is Amlodd; the institution is clearly of Danaan, Children of Don, origin.

ANDERIDA (pp. 74–5):

A people, of the Weald and Pevensey. Their chief, Andr-auc.*
Possibly a sect akin to the Brigant,* cf. classical Androgeus, son of
Minos.* Connected with the Eagle* folk of the Lake, as Pevensey
Castle called 'the Honour of the Eagle' by Normans; hence *De Aquila.*
Eagle of Pevensey has descended through Edward I to John of Ghent
and Beauforts, thence to Cambridge colleges of St John and Christ.

ANDRAUC (*Androgeus*) (p. 74):

Chief of the Ander-idi;* in classical history Mandubrauc. In Caesar's
first campaign, medium between Caswallon and Caledon; in second,
quarrelled with Caswallon and gave Caesar safe landing in Thanet
(G/M and Boece). For family, *see* CYMBELINE* and CALEDON*; hence
his granddaughter Cartimandua's jealousies. *See also* MINOS.*

ANNA (pp. 39, 49, 97, 103–4, 224):

At least three Welsh Saints—Beino, Cadoc, and Carranog—are
traced to 'Anna, cousin of the Virgin Mary, the mother of Christ', and
St David to the sister of the Virgin Mary. Fictitious generations have
been invented to suit a supposed Saxon period; discarded, the remainder evidence her real kindred.

ANNWVYN (pp. 42, 226):

Ann-dale, the valley of the Ann or Anton, the Test (*vide* the
reviewer of Eckwall's *River Names* in the *Geographical Journal*, 1929).
Wvyn is a variation of *dwfyn*, and the sequence *glyn*, *dwfn*, *gwaelod*
corresponds to glen, dale, strath; thus Annwvyn is the middle part of
the Test valley, between its upper reaches and estuary.

The synonymity of Annwyn and Avalon is instanced in:
   (i) Modron* daughter of Avallawch calls herself daughter of the
       king of Annwn.
   (ii) Morgan le Fay of Avalon is 'goddess of Annwvyn', *see* MORGAN.*
       She is one of nine sisters, cf. the nine maidens who warmed
       the cauldron of Annwn (Skene, viii).
It was the domain of—Nudd (p. 226).
                     —Pwyll Avallawch* and of Dyfed;* he was
                     Pelles of the Lower Folk, i.e. Lower Ann.
In it was Caer Sidi (Taliesin's *Spoils of Annwn*, Skene, viii and xii);
its resemblances to the island of the Graal in *Perceval le Gallois*, xxxv,
are several (*see* Loomis' *Wales and the Arthurian Legend*, amended as in
(*d*) below):
   (*a*) 'an island of the sea' and 'around it the streams of the ocean'.

(b) 'the four corners of the town' and 'the four-cornered caer (Pedryvan)'.

(c) 'underneath a tree a fountain' and 'the fruitful (i.e. wonder-working) fountain is above it'.

(d) the fountain of Iweret won by Lancelot can be identified with this; its custom the creed of Perpetual Youth, cf. Taliesin—'age does not harm him who dwells therein' (Skene, viii).

(e) the vessel of glass (in the *Perlesvaus* version) and cf. the Glass Caer (*Wydyr*) of Annwn.

In *Pwyll Prince of Dyfed* (Mab.) Pwyll had a neighbour Arawn of Annwvyn, who owned Havgan which seems to be Havant by Portsmouth. They agreed to exchange kingdoms, suggesting rival claims to these lands; hence Arawn of Annwvyn would appear to be Urien Rheged* of Chichester. Cf. marriage of Modron* to Urien.

Hounds of Annwn probably astronomers of Nudd.

APPLE-TREE (pp. 34, 50):
Associated with Justice, cf. crab-apple badge of Clan Lamont 'law-men' and Lamas apple festival when disputes settled. Ref. also Hesperides (p. 265), and Geraint's maze (p. 143).

ARGYLL: *see under* ALBANY.

ARIANRHOD (pp. 26, 256):
Caswallon's sister (Hengwrt MS. 536, Tr. xxxii); her sons accompanied him to Gascony, against Romans. As Caswallon and Lear were Belgic, while the name Arianrhod is 'Children of Don',* it is inferred their mother was East Anglian Gael.

ARIMATHEA (pp. 49–54, 102–6, 209, 215, 224):
The memory of Joseph's Church has suffered from the general contempt for oral tradition, which followed the development of printing and disappearance of illiteracy, also from a Church of England predilection to trace itself from St Augustine. Contrarily in the Middle Ages the British tradition was respected internationally; e.g. Ussher— 'Upon this ground the ambassadors of the kings of England claimed precedency of the ambassadors of the kings of France, Spain, and Scotland in several councils held in Europe: one at Pisa, A.D. 1409; another at Constance, A.D. 1414; another at Siena, A.D. 1424; and especially at Basle, A.D. 1434, where the point of precedency was strongly debated (and conceded to England). The ambassadors from France, insisting much upon the dignity and magnitude of that kingdom, said " 'Twas not reasonable that England should enjoy equal privileges with France"; but the ambassadors of England, insisting on

the honour of the Church, declared that the Christian faith was first received in England, Joseph of Arimathea having come hither with others, in the fifteenth year after the assumption of the Virgin Mary (etc.).' And the Council upheld the English claim.

Salient traditions are these:

(i) Gildas states that these islands received Christianity in the last year of Tiberius Caesar, i.e. in A.D. 37. Council of Constance, 1414, stated 'immediately after the Passion of Christ' (Morgan, p. 113).

(ii) The Welsh Triads and Achau y Saint state that Christianity was first brought to this island by Vran, for which he was styled Bendigeid 'the Blessed'; he brought with him Ilid and two or three other teachers. The supposition that Vran came from captivity with his son Caradoc has arisen from this tradition of the original Inys-witryn having become mixed with the foundation of the Glastonbury Inys-witryn, which latter took place on Caradoc's return from captivity in Rome. Correctly, Christianity was brought by Ilid who was given sanctuary by Vran, in A.D. 37. Ilid is stated to have been a 'man of Israel', and other tradition tells of his having been a cousin of Arthur and thus of Vran; Charles Cooksey, in the *XIXth Century*, 1924, pointed to the identity of Ilid with Joseph of Arimathea; and the family table on p. 224 explains the relationship, making clear how intimate it will have been to the Britons.

(iii) The Vatican MS. quoted on p. 52. There is a Welsh Triad of Lazarus; it is unlikely to have borne his name unless he had had some connection with Britain.

(iv) William of Malmesbury, *c.* 1135, records the Glastonbury tradition that twelve disciples of Philip, headed by Joseph of Arimathea, came from France and were granted Inys-witryn in A.D. 63, and that Arwiragus and subsequent kings gave it twelve hides of land. This is a mixture of two traditions: the one, of Joseph's arrival in A.D. 37 at the original Inys-witryn, the Isle of Wight; the other, of his return to Glastonbury in A.D. 63 from South Wales, to which the name Inys-witryn was transferred and the twelve hides were granted. *See also* PASSION.*

(v) *See* L. S. Lewis, *St Joseph of Arimathea at Glastonbury*, and R. W. Morgan, *The Origin of British . . . Christianity*, who quote many early writers, e.g. Dorotheus Bishop of Tyre, A.D. 303: 'Aristobulus, who is mentioned by the Apostle in his epistle to the Romans, was made bishop in Britain'; this corroborates the Triad statement that Arwstli accompanied Ilid when he brought Christianity to Britain; it treats him as contemporary with St Paul.

(vi) The international acceptance of the Grail legend, and the honour paid to the Three Crowns device (Ch. 16), testify to a genuine foundation; in connection with p. 265 and the note ECCLESIASTES below, cf. the legend—When Lucifer was cast out of heaven, he had been offered a crown by the angels; a stone from it fell, and from it was carved a cup of great beauty which eventually came into the hands of Joseph of Arimathea and became the Holy Grail; it was used at the Last Supper, and in it some of the blood from Christ's side was caught.

Joseph's name Ilid or Illtyd (the Saint of Ili) refers conceivably to the descendants of Ili-um, Troy, prided by the Cornish as their origin (*see* G/M). Hence the Isle river, and names Il-, Somerset; cf. the Ilidh river, Sutherland. He is called soldier-saint apparently because of his former appointment as decurion in Palestine. His mother was a daughter of Amlodd, thereby bringing him into relationship with most of the leading Cornish families; his father was Bicanys of Llydaw,* the West Country, evidently a half-Phoenician trader. Joseph's burial in the old wattle church at Glastonbury is recorded in a manuscript attributed to Maelgwn of Llandaff, also said to have lived contemporarily. (For St David's connection with it, *see* DEWI.*)

The traditional date for Joseph's death is A.D. 82, but as will be seen that is improbable, and A.D. 72 more likely, on the assumption that an extra 'X' has slipped into the Roman numeral. In Malory, xv, iv, it is stated that Joseph preached forty years after the Passion,* which (*q.v.*) implies until A.D. 73 or thereabouts, giving the A.D. 72 some corroboration. As regards his birth: being the Virgin Mary's uncle he is unlikely to have been born later than her; and her birth, *vide* Hastings *Dict. Bible*, must have been in about 23 B.C.; that date is therefore the latest reasonable one for him, making his age in A.D. 72 ninety-five or over.

Thus Joseph will have been nearing seventy-five years of age at the time of Arthur's captivity at Rome, when the Church's welfare suffered a complete set-back everywhere. It may be concluded therefore that, like Geraint's sons, he crossed the Severn estuary into South Wales, and there lived with a small following at Llantwit Major, away from Roman rule. After Arthur's restoration, in about A.D. 63, he will have returned to Glastonbury at the age of eighty-seven; and in this elderly state he presided at Glastonbury until his death.

ARLLECHWEDD GALEHEDIN:

The Down-land between Kent and the Severn (Iolo MS.); it belonged to the southern Belgae (Tr.). The men of Galedin came to Wight from the land of Pwyl* when it was drowned by the sea (Tr., Guest II, 20). Its corruption was 'Harlech', where birds of Rhiannon sang; she was wife of Nudd of Annwvyn. Land in Arllechwedd given to Taliesin, thus adjoining the Itchen and Lowland Hundred, see DYFED.*

ARMORICA (p. 58):

Beside the Sea (McClure). North-west Devon and Brittany; the Devon Armorica contained LLYDAW.*

ARUNDEL:

Briton name Magouns (Malory x, xxxiii), 'the Honour of the Bear', from Gaelic *maghavenn, mathghaimhain,* bear. Alternatively 'the Honour of the Swallow', *see* CALEDON*; Norman-French *hirondelle* anglicized into *Harundel* (Domesday). A.-S. derivation improbable. For 'The Bear' as the chief's designation *see* p. 21.

ARWIRAGUS (pp. 16, 81, 123, 131):

The Gaelic-Pict name it represents appears to be Arc-wyr-auc, Ar'wyrauc, 'the Bear-folk chief'. The Gaelic '*c*' could become '*t*' in Pictish, both aspirated, giving Arth-wyr, 'The Arthur' (cf. Skene, Ch. viii).
Below is a comparison of that name with Caratacos:

Classical	Geoffrey of Monmouth and Hector Boece	Cambrian Biography
Togodumnus and Caratacos the sons of Cymbeline	Gwydr and Arwiragus, the sons of Cymbeline	Gwydr and Gweirydd* Adarweinidog, the sons of Cymbeline.
Togodumnus slain, and Caratacos succeeded him as king of the Britons	Gwydr slain, and Arwiragus succeeded him as king of the Britons	Caratacos (Caradoc), the son of Bendigeid Bran, 'the Blessed Chough'
Claudius received Caratacos' submission at Camulodunum	Claudius received Arwiragus' submission at Camelot Dun	
Vespasian fought a heavy campaign, including the Isle of Wight; his legion was at Exeter	Vespasian landed at Totnes and took Exeter. Arwiragus led the resistance	
Caractacus defeated and taken to Rome	Arwiragus taken to Rome (*vide* Boece/Stewart)	Caradoc ab Bran taken to Rome
Caractacus famed throughout the provinces and Italy	Arwiragus famed throughout Europe and at Rome	

AVALLAWCH, AVALON:
Anglicized to Evelake (Rhys xiii). Adjoined Annwvyn;* hence Pwyll pen Annwvyn is Pwyll Avallawch.

Rhiannon,* i.e. Royal Anton, the domain of Avallawch and of Nudd of Annwn; Avallawch's family were termed 'of the Valleys of Camelot'.

Avalon is also called the Joyous Isle; in *Sir Launfal*, Lancelot's 'mistress' is the king of Avalon's daughter, with whom he goes to live in the 'jolyf ile' for ever. Also called 'the Four-cornered Isle', *see* CARBONEK* and ANNWVYN.*

Thus Avalon, a four-cornered island off the lower Test, close to Camelot (Winchester) and adjoining the Dyfi which was flooded by the sea, *see* LOWLAND.* It is plainly the Isle of Wight.*

Its meaning: 'Apples', a clan name, *see* APPLE-TREE.*

BAN OF BENEWICK (pp. 53, 54, 61, 242):
Son-in-law of Cymbeline, and father of Lancelot.* Classical Adminius. For his death *see* Keightley's *Fairy Mythology*, pp. 30, 31.

For BENEWICK *see* CARBONEK.*

BEAR (pp. 15–16, 21, 82, 184):
A Gaelic-Pict clan, the *Arc*, closely akin to the Boar,* *Orc*. Their peoples Arcadians and Orcadians; their chieftains 'The Bear' and 'The Boar'.*

BENEWICK: *see* BAN.

BLACK COUNTRY (pp. 75–7, 157):
Named from the widespread charcoal burning for iron smelting. Dobona from British *dubo-*, black.

Alternatively sometimes refers to the Black Man fraternity (Ch. 13), as in Dyfi;* cf. Dewi,* and Balthazar (Ch. 16), and Black Prince (Ch. 17).

BOADICEA (pp. 47, 88, 117–19, 121–5, 138, 155, 178, 193–4, 200–1, 214, 254–6, 262):
Correctly Boada or Voada (Boece); mistakenly given her daughter's name (p. 255). She was daughter of Cadallan* and Cartimandua *see* CALEDON,* with a half-brother Caratak of Caledon. The agreement that she should marry Caratac, son of Cymbeline, abandoned (pp. 115, 121); kidnapped by Prasutawg (p. 126); repercussions (p. 119). Her two daughters' affairs (Chh. 11, 15).

BOAR (pp. 72–3, 84, 104):

A Gaelic-Pict clan, *see* BEAR.* *Twrc Trwyth*, the Boar ravaging Caledon, alludes to a traditional rival enmity; in this case not a native Boar, but foreign. Probably an allusion to Claudius' Tuscan origin; Etruscan emblem a Boar. *Trwyth* has been suggested as a corruption of Ostorius; mistaken for Plautius.

The sequence of Arthur's hunt after it may preserve names of forgotten skirmishes; it should be compared with the sequence tabulated under WEALDEN* BATTLES.

(i) Arthur seizes a 'cauldron' in 'Ireland' (the Gaels' islands of the Lake), and takes it to Porth Kerddin in Dyfed. (This appears to refer to the removal of the stones from 'Ireland' to Stonehenge.)

(ii) The Boar with seven young pigs is in the Gaels' country; on the first day he is fought by the Gaels, on the second by Arthur's household, and on the third by Arthur himself. (This resembles the Roman landing on the shores of the Gaelic area.) The Boar then says—'We will go into Arthur's country, and there will we do all the mischief that we can', referring to the mainland of Britain.

(iii) The Boar lands at Porth Cleis in Dyfed; Arthur comes to Mynyw, the Meon river.

(iv) Fighting follows at:

Aber Gleddyf
Preseleu
Glyn Nyver
Cwm Kerwyn—twice, and on the second occasion Arthur's 'son' (i.e. brother) Gwydr was killed.
Pelumyawc
Aber Teivi—where the Gauls ('king of France') were engaged.
Glyn Ystu—by Gwyn ab Nudd's domain of Annwyn.
Dyffryn Llychwr—In Urien Rheged's domains, around Chichester.
Mynydd Amanw
Dyffryn Amanw
Llwch Ewin
Llwch Tawy ⎫
Din Tywi ⎬— ? on Dartmoor (unrecorded).

Ystrad Yw—in Armorica (Devon), where two of Arthur's uncles were slain. This resembles the battle of Llongborth, where the Yeo flows into the Parret.

Severn estuary—this corresponds with the battle at the mouth of the Brue, and the one at Bath.

Cornwall—where the Boar disappears.

BODUNNI (p. 77):

Commonly assumed a mistake for Dobunni (*see* DUBNO*), but not certain; alternative 'Bedegraine' suggests Boduag'ni, a Belgic name from Hainault.

BRIGANCE, BRIGANT:

A sect rather than a tribe, found all over England, e.g. Brentford by London, Brent, Brig-stow in Somerset. In this case East Sussex, near Caledon;* cf. Boece, 55 B.C.—'Near Brigantia coast Ederus (of Caledon) lay with a royal host, adread the Romans should his land invade'. Also Brigance had a stronghold in Calidon wood. Brigance probably synonymous with Moray (p. 197).

Compare Caswallon's three allies in Boece with his three vassals in G/M:

Hector Boece	*Geoffrey of Monmouth*
Eder of Scots (Caledon)	Cridious of Albany
Geth of Picts	Guerthaeth of Gwynedd
Cadallan of Brigance	Britael of Dyfed*

Gwynedd, the valley of the Gwyn (Itchen), was regarded as Pictish. Brigance thus adjoined Dyfed.*

Brig- implies 'Bright', with reference to 'Light', Reason. Note their feminine deity canonized as St Briget; and note the legend of her at Bethlehem.

(P. 178): Cartimandua's designation as queen of the Brigant (Tacitus) is not clear; her first husband Cadallan* had been its chief, and his son Caratak of Caledon will have succeeded him; perhaps she was known by her old style. Her family belonged to the Kent-Sussex area, her grandfather Mandubrauc having treacherously let Caesar land in Thanet; possibly they claimed Brigance. The classical Beric of Brigance may be another unidentified claimant.

BRYNACH WYDDEL (pp. 234-9):

Two men of this name—one, Arthur's treacherous seneschal (Ch. 14); the other a saint, 'son of Israel', who lived in great austerity. The latter will have been the Brynach of Affaraon, given a wolf-cub in the Cat* Palug tale, because—'there was much talk concerning the wolf of Brynach'—and a wolf figures in the life of St Brynach.

CADALLAN:

Prominent in Boece as chief of BRIGANCE,* both temp. Caesar and Cymbeline; the two cannot be the same person. Cadallan jr. was Cartimandua's first husband, and father of Boadicea, see CALEDON.* Cadallan sen. was the slayer of Murkthet, a traitor of Caesar's day; Mwrchan in Tr., cxxiv and cii. He slew him in 'Ireland',* thus indicating Brigance as near the Lake.*

CAITHNESS:

In G/M's expression 'Humber to Caithness' (III, i and IX, i), which is regarded as Northumbria, it seems that Caithness is a transcription for 'North Sea', Mor Tawch, cf. Iolo MS. 'Caint about the river Tain and the Mor Tawch'. Thus Humber to Caithness correctly is Tarrant (Arun) to Kent—perhaps to 'Caintness'.

CALCHFYNYDD:

'Chalk Hills', the Chilterns. Described in Iolo MS. as between the Trent and Thames. The country of the Catuuellauni. In a heraldic MS. temp. Elizabeth, certain Welsh families are traced to 'Kadrod Kalch-vynydd, Earl of Dunstable' (Guest II, 49).

The cattle raid of the men of Calchvynyd on Dyfed (Skene, xlvi) was a deep penetration, suggesting Silchester's collaboration; it lay in the direct line of movement, and evidently still acknowledged itself as Lear's dowry for Cordelia (p. 226 above).

CALEDON:

Its chief 'The Bear' (p. 21); for 'the Honour of the Bear', Magouns, see ARUNDEL.* Also allusive is the Greek caledo, Swallow, representing Caledonian druids, cf. Culdees; hence the swallows, martlets, in the arms of Sussex and Surrey.

It is called the Daneian Wood by G/M.

(Pp. 33, 58, 88): The chieftainship oscillated greatly, and was a great bone of contention. Its descent is shown in the table opposite (from Boece); Lear's family have been entered in italics; see also under CARATAK.*

(i) Some of the variations in name are as follows:

Chief of Caledon, or King of Albany (temp. Julius Caesar)
  Boece—Eder, cf. Ider son of Nudd.
  G/M—Lear's son-in-law Maglaun, see MAELGWN.*
  G/M—Cridious, possibly Greidiawl (ref. Silchester claim, p. 226).

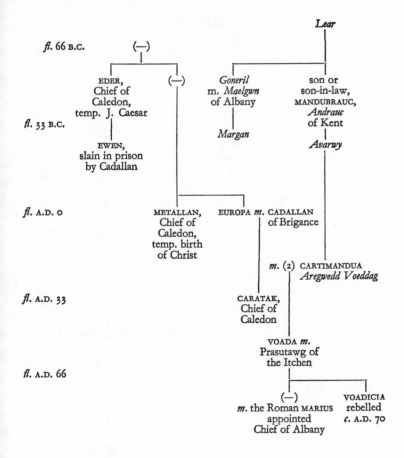

Lear

(—)

EDER,
Chief of
Caledon,
temp. J. Caesar

(—)

Goneril
m. *Maelgwn*
of Albany

Margan

son or
son-in-law,
MANDUBRAUC,
Andrauc
of Kent

Avarwy

EWEN,
slain in prison
by Cadallan

METALLAN,
Chief of
Caledon,
temp. birth
of Christ

EUROPA *m.* CADALLAN
of Brigance

m. (2) CARTIMANDUA
Aregwedd Voeddag

CARATAK,
Chief of
Caledon

VOADA *m.*
Prasutawg of
the Itchen

(—)
m. the Roman MARIUS
appointed
Chief of Albany

VOADICIA
rebelled
c. A.D. 70

Chief of Kent (temp. Julius Caesar)

G/M—Andrauc, Caswallon's nephew and chief of the Trinovant, Thames estuary.

Boece—Andrauc, not mentioned as chief but as envoy between Caswallon and Caledon.

Welsh Triads—Mandubrauc; called son of Lear, but perhaps son-in-law intended.

Caesar's Commentaries—Mandubrauc, son of Inianu Vetitius (*see* p. 27).

Chief of Caledon (temp. Nero)—p. 188:

Boece calls him Corbreid brother of Caratak, said to be in Rome. The Caratac in Rome, though, was son of Cymbeline; Caratak of

Caledon's circumstances are unknown. So in this text the chief has simply been called 'Caledon'.

(ii) Their dates are derived from Boece:

> Eder 58–11 B.C. Caesar's invasion of 55 B.C. was in the fourth year of his reign; he died in the forty-eighth year of it.
> Ewen 11–4 B.C. Deposed in the seventh year of his reign.
> Metallan 4 B.C.–A.D. 34. Died in the thirty-ninth year of his reign.
> Caratak A.D. 34–54. Died in the twenty-first year of his reign, which was A.D. 54 (Stewart ll. 8317–19).

Boece's remark that Christ was born in the tenth year of Metallan's reign, i.e. in A.D. 5, bears out this chronology. The word 'born' is evidently in error; it will have come from a Gaelic dialect, and as for example in modern Gaelic the word *breith* can mean either 'birth', or 'judgement', or 'interpretation', the translation 'nativity' is mistaken; some other occurrence in Christ's life will have been intended. Busch in *The Five Herods* has identified Christ's birth with 7 B.C. (*see more fully* DATES*); in 5 A.D. therefore he will have been twelve years old, which is the age given by St Luke as when he conducted his disputation with the doctors in the Temple, who were amazed at his understanding. As British tradition avers that Christ in his childhood accompanied his uncle Joseph of Arimathea to Britain, his argument in the Temple will have been of especial admiration to the British druids, whose teaching he will have learnt; hence the record of his 'interpretation' (of the Law) as having taken place in the tenth year of Metallan's reign. Cf. the A.S. Chron. date of Caesar's 55 B.C. invasion as sixty years before Christ's birth, i.e. *breith*.

Cartimandua—in A.D. 53 she was the wife of her second husband, Venusius of the Iugant, but was deserting him in favour of his standard bearer; this gives her the appearance of being aged, say, 45–50, which means that she will have been born in about A.D. 5; when her daughter Voada rebelled in A.D. 61 the daughter herself had daughters who were violated, so Cartimandua's marriage to Cadallan can scarcely have taken place later than A.D. 25, and must have been the wedding of a girl of less than twenty with a fairly elderly man—in fact a political affair.

(iii) Their names:

Metallan can be recognized as Verica, who, until the appearance of his coinage in about A.D. 10, was evidently subordinate to his brothers Tincommius and Epillus. In his being followed by Caratak, the coinage corroborates tradition. Commius was father of the three brothers Verica, Epillus, and Tincommius; and from Boece's indication (in the diagram above) he will have been married to a sister of Eder, who was thus his brother-in-law. More probably their relationship was even more tenuous, in that he was married to the sister of Eder's wife. In that case Commius could be the Atrebatan of Caesar's narrative, a Gaul from Arras, married to Lear's daughter Cordelia, while Eder would be her sister's husband Maelgwn of Albany. The discrepancy of name between Eder and Maelgwn is less than is at first apparent, because the -gwn in the latter has been compared with Gwyn the son of Nudd, while Yder (Ider, pronounced Eder) was also a son of Nudd; MAELGWN* certainly seems a designation, the two could have been one.

According to G/M, the son of Lear's daughter and Maelgwn (? Eder) joined with his cousin of Cornwall in wresting from Cordelia her land, the Silchester district; conceivably therefore the nature of Ewen's iniquity, as told by Boece, was that he and his Cornish cousin Tasciovan had joined together to dispossess the sons of Commius, but failed. It is apparent that tradition varies according to its source; in this case both Albany and Cornwall claim to have been in possession of the same place at the same time; actually they were engaged in struggling for it.

Tincommius and Epillus do not figure in the British records.

All of these, it is clear, were petty chieftains in a very disintegrated province. The principal divisions of Albany at Caesar's time are shown under BRIGANCE*; they were Caledon, the Pict land of Gwynedd which is the Itchen valley, and Brigance or Dyfed. Separate from them were the disputed district of Silchester, and the Trinovant territory of North Kent.

CALIBURN (pp. 106–11, 227, 280):
Anglicism of *Calebwlch*, Welsh *Caledvwlch;* in romance (Ex)calibur. The *Hard Cleaver* (*see* p. 280).

CAMEL (p. 245): *see* CAMELOS* and CAMLAN.*

CAMELOS (pp. 99, 268):
The personal name from which has come the river name Camel. It belonged to a sect of druids, 'rainmakers', the Black Man guild of Ch. 16. Meaning 'wavy', it refers to the wavy water-line of Aquarius. Though said to be the god of war, this is impossible except in so far as war correctly is determination to uphold right; Camelos, as the Black Man, was representative of the whole creed of Light.

CAMELOT:

Derivation as for Camelos,* the Black guild being spread over the Dyfi* valley. Note the theory that the upper Avon once flowed into the Test (Clement Reid, on the ancient river Solent, in *Geology of Ringwood*).

CAMLAN:

Welsh sources call Arthur's last battle Camlan; G/M says, on the river Camel, so does Wace; Malory noticeably differs in saying that Arthur and Modred agreed to meet—'upon a down beside Salisbury'. As the Upper Avon in Wiltshire used to be called Camel* (Eckwall, under Cam Brook), and as this lay in what used to be called 'Cornwall', it is straightforward to accept Malory's tradition that they fought near Salisbury; any idea of the modern Cornwall would not have arisen until Camelham in Wilts. had been forgotten, yet Camelford in Cornwall was known.

Boece has called the battle 'Humber', mistaking it for the earlier fight on the Trisanton (Stour or Dyfi).

Arthur's endeavour to come to terms: see Malory and Boece.

Caledon under the rule of Owein: see Wace, 'Owein' being 'Yvain'. Wace continues that Aguisel used to claim it; cf. under Rheged.*

Numbers engaged: Wace tells of Modred's flight from Winchester with a few adherents; what other memories are preserved of the fight give the view that numbers were small. 'Cornish loyal country' means from Hampshire westwards. G/M mentions 'Saxons' among Modred's force; his Irish, Scots, and Picts is accurate, picturing malcontents from the Lake and Caledon; the question arises whether half-mutinous Roman auxiliaries were helping Modred. It seems so.

Alan Fyrgan's household: see Tr. xxvii of Hengwrt MS. 536 (Skene).

Gwynnhyvar's reserve: see Mab. *Kilhwch and Olwen*, and Notes on 'The Ninth Man that rallied Camlan' and on 'Camlan' itself.

Kynwyl Sant: for other reputed survivors *see* Mab. *K. & O.*, also its Note on Glewlwyd Gavaelvawr.

CARADOC (pp. 26, 81, 258):

I.e. Caratac of Britain; for his family, *see* CYMBELINE.*

CARATAC-US (pp. 18, 180):

I.e. Caratac of Britain; for his family, *see* CYMBELINE.*

CARATAK (pp. 33, 46, 58, 121–6, 154–61, 178):

I.e. Caratak of Caledon and Brigance. In Boece, Caratak of Scotland, here altered to Caledon. He is Malory's Carados of Scotland, and the CARA of a coin found in the Weald. For his family, *see* CALEDON.*

CARBONEK (pp. 50, 214):

The scene of Malory's Grail romance (Chh. XIII–XVII); anglicism of Caer Bannawc, which Rhys translates as 'having points' or 'horns'. Corruptions are—Benoic, Benewick, Vannawc, Corbenic, Corbyn, Corbiere.

It was the four-cornered caer in AVALON,* the Joyous Isle (*see also* ANNWVYN*), owned by Pwyll Avallawch or Pelles of Carbonek, who gave the Joyous Isle to Lancelot, married to his daughter Elaine. Thus called Joyous Garde, it was near Caer Leon Camelot, 'Carlisle' (Malory, xx, xiv), while Pelles of Carbonek and of the Lower Folk was brother to the Widow Lady who claimed the Valleys of Camelot; it lay therefore on an island near Camelot and the Lower Folk, i.e. Wight. Lancelot* was son of Ban of Benwick.

In *The Spoils of Annwn* (Skene, viii) Pedryvan means 'the fourfold corners' (Rhys, xiii); this seems to indicate a square or diamond-shaped island, or alternatively a rectangular enclosure such as a Roman camp; cf. 'They saw a castle and an island of the sea . . . and saw four that sounded bells at the four corners of the town' (Grael, xxxv, i). It contained the cauldron of Pwyll pen Annwn (Skene, viii).

The nature of the rivalry between Ban of Benwick's family and Pwyll Avallawch is clear: both claimed the Isle of Wight.

CARTIMANDUA (pp. 41, 46, 178–81, 188):

For her family, *see* CALEDON;* claim to BRIGANCE* (*q.v.*); betrayal of Arthur, possible cause, *see* CAT PALUG.*

CAT PALUG (pp. 183–4):

Also called the Cat of Lausanne, which seems to mean 'of the Lake', Lausanne on Lake Leman (Geneva) being substituted for Lake Leoman (Britain). It was reared in Mon, an island of the Lake,* and was a voracious feeder:

> Cai the fair went to Mon, to devastate Llewon.
> His shield was ready against Cath Palug when the people welcomed him.
> Who pierced the Cath Palug?
> Nine score before dawn would fall for its food. Nine score chieftains.
>
> (Skene vii)

For its origin *see* Mab., Notes to *Kilhwch and Olwen*. The sow of Dadweir Dallpenn in Cornwall became with young, so Arthur sought to destroy her. She plunged into the sea, and landed at various places:

in Gwent she left three bees, in Dyfed a pig, in Arvon a wolf-cub given to Brynach of Affaraon, and an eaglet to the lord of Arllechwedd; then at Maen Du in Arvon she left a kitten, and Coll ab Collfrewi took it and threw it into the Menai; but the sons of Palug in Mon reared this kitten, to their cost, for it became the Palug Cat and one of the three plagues of Mon. (Is Menai—Mynyw, Meon?)

Conceivably it was a foreign trading concern expanding and establishing new branches; the creatures left by her might represent the people with whom agreements were made: e.g. bees, Ambrose;* pig, the Orcin; eaglet,* Leoman; kitten, Chatti ('St. Catharine'). It is possible that Cartimandua was in debt to the last mentioned, and sold Arthur to redeem her dues.

CHATTI: see CAT* PALUG:

A very widespread Cymric clan, instanced in the Rhine Valley, Hesse; in Kent (p. 78); in Clan Chattan, Scotland. The many St Catharine Hills bear their feminine priesthood's name canonized. Their Saxon branch were Whitti, e.g. Whit-inga-ton, with their Cat emblem.

CLAUSENTUM (p. 171):

Known to the Britons as 'Camp of Ostorius' men'. Urien Rheged* used to hold a national and royal court at Caer Gwyr Oswydd, or Ystum Llwynarth (Mab. Notes, *Taliesin*); it was connected with the cantred of Iscennen, Itchen.

COLLEGES (p. 266):

The equivalent modern term for the old-world 'gardens', i.e. tree groves, in which wisdom was studied and taught. Apart from their proper names, they were known colloquially by the seven colours of light, alluding to the particular aspect of wisdom emphasized. These probably explain the tinctures of the field in old heraldic shields of Three Crowns, and others; cf. too the various coloured knights fought with in romance.

The Black: Its code was apparently an austere renunciation of worldliness, perpetuated by St David, see DEWI.* Instanced in Malory:

> They came to a black land; and there was black hawthorn, and thereon hung a black banner and . . . a black shield . . . (and) there sat a knight all armed in black harness, and his name was the knight of the black land. (VII, vi.)

The Green: Similarly Unworldliness, but embodying a feminine element, e.g. Glastonbury, see DEWI.* Typified by the Green Man, and apparently headed in its Christianized form by Gawain (*see* romance *Gawain and the Green Knight*).

The Purple: Goodwill; typified by St George (see *The Seven Champions of Christendom*). Its colour derived from the wine used ritually for stimulating it. His red cross ought to be the old-rose tint of purple. The college name presumably Ambrose.*

The White: Typified by the White Hart (p. 210). The explanation of white as Youth (in Malory XVII, ix) is a wrong supposition.

The Gold: Ideal Wisdom, as the golden 'light' of the Sun (not Prosperity). Possibly associated with the Apple-tree;* cf. the Golden Apples of the Hesperides.

The Red: Justice; characteristically Gaelic.

The Blue: Simplicity, the ideal renunciation of the desire for wealth; characteristically Pictish.

COREMYN (pp. 120, 160, 168):

Boece calls it Shrewsbury, though Stewart adds 'Coremyn now called Shrewsbury'. Evidently a hill; Shrewsbury seems introduced through its Welsh name Pen-gwern, 'head of the marsh'; accordingly that translation adopted here.

(Pp. 160, 168): This Corymyn not necessarily the same as above, but possibly so; in which case Cori- could refer to the Coranians/Coritanians at the mouth of the Arun. *See also* TEGN.*

CORIN, CORNWALL *see also* ALBANY*:

The Cornish Britons' traditional origin is given in G/M I; they are the Corini who conquered all Wessex, leaving their name in Corini-um, Ciren-cester (cf. Cyren-ica). They are traced from Greeks who sailed to Rome after the fall of Troy; their badge, the Chough, is the Greek Coronis. Thus Corineus, their leader, is themselves personified—the Corini-ys, the Corini-folk. The Corna-wys* are an earlier stock of the same race. The Corin druids, Merlin, took over Stonehenge from its former druids Myrddin, to whom belonged the cognomen Ambrose.* For the Trojan name Ila in Somerset, *see* ARIMATHEA.*

Most of pre-Arthurian history is a tale of constant rivalry with Albany over control of the Trisanton (Southampton) trade.

In Arthur's day the Corin Britons possessed South-west England as far as Hampshire; the Itchen-Arun district was debatable ground with Gaelic Albany, as also was Silchester.* In the romances 'Cornwall' implies all Wessex; the Cornish March was the Sussex Border, thus Breton romance calls King Mark of Cornwall '*le roi de Portzmarch*', i.e. Portchester.

Arthur's kinship to the Cornish chief's family is roughly as below:

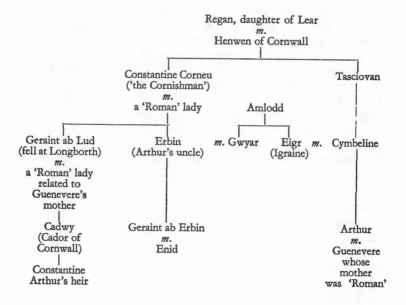

'Roman lady' cannot have its literal meaning; and it is noticeable that Merlin and Aurelie Ambrose each is called son of a 'Roman consul'. Perhaps the institute of Amlodd was invested with Roman authority later, so that 'daughter of Amlodd' became replaced by 'Roman' lady. Cf. A. Wade-Evans, *Welsh Christian Origins.*

CORNAWYS (pp. 190, 212):

The Cornavii of classical record; found at either end of Britain, in Cornwall and Caithness, as well as Cheshire-Salop. Corn-wall is Saxon -*wealas* in place of Briton -*wys*; they are an earlier stock than the Corin Britons, *see* CORIN above. Corna-wy or Cerne-wy means Horns-folk; for present-day survivals of them *see* p. 211.

COXALL KNOLL (p. 175):

The *Seven Champions of Christendom* account mentions—'The sun also lying in the Pagans faces, to their great disadvantage'. Perhaps having crossed the river, the Romans turned westwards to attack the hill, thus at the crest facing the afternoon sun.

CYMBELINE (pp. 18, 31–58, 97, 123, 155, 224):

His family—

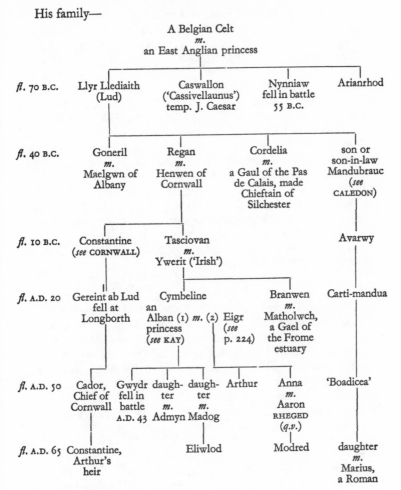

Notes on Lear's* family are under his name. Tasciovan will be G/M's Cunedag, son of Regan and Henwin; he recovered much of Lear's kingdom, including perhaps suzerainty over Atrebatan Silchester, reigning for thirty-three years (G/M), i.e. *c*. 27 B.C.–*c*. A.D. 5. The first half of the names Cunedag and Cymbeline (Cuno-belin) is *cunos*, hound; it seems to have some Cornish significance, because Gildas terms Constantine of Cornwall 'whelp', and his epithets for other men have specific meaning—Cynlas 'the Bear', Maelgwn 'the Dragon'.

The varying names of Cymbeline's sons are:

Gwydr (Guiderius)	G/M	Arwiragus	G/M
Gwydr	C.B.	Arwiragus	Boece
Togodumnus	Dio	Caratacos	Dio
		Caradoc son of Bran	C.B.
		Gweirydd	C.B.

See DUBNO* for the implication of Togo-dubnus. That Gweirydd and Arwiragus are the same is evidenced by both having a 'son' and successor Marius.*

Sons-in-law of Cymbeline, by his first wife, are evidenced—Madog, said to be son of 'Uther';* his son Eliwlod a knight of Arthur's Court, and an Eagle.* Had he been a blood son of Cymbeline, he would have had a prior claim to Arthur for the crown; presumably therefore a son-in-law. As an Eagle, Eliwlod's family will have been Gaels of the Lake, corroborating that Cymbeline's first wife came from Albany.

Admyn, mentioned by Suetonius, who says that he sought help from Caligula; for the same reason as Madog, although called 'son', must have been son-in-law (*see* BAN*).

CYMRY (pp. 78, 145):

Here applied as in Tr., iv, to the Celts who came across the North Sea from South-east Europe, under Hu the Mighty, i.e. under the creed of Hesu. They seem to have been a mixed Gaelic-Brythonic stock, e.g. the Morauians whom Boece says came from the Rhine (though at an earlier date than his); and they contributed to Anglo-Saxon stock, e.g. the names Pilk-inga, Ingavoni. Although the name implies a united nature, as 'fellow-countrymen', they did not exemplify it. J. E. Lloyd, *History of Wales*, Ch. VI, note i, considers it possibly to have been a legal term before adoption as a national one.

DATES:

Joseph of Arimathea's arrival—A.D. 37. Gildas, *see* ARIMATHEA; 'immediately after the Passion of Christ' (Council of Constance, 1419, *see* Morgan, p. 113).

Death of Vran, Cymbeline—A.D. 39 (*see* p. 55).

Flooding of Lowland Hundred—in the time of Ambrosius (Tr., xxxvii), presumably the father of Owain son of Ambrosius; the latter buried the head of Vran (Tr., liii), and lived at the time when the Britons resumed the sovereignty from Rome (Tr., xxxiv). Thus the flooding was in the generation before A.D. 39. *See also* LOWLAND.*

Arthur's Court—Cadeir, adopted son of Seithin Saidai, was one of its knights (Tr., cxix), and Seithin lived at the time of the flooding, above. Thus Arthur's Court was soon after A.D. 39. Manawyddan, brother of Vran, and other persons of the Court were present at the battle of Traeth Brue, Trywruit (Skene, vii), indicating the same generation as A.D. 39.

Birth and death of Christ—referred to by Boece, *see* CALEDON, and Malory as below. F. O. Busch (*The Five Herods*, p. 54) dates his birth as 7 B.C., from—classical date of Quirinius' first census; astronomical date of conjunction of Saturn and Jupiter in Pisces; correct translation of ἐν τῇ ἀνατωλῃ; and date of Herod Achelaus' succession to Judea, 4 B.C. 7 B.C. corroborates Boece. His death, Busch states, is placed by latest research as A.D. 33. This was the traditional one—cf. Susebius, and A. S. Chron. Susebius was closely related to Helen of Colchester's family.

Glastonbury's foundation—A.D. 65, i.e. thirty-two years after the Passion (Malory, XIII, x). William of Malmesbury's A.D. 63 represents the Isle of Wight Church's resuscitation on Arthur's return.

DEWI, *St David* (pp. 172, 175–7, 224, 227, 234):

He was born at Hen Meneu, i.e. Old Meneu, the Mynyw river of Hampshire, as distinct from the later Menewia of Wales. He was educated at the school of Iltyd, which will have been at Glastonbury, and later established a monastery in Rhos, the valley of the Mynyw (Meon). There he and his followers practised severe austerity. On the death of Dubric, the prelate at Caerleon, the choice of a successor lay between him and Gildas, son of Kaw; Arthur chose David, which Gildas much resented.

His family is shown overleaf; he is said to have been Arthur's uncle, and of the kindred of the Virgin Mary (i.e. of the family of AMLODD*). 'Uncle' can hardly be correct, as he can only have been a cousin through Amlodd, or a foster connection. His grandfather having been Arthur's foster-father suggests that Cymbeline's first wife was Cynyr's daughter, *see* KAY.*

For his college* of 'Watermen', *see* Wade-Evans' *Welsh Christian Origins*. But the idea that their name came from drinking water is a fallacy, they were the Christianized form of the Black Man of the Fountain (p. 229), with selflessness practised as austerity; hence his traditional colour black, and the black field of his arms.

For legends, *see* Lewis' *Glastonbury and Her Saints*. A material one is that, hearing of the sanctity of the 'Old' wattle church at Glastonbury, he wished to dedicate it, and journeyed thither with seven associates; but during the night before the service he had a curious dream—he saw our Lord standing beside his bed, who asked him what he intended; and when David had told him, our Lord forbade him, saying that it had already been dedicated by himself, long ago, in honour of his

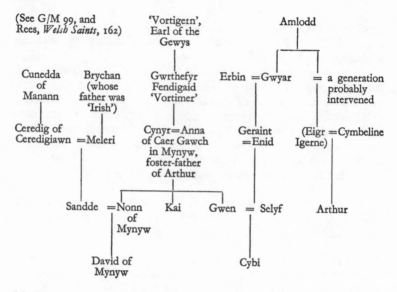

Mother, and that it was unseemly for it to be re-dedicated. As a result of this, David added another building instead, as a sort of chancel to the old church. The tradition was recognized by St Augustine, when writing to the Pope, in A.D. 600:

In the western confines of Britain, there is a certain royal island of large extent, surrounded by water, abounding in all the beauties of nature and necessaries of life. In it the first neophytes of the catholic law, God beforehand acquainting them, found a church constructed by no human art, but by the hands of Christ himself, for the salvation of his people. The Almighty has made it manifest by many miracles and mysterious visitations that He continues to watch over it as sacred to himself and to Mary the mother of God.

This legend indicates an evident desire of St David to alter an existing custom; it is reflected in a comparison between the green of the Glastonbury arms and the black of his own see (*vide* ECCLESIASTES*).

In Ricemarch's *Life of St David* he is recorded as having travelled as follows:

Glastonbury—built a church.
Bath—blessed the warm springs.
Cowlan—
Repicwn (queried as Kilpeck, Herefordshire)—
Collan (Colva, Radnorshire)—

Glasgwm (Radnorshire)—here used to be a hand-bell, traditionally given to the church by St David (*see* Giraldus Cambrensis, *Iter.*).

Leominster—founded the monastery.

Erging (Archenfield, South Herefordshire)—cured the blindness of Bebrawc or Pebiau, its chieftain. In Archenfield are Dew-church, Dewys-welle, and Llan Dewi Cil Peddeg (Kilpeck).

Raglan (Monmouth, Bryn Llyngwren 'Bird Cherry Hill')—built a church.

Llangyvelach (Gower)—founded a monastery, and placed there an altar sent by Pebiau of Archenfield.

Kidwelly—

It is impossible not to notice that this area corresponds with the Welsh borderland of Ostorius' campaign. It gives a strong impression that St David, in later life, revisited the scene of his fighting and founded there various churches, literally as war memorials. In South Herefordshire were the sons of Geraint, who had settled there after Llongborth; they were his uncles through their mother Gwen, sister of his mother Non; family relationship seems naturally to have entered into his actions. As regards his leek (p. 177): Taliesin writes—Pleasant the camp where the leek flourishes' (Skene, xcviii); it corroborates the significance of 'Neighbourly Aid'.

DON (p. 26):

For the identity of Don and Danaan *see* pp. 263–4. Note also the Cornish tradition of descent from Greek Danaos, and G/M's name Daneian Wood for Caledon, also Ogier the Dane, and 'Denmark' in the Lake;* they instance a single race name.

In classical tales the descendants of Daneos are often called 'the Cock', referring to the same racial emblem as the present-day Gallic cock, *galli*; they were identical with Gaels or Gauls. But the bird varied; today in Kent the galli-bird is the woodpecker, the Greek *druops*, 'tree-worker', i.e. druid. Thus the Gaels of the Lake were Children of Don, also the Chatti*-Irish. St Catherine, their patron figure, is conceivably Arianrhod daughter of Don, whose name 'Silver Wheel' will mean the moon.

Another Arianrhod, mother of Llew Llaw Gyffes of Gwynedd, is called Rhianon in the *Camb. Biog.*; this indicates the Rig-Anton, Annwvyn,* astronomers of Nudd as having been Children of Don. For the Don feature as astronomers *see* Mab. Notes, *Math*; and for their 'cauldrons' (p. 142) *see* Mab. Notes, *Branwen*.

DRUIDISM (pp. 34, 102, 110, 192, 222, 230):

Druids literally 'tree-men', i.e. men of tree-grove temples, cf. Greek 'sprung from trees' and Scottish MacDara 'son of oak', etc., in point of fact temple-born. *See also* DON.* This points to an origin older than Homeric Greece, as does Boece (St., ll., 3400 *et seq.*) and the Cecrops of Athens traditions (Miller's *Legends of North Scotland*, Harverty's *Hist. of Ireland*).

Their functions—science in general, judicial, historian, priesthood, medical. All learning transmitted orally, with trained scruple over strict accuracy; hence oral records, though liable to corruption, can possibly contain contemporary verbatim relics.

'Civil laws codified by Dyfnwal Moelmud have since remained the common, unwritten, or native laws of the island . . . these druidic laws have been always justly regarded as the foundation of British liberties' (Morgan, pp. 53–4. J. E. Lloyd, *Hist. of Wales*, Ch. IX, is perhaps unduly sceptical). Their purpose—'that all might obtain Justice and Protection' (Tr.). A much prized tradition.

Religion: pure humanity based on Reason.

(*a*) The essence of the universe is pure mind, spoken of as mental light, *Duw* (French *Dieu*), corresponding with Virgil's—

> In the beginning, the earth and the sky and spaces of night,
> Also the shining moon, and the sun titanic and bright
> Feed on an inward life; and, with all things mingled, a Mind
> Moves universal matter, with Nature's frame is combined.

(*b*) This 'light' was also called the Word, Reason (p. 105).
See Taliesin's *Hanes* (Giles' *Nennius*, App.)—'John the Divine called me Myrddin.' For the pre-Christian Word symbolized as a White Hart *see* Malory, XVII, ix, and p. 210 above.

(*c*) For their principles governing reasoning, with their colour mnemonics, *see* pp. 266–8 above.

(*d*) The 'Light' of Reason, *Dieu*, was commonly represented as three rays: that which created the past, that which preserves the present, and that which will renovate the future. For 'Strength the Preserver' as a Bull, *see* HERALDRY.*

When the spirit of Nature was considered as dwelling in the earth, it and its druids were pictured as the serpent, the creature which penetrates into rocks (cf. the sword in stone, p. 109), or as the water-serpent, the dragon; both signified wisdom and justice. But when ideas had progressed, and the spirit of Nature was conceived as a heavenly Mind, it and its druids were designated 'fish' of the 'cloud sea', e.g. the salmon of knowledge; or as 'birds', e.g. the birds of Rhiannon (and p. 48); or as 'sky hounds', the *cwn wybyr*, who hunted for departed souls, cf. the hounds of Annwn. Arthur's epithet *Adarweinidog*, 'Birds Warrior', presumably refers to his support of religion.

DUBNO (pp. 65, 157):

Evidently a title. Dubno-uellaun of Essex and North Kent held it shortly after 54 B.C.; he was dispossessed by Cymbeline, in whose son it reappears. Togo-dubn; after the defeat of Cymbeline's family it was granted by the Romans to a Chichester chief, Cogi-dubn; after whom it was borne by Modred's son, Dubn-auc (Dyfnog). It would seem therefore to relate to land between Kent and Chichester, i.e. the Weald, and may have applied to the Dobunni (Bodunni) who surrendered early to Rome (*see* p. 77).

DYFED, DYFI (pp. 42, 44–5, 100, 243):

The following indicate its geographical position. It caused the flooding of the Lowland* Hundred and Enlli*

> Around the land of Enlli the Dyfi has poured,
> Raising the ships on the surface of the plain.

It adjoined Arllechwedd* and Caer Leon on Itchen, and Gwynedd* of the Itchen, Taliesin being given land in Arllechwedd by the chieftain who owned a fishing weir on the Dyfi and land at Caer Leon; Taliesin was dispossessed of this land by Maelgwn Gwynedd. At Caer Leon, Taliesin was bard to Arthur, after which he went to Rheged, Chichester. Dyfed adjoined the lower Test, Annwvyn;* its seven cantreds were Rhiannon's dowry, thus identifying Dyfed with the Anton, Test. It was near the Meon (*Mynyw*), *see* Twrch Trwth *under* BOAR,* and DEWI.*

Hence the Dyfi once ran through the submerged valley, now the Solent and Spithead, which was a continuation of the Christchurch Avon and Stour. Its name, from *Dubro*, black, appears to have come from Camelos* as 'the Black', now the Avon, which flowed into it, Avon only meaning 'river'. In corroboration, the flooding of the Lowland Hundred was attributed to the Black Maiden; and at the lower end of its valley Dewi became 'Saint' of the Black brotherhood.

EAGLE (pp. 48, 144, 226):

Eagles of the Lake (G/M, IX, vi).
Eagle of Shaftesbury (G/M, II, ix and XII, xviii).
Eagle of Gwern Abwy, *see* KAW.*
Eaglet given to the lord of Arllechwedd, *see* CAT* PALUG.
Eagle of Gwidien, his grandson at Catraeth, *see* KAW.*
Eagle Eliwlod, Arthur's nephew (Rhys III, referring to *Myvryian Archaeology*, i, 176).
Eagle badge of Pevensey, *see* ANDERIDA.*
Eagle borne by Gawain on his shield (Malory).

ECCLESIASTES (pp. 51, 103, 211, 230, 234, 268, 274):

The Ossianic 'Exult thee, O sun, in the strength of thy youth' is the Celtic counterpart of *Ecclesiastes*' 'Rejoice, O young man, in thy youth', and of the Egyptian 'Lay of the Harper'. The two latter provide written survivals of the very ancient creed of 'Youth', which was personified in Celtic (Irish) myth as 'The Great Youth' of the Danaan, or British Children of Don. The creed constitutes an important factor in the social dissensions at Arthur's time, since in essence it was very close to the new creed of Christianity which he was sponsoring; in practice, though, the old creed will have been corruptly used.

The five essays and epilogue of *Ecclesiastes* (*vide* the *Modern Reader's Bible*) are the six precepts of the creed after it had been revised from pagan to theistic belief. This theistic form was held in Britain, where God was *Duw*, identical with the French *Dieu*. The six precepts are denoted in Celtic lore by colours, symbols, and in various other ways; opposite are examples.

Herrick's calendar of decorations shows that the pagan creed of 'Youth' year began on the 1st April, or more correctly on 22nd March when the sun rose due east. The Teutonic Eostre being the goddess of dawn, and Venus being the star of the east and of dawn, it is also recognizable that this was the creed of the East-men, the Greek Kadmeans and Danish Ost-men. They observed, though, the revised theistic version given here.

Venus, the star of the east, is the Celtic Cyridwen, 'Mother Earth', with Teutonic equivalents in the several Venus-bergs. Thus her colour was green; but when the pagan creed was adapted to a theological character she became the 'spinster', the selfless virgin, and 'youth' was personified by Saturn (a godly, not pagan, conception). Thus Saturn was the 'green man', and Venus became black; however, conservative affections ruled, and the colours became popularly reversed to what they have since remained—Saturn black, and Venus green. Classical legend tells that Saturn lingered long in Britain (*see* Ch. 16); he was in fact the popular Black Man of the Fountain, of Arthur's day.

ENLLI:

A district of repute, turned into an island by the flooding of the river Dyfi; commonly supposed to be Bardsey, but actually by the Hampshire Dyfed.* When Merlin left Britain he and nine bards went to sea in a glass house from Enlli, taking with them the thirteen treasures of Britain.

The name may originally have been Venlli or Benlli, who was

Precepts	Colours	Symbols	Calendar
for achieving Happiness	e.g. the Black Man of the Fountain and his knights, in Ch. XIII	e.g. ceiling at Longthorpe	e.g. Herrick's rhyme on seasonal decorations
1. Belief in God (Ideals)	Blue (Heaven i.e. unworldliness)	Figure at the centre of a five-spoked wheel	Dec./Jan.: Mistletoe (the plant without earthly root)
2. Knowledge	White (colour of moonlight, the moon denoting the heavenly power that influences the Mind)	Ape (cf. Egypt— Thoth, wisdom)	Feb./Mar.: (properly Willow, *lug-*, 'light')
3. Health and Strength ('Youth')	Green (the youth of the year)	Vulture (caricature of eagle; cf. Psalm ciii, 5, and phoenix eagle of 'perpetual youth')	April/May: Yew ('ever green') Celtic *yw* = green
4. Selflessness (originally 'Luck')	Black (colour of the lucky rain cloud; subsequently Black Venus, *see* LOWLAND HUNDRED)	Spider (the 'spinster', and regarded as lucky)	June/July: Birch (Gaelic *vergan*, cf. Virgin, properly spinster, i.e. type of selfless devotion)
5. Justice	Red (for Mars or Ares who was Justice, cf. Areopagus, 'Hill of Mars')	Cock (the Gallic bird; Gaels particularly devoted to justice; also the bird of Ares)	Aug./Sept.: the Reed (correctly the 'Rod' of justice)
6. Simple Livelihood	Gold (prosperity)	Boar (Gaelic *orc*, cf. Orcus, Pluto, wealth)	Oct./Nov.: (properly Corn, the harvest— prosperity, cf. Proserpine)

N.B.: symbols varied and there were others

a pagan giant consumed by fire from heaven for having refused Christianity (Rhys).

Dubric of Caer Leon Camelot was buried in Enlli.

GLASS ISLAND:

The domain of Melwas or Meliagrance, whom Rhys regards as devoted to 'Perpetual Youth'; located seven miles from Arthur's Court at 'Westminster' i.e. Caer Leon Camelot, on 'the other side of the Thames'. He is called a 'prince from Alban' in the *Myvyrian*.

Caradoc of Llancarvan describes his domain as *Aestiva Regio*, which is to be queried as *Aestu Regio*, i.e. 'tidal'. He latinizes Glaston as *Urbs Vitrea*, conceivably corrupted from *Wytryn*.

See the glass house under ENLLI.*

GLASTONBURY (pp. 215, 225, 230, 237)

The root of the name seems to be glas, 'green', with reference to the colloquial term for the abbey's religious denomination; it is indicated by its arms and by the legend of St David, *see* DEWI.*

The A.D. 601 name for Glastonbury, Inyswytryn, is apparently a survival of the name Isle of Wight (*wytryn*), the alternative for Avalon, transferred to it when the headship of the Church was transferred there in A.D. 65 from the Isle of Wight.

For its traditions *see* William of Malmesbury's *Antiquities* and below under PASSION.*

GOAT: (p. 41):

Not necessarily always associated with elder-trees, but sometimes —'I have been . . . a goat on an elder-tree' (*Taliesin*. Skene, xxviii). 'Havering-atte-Bower', village, meaning 'Buck Goat by the Elder-trees'.

These refer to a device (probably tattooed) of a Goat browsing off a Tree; cf. Ince and Inys crests, in the latter indifferent artistry has caused the goat's horns to be mistaken for rabbit's ears. It comes from the Iñg-ys folk (p. 27), cf. Haddington town arms; Haddington derived from Heardingas, mentioned in an A.S. rhyme on the rune 'Iñg':

> Ing was first among the East Danes
> Seen by men, . . .
> So the Heardingas named the hero.
> (B. Dickens, *Runic and Heroic Poems*)

Browsing is the equivalent of the Greek metaphor for acquiring wisdom—'to partake of the acorns of Zeus'; it depicts a Goat druid browsing in an elder grove. For the ceremonial installation of a Goat on a mound, *see* LEUIS*; and cf. the Norse enthronement of a 'Dog' on a mound, to receive the spring and harvest payments of meal and butter; the Dog used to bark two words but speak the third (H. Marwick *Orcadian*, 30 Jan., 1958).

GOGLED:

Commonly 'the men of the North', but properly *Celyddon yn y Gogled*, Caledon of the North (Skene, Preface). The people referred to were of Caledon; 'of the North' is mistaken embellishment, the Caledon* intended was the Weald.

GUNWASIUS (p. 119):

Rhys analyses this as Gwyn-gwas, *gwas* meaning 'The Youth'. Gunwasius of Orkney is often coupled with Melwas of Iceland, *see* LAKE;* Orkney and Iceland are corruptions of two of its islands. The first syllables Mael and Gwyn bring to mind Maelgwn; he was of Gwynedd, the land round the Gwyn, Itchen, suggesting a connection; it corresponds with Boece, that the men of Itchen (Icenia) and of Gwynedd ('Wales') rebelled, together with the Isle of Wight.

For Gunwasius' (Ganus) shipment to Rome, *see* Boece (St. ll. 6773–6).

Subsequent to this, G/M records (ix, x) that 'Gunfast King of the Orkneys' did homage to Arthur; this is not necessarily the same person, because 'Youth of the Gwyn' sounds very like a designation, in the creed of Perpetual Youth. Cf. Melwas, *The Princely Youth;* his attempt to carry off 'the queen' when she was Maying sounds like an attempt to pervert the kingdom back to the old creed.

Gwynwas and Melwas both involved in the death of Ursula, daughter of Noth, a British prince, which took place off the mouth of the 'Thames', i.e. Nudd of Annwvyn and the river Itchen (*see* Baring-Gould, *Curious Myths*).

GWAELOD: *see* LOWLAND* HUNDRED.

GWEIRYDD ADARWEINIDOG:

The son of Cymbeline, and successor to his brother Gwydr (C.B.), thus identical with G/M's Arwiragus. It means 'Birds' Warrior' or 'Birds' Ranger', apparently referring to his support of religion.

Lewis analyses *weinidog* (*Glossary of Mediaeval Welsh Law*, Introduction), quoting Kuno Meyer's *Fianagecht*—'In its stricter sense *fian* denoted a larger or smaller band of roving warriors, who joined for the purpose of making war on their account. This was called *dul for fianas* (*fenidecht*). They were, however, not mere robbers or marauders;

indeed their mode of warfare was considered honourable and lawful, and is so recognized by the laws.' Lewis then goes on to show that some of the early warriors, styled *gwyn*, may have been mistaken for saints from its other meaning 'blessed', e.g. Sir Kay.

GWYDR (pp. 155, 169, 233):

For Arthur's son Gwydr, *see* Boece. Although said to be Boadicea's child, he must have been Guenevere's (p. 155); born therefore in about A.D. 46. The C.B. states that Arthur's son was slain at Llongborth, naming him Llechau; but the interpretation here, captivity, seems more probable. Kay's treachery (Graal XIX, vi) is probable a confusion in names, cf. p. 233.

GWYN (pp. 55-7, 99, 114, 119, 227):

Gwyn an alternative name for the Itchen, modern Win or Winnal (*see* Skues, letter to *The Field*, 11.5.40). The first syllable in Win-chester. Meaning 'clear'.
Instances:

Garan Wynion (Gwynion River)—also Gwenystrad (Gwyn Valley) mentioned with Catraeth, 'Battle of the Estuary' (Skene, XXXVIII), and with Ardderyd of Caledon (Skene, XLIX-L).

Eccluis Gunnion (Gwynion Church)—birthplace of St Teilo, near Caer Leon (on Itchen) where St Dubric taught, and near the Lowland* Hundred whence Maelgwn Gwynedd's death was caused by the Yellow Plague of Rhos.

Guinn Liguiac—for comparison (*see* McClure). Guinn later became Gwent; thus Gwent in the story of the Sow of Dallpen (*under* CAT* PALUG) may have been the Gwyn Itchen.

Gwynlug—birthplace of Cadog, whence he went to Penychen, 'head of the Itchen' (?), and later to 'Ireland' (the Lake*) and to the Alclud of Kaw*; all near Winchester.

Caer Guinion (Gwynion Camp)—Arthur's eighth battle. This may have been Win-chester (Gwyn Camp), or the site of the later Caer Leon, Bitterne.

Bryn Gwyn (Gwyn Hill)—the knoll on which Vran's head was buried; St Catherine's, Winchester.

GWYTHUR mab Greidiawl (p. 226):

Father of Gwenhwyvar (C.B.), *see* OGYRVEN.*

HAND of God (p. 105):

Either hand or arm, e.g. the hand from a cloud, with rays also, on a roof boss in London Guildhall porch; and cf. the figure of the

Creator from a cloud, wearing a triple crown, in the Castile Book (Br. Mus.).

HERALDRY (Frontispiece, 29, 105, 256, 260–7):

(Frontispiece): The banner is reproduced from C/A MS. I, 2, in which the field is marked alternatively blue and red; blue has been chosen to correspond with Sir David Lindsay's Scottish MS.; this corresponds also with Arwiragus' supposed 'arms' in C/A MS. L, 14, ii. The usual red field assigned to Arthur was evidently to distinguish him from the house of Cymbeline; but it is noticeable that in some versions the distinction was not made.

In many lists of arms Arthur is attributed arms of thirteen crowns on a blue field; they surely allude to the thirteen stars of Cassiopeia, *Llys Don*, 'The Court of Don', and corroborate the Children of Don inference on p. 253 above?

All of these shields may have originated in the twelfth century, with the Three Crowns tradition.

The black bull supporting his banner presumably refers to Nennius, §19, in which Beli is called 'son' of Minocannus of the Tyrrhene Sea, i.e. of the Minotaur of Crete. This infers that Taran the second person of the Celtic trinity, 'Strength the Preserver', was derived from a Cretan origin. Cf. the legend of Minos' son Glaucos, which also has a reflection in Britain. And cf. 'the herd of the roaring Beli' (*Gododin*, Skene, L).

(P. 28): The shield with three crescents and suns grouped at the centre is conjectural, based on parallel instances, e.g. Paplay (Kirkwall cathedral); Poulet, Pallet (Harl. 6163); Plantagenet of Lancaster, and Carey (Gwillym). These seem to illustrate a popular practice, if not in the best heraldry, of grouping charges round the centre point; conceivably it may have been popular with tattoo artists.

(P. 256): Arms of three gold crowns palewise on a blue field are assigned to Llyr and Cymbeline in C/A. MS. L, 14, ii; which states that they were borne by Belinus and his successors until the time of Arwiragus. The writer of the MS. evidently intended them to represent the creed of Beli as well as blood descent, because he pictures Arwiragus changing them to a St George's cross after his baptism by Joseph of Arimathea.

Coel's similar shield, but with the crowns bendwise, is from Harl. 619.

(P. 265): The shields of the Three Wise Men are from Harl. 2169, but with Balthazar's youth coloured as in Sir David Lindsay's MS. For his Black Man implication *see* p. 229.

(P. 306): St David's see: black, a gold cross with five black cinquefoils on it. Glastonbury: the green second quarter of Arthur's banner. Their difference, *see* DEWI.* They are a direct survival from the oldest philosophy in the world. The five cinquefoils on St David's cross allude to the five-principled origin of *Ecclesiastes**; they are a variation of the five-pointed star (cf. Frazer, Murray, and Three Crowns) which signified Health and Strength, e.g. the quinguangle 'symbol of health' of the Phisicke Reader, Cambridge, and Gawain's quinquangle in *Gawain and the Green Knight*. For the rune Ing* in heraldry, *q.v.*, and pp. 27, 264.

HYPER-BOREANS (p. 265):

When Hekateos wrote (*c.* 500 B.C.) of an island opposite the Celts, the Gauls were in North-west Germany; so, the island will have been at the north end of the North Sea. The name 'Extreme Northerners' indicates the same. As it is known that islands have disappeared from it, and as the deepening of the Thames between 60 B.C. and A.D. 0 (*see* p. 41 and ROADS*) points to the sea-bed having sunk about then, it is for consideration whether a large island may not have lain off the north coast of Britain. The Orkney islands have the distinct appearance of sunken down-land; and *c.* 100 B.C. a new type of defence work, the broch, made its appearance all along the present coastline of the Orkneys and Shetlands; it seems possible, therefore, that they are the remains of the island, which *c.* 100 B.C. sank with the sea-bed.

Note Pausanias, Baeo, and the Triad that Alon the Hyper-Borean originated the Delphic oracle and creed of Apollo (C.B. under Alon); cf. Apollo's cyclic visits to the island, Latona's birth, Saturn's retreat, and Apollo's arrow emblem of 'Light' being kept there, until eventually presented to Pythagoras. It was the source of his philosophy.

Their traditional happiness refers to their creed of Reason as the Way to happiness.

ICEN (pp. 17, 29, 170, 193–7, 238, 262–3):

Dio Cassius' sentence that 'the Britons retired to the river Thames at a point where it empties into the ocean, and at flood-tide forms a lake' has long been recognized as inapplicable to the London Thames. Horsley, in 1732 (*Claudius' Invasions*), quotes a Mr Ward's analysis of it—'However I am rather inclined to think he designed the former construction. For, as I take it, here are two things expressed, an overflowing of the water, and the effect of it, which was a stagnation upon the land; and that the verbs πλημυρειν or πλημμυρὲιν (for it is written both ways, as Constantine remarks) and λιμαξειν are so joined to express both these, is plain from a passage in Philo, cited by Stevens: Ἀναχεομενος πλημμυρὲι, ἱγ λιμαζει τας αρουργς: that is, the water swelling it overflows, and stagnates in the fields, or covers them in the manner of a lake. The sense of this passage seems much the same with that before us.' He also quotes the use of the word τὸ χωρριον as evidence of the place being one recently inundated giving a passage from Herodian in support, where the word is used distinctly in connection with a place which, overflowed by the sea, upon the recess of the tide becomes fenny. This would be particularly appropriate to the Solent.

Cf. Melwas' realm, *under* GLASS* and GUNWASIUS*; *also* Lancelot at Camelot seeing the Fair Maid's body on the Thames; *also* the mistake over *Colonia Londin* under LONDON.*

ICTIS (pp. 22, 42):
Icht, the English Channel. Witsand was *Portus Itius*, the Caer Icht of G/M, II, xii; Cape Griz Nez, the Ition or Ikion promontory (McClure p. 74, fn.). The fact that the tin trade port was on an island reached by wagons at low water suggests that after its establishment tidal erosion set in. This is to be expected, as it will have been constant.

IGNOGE (pp. 27, 264, 270):
Married to 'Brute' the personification of the Britons, she was daughter of Pandrasus, king of the Greeks (G/M, I, x); his name corresponds with Pandrosos, daughter of Cecrops of Athens who was traditional forbear of the Gaels. Thus the 'arms' assigned to Brute in Harl. 619 and C/A., I, 2, illustrate the Brythons quartered with the Gaels, a blood union; the three crowns of her quarter are also assigned to Coel, father of Helen of Colchester.

For the circumstances under which the Gaels (Pandrosos) left Athens, *see* R. Graves' *Greek Myths*, §25. It appears that the Cornish Choughs (Coronis) were expelled at the same time, and so were already connected. Cf. the Greek Oenone (Ignogne) with her son Corythus (Corin-thus).
See also JANUS.*

ING (pp. 27, 264):
The rune is illustrated heraldically by two intertwined snakes or swans' necks; e.g. the (Moray) crest of Stewart, *see* Map, p. 261.

IRELAND (pp. 24, 73, 99):
Cf. 'these isles of Ireland' where Bran (Brandiles) kept the Grail (Rhys, XIII); accordingly here Briant of the Isles is rendered Brynach* the Gael.

Ireland Border: *Margo Hibernensium*, mistranslation of Are-gaithel, Gaelic Border, Argyll (Skene, I, 173).

IUGANT (p. 179):

Perhaps a religious sect of no location, related to 'yoke' implying self-control; cf. *Iug-alis* for Juno's marriage 'yoke', and Hindu *Yoga*.

JANUS (pp. 27, 31):

Associated with Britain also in Lear's burial (G/M, II, xiv). His name was originally the moon, the masculine form of Diana, Di-jana (Keightley, *Classical Mythology*); later it became the sun. An old name for Venus was Dione, thus instancing the combined crescent moon and star as Iana-Ione; cf. Oene-one, and Lear's Ini-anu (p. 27).

Janus' two faces are those imagined in the curves of waxing and waning moons; one looks at the past, the other towards the future, hence he was said to know past and future.

Latin myth tells that he acknowledged Saturn, i.e. ECCLESIASTES.*

JOSEPH OF ARIMATHEA: *see* ARIMATHEA.*

JOSEPHUS (p. 14):

Lived 37– post A.D. 97. Imprisoned by Vespasian, A.D. 67–70, for taking part in a Palestine rebellion, he gained some clemency by fore-telling he would become emperor. Although no record that he wrote about Britain, it is likely that he wrote Vespasian's military career for the same purpose. This would have covered the 43–45 operations, and have included the early Church's influence, in view of Vespasian's curious capture of a 'sword and crown' at Camelot, which he used all his life (p. 149). He had a flair for topical detail in his writing.

KAW (pp. 233–4):

'Of Pictland', lord of Cwm Cawlwyd near Alclud* (C.B.); he had land in Mon* from Maelgwn Gwynedd, and his children land in Siluria* from Arthur. A daughter Gwenabwy was married to the son of Nwython, whom Rhys (XIII) regards as Natiien, thus introducing the places Netley and Caledon. All indicate the Hants/Sussex border.

He had many children, including Gildas, Aneurin, Samson disciple of Illtyd, and Aeddan Foeddog disciple of Dewi; Aeddan introduced bees to 'Ireland', so presumably an Ambrose* druid.

The murder of Gwenabwy's son Gwydr, by her brother Hywel, caused enmity between Arthur and the sons of Kaw; but it seems likely that Gwenabwy was a druid college, not a girl, and the murder was a sectarian quarrel. Gwenabwy is grandson of the Eagle of Gwydien, in the *Gododin* (Skene, L).

Cf. the quintet of creatures in *Kilhwch and Olwen* (Mab.)—Ousel of Cilgwri, Stag of Rednyvre, Owl of Cwm Cawlwyd, Eagle of Gwern

Abwy, Salmon of Llyn Llyw; and cf. the earliest Gaels—'Tuan the son of Starn ... one hundred years was he in man's shape, eighty as a stag, twenty as a boar, one hundred as an eagle, twenty as a salmon. ...' The sequence Stag, Owl (Boar), Eagle, Salmon is in metaphor the evolution of a druidic philosophy. The Owl* was daughter of a chieftain of Mon (Mab. *Math*, Notes).

KAY (pp. 39, 148, 158, 208, 227–8, 233–9):

From Caer Gawch in Mynyw (the Meon); uncle of St David. His father's appointment as foster-father to Arthur looks like compensation for loss of Court influence on his daughter's death (apparently Cymbeline's first wife—*see* DEWI*). Kay's behaviour at the choice of a king after Gwydr's death is significant—the test was to 'draw a sword from a stone'; Arthur drew the sword, but lent it to Kay, who thereupon presented it as testimony that he himself was the proven king. He was thus making a claim of some sort to Cymbeline's kingdom, possibly in a pretended right as Gwydr's uncle.

KENDAL (p. 187):

Westmorland is out of the question; cf. Caer Leon mistaken for Carlisle. Kendal, Westmorland, is Kent Dale abbreviated; so as there was a Kent Water in Kent, there can also have been Kent Dale. Boece brackets Kendal with Ordul,* i.e. Caer Leon on Itchen, in Boadicea's rising; and after it, says Marius made ruler of Kendale; it must have been the Kentish Weald.

LAKE (pp. 22–4, 52, 73, 97, 101, 128, 150–1, 170, 227, 251):

For the classical description—'at flood-tide forms a lake' *see* ICEN;* 'lake' still used for a stream estuary in Southampton Water. Three names in tradition—Lemane, Lumonyw, Llychlyn:

Lemane—correct; 'of the Elm-folk', cf. Gallic Lemovic 'Warriors of the Elm'. Lake Geneva was *Lacus Lemannus*, later Lausanne, *see* CAT* PALUG.

Lumonyw—Lemany, mistranslated 'Lomond'; Lymington probably a similar survival (Eckwall, under Lympne).

Llychlyn—corrupted to Lochlann and 'Norway'; it 'at first meant the fabulous land beneath the waves of the sea' (Rhys, 1).

Its several islands, and the foreign lands confused for them, were:

Orkney—near Chichester, *see* ORCIN.*

Benewick—the Isle of Wight, *see* CARBONEK.*

Ganys—the land of Bors, ravaged by 'King Claudas'; apparently close to Benewick; alternatively called 'Gaul', i.e. Gael.

Mon—often associated with the Mynyw (Meon); in Boece, an hour's sail from Brigance* (Sussex), near to Ordul* (Caer Leon on Itchen), and in the same area as Camelot, 'York' (by Chichester), and Kent. *See also* MAELGWN* and CAT* PALUG.

Iceland, Orkney, Gothland, Finland, Norway, Denmark—(p. 151) conquered by Arthur after 'Ireland', and the last two given to Loth* of Chichester. In the *Brut*, Ireland, Iceland, Gothland, Orkney, Llychlyn, Denmark, are islands added to the British possessions by Maelgwn Gwynedd; thus they were near Gwynedd* (Itchen), and as he died of the Yellow Plague after the flooding of the Lowland* Hundred, they are likely to have been formed then.

(The names are noticeably Scandinavian, and possibly arose through the equivalent of *kenningar*, poetic synonyms, in which islands in particular used to be spoken of allusively):

Norway—as for Llychlyn, above.

Finland—its native name 'Land of Lakes and Marshes' (*Suomesimaa*) applies here.

Den-mark—the same as Don-marc, 'Borderland of the Children of Don'.

Goth-land—presumably Goddeu, adjoining Rheged, Mureif, and Annwvyn (*see* Rhys, XI).

Iceland—in the Welsh text of G/M this is *Inys yr ia*, Yria Island; if the *yr* is Norse 'yew', then it is the equivalent of 'Ireland', and evidently the Gaels' name for their territory. Its king was Melwas, of the Itchen estuary, *see* GUNWASIUS.*

Hun-land—Gunwasius of Orkney was also called king of the Huns, i.e. Ungs, referring to Prester* John of Chichester, called Ung Khan in the East.

Winet-land—in Layoman: it stands for Gwynedd.

LANCELOT (pp. 149, 189, 208–14, 224–5, 235–43, 278):
Son of Ban* (Adminius); thus presumably the Lucullus son of Adminius who dedicated an altar at Chichester, and became Lieutenant General of Britain *temp*. Agricola (A.D. 78–85). Lucullus might be latinized Lugncullo, the 'gn' mute as in Lugn-dun, Leyden.

So prominently does he figure in seeking the crown, that he must have had some legitimate right; what it was is just discernible. He and his cousin Bors, and relatives, form a distinct group derived from the two brothers Ban of Benewick and Bors of Ganis. There are signs, though, that these two were not blood brothers but brothers-in-law; and as Bort is especially mentioned as having wed a daughter of Bran de Gore (Cymbeline), it is possible that Ban married her sister, both of them children by Cymbeline's first wife and sisters of Gwydr. That

Cymbeline did have two daughters is in a note under his name; the one's family was loyal, the other's plotted with the Romans from the outset.

Lancelot's story is told in a French-German legend (Rhys, VI). His father was Pant of Genewis (Ban of Gwynwys ?), killed in a rebellion when Lancelot was a baby; the mother's name was Clarine, but Lancelot was taken from her by a fairy, the Lady of the Lake, and brought up by her in an island surrounded by the sea. Under Leuis* it is clear that his father was the Adminius banished by Cymbeline, whose son Gwydr he murdered, for which he was slain by Arthur. Thus it was that the fatherless Lancelot was brought up by the Lady of the Lake; for she was his aunt, Arthur's sister Anna. Lancelot's claim to the crown is as below:

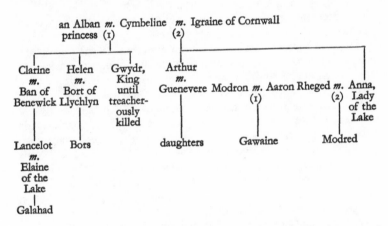

He is more likely to have sought nomination as heir-apparent than the crown at the moment; and his allegiance to Arthur oscillated with his chances, his rival being Modred. This explains why he has been treated kindly by legend, in that from one point of view his claim was just; and it explains Gawain's middle-course behaviour, through having no personal title. But what tradition ignores is the position of Arthur's own daughters, too young to be counted in the catch-as-catch-can struggle.

Lancelot enters also into rivalry over headship of the Church, 'achievement of the Grail'. For some reason he was passed over in favour of his son Galahad; probably this was in order to keep it within the 'kindred of Joseph of Arimathea', as was Galahad through his mother Elaine; but alternatively Lancelot's character may have been doubted, for it had disclosed itself when he deserted Elaine at the crisis. More about this is told in the French-German legend, continued later. In short, he was more concerned with effecting his father's old claim to Benewick.

The site of his main interest must have been, within narrow bounds, the Isle of Wight, *see* CARBONEK;* it had been claimed by his father but granted to Pwyll Avallawch, thereby causing his father to rebel; Lancelot eventually obtained it by marrying Pwyll's daughter Elaine.

His claim to the succession cannot be judged tabularly; the comparative suitability of the claimants had to be taken into account by the custom of the day. In giving Modred preference, Arthur may appear to favour a sister's son over a step-sister's, but other factors can have intervened. Modred may have commanded more influence in Rheged, where Owain was *persona grata* with the Romans, while Lancelot was not (p. 240); or it may have been a matter of character.

The French-German poem tells more about the rivalry over Carbonek. The Lady of the Lake was oppressed by a giant Iweret; that is to say, Avallawch's domain or Church was threatened by an 'Irish' rival. Lancelot was to rid her of the threat. In his quest he becomes a famous knight at Arthur's Court, and marries a lady; but after a time he falls beneath an enchantment and becomes a coward, and his wife leaves him. He recovers, and challenges Iweret. This is done by the Custom of the Fountain (p. 229): he goes to a well, over which stands a lime tree, and strikes a cymbal hanging from the tree, whereupon Iweret hastens to the scene armed for battle. He defeats and slays Iweret, but marries his daughter and takes possession of the domain.

The main features in this correspond to the rest of the Lancelot romance—his 'enchantment' when he left his wife, and his possession of Wight. As in the end the Church had to be removed to Glastonbury, it seems that the Custom of the Fountain continued, and that his chief concern had been to gain ownership of the domain.

LAVANT: *see* LLIVAN:*

LEAR (pp. 29, 77, 226, 254–6, 263):
For his family, *see* CYMBELINE.* Besides his three daughters and sons-in-law is a fourth, Mandubrauc or Andrauc,* in Welsh Avarwy son of Lud (C.B.). As Boadicea is called Avarwy's daughter (C.B.), a generation seems to have been omitted between him and Lear, cf. Bran ab Lud and Geraint ab Lud. This points to Andrauc having been a son-in-law rather than son.

LEEK (pp. 176–7): *see* DEWI.*

LEGIONS (pp. 71, 164):
Their distinctly non-Roman character needs to be emphasized. Of those serving in Britain, two were Celtic, and of the two Italian one was perhaps partly mixed; but the Italian itself comprised a large proportion of freed-slave foreign stock (*see* A. R. Burn, *Agricola*, Ch. 1). It is noticeable that for the conquest of Anglesey the two Italian were taken, the Celtic ones being used for holding purposes.

LEMANE, LENNOX, LEVEN: *see* LLIVAN.*

LEUIS, LEWIS
(P. 85): G/M's treatment of his second name, Hamo, is perhaps popular etymology. He is likely to have been either the Adminius or Bericus of classical history, who deserted to Rome beforehand. As Adminius was son (in-law) to Cymbeline, and so was Ban of Benwick, *see* LANCELOT,* it is probable that Leuis is the same person.
    The name is a style rather than personal, cf. the kings of France, Louis, correctly Llouis, 'Clouis', Lleu-wys, 'The' Light-folk, i.e. their Head. Cf. the Welsh designation Lleu for Lot of Lothian, *see* Rheged*; the present-day arms of Lothian, a Sun, preserve it—'The Light'.
    Ban therefore was claimant to the title Leuis; he was brother to Bors of Lychlyn, but as Aaron Rheged became Lot of Lychlyn, it can be seen that he failed. Hence Lancelot's position.
    (P. 41): Lewy's Fair, the name given to the 1st August Lammas fair at Kilorglin, Kerry (E. E. Evans, *Irish Folk Ways*, xviii). Lammas being a quarter-day, at which first fruits were offered, they will have been given to the spiritual head, 'The Light', thus the term Lewy's.

LIME (p. 77):
Cf. the Lime-tree where Lancelot* overcame the Custom of the Fountain.

LLIVAN, LLWYVEIN:
Lavant, Lemane, Lennox, Leven, Lomond, and Lympne, all variations of Lemana (Brit.), Leamhain (Gael.), Llwyvein (Welsh), 'Elm'-tree. Given to the Lake because its people's sacred tree, of which their groves formed. The area stretched from Lympne in Kent to Lymington, Hants.
    Rhys (Ch. xv) identifies Llivan with the Irish Liban, the maiden responsible for an inundation like the Lowland* Hundred flood; through her he connects Lyonesse with Llivan, and Lunet handmaiden of the Lady of the Fountain. Hence the 'Black' philosophy of Ch. 13 above is connected, corresponding with the valley's name Dyfed.*

LLYDAW:

In Devon Armorica*; it contained Ystrad Yw, the Yeo valley, which includes the Parret. Accordingly, the record that men of Armorica fought the Twrch Trwyth in Ystrad Yw, where two of Arthur's uncles and the king of Armorica were killed, seems to represent the battle of Llongborth, Langport. The king's name, Hirpeissawc, means 'of the long tunic' and was an epithet of distinction.

Bicanys was a nobleman of Llydaw, and thus also will have been his son Joseph of Arimathea,* or Illtyd. Breton tradition corroborates Bicanys of Devon.

LOEGRIA (p. 50):

The Lloegr-wys came from Gascony (Tr.) between the arrivals of the Cymry and Saxons, and were hostile to both (Rees, *Welsh Saints*, p. 167, n.); thus they are the Cornish Britons.

The divisions of Britons in G/M are personified:

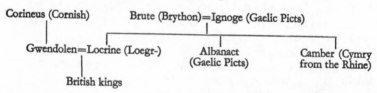

Locrine's name has been taken apparently from the incoming stock, with which the existing one fused. The table is inconsistent, though, in that there always have been two main divisions, Albanact and Briton (Skene, Ch. VII); they are represented in the 'marriage' Brute/Ignoge. This differentiation between Gael and Briton has continued to the present day: in Boece it is very marked, as Albany's feud with the Cornish, called Britons; then, after the Saxon invasion, it was Cymry/Loegrians, the Welsh calling England Loegria; today it is rivalry, Welsh or Scots/English. Loegria of Malory therefore was Wessex, in a Wessex/East Anglian or Briton/Albanact feud.

The ending of the Grail story, when it was taken from Loegria to Sarras, the 'spiritual place', is not clear. Sarras is where Joseph of Arimathea first landed, in Avallawch's land on the north shore of Spithead; it could not have gone back there, where anti-Christian belief was spreading. It would seem that Sarras is a faulty addition, and that the 'spiritual place' to which it went was Glastonbury, also called Avalon, for which name Avallawch's Hampshire domain was substituted. The Loegria the Grail left was the Cornish border-land, Wight; and the reason is under Lancelot,* he had turned to the old Custom of the Fountain.

LOMOND: *see* LLIVAN.*

LONDON (pp. 29, 66–7, 96, 99, 126, 157, 164, 193, 196–8):
   Llyr's name probably Lugn-dun, 'gn' being the obsolete letter now 'ñ' or 'g' (p. 13); the same as Lug-dun in Holland, Leyden. Lugn meaning 'Light', e.g. p. 27 and *see* LUGH.*
   Several mistakes connected with the name:
   (*a*) A Welsh text Llyndain is altered by G/M to Trinovant, implying London; but Llyndain is quite different, meaning Lake Dain and referring to . . . ? (*see* Griscom and Jones, *Geoffrey of Monmouth*, p. 298).
   (*b*) Because Itchen misrendered 'Thames' (p. 17), Camelot Colonia is wrongly called 'London'.
   (*c*) As early as A.D. 314 some confusion between Camelot and London. At the Council of Arles, three bishops are recorded as representing Britain—Eborac, Londin, and Colonia Londin; cf. G/M (XI, x), three archbishops—Caerleon, London, and York. These correspond to the three main Roman provinces— Britannia Prima (south of Thames), Flavia Caesariensis (north of Thames), Maxima Caesariensis (beyond the Humber); to-gether with a fourth, Britannia Secunda (Wales), for some reason omitted at Arles. Thus London and York are the provinces F.C. and M.C., while 'Colonia Londin' is B.P. which furthermore is placed first by G/M as most senior; it seems clearly Colonia Camelot.

LOTH (pp. 87, 97–100, 137–40): *see* RHEGED.*

LOWER FOLK: *see* ANNWVYN.*

LOWLAND HUNDRED (pp. 42, 44–6, 50):
   Cantred y Gwaelod. For the old Solent river basin being recent, *see* SOLENT* and the Needles track to the mainland (p. 21 above); fossil freshwater fish at Brading testify to a sudden inrush of salt water. As regards date: the tin island Ictis mentioned 45 B.C. by Diodorus, but not in A.D. 150 by Ptolemy; also, Wight was an island in A.D. 44 when taken by Vespasian. An island Mictis mentioned A.D. 77 by Pliny may or may not be Ictis, a disappearing relic under tide erosion. Epaticcus possibly connected with the event (*see* MANAWYDDAN*); an approximate year therefore A.D. 30; *see also* DATES.*
   Seithenyn only partly to blame, the Maiden of the Fountain of Venus also the cause (*Black Book of Caermarthen*, xxxviii, in Skene, xxiii). Rhys connects several names with the Lyonesse of romance Ch. xv), including Liban.

Liban also called Muirgen, whence Morgen 'sea born' and Morgan le Fay, Arthur's sister Anna (Rhys, 1). Much old philosophy in this; Venus originally the Black Maiden (cf. Dyfed*), formerly Luck but latterly Selflessness (Ch. 16 above), the sea she came from metaphorical 'the cloud sea' of heaven, i.e. Unworldliness. The cause of the flooding probably attributed to Bad Luck.

The refugee problem (p. 45) conjecture, but inserted as a reminder of the essential part played by ownership of land. Without it, or without a trade or tools, nothing between men and starvation; no surplus for charity. Conceivably this problem is the substance of the Mabinogi *Pwyll Prince of Dyfed*, who received Rhiannon,* a domain in the Test valley, from Arawn Rheged.

LUGH:

The Irish 'Light', *see* LEUIS* and LONDON.* His epithet Lavada refers to the rainbow.

'Lugh's Hound', the Moon, 'a ball of fire every night'; also allusive to Wisdom—'irresistible in hardness of combat, better than wealth ever known', cf. the 'Hard Cleaver' (p. 280), probably the sword in the arms of the City of London.

'Lugh's Chain', the Milky Way, the 'Soul's Way' to heaven, in Welsh Caer Gwydion—son of Don.

MAELGWN:

Mael, lord, *cunos*, hound; perhaps titular head of the Hound astronomers of Annwvyn.* It associates Gwynedd with Annwvyn, and with the Lowland* Hundred on account of his death from the Yellow Plague, and with Mon* (Skene, xciii). Cf. Maglaun of Albany, *see* CALEDON.*

MANAWYDDAN (pp. 43–4, 57):

Brother of Cymbeline (Vran) he figures in two Mabinogi—*Branwen* and *Manawyddan*. The first opens at Harlech (*see* ARLECHWEDD*); both centre about the Dorset Frome (Aber Ffraw*), the Test (Rhiannon*), and Lowland* Hundred (Dyfed), thus he was associated with that area. Identifiable with Cymbeline's brother Epaticcus, whose coins show him acting south of the Thames.

MANDUBRAUC (pp. 27, 30, 41, 63, 74–5, 178): In Boece and G/M Andrauc.*

MARIUS (pp. 254–6):

On Arthur's death can only have been made chief of Albany, Constantine succeeding to Cornwall. But as he gave land to Glastonbury, and is called king of Britain, it seems eventually made ruler of both.

MAURIN (p. 93): *see* p. 343.

MELIAGRANCE, MELWAS (p. 238):
    See GLASS* ISLAND and GUNWASIUS.*

MERLIN (pp. 34–6, 48, 86, 99, 103–12, 138–47, 157, 223, 250, 258, 279):
    Druid of the Corin Britons, *see* CORNWALL.* Means 'Black Bird', i.e. Cornish Chough; cf. Scots merle. In one Anglo-Welsh family the Chough still known as a merlin. A titular name, though Merlin of romance a distinct individual.
    For the Breton version of his eclipse, enchantment by Viviane beneath a white-thorn, *see* Mab. Notes to *The Lady of the Fountain*. In it, Arthur sends several knights to search for him, including Gawain; this perhaps relates to Ch. 13 above.

MILE (p. 130):
    Probably those of Dyfnwal Moelmud, about four English ones. The Laws' measure ran:

3 barleycorns, 1 inch;	3 inches, 1 handbreath;	3 handbreadths,	1 foot
3 feet, 1 step;	3 steps, 1 jump;	3 jumps,	1 land or ridge;
1000 lands, 1 mile.			

The inch likely to be the old 'long' inch of 1.03125 standard inches, of which 256 to the chain (*see* Sewell, *Royal Engineers Journal*, September, 1929), making a Welsh step of .77 yard.

MINOS (of Crete):
    The creed of Strength, as the source of Perpetual Youth.
    Father of Beli, and signified by a bull, *see* HERALDRY.*
    Father of Andrauc,* in classical myth; perhaps titular name.
    Father of Glaukos, connected with a cow the colours of a brambleberry, those of the patron saints of Britain.

MODRON (p. 46):
    Daughter of Avallawch—'Owein and Morvudd, his sister, at the same time in the womb of Modron daughter of Avallawch' (Tr.).
    A Denbeighshire legend tells of the Ford of the Barking—'The

dogs of the country would come there to bark, and no one would venture to go to see what was there until Urien Rheged came. And when he came to the ford, he saw nought but a woman washing. And then the dogs stopped barking, and Urien took hold of the woman, and had possession of her. Then she said—". . . it is my destiny to wash here until I have a son by a Christian; and I am the daughter of the king of Annwn. Do thou come here at the end of a year, and thou shalt have the son. And so he went and got a son and a daughter, none other than Owain ab Urien and Morfudd, daughter of Urien' (c. 1556, quoted by R. S. Loomis, *Wales and the Arthurian Legend*, Ch. VII).

Cf. the barking of a Scandinavian 'Hound King', *see* GOAT.* It will have been an ordained marriage.

MON:

Both Anglesey and the Isle of Man and an island of the Lake* (q.v.). It contained a noted druid temple (Boece); Boadicea's nephew brought up there (St., l. 9983).

MORAY (pp. 137–8, 197, 201, 260–3):

The land containing 'Loch Lomond' with its sixty islets and eagles (G/M IX, vi), i.e. the Lake.* The word a contraction of Moravia. Its people came from the Rhine (Boece, St., 9412—though at an earlier date); cf. Moravia of the Danube, with its eagle arms. For their migration to the Moray Firth, *see* St., 9934–41. Urien Rheged lord of Moray and Leven (Llivan,* the Lake). *See also under* YORK.*

MORGAN LE FAY:

Lady of the Lake, Argante (p. 250), *see* LOWLAND.* The fable that she murdered her husband is due to her name being mistaken for Morken or Morcant of Alclud, who killed Urien Rheged.

The Welsh 'Morgan goddess from Annwvyn' (Loomis, p. 99) identifies the Lake with the Lower Test. Said to be one of nine sisters, cf. the nine maidens who warmed the cauldron of Annwvyn.

MYRDDIN (pp. 145, 279):

See also PRESTER JOHN.*

NENE (p. 162):

Tacitus' text has two different readings—Avona and Antona. The latter has been needlessly conjectured Trisantona by dividing the preceding word *castris* into *cis Tris*, thus supposing the river to be Trent. This does not fit the military situation: from the road alignments (Map, p. 163) the frontier was not so far north at that date, nor likely to have been, with unsubdued Welsh on the left flank.

Avona, Nene, is entirely suitable. Its old name Avon, e.g. Drayton (1613) referring to Nene—'Avon which of long the Britons called her', and 'whom by Aufona's name the Roman did renown' (McClure). ANTONA apparently a misreading of AUFONA in Roman capitals.

NORTH: *see* GOGLED.*

NORWAY: *see* LAKE.*

OENONE: *see* JANUS.*

OGYRVANS (p. 147):

Alternatively Gogyrven; Guenevere's father, for whom the C.B. gives two other names—Gwryd Gwent, and Gwythr ab Greidiol; Malory adds a fourth, Leodegrance. As Gwythr he contested with Gwyn for Cordelia's domain, Silchester (p. 226); and as Leodegrance he owned the Round Table; thus he will have belonged to the Stonehenge district.

Ogyrven is the equivalent of 'God', cf. 'Cyridwen the Ogyrven (goddess) of various seeds'; she was the generative power of Nature, and Ogyrven a similar personification of it (Skene, lxxii and Notes, p. 324), linked with the wisdom emanating from her 'cauldron', i.e. stone circle. The impression given is that Leodegrance's (Ogyrven's) circle of Stonehenge was originally dedicated to Cyridwen; which dedication had continued down to Guenevere's day, her father being its chief druid or 'Dean', while Merlin was arch-druid of the realm.

If it be assumed that Ogyrven is the same as the Gaulish Ogmios, the inventor of Ogham script, and as Ogier the Dane, i.e. of the race of Don, then we see the survival of an extremely ancient Aryan creed. Mandeville relates that Ogier the Dane conquered North India, which he divided amongst his followers, and that he became ancestor of Ung Khan, 'Prester John',* of Central Asia. This is an accurate memory of the Aryan invasion of North India, under 'Herakles', bringing with it the creed of 'Light' recorded by Megasthenes (p. 105 above), which the Chichester figure of Prester John illustrates. Thus Ogier was its antecedent. Ogmius correspondingly was Herakles, Era-lleuys, the 'Aryan Light'; he was Reason, 'he conquered mostly by persuasion' (Lucian). So, if Ogyrven's identity with him and Ogier be accepted, we see in him a rightly revered Dean of the Round Table.

Ogier is with Arthur in Avalon. When an old man he was taken thither by Morgan le Fay; but when the good land of France was threatened by the Moors, she sent him to defend it as one of Charlemagne's paladins. After its safety had been won, she brought him back to Avalon; and there he remains, waiting to be called again.

ORCIN (pp. 100, 118–19, 124):

Not the Orkney Islands of North Scotland. Nennius, §21, tells that
Claudius sailed to them and made them tributary, which Bede (c. A.D.
700) repeats. Tacitus however, A.D. 97–98, remarks that Agricola's
fleet—'discovered and subdued the Orkney islands, hitherto unknown'.
Tacitus contemporary; the British tradition relates to islands of the
Lake.*

Orc the Gaelic for 'boar'; orchin, the 'little boar', the hedgehog,
hence urchin, the 'little fellow'. A tribal term, cf. the miniature bronze
boar emblems dug up near Brighton.

ORDUL (pp. 43, 195, 248):

Two distinct districts in Boece—one the North Welsh, Tacitus'
Ordovic, the other at Caer Leon Camelot. Ordovic meaning 'Warriors
of the Hammer', and the Hammer being the equivalent of Thor's, the
divine power of Nature typified in thunder-storms, their relation to
Camelos the Black Man, and Camelot, is clear.

In Boece's account of Boadicea's rising, the Ordul of Caer Leon
figures twice: the first is a repetition of Tacitus' story of the storming
of the temple; the second is from native sources, with the storming
repeated and reduplicated, once as 'Berwick', again as 'Carlisle'.
Stewart however doubted the name Berwick, for he qualifies it with
'as my author did say'; in Bellenden it is near Camelot. Both are near
where the Morays* landed.

OWL: see KAW:*

The Owl of Cwm Cawlwyd was daughter of the lord of Mon, but
fell in love with Goronwy son of a 'Heron' (presumably one of the
clan of Gwydno of the Lowland* Hundred); for which she was
changed into an Owl. Goronwy was in conflict with Gwynedd. The
story seems one of rivalry between the Herons of the Estuary and
Gwynedd for a possession of Mon. Heron is the generic name for the
'Irish' Picts, the Cruithen or Cranes.

OXFORD (pp. 17, 62, 257, 262):

Rhyd-icen, Icen-ford (see G/M, x, vi). Icen evidently an alternative
name for the Thames.* Icen mistaken for ychain, oxen.

In Lludd and Lleuelys (Mab.) Oxford is the centre of the kingdom;
this is actually so for Llyr's or Cymbeline's, the half-way point between
London–Gloucester and Portsmouth–Leicester. For Dinas Emrys in
the tale, however, see AFFARAON.*

PALUG: see CAT.*

PASSION (p. 14):

The event referred to is the conversion of Evelake, Avallawch.*
Malory's tradition runs—Joseph of Arimathea, thirty-two years after
the Passion, left Jerusalem with many of his kindred and came to
Sarras, where dwelt Evelake; Joseph succeeded in converting him, and
together they came to Britain, where Joseph was put into prison but
eventually released; after which the whole land turned to the Christian
faith.

This date is intended for the reputed one of the grant of land at
Glastonbury, A.D. 63; the discrepancy is that the latter is when Joseph
returned from South Wales (see ARIMATHEA*) and when Arthur came
back to Britain; the former when the Church was moved from the Isle
of Wight to Glastonbury, and euphemistically 'the whole land'
responded. Joseph's arrival from Palestine was in A.D. 37 (p. 49); his
imprisonment probably represents the disaster the Church suffered
when Arthur was taken to Rome, and when Avallawch received the
'dolorous stroke'. For A.D. 33 see DATES.*

PELLES, PELLINORE (p. 100, 106, 139–41, 146, 236):

Pelles in the earlier part of Malory becomes Pellinore later; Pelles
is called the 'Maimed King', as is Evelake, so Pelles Evelake is Pwyll
Avallawch. Malory mistakenly calls him Pellam, i.e. Palomides, Pellinore's 'next kin'. Palomides' character different: a Black Man (Ch. 13
above) and unchristened until Galahad's time, see Tristram romance.
However the wounding of Pellam with the holy spear (Malory, II, xv)
is certainly the same as the 'dolorous stroke' given to Pelles (Malory,
XIII, v).

His various designations are:

Pwyll Avallawch—for his domain of Avalon.

Pwyll pen Annwvyn—for his domain of the Anton valley.

Pelles of the Lower Folk—as above, the Lower Anton valley.

Pelles the Maimed King—'wounded in the two thighs in a
battle of Rome'.

Pelles of the Foreign Country—probably a confusion with his
'Saracen' Black brother.

Pellam of Listinois—

His father's name was Evrawc, i.e. chief of 'York'* by Chichester;
in the French Grael he is Alain of the valleys of Camelot, evidencing
a shorn territory once stretching from the Test to the Lavant, but since
deprived of its eastern uplands. It illustrates the border ebb and flow,
Rheged/Avallawch or Albany/Cornwall. So, when Arthur knighted
Pellinore's son before Rheged's it stirred old jealousy, repeated when
Pellinore helped Arthur against Rheged's Orcin, and finally vented in

Gawain's 'dolorous stroke'. Hence Arthur's choice in posting Gauls at Alclud (Butser Hill): the ground was debatable, and Rheged's inaction against the Romans justified his putting it in neutral hands, reserving his judgement.

Malory's story of Pwyll in outline is—Arthur met him shortly after succeeding to the crown, before Claudius landed in person; Pwyll was then following the 'questing beast', i.e. Christianity, alluding to Yesu the renovating spirit of the Celtic trinity, the three-headed hound. Arthur asked to take his place, but Pwyll replied the quest would only be achieved by himself or his next of kin—and rode off with Arthur's horse. The meaning is uncertain: his horse (p. 148) is 'proper pride', while his mare Llamrei is 'full of vigour'; can it be a warning against over-confidence? The disclosure of Vran's head had been over-confidence, and the cause of the present trouble.

Next, Pwyll aided Arthur in punishing the Orcin; this will have been A.D. 44, so romance is accurate when it says that Gawain avenged his father ten years later, with the 'dolorous stroke', i.e. A.D. 54 when Arthur had been taken to Rome. From A.D. 44–54 Pwyll was fostering the new Church, its centre at Carbonek;* it was he who brought to Arthur's Court the damsel of the Lake who caused Merlin's eclipse. During this period Lancelot married his daughter Elaine. After the 'dolorous stroke' he lay maimed, and the Church languished; then, on Arthur's return, there set in the famous Quest of the Grail, in which he is the Maimed King or King Fisherman.

PENGWERN (see COREMYN):

There was a Pengwern near Celyddon (Caledon) and Ardderyd, the region of Maelgwn Gwynedd (Skene, L).

PRESTER JOHN (pp. 111, 147, 266):

Presbyter John, the Asiatic Ung Khan; see OGYRVEN,* and fuller in Baring-Gould, *Curious Myths*, who quotes Otto of Freisingen (1145) that he ruled in central Asia and was descended from the Magi.

A Celtic figure, instanced in the arms of Chichester see and in 'Hun-land', the Lake,* to be associated with the crescent and star of Portsmouth (p. 28); instanced also in the old seal of Dartmouth, seated in a boat with a crescent and star on either side.

In the East he represents a sect of Nestorian Christians; they paid especial regard to the Word, cf. the sword from his mouth (pp. 105–12). Said to be descended from the Hebrews who accompanied the Queen of Sheba back from Solomon's court; cf. the branch of Solomon's Temple which came to Britain (Malory XVII, vii); however, in Britain before then. Conceivably the same as Myrddin; Nennius, §7, enters

Caer Merdin between Caer Guin truis (? Winchester) and Porchester; not listed systematically, but might indicate Chichester. His emerald sceptre and the Green Isle, *Clas Myrddin*, to be noted; for green, *see* pp. 267–8, and cf. the Glastonbury arms.

PWYL: *see* ARLLECHWEDD:

Guest, vol. II, p. 20, considers it to be identical with the Netherlands *Peel*. Subsidences of land all along the shores of the North Sea may have been occurring, *see* HYPER-BOREANS.* Pwyll Avallawch's land does not seem intended, as the Triad implies people from abroad. Conceivably the people are the Morays,* not reft of their lands by the Romans but by the sea; their arrival must have been at an earlier date than Boadicea's rebellion, though.

QUESTING BEAST: *see* PELLINORE.*

RAYS (p. 274): *see* HAND.*

RHEGED (pp. 46, 48, 87, 96–8, 123, 138, 150, 155, 157, 171, 180):

Tradition makes Urien Rheged, Arawn, and Loth three brothers (Mab. Notes); but Urien certainly the same as Loth, both being husband of Morgan le Fay, Lleu and Loth designations, not personal names, so Arawn likely the same as Urien; all three one person.

Lleu means 'The Light', titular head of the people. Loth derived by Rhys from Lleuddun, whence Lleudduniawn, Lothian; similar, *see* LEUIS.*

The various names tabulated are:

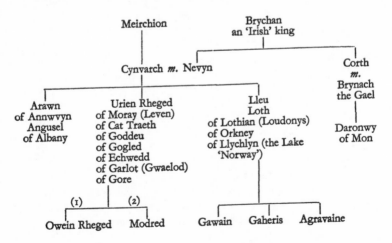

Angusel derived by Rhys (xi) from Aengus, the 'Great Youth' of the Irish, a religious designation; cf. under Gunwasius,* Melwas 'Princely Youth' and Gwynwas 'Youth of the Gwyn'.

Rheged here identified with the classical Regni of Chichester; it does not seem reasonable to suppose otherwise. A member of this family, therefore, must have been Cogi-dubnus, whom Tacitus says was always loyal to Rome; *see* DUBNO,* and note Modred's son Dubn-auc.

For Urien's court at Caer Leon, *see* CLAUSENTUM* and pp. 170–1.

Loth's claim to Llychlyn as an inheritance from his grandfather, probably maternal; Tr., iii, 122 calls Bors its king.

RHIANNON (pp. 43, 58):
A domain, Royal Anton (Squire, *Celtic Myth*), rather than a personal name. The estate's history was—'wife of', i.e. belonged to, Nudd of Annwvyn, father of Pwyll Avallawch; then 'wife' of Pwyll, whose son Pryderi bestows her on Manawyddan after his father's death. Contested for by Gwawl son of Llwyd, who revenged himself on Pryderi, but was baffled by Manawyddan (Mab. *Pwyll and Manawyddan*). The Widow Lady, though, complained of being unjustly reft of the Valleys of Camelot (*Perceval Le Gallois*, xv, xxi–xxvi).

RICHBOROUGH (pp. 18, 114, 126, 164):
Its long shallow front indicates a main purpose of covering a beach. Length of 700 yards would hold about 70 ships. The camp likely to have been rectangular, maximum area 670 × 130 square yards. Deducting one-eighth for perimeter and camp roads, 75,000 square yards would hold 5,000 men less the area required for depot storage.

Probably built in A.D. 44 when Vespasian's West Country operations brought the Albanys into revolt again, and communications around Chichester became unsafe; a subsidiary base depot, which quickly became redundant. Note G/M's version of the enemy sheltering then in Thanet (IX, v). In A.D. 49, however, when the Albanys again revolted, Ostorius likely to have re-established and reconstructed it, with its damp-proof grain stores.

(P. 243): G/M's version: Stour-mouth, Kent, mistaken for Stour-mouth, Hants, the old estuary of the Dorset Stour, in its lower reaches the Dyfi after being joined by that river.

ROADS (pp. 75, 93, 126, 154, 156, 163, 172–3):
Alignments contradict the supposition of an invasion through Kent; conversely they show it from a base area Portchester/Chichester.

The first feature to be observed is that four main roads to London converge on a single point in the City (junction of Mark Lane and Fenchurch Street); they run from Chichester, Pevensey, Colchester, and Royston, and are evidently the initial system after Plautius had captured the South-East. From the junction they have been aligned directly on their starting points; but at their starting points they mostly deviate from the direct line for local reasons, though afterwards are noticeably realigned on to the City. They represent extremely accurate survey.

Main base, Portchester/Chichester; subsidiary, and connected with Boulogne, were Pevensey, Richborough, and Colchester. Pevensey coupled with Newhaven; Richborough connected with Pilgrims Way at Canterbury. Frontier ran approximately: just west of Winchester and Silchester, then along Icknield Way; Royston a frontier post.

These roads will not have been metalled, but drained and bridged, and with wide clearance of trees and undergrowth to prevent ambushes. When metalled later, considerable alterations made.

After Vespasian's conquest of the South-West, a bigger system laid out (*see* Map, p. 163, except that the frontier ran Gloucester–Alchester–unfinished road heading north-east). Silchester headquarters based on Portchester/Chichester. *Refer also to* RICHBOROUGH* and THAMES.* Colchester and Richborough connected with Boulogne; Pevensey and Newhaven commercial only. The Silchester road entered London indirectly down Oxford Street and Newgate, then joined an apparently local road running to the Mark Lane crossroads.

The direct alignments of the old British tracks mentioned under THAMES* are remarkable, and appear to corroborate the tradition of their having been planned by the son of Dyfnwal Moelmud (G/M, III, v), who—'commanded a highway to be builded from the (Cheshire) sea to the coast of (Kent), and should run in a straight line from one city unto another, the whole of the way along'. Here, 'Cheshire' has been substituted for 'Cornish' in view of the *Cornavii* of Cheshire, and 'Kent' for 'Caithness'* (q.v.) which seems to represent Caintness. This identification is not essential, though, because other roads were laid out at the same time, 'slantwise' across the country; and as there was then no convention about facing north, the expression is indefinite. The tradition appears to have a basis of fact; and although the tracks themselves are not to be supposed as straight, yet ruling points upon them, such as fords and market towns, were (by some means) accurately sited. The supposition of straightness may partly have been derived from the later Roman roads; but the accurate choice of the Gravesend and London fords is pre-Roman, and seems scarcely accidental when viewed in conjunction with the general straightness of the line Lympne–Gravesend–Wheathampstead–Brickhill–Flint.

ROMNEY (p. 243):
   Wace's version; a guess at 'the Dover marshes'.

SALURIA (pp. 137, 156, 160, 170): *see* SILURIA.*

SARRAS (pp. 50, 52, 215): *see* LOEGRIA.*

SATURN (p. 268):
   Cf. mediaeval Church—'Treachery of Saturn was it, not the holy Sabbath day' (Angilbert, *Fontenoy*, *c.* A.D. 841).

SILCHESTER: (pp. 21, 29–33, 75, 126, 157, 164, 166, 180, 196, 225):
   Formerly Calleva, in which Cal- represents that of Caledon (p. 21).
   Given to the Atrebati by Lear, in alliance (p. 29).
   Its connivance in Chilterns raid on Dyfed (Calchfynydd*).
   Roman headquarters (p. 164).
   Striven for by Gwyn ab Nudd and Gwythur (p. 226 above, and Rhys, XIII).

   Coins evidence a ruling family with approximate dates as below; *see also under* CALEDON:*

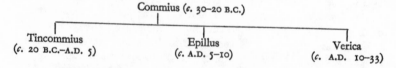

Commius (*c.* 30–20 B.C.)

Tincommius (*c.* 20 B.C.–A.D. 5)   Epillus (*c.* A.D. 5–10)   Verica (*c.* A.D. 10–33)

   Excavation evidences the following building periods:
   A Belgic town encircled by a ditch, up to about A.D. 45.
   A Romano-British town in the same perimeter, from *c.* A.D. 45–65.
      The four gateways made across the ditch, for the new Roman roads, indicate the original main roads: south from Winchester, east to London, north to the Thames, and west to Cirencester.
   An expanded Romano-British town protected by a new earthwork, dug *c.* A.D. 65, after Boadicea's rising.

SILURIA (pp. 137, 160, 169, 175, 183–9):
   Alternatively Saluria; enters considerably into Boece's narrative, where usually regarded as Strath-Clyde, Scotland. This has led, in one instance, to Caerleon of southern England being translated as Carlisle. Strath-Clyde correctly does not enter into Roman operations until Agricola's A.D. 80 campaign. Boece's account of Agricola's first year confuses the Ordovic ('Ordulus') of North Wales with those of Hamp-

shire; thus Hampshire Saluria and Camelot are introduced, and the whole transferred to Scotland.

For Arthurian history there are two Silurias: the well-known South Welsh district, and the hitherto unrecognized one of the Hampshire–Sussex border, recognizable through place-names beginning Sel-.

Lady Guest (Mab. Notes) comments that the Seisyllwch cantreds of Dyfed are not to be confused with Essyllwg the country of the Siluri (Wales); actually, though, they correspond with those of the Hampshire Siluri.

SOLENT (pp. 21–2, 42):

See *British Regional Geology, Hants Basin,* p. 82. The final encroachment causing the flooding of the Lowland* Hundred must have been preceded by steady erosion ever since tides flowed through the Dover/Calais straits. An intermediate stage is presumed here, accounting for an Aber Ffraw* at the mouth of the Frome.

SOW OF DADWEIR: *see* CAT* PALUG.

STOUR (pp. 21, 29):

G/M (II, xiv) says that Lear died three years after a successful fight against his sons-in-law, and was buried by Cordelia and her Gallic husband beneath the Soar at Leicester. But judging from Caesar, he lost his life in a fight against the Trinovant of Kent (where Gallic aid could readily have been provided). Eckwall, in a footnote on the Soar, says a 't' has been dropped; hence the Stour of Kent is inferred here. For his burial chamber, *see* JANUS.*

SUPPLIES CONTRACTOR (p. 117):

Mark Terebell appointed (Stewart, ll. 6105–8); Castle Terrabil seized by 'Uther' (Mal. I, ii), and re-assailed unsuccessfully by Rience (Mal. II, vi). Evidently near Camelot (Mal. II, x).

TEGN (p. 168):

Boece's Tegens could refer to a Stagra or Staer; conceivably the Sussex Stor or Storge, of Storrington (*see* Eckwall, *under* Teign, *and* Stor).

THAMES (pp. 17, 41, 63, 83, 197):

The deepening of the river-bed is evidenced by the old British route 'Watling Street', which evidently ran in a fairly direct line from Lympne, across a ford at Gravesend, through Wheathampstead, to Brickhill, Towcester, and North Wales. The Roman road more or less followed it; hence the change in direction at Brickhill, where the road from the Westminster ford regains the old route. The Gravesend ford evidently became unusable before Roman times. It will be seen that London lies on a direct line from Wheathampstead, Lear's capital, to Pevensey the port for the Wealden iron trade; thus Lear's choice of London to replace the Gravesend ford.

The Romans continued to use the London ford, or fords, for their initial road system (*see* ROADS*), but subsequently aligned the Canterbury–Rochester stretch of Watling Street to cross at Westminster; whether this was because the river-bed at London was still deepening, or whether because as a military route they wished it to avoid the town (like the Silchester–Colchester road), is uncertain. All in all it seems more probable that the bed was still deepening, and the London fords had become precarious.

See also HYPER-BOREANS.*

For the misrendering of Thames as Icen,* q.v. and p. 17.

THREE CROWNS (pp. 26, 257, 260–6, 271, 274):
The creed of mental 'Light' or Reason, and the race whose creed it was. Originally rayed ones, of light, but the later leaved ones mean the same. Numbers vary, e.g. 13 of Arthur, 6 of Winchester earldom, but usually 3; three probably imply the mediaeval—*pour symboliser le sainte Trinité*, the universal triple aspect of Wisdom as Creator of the past, Safeguard of the present, renovating Spirit of the future. Cf. the triple crown of the Almighty, and three raised fingers of His Hand.*

They indicate St George as Beli, in a Cornish play:

Here come I, St George, that worthy champion bold;
And, with my sword and spear, I won three crowns of gold.

TRISANTON (pp. 21–2, 44, 50):
Recorded by Ptolemy, it must have been a well-known feature. Eckwall identifies it as the mouth of the Arun; but the Dorset Stour also called Tarrant (i.e. Trisanton), and used to flow through the Solent to the same estuary as the Arun shortly before this date. Alternatively known as the Dyfi;* the differences explained by the tributaries to the main stream having come from different tribal areas. To the Dorset and Lake 'Irish', the estuary will have been Trisanton; but to the Cornish from Salisbury Plain it will have been Dyfi, after their own river, now the Avon.

As regards the name's derivation, it is for consideration whether Santon may not be the Anatolian Sandon 'the Strong', who was the same as the British Bel; that land was the traditional home of the Gaels.

TWRCH TRWYTH: *see* BOAR.*

UTHER PENDRAGON (pp. 86, 101):

Son of Constantine, a fiction generated by oral tradition. For its origin cf. Tr., i, 61 and iii, 122 (Rhys, VII), which say that—'Bors son of Bort begat (Helyn) on Brangor's daughter, who was empress in Constantinople'; Helyn has here been added from Malory. The course of the corruption seems to have run as below; in which Brangor is Bran de Gore, Cymbeline, and the empress is Helen of Colchester, wife of Constantius and mother of Constantine the Great. These personages are three centuries apart, but can have been confused through the expression 'king of Camelot', meaning either Cymbeline of Winchester or Coel of Colchester, Helen's father.

> Bort, son of Bort and Brangor's daughter, begat a son Helyn
> Bort, son of Bort and Camelot's daughter, begat a son Helyn
> Bort son of Bort and Camelot's daughter begat a son Helyn
> Bort begat a son by Camelot's daughter, Helyn
> Bort begat a son by Colchester's daughter, Helen.

But the father of Helen of Colchester's son was Constantius, in British Constans, so Bort and Constans became regarded as the same person; and Bort son of Bort became Constans son of Constans, which in turn changed to Constans son of Constantine, probably derived from Constantine the Great and his son Constans. Thus Bort son-in-law of Brangor, and Arthur son of Brangor, became Constans and Uther sons of Constantine; to whom was added Aurelie Ambrose in place of Arthur's brother Gwydr.

When a comparison of the exploits of Aurelie and Uther is made with those of Gwydr and Arthur, and Uther's death with Gwydr's (as is done under WEALDEN BATTLES*), it corroborates markedly that Uther was Gwydr. Guest suggests the idea of Arthur having been Uther's son came from *Arthur mab uthyr*, 'Arthur the terrible boy', being misconstrued as *mab Uthr*, 'son of Uthr'. Boece makes Arthur's sister Anna to be the sister of Uther.

(P. 86): Likewise the comet seen by Uther must relate to Arthur, unless it is pure fantasy; but in part it seems genuine. The beams pointing towards the 'Irish' Sea and Gaul might be real, as there lay the enemy; but the portent of a son and daughter seems far-fetched. Wace's version that the daughter should become queen of Scotland illustrates 'Scotland' as Caledon, adjacent to the 'Irish' islands of the Lake.

WEALD, i.e. FOREST OF CALEDON (*see* p. 19):

(P. 120): Boece's original is—'the lords of Carlisle, Kendal, and Durham'; but *see* KENDAL* and SILURIA* for the error.

WEALDEN BATTLES (pp. 82, 89):

For the misapprehension Uther,* q.v. The comparison between his battles and Gwydr's is as follows; *see also* the fights under BOAR:*

'AURELIE AND UTHER'	GWYDR AND ARTHUR
Enemy establish themselves on the Kent side of the Humber (Arun). (G/M, vi.)	Romans land, and two Briton brothers fight an unnamed series of battles in swamps; there is a fight on a river, in which Gnaeus Hostidius distinguishes himself. (Dio Cassius.)
The account, though, is tied up with the actual Saxon invasion.	
	Romans land at Portchester; Gwydr heads the opposition. (G/M, iv, xii.)
	Arthur's first six battles: the Glein (Sussex), Duglas (Kent), Lusas (Medway). (Nennius, 50.)
Enemy withdraw to concentrate in the neighbourhood of the *Arun*, and of Caledon. (G/M, viii, iii.)	Scene of the fighting removed to the neighbourhood of the *Itchen*. (Dio Cass.)
After a battle at Maesbeli, towards Caledon, the enemy withdraw to Caer Conan, 'York' and Alclud. Caer Conan falls to the Britons. Aurelius is successful at 'York', but allows the enemy to remain on the borders of Caledon, while he himself goes to Winchester. He sends his brother to remove some venerated stones from the 'Irish' Islands and incorporate them in Stonehenge. (G/M, viii, v–xii.)	
'Irish' and enemy assemble on the river Meon, to avenge the removal of the stones. The 'Irish' chief murders Aurelie at Winchester; the younger brother then takes the lead, defeats the enemy on the Meon, and is accepted by the Britons as king. (G/M, viii, xiv–xvii.)	Battle on the *Itchen*, the elder brother is slain, but the Britons unite the more firmly to revenge his death. Romans consider it wise to go on the defensive, and to await reinforcements. (Dio Cass.)
	Romans had decided to abandon Britain, when Gwydr was treacherously killed by a native near Southampton; his younger brother takes command. (G/M, iv, xiii.)
Fighting at 'York'. (G/M, viii, xviii.) Uther dies, his 'son' Arthur appointed king. The enemy is recorded as controlling from 'Humber to Caithness',* meaning from the Arun to the North Sea coast of Kent. Arthur defeats the enemy on the Duglas, and pursues them to 'York'. (G/M, ix, i.)	

Enemy is reinforced from oversea. (G/M, IX, i.)	Claudius brings reinforcements to Britain, and lands near the *Itchen*. (Dio Cass.)
The 'Kaiser' arrives with 'all the strength of Rome'. (Layamon.)	Claudius reassembles the Romans at Portchester. (G/M, IV, xiv.)
Arthur fights the enemy at Lindecoit, then at Caledon. (G/M, IX, iii.)	Arthur's seventh battle, Celidon. (Nennius, 50.)
	Claudius fights on the *Itchen* and captures Camelot (Winchester), and then makes peace. (Dio Cassius.)
	Claudius defeats the Britons at Winchester, and makes peace. (G/M, IV, xiv.)
	Arthur's eighth battle, Winchester, Caer Gwyn. (Nennius, 50.)
Enemy makes peace, but treacherously sails to Totnes. (G/M, IX, iii.)	Vespasian sails to Totnes, and fights at Exeter. (G/M, IV, xvi.)
	Arthur's ninth battle, Caer Leon, Exeter. (Nennius, 50.)
Enemy takes possession of the country as far as the Severn.	Arthur's tenth battle, the Brue estuary. (Nennius, 50.)
Arthur fights a stern battle at Bath. (G/M, IX, iii, iv.)	
Arthur subdues 'Ireland'. (G/M, IX, vi.)	Vespasian makes peace with the Britons, and both send their soldiery to 'Ireland'. (G/M, IV, xvi.)

In the above, except for a single action in the land of 'Hergin' (unidentified), the two brothers' operations begin with the enemy's withdrawal across the Humber to 'York', i.e. across the Arun to the Caer Evrawc outpost of the Portchester–Chichester area. The fight at Maesbeli (assuming it to be against a Roman enemy, though perhaps it is an actual Saxon battle which has intruded) is well described by Wace; the Britons by assembling threateningly caused the enemy to march out and attack them, and by making good use of their ground repulsed them successfully. They then followed them up, and stormed what appears to be another outpost, Caer Conan. Neither of these actions have had sites suggested for them here. The Britons then besieged 'York', which the enemy were able to hold; and after that they 'allowed' the enemy to remain on the borders of Caledon, in other words made no further attempt to harry Plautius' winter quarters' outposts.

After the elder brother Aurelius'/Uther's death, owing to the illusory introduction of Uther, the romances' accounts of the fighting become duplicated: firstly there is narrated the fighting under Aurelius' younger brother Uther, which can be accepted as that of Gwydr's younger brother Arthur; then secondly there is the fighting under Arthur's own name, immediately after his accession. These two separate narratives are here woven into one.

Celidon (p. 89): This is a series of engagements, which begin with the battle under Arthur's own name, on the Duglas; the account is quoted from Layamon, with 'foreigners' substituted for 'Saxish men'. It is followed by the attack on the Lindecoit fort, miscalled 'Lincoln', after which according to the romances the enemy retreat to the Wood of Caledon. As explained in the text, the retreat must have been on Pevensey, though, and thence by sea to Caledon, i.e. Portchester, the land on the borders of Caledon where they were 'allowed' to stay.

There is then a gap in the romance account under the name of Arthur; so here the narrative takes up the story from the deeds of Uther as the younger brother. He, Wace tells us, had already punished the 'Irish' on the Meon for his brother's murder. There is no mention of his fighting on the Duglas or at Lindecoit, but only that the enemy had overrun the realm 'from Humber to Scotland', i.e. beyond the Arun; the fighting then is transferred to 'York', which here is being quoted as Uther's attack on it and at Mount Damen afterwards. In the text accordingly, on p. 91, the next quotation is from Wace, with the word 'camp' substituted for 'city'; after that the Cornish chieftain's counsel is taken from Geoffrey of Monmouth (VIII, xviii), and the night attack's success from Wace again. The story then continues under Arthur's own deeds at 'York', taken from Wace, and with the tale of British duplicity from Layamon, and ending with a short extract from Wace (p. 94).

After this the romances tell of the Gauls' arrival and of the enemy sailing to Totnes; but before the latter event happened, much more took place, as is told in the text.

WIGHT, Isle of (pp. 17, 22, 43, 50, 68, 84, 103, 119, 137, 215, 242, 245):
Wytryn, 'fractured', latinized into *Vitrea*, 'glass',* (q.v.) *See* LANCELOT.*

AVALON,* Pwyll Avallawch's land (p. 50).
CARBONEK,* the 'Four Cornered' and the 'Joyous Isle'.

YORK (pp. 24–5, 79–99, 102, 124, 126, 136–7):
Contraction of Ebor-auc, 'Chief Yew', the druidic style still retained by the Archbishop, 'Ebor'. It relates to the widespread clan who gave

Ireland the name (H)ibernia; cf. Iwerne, Dorset, and Gwenevere, Gwen-hwyvar, 'of the Yew'.

In romance an important outpost of the Roman base at the period, i.e. Portchester–Chichester. From the lie of the ground, seems to have been Bow Hill, held perhaps by Briton friendlies. *See also* ALCLUD.*

Scottish tradition (Miller, *Legends of North Scotland*) says York founded by the brother-in-law of the Cromarty Gael; corroborates British tradition (Ignoge*) and confirms that the Moray men who migrated to Cromarty after Boadicea's disaster were from the 'York' of Sussex.

ADDENDA

MAURIN (p. 93)

Presumably the leading character in the Dutch *Romance of Morien* Related to Perceval; i.e. Arthur's kin through Avallawch and Amlodd (p. 224). His mother 'Moorish' means of the 'Black' persuasion (ch. 13). Evidently the Black creed hostile to Arthur at this period; *cf.* Palomides the Black at issue with Pellinore, and *cf.* Arthur challenging the Custom of the Fountain, i.e. the Black Man (pp. 106–7).

Romance of Morien tells that Arthur was taken prisoner by the 'Saxons'; and in his absence the 'Irish' made inroads.

PRONUNCIATION

It is to be remembered that the original British pronunciation corresponded with French, not English, practice. Camelot was Camelo, Lancelot was Lancelo. The Latin terminals 's' and 'm' should be disregarded, and the Latin 'v' be pronounced 'u' or 'w'; thus Cassivellaunus was Cassivellaunu, and Arviragus was Arwiragu. Similarly Beli should be as in French, Bayley. 'Y' is the Greek long 'e', η; thus Yder, Ider, Eder are all the same, Eeder.

Bibliography

ALLEN, D.F., article on 'Belgic Dynasties of Britain and their Coins' in *Archaeologia*, XC, 1944.

ANTIQUARIES SOCIETY, *Reports of the Research Committee*, on Richborough, 1926, '28, '32, '49.

ASHE, G., *King Arthur's Avalon;* Collins, 1957.

BARING-GOULD, S., *Curious Myths of the Middle Ages;* Rivingtons, London, 1884.

BELLENDEN, J., translation of Boece; Tait, Edinburgh, 1821.

BOECE, HECTOR, *History and Chronicles of Scotland;* translations by Bellenden and Stewart (qq.v.)

BOON, G.C., *Roman Silchester;* Max Parrish, London, 1957.

BROOKE, G.C., article on 'Distribution of Gaulish and British Coins in Britain, in *Antiquity*, September, 1933.

BURN, A.R., *Agricola and Roman Britain;* English Universities Press, 1933.

BUSCH, FRITZ-OTTO, *The Five Herods;* Robert Hale, 1958.

Chichester Guide, The; 1794.

COLLINGWOOD, R. G. and MYRES, J.N.L., *Roman Britain and the English Settlements;* Oxford, 1937.

COLLINGWOOD, W.G., article on 'Arthur's Battles', in *Antiquity*, September, 1929.

COOKSEY, C.F., article on 'The Morte D'Arthur', in *XIXth Century*, June, 1924.

COPLEY, G. J., *Archaeology of South-East England;* Phoenix House, 1958.

CURWEN, E. C., *Archaeology of Sussex;* Methuen, 1954.

DICKENS, B., *Runic and Heroic Poems;* Cambridge University Press, 1915.

DIO CASSIUS, *Roman History;* Loeb Classical Library, London, 1925.

ECKWALL, E. ⎰ *English River Names;* Clarendon Press, 1928.
⎱ *The Oxford Dictionary of Place Names.*

EVANS, SEBASTIAN, translation of *Perceval Le Gallois;* Everyman's Library, 1921; translation of Geoffrey of Monmouth (*q.v.*)

344

GEOFFREY OF MONMOUTH, *Histories of the Kings of Britain;* translations by Griscom & Jones, Longmans Green & Co., 1929, and by Sebastian Evans, Everyman's Library, 1911.

GILDAS ⎱ Gildas' *Epistle,* translated by J. A. Giles; Bohn,
GILES, J. A.⎰ London, 1841.

GIRALDUS CAMBRENSIS, *Itinerary Through Wales;* edited by W. Llewelyn Williams; Everyman's Library, 1908.

GRINSELL, L. V., *The Archaelogy of Wessex;* Methuen, 1958.

GRISCOM, ACTON, *under* GEOFFREY OF MONMOUTH.

GUEST, LADY CHARLOTTE, translation of and Notes on the *Mabinogion;* Everyman's Library, 1919.

GUEST, E., *Origines Celticae;* Macmillan & Co., London, 1883.

HAWKES, C. F. C. and HULL, M. R., *Camulodunum;* Oxford, 1947.

HERALDIC MSS. ⎧ Harleian nos. 619, 2169, British Museum, London.
⎨ College of Arms nos. L.8, L.14ii, London.
⎩ Sir David Lindsay's.

HORSLEY, *Claudius' Invasions and Roman Transactions in Britain;* 1732.

HULL, M. R., *Roman Colchester;* Oxford, 1958.

JOHNSON, RICHARD, *The Seven Champions of Christendom;* Blackie & Son, 1926.

JONES, R. E., *under* GEOFFREY OF MONMOUTH.

JONES, W. L., *King Arthur in History and Legend;* London, 1911.

JOYCE, P. W., *Old Celtic Romances;* David Nutt, 1894.

LAYAMON, *Brut;* Everyman's Library, 1921.

LEWIS, L.S., *St Joseph of Arimathea at Glastonbury* and *Glastonbury and her Saints;* Mowbray & Co., London, 1927.

LLOYD, J. E., *A History of Wales;* Longmans Green & Co., 1911.

LOMAX, F., *under* WILLIAM OF MALMESBURY.

LOOMIS, R. S., *Wales and the Arthurian Legend;* University of Wales Press, 1956.

MCCLURE, E., *British Place Names in Their Historical Setting;* S.P.C.K., London, 1910.

MALORY, SIR THOMAS, *Morte D'Arthur;* Everyman's Library, 1919.

MARGARY, I. D., *Roman Roads in Britain;* Phoenix House, 1955.

MEYER, KUNO and NUTT, ALFRED, *The Voyage of Bran;* David Nutt, 1895.

MILLER, HUGH, *Scenes and Legends of the North of Scotland;* 1834.

MORGAN, R. W., *St Paul in Britain, the Origin of British Christianity;* Covenant Publishing C., 1933.

MYRES, J. N. L., *under* COLLINGWOOD.

NENNIUS, translated by J. A. Giles; Bohn, London, 1841.

Ordnance Survey Map of Roman Britain; 1956.

OWEN, WILLIAM, *Cambrian Biography;* Williams, London, 1803.

PATON, LUCY, *Studies in the Fairy Mythology of Arthurian Romance;* Boston, 1903.

REES, RICE, *An Essay on the Welsh Saints;* Longman Rees, 1836.

REES, W. J., *Lives of the Cambro-British Saints;* W. Rees, Llandovery, and Longman & Co., London, 1853.

REID, CLEMENT, referred to in *British Regional Geology, the Hampshire Basin,* 1948/56; and in *Geology of the Country Around Weymouth;* Stationery Office, 1947.

RHYS, SIR JOHN, *The Arthurian Legend;* Clarendon Press, 1891.

RICEMARCH, BISHOP, *under* REES, W. J.; *The Life of St David.*

RICHMOND, I., *Roman Britain;* Pelican Library, 1955.

SEWELL, COLONEL, article on Ancient Measures, in the *Royal Engineers' Journal;* September, 1929.

SKENE, W. F., *Four Ancient Books of Wales;* Edinburgh, 1868.

SPENCE, LEWIS, *Boadicea;* Robert Hale Ltd., 1937.

SQUIRE, C., *Celtic Myth and Legend;* Gresham Publishing Co., London.

STEWART, W., translation of Boece; metrical; Longman Brown Green, London, 1858.

SUETONIUS, translated by J. C. Rolfe; Heinemann, New York, 1920.

TACITUS, *Agricola;* translated by H. Mattingly; Penguin Books, 1948; *Annals;* translated by A. Murphy; Everyman's Library, 1928.

WACE, *History of the Britons* (Roman de Brut); Everyman's Library, 1921.

WADE-EVANS, A. W., *Welsh Christian Origins;* Alden Press, 1934.

WESTON, JESSIE L., translations of *Arthurian Romances Unrepresented in Malory's Morte D'Arthur;* David Nutt, 1900.

WILLIAM OF MALMESBURY, *Antiquities of Glastonbury* (c. 1135); translated by Frank Lomax, Talbot, Paternoster Row.

WINDLE, B., *The Romans in Britain;* London, 1923.

Index

An asterisk (*) means a reference to the Glossary

347